THE
BEST
OF
Gourmet

THE
BEST
OF
Gourmet

1998

FROM THE EDITORS OF GOURMET

PHOTOGRAPHS BY ROMULO A. YANES

CONDÉ NAST BOOKS · RANDOM HOUSE, NEW YORK

Copyright © 1998
The Condé Nast Publications Inc.
All rights reserved under International and
Pan-American Copyright Conventions.
Published in the United States by
Random House, Inc., New York, and
simultaneously in Canada by Random
House of Canada Limited, Toronto.

LIBRARY OF CONGRESS
CATALOGING-IN-PUBLICATION DATA

The best of Gourmet: featuring the flavors of
India / from the editors of Gourmet;
photographs by Romulo A. Yanes. — 1st ed.
        p.   cm.
    Includes index.
    1. Cookery, India. I. Gourmet
TX724.5.I4B46   1998
641.5954--dc21   97-35517
                                        CIP

ISBN 0-375-50138-X
ISSN 1046-1760

Random House website address:
www.randomhouse.com/

Most of the recipes in this work were published previously in *Gourmet* Magazine.

Printed in the United States of America
on acid-free paper.

98765432
First Edition

New recipes in this book were developed
by: Leslie Glover Pendleton (Gifts from
Your Kitchen, pages 276-287); Lori
Walther (A North India Dinner, pages
249-257); Elizabeth Vought (An Indian
Vegetarian Dinner, pages 259-267); and
Alexis Touchet (A South India Dinner,
pages 269-275).

Informative text in this book was written
by Diane Keitt and Caroline A. Schleifer.

The text of this book was set in Times
Roman by Media Projects Incorporated.
The four-color separations were done by
American Color and Applied Graphic
Technologies. The book was printed and
bound at R. R. Donnelley and Sons. Stock
is Citation Web Gloss, Westvaco.

For Condé Nast Books

Jill Cohen, President
Ellen Maria Bruzelius, Division Vice
    President
Lucille Friedman, Fulfillment Manager
Tom Downing, Direct Marketing Manager
Jill Neal, Direct Marketing Manager
Paul DiNardo, Direct Marketing Assistant
Serafino J. Cambareri, Quality Control
    Manager

For *Gourmet* Books

Diane Keitt, Director
Caroline A. Schleifer, Editor

For *Gourmet* Magazine

Gail Zweigenthal, Editor-in-Chief

Zanne Early Stewart, Executive Food
    Editor
Kemp Miles Minifie, Senior Food Editor
Alexis M. Touchet, Associate Food Editor
Amy Mastrangelo, Food Editor
Lori Walther, Food Editor
Elizabeth Vought, Food Editor
Katy Massam, Food Editor
Shelton Wiseman, Food Editor
Alix Palley, Food Editor

Romulo A. Yanes, Photographer
Marjorie H. Webb, Style Director
Nancy Purdum, Senior Style Editor

Produced in association with
Media Projects Incorporated

Carter Smith, Executive Editor
Anne B. Wright, Project Editor
John W. Kern, Production Editor
Marilyn Flaig, Indexer
Karen Salsgiver, Design Consultant

Front Jacket: Coconut Tiger Prawn Curry
(page 272).
Back Jacket: Deviled Drumsticks (page
144); Macaroni Salad with Ham and Peas
(page 186); and Fallen Chocolate Cake
Squares à la Mode with Butterscotch
Sauce (page 200).
Frontispiece: Peppermint Chocolate-
Chunk Ice Cream (page 216); Strawberry
Ice Cream (page 214); Blueberry Ice
Cream (page 213).

ACKNOWLEDGMENTS

The editors of *Gourmet* Books would like to thank everyone who contributed to this thirteenth edition of *The Best of Gourmet*, especially Zanne Early Stewart, *Gourmet*'s Executive Food Editor, who acted as consultant.

Menus for this year's Cuisines of the World section, featuring the Flavors of India, were created and styled by Lori Walther (A North India Dinner), Liz Vought (A Vegetarian Indian Dinner), and Alexis Touchet (A South India Dinner). Alexis also styled her tiger prawn curry for the jacket. Yamuna Devi, a well-known cookbook writer and cooking teacher, acted as consultant, ensuring that recipes and text are true to the spirit of India, her adopted homeland. Margo True shared her first-hand knowledge of Indian food and introduced us to Maya Kaimal MacMillan, author of *Curried Favors*, who further explained customs and traditions. Jacket and menu photographs by Romulo Yanes, with Jeannie Oberholtzer as stylist; photos of India by Jean-Marc Giboux, Ted Voigt, and Roberta Gleit; and line drawings by Laura Hartman Maestro visually transport us to magical India.

Leslie Glover Pendleton created 24 unique recipes for this year's Addendum—Gifts from Your Kitchen. They are accompanied by Alexis Seabrook's charming drawings.

The Recipe Compendium is enlivened with line drawings by many gifted artists: Leland Burke, Jean Chandler, Beverly Charlton, Suzanne Dunaway, Maurie Harrington, Vicky Harrison, Tina Lang, Elisa Mambrino, Jeanne Meinke, Bob Palevitz, Rowena Perkins, Kristen Reilly, Agni Saucier, Jim Saucier, Alexis Seabrook, Harley Seabrook, Meg Shields, and Susan Hunt Yule.

Finally, thanks to Anne Wright and John Kern of Media Projects; to Karen Salsgiver for her clear designer's eye; and to Hobby McKenney, Elaine Richard, Kemp Minifie, and Kathleen Duffy Freud for their editorial contributions.

CONTENTS

INTRODUCTION

Sometimes we harried city dwellers, too busy to cook, rely on restaurants when we want to entertain. After all (we rationalize), there is such a great selection of beautiful *and* delicious places from which to choose. Of course, we also know that there is nothing quite as special as cooking for guests at home, so many of us are making the effort to do just that. *The Best of Gourmet, 1998*, filled with 26 of the *best* menus from *Gourmet's* kitchen, is designed to tempt you back into yours.

Over the years, I have come to realize that a cocktail or buffet party for 20 guests can be as easy to prepare as a formal sit-down dinner for 8. *Gourmet's* food editors agree, and throughout 1997 they developed an array of larger gatherings. One of my favorites, "Come for Cocktails," offers an exciting mix of flavors in tasty bites, like Crab, Mango, and Mint Nori Rolls. (Every recipe can be made, at least in part, ahead of time.) Our New Year's Eve Buffet of indulgent recipes, like Brie and Saffron Phyllo Tartlets, and a heavenly Dessert Party, with temptations such as Triple-Chocolate Hazelnut Truffles, also are worth a look. Naturally, you'll find exceptional smaller menus for intimate occasions, alfresco excursions, and holiday cheer too.

Three brand-new menus were created for our Cuisines of the World section, featuring The Flavors of India—a vegetarian sampler of regional favorites; a North India dinner, highlighting tandoori cooking; and an exotic South India dinner, with coconut and rice specialties. And 24 more new recipes follow in the Addendum—Gifts from Your Kitchen. Extraordinary homemade treats like Butter Pecan Bourbon Sauce and Coconut Macadamia Macaroons are unbeatable.

This thirteenth volume of *The Best of Gourmet* contains over 400 of the *best* recipes from *Gourmet's* food columns. Almost half can be made in 45 minutes or less. You'll also find many leaner/lighter recipes, complete with calorie and fat gram counts, to help you watch your waistline. This year, we've even included a few of our favorite readers' recipes for you to enjoy.

Cooking for someone is the ultimate gift. With *The Best of Gourmet, 1998*, it is also a joy.

Gail Zweigenthal, Editor-in-Chief

A sumptuous crisp-skinned roasted goose for the holidays ... a table set, Parisian-style, with a charming vase of asparagus crudités ... luscious chocolate-chunk cookies, the perfect finale to an end-of-summer picnic on a sparkling pond—special occasions enjoyed with friends and family are priceless, and *Gourmet*'s exceptional menus, planned to the minutest detail, make them memorable. Whether you're preparing an elegant affair for 20, a romantic breakfast for 2, or something in-between, let this collection of *Gourmet*'s 23 best menus from 1997 inspire you. Seventy pages filled with outstanding full-color photographs await.

This year, large cocktail parties are more dazzling than ever. Whether it's Asian Pork Crêpes at a New Year's Eve Buffet, or Pernod-Marinated Mussels at a "Come for Cocktails" autumn soirée, each exotic bite is sure to impress. Of course, not every gathering needs to be formal. A volleyball Picnic on the Beach is the ideal time for hearty focaccia sandwiches stuffed with either grilled tuna and peppers, or prosciutto, mozzarella, and olives. A "Lazy Sundaes" ice-cream party with chocolate velvet and lemon meringue flavors is another delightful way to please a group.

On the other hand, it's always fun to pamper someone special. Passion-Fruit Mimosas will wake up your Valentine to a lavish Breakfast in Bed of Herbed Yellow Pepper Scrambled Eggs on buttery brioche. On any important day (or better yet, for no reason at all), you could even surprise a friend with a totable lunch at the office. Chicken Cashew Chili, Cheddar Cornbread, and Poached Pears with Ginger and Port give new meaning to Desktop Dining.

Sometimes, the most thoughtful treat is a simple dinner that's sensible yet completely satisfying. Our leaner/lighter menus (we've chosen 3 of the best) meet the requirements with delicious, unexpected options. Poached Filets Mignons with Horseradish Sauce, Veal Scallops with Squash, Tomatoes, and Roasted-Garlic Basil Sauce, and Roasted Peppers Stuffed with Chick-Pea and Eggplant Purée make tempting fare *without* the guilt.

With *Gourmet*'s menus in hand, bold flavors, inspired combinations, and lovely tablesetting ideas are assured. Here's to future memories.

Mâche, Pomegranate, and Walnut Salad

DINNER FOR TWO

Crisp Potato Canapés with Caviar, p. 104

Baked Oysters in Jackets with Bacon Cognac Butter, p. 129

Mâche, Pomegranate, and Walnut Salad, p. 187

Billecart-Salmon Brut Champagne

•

Roast Lamb Loin Persillade, p. 140

Parmesan-Potato-Stuffed Roasted Onions, p. 176

Sautéed Radicchio and Fried Kale, p. 177

Robert Mondavi Napa Valley Reserve Cabernet Sauvignon '91

•

*Mocha Mousse with Kumquat Cranberry Sauce
and Phyllo Pecan Crisps*, p. 226

•

Serves 2

Baked Oysters in Jackets with
Bacon Cognac Butter; Crisp Potato
Canapés with Caviar

Mocha Mousse with Kumquat Cranberry Sauce
and Phyllo Pecan Crisps

Roast Lamb Loin Persillade; Parmesan-Potato-Stuffed
Roasted Onion; Sautéed Radicchio and Fried Kale

Apricot Almond Shortbreads

NEW YEAR'S EVE BUFFET PARTY

Exotic Mushroom Pâté, p. 106

Smoked Salmon, Cucumber, and Dill Mousse, p. 108

Tempura Shrimp Nori Rolls, p. 98

Brie and Saffron Phyllo Tartlets, p. 90

Miniature Olive Focaccias with Marinated Peppers, p. 96

Individual Yorkshire Puddings with Rare Roast Beef, p. 100

Asian Pork Crêpes, p. 97

Etude Carneros Pinot Blanc '95

•

Chocolate Walnut Biscotti with Chocolate Custard Swirls, p. 206

Apricot Almond Shortbreads, p. 203

Schramsberg Blanc de Blancs '91

•

Serves 30

Smoked Salmon, Cucumber, and Dill Mousse;
Asian Pork Crêpes; Exotic Mushroom Pâté;
Tempura Shrimp Nori Rolls

Crisp-Skinned Roast Duck with Mock Mandarin Pancakes

CHINESE NEW YEAR

Chinese Chicken Noodle Soup with Spinach and Garlic Chives, p. 119

Crisp-Skinned Roast Duck with Mock Mandarin Pancakes, p. 147

Gingered Vegetable Stir-Fry, p. 180

Handley's Dry Creek Sauvignon Blanc '95

•

Fresh Tangerine Sorbet, p. 218

Litchi Five-Spice Ice Cream, p. 218

Almond Fortune Cookies, p. 202

•

Serves 6

Chinese Chicken Noodle Soup
with Spinach and Garlic Chives

Macerated Grapes   Cappuccino

BREAKFAST IN BED

Passion-Fruit Mimosas, p. 230

Herbed Yellow Pepper Scrambled Eggs with Chive Sour Cream on Brioche, p. 153

Broiled Brown-Sugar Apples with Bacon, p. 154

Macerated Grapes in Clove and Cinnamon Syrup, p. 219

Cappuccino

Serves 2

Herbed Yellow Pepper Scrambled Eggs with
Chive Sour Cream on Brioche; Broiled Brown-Sugar
Apple with Bacon; Passion-Fruit Mimosa

Shrimp, Fava Bean, and Asparagus Salad

EASTER DINNER

Shrimp, Fava Bean, and Asparagus Salad, p. 185

Handley Cellars Anderson Valley Gewürztraminer '95

•

Pork Loin with Morel Stuffing, p. 136

Roasted Celery Root, p. 172

Minted Spring Vegetables, p. 180

Villa Mt. Eden Santa Maria Bien Nacido Vineyard Pinot Noir Grand Reserve '94

•

Rhubarb Raspberry Meringue Cake, p. 198

•

Serves 6

Rhubarb Raspberry Meringue Cake

Pork Loin with Morel Stuffing; Roasted Celery Root;
Minted Spring Vegetables

Poached Pear with Ginger and Port

DESKTOP DINING

Chicken Cashew Chili, p. 145

Cheddar Corn Bread, p. 112

Frisée and Watercress Salad with Jícama and Oranges, p. 187

•

Poached Pears with Ginger and Port, p. 221

•

Serves 2

Warm Camembert Croûte with Dandelion Greens and Red Currants

SPRING DINNER

Asparagus Crudités with Mayonnaise Verte, p. 110

Columbelle, Vin de Pays des Côtes de Gascoyne '96

•

Lavender and Thyme Roasted Poussins, p. 142

Vegetables Printanier, p. 181

Warm Camembert Croûtes with Dandelion Greens and Red Currants, p. 186

La Digoine, Bourgogne Côte Chalonnaise '95, Aubert de Villaine

•

Frozen Lemon Mousses with Strawberry Mint Sauce, p. 215

Château Suduiraut Sauternes '94

•

Serves 4

Asparagus Crudités with Mayonnaise Verte

Lavender and Thyme Roasted Poussin;
Vegetables Printanier

Frozen Lemon Mousses with Strawberry Mint Sauce

Walnut Maple Torte with Maple Meringue Frosting

DESSERT PARTY

Pistachio Rosewater Turkish Delight, p. 225

Mint Turkish Delight, p. 224

Chocolate Tangerine Roulade, p. 195

Raspberry and Lime Custard Tart, p. 212

Brandy Snap Twirls, p. 202

Elderflower and Strawberry Bombe, p. 212

Triple-Chocolate Hazelnut Truffles, p. 223

Walnut Maple Torte with Maple Meringue Frosting, p. 200

Coconut Caramel Panna Cottas, p. 227

Perrier Jouët Extra Dry Champagne

•

Single-Vineyard Grappas

•

Serves 30

Pistachio Rosewater Turkish Delight;
Mint Turkish Delight

Chocolate Tangerine Roulade; Raspberry and Lime Custard Tart;
Brandy Snap Twirls; Elderflower and Strawberry Bombe;
Triple-Chocolate Hazelnut Truffles

"Aquavit"   Herring Canapés

A SWEDISH MIDSUMMER PARTY

Herring Canapés, p. 101

Scandinavian Cheeses (Vodcheese and Västerbotten) and Rye Crisp-Bread

Shrimp Tart, p. 103

Matjes Herring with Red Onion and Dill, p. 102

Smörgåstårta, p. 102
(Savory Sandwich Torte)

Grilled Swedish Meatball Kebabs, p. 100

Pickled Cucumbers, p. 101

Boston Lettuce with Radishes and Lemon Dressing, p. 187

Christer Larsson's Spiced "Aquavit", p. 229   *Blueberry Citron "Aquavit", p. 229*

Carlsberg Beer

Maximin Grünhäuser Abtsberg Riesling Auslese '95

Strawberry Cream Cake, p. 199

Serves 10 to 12

Strawberry Cream Cake

Matjes Herring with Red Onion and Dill, Boiled Potatoes;
Savory Sandwich Torte, Shrimp Tart;
Grilled Swedish Meatball Kebabs; Pickled Cucumbers,
Boston Lettuce with Radishes

Chunky Clam and Bacon Dip with Pita Toasts

CELEBRATING FATHER'S DAY

Chunky Clam and Bacon Dip with Pita Toasts, p. 107

Chehalem Willamette Valley Pinot Gris '96
Samuel Adams Boston Ale   Paulaner Hefe-Weizen

•

Grilled Porterhouse Steaks, p. 131

Mixed Olive Relish, p. 192

Skillet-Crusted Potatoes, p. 177

Arugula Salad with Garlic Balsamic Vinaigrette, p. 186

Château Montelena Napa Valley Estate Cabernet Sauvignon '93

•

Fallen Chocolate Cake Squares à la Mode with Butterscotch Sauce, p. 200

Cossart 10-Year-Old Malmsey Madeira

•

Serves 6

Fallen Chocolate Cake Squares à la
Mode with Butterscotch Sauce

Grilled Porterhouse Steaks; Mixed Olive Relish; Skillet-Crusted
Potatoes; Arugula Salad with Garlic Balsamic Vinaigrette

Watermelon Slices

PICNIC ON THE BEACH

Spicy Yogurt Dip with Chips and Vegetables, p. 110

Grilled Tuna and Roasted Pepper Sandwiches on Thyme Focaccia, p. 126

Prosciutto, Mozzarella, and Olive Sandwiches on Parmesan Focaccia, p. 157

Blackberry Lemonade, p. 230
Weingut Dr. Loosen Riesling Kabinett '95
Bonny Doon Vin Gris de Cigare '95

•

Raspberry Linzer Star Bars, p. 204

Watermelon Slices and Grapes

•

Serves 8

Blackberry Lemonade; Spicy Yogurt Dip with Chips and Vegetables; Raspberry
Linzer Star Bars; Grilled Tuna and Roasted Pepper Sandwiches on Thyme Focaccia;
Prosciutto, Mozzarella, and Olive Sandwich on Parmesan Focaccia

Piquant Crab on Jícama Wedges; Cucumber Coolers

¡TAQUIZA!

A MEXICAN TACO PARTY

Chorizo and Potato Empanaditas, p. 93
(Sausage and Potato Mini-Turnovers)

Guacamole, p. 108   *Fresh Tomato Salsa, p. 193*

Piquant Crab on Jícama Wedges, p. 93

Frozen Watermelon Margaritas, p. 230   *Agua Fresca de Pepino, p. 231*
(Cucumber Cooler)

•

Warm Tortillas, p. 127

Pollo en Pipián Verde, p. 142   *Camarones Adobados a la Parrilla, p. 126*
(Chicken in Pumpkin-Seed Sauce)   *(Grilled Shrimp with Ancho Pasilla Sauce)*

Arrachera con Ajo´y Limón a la Parrilla, p. 134   *Rajas con Crema, p. 171*
(Grilled Garlic-Marinated Skirt Steak with Lime)   *(Poblano Strips with Onions and Cream)*

Cebollitas Asadas, p. 174   *Frijoles Borrachos, p. 182*
(Grilled Spring Onions)   *("Drunken" Beans)*

Tomato and Herb Salad, p. 191

F.E. Trimbach Pinot Blanc '95   *Isole e Olena Chianti Classico '94*   *Dos Equis Dark Beer*

•

Mango, Cactus-Pear, and Lime Sorbets, p. 217

•

Serves 16

Frozen Watermelon Margaritas,
Chorizo and Potato Empanaditas; Guacamole; Tomato
and Herb Salad; Grilled Spring Onions, Drunken Beans,
Warm Tortillas Filled with Chicken in Pumpkin-Seed Sauce

Grilled Garlic-Marinated Skirt Steak with Lime; Poblano Strips with Onions and Cream; Grilled
Shrimp with Ancho Pasilla Sauce; Fresh Tomato Salsa; plated serving; Chopped Avocado

Mango, Cactus-Pear, and Lime Sorbets

Fresh Figs   Chilled Tarragon Tomato Soup

AN HERB GARDEN LUNCH

Elderflower Coolers, p. 231

Fresh Figs with Rosemary Goat Cheese, p. 94

Chilled Tarragon Tomato Soup with Vegetable Confetti, p. 122

Baguette Toasts, p. 122

Cloudy Bay Sauvignon Blanc '96

•

*Grilled Shellfish and Potato Salad with Avocado Salsa, Scallion Oil,
and Plum Coulis, p. 183*

*Domaine du Clos Naudin Vouvray Sec '95
Brigaldara Valpolicella '95*

•

Summer-Berry Basil Kissel, p. 218

Sweet Lemon-Thyme Crisps, p. 204

Val d'Orbieu St.-Jean-de-Minervois

•

Serves 6

Grilled Shellfish and Potato Salad with Avocado
Salsa, Scallion Oil, and Plum Coulis

Summer-Berry Basil Kissel;
Sweet Lemon-Thyme Crisps

Peppermint Chocolate-Chunk and Blueberry Ice Creams

LAZY SUNDAES

Deviled Drumsticks, p. 144

Macaroni Salad with Ham and Peas, p. 186

Pickled Cucumber, Squash, and Red Pepper Salad, p. 190

Molasses Corn Bread, p. 113

De Loach Sonoma Cuvée '95   *Iced Tea*   *Lemonade*

•

ICE CREAMS

Lemon Meringue, p. 214   *Chocolate Velvet, p. 213*   *Strawberry, p. 214*

Peppermint Chocolate-Chunk, p. 216   *Maple Butter-Pecan, p. 214*   *Blueberry, p. 213*

Assorted Ice-Cream Cones

•

SAUCES AND TOPPINGS

Chocolate Sauce, p. 193   *Blackberry-Raspberry Sauce, p. 193*   *Marshmallow Sauce, p. 193*

Crystallized Mint Leaves, p. 194   *Candied Orange and Lemon Zest, p. 194*

Almond Praline, p. 194   *Chocolate Curls, p. 194*   *Maraschino Cherries*

•

Serves 8

Deviled Drumsticks; Macaroni Salad with Ham and Peas;
Pickled Cucumber, Squash, and Red Pepper Salad;
Molasses Corn Bread

Ice-cream fixings; Peppermint Chocolate-Chunk Ice Cream with Chocolate Curls, and Maple Butter-Pecan Ice Cream; Chocolate Velvet Ice Cream Sundae with Marshmallow Sauce and Almond Praline; Blueberry Ice Cream with Candied Orange and Lemon Zest

Strawberry Ice Cream Sundae with Blackberry-Raspberry Sauce and Crystallized Mint Leaf; Lemon Meringue Ice Cream with Candied Orange and Lemon Zest

PICNIC ON THE POND

Minted Honeydew Limeade, p. 231

Roast Beef, Basil, and Spicy Tomato Chutney Lavash Sandwiches, p. 133

Smoked Salmon, Horseradish Sour Cream, and Cucumber Lavash Sandwiches, p. 125

Corn and Tomato Salad with Lemon Thyme and Roasted Poblano Chili, p. 189

Explorateur Cheese and Assorted Crackers

Laurent-Perrier Rosé Brut Champagne
Sierra Cantabria Rioja '94

•

Nectarines, Plums, and Blueberries in Lemony Ginger Anise Syrup, p. 219

Chocolate-Chunk Cookies with Pecans, Dried Apricots, and Tart Cherries, p. 204

•

Serves 4

Roast Beef, Basil, and Spicy Tomato Chutney Lavash Sandwiches;
Smoked Salmon, Horseradish Sour Cream, and Cucumber Lavash Sandwiches;
Corn and Tomato Salad with Lemon Thyme and Roasted Poblano Chili;
Spicy Tomato Chutney

Nectarines, Plums, and Blueberries
in Lemony Ginger Anise Syrup;
Chocolate-Chunk Cookies with Pecans,
Dried Apricots, and Tart Cherries

Explorateur Cheese and Assorted Crackers

Minted Honeydew Limeade

Lemon Meringue Bites

COME FOR COCKTAILS

French 75 Cocktails, p. 230

Snap Bean and Radish Crudités with Caesar Mayonnaise, p. 111

Gorgonzola, Fava Bean, and Purple Potato Canapés, p. 105

Smoked Bocconcini and Tomato-Olive Salsa Canapés, p. 104

Lemon-Vodka Cherry Tomatoes with Dill, p. 99

Crab, Mango, and Mint Nori Rolls, p. 94

Pernod-Marinated New Zealand Mussels with Chervil Oil, p. 95

Chicken Negimaki with Spicy Red Pepper Dipping Sauce, p. 91

Grape Leaves Stuffed with Prosciutto, Dried Fruit, and Herbed Rice, p. 94

Goat Cheese and Onion Tarts, p. 92

Millbrook Vineyards Chardonnay '95

Château de Jau Clos de Paulliles Rosé '96   La Vigne Bourgogne Rouge '95

•

Lemon Meringue Bites, p. 209   Chocolate Raspberry Bites, p. 208

•

Serves 20 to 30

Snap Bean and Radish Crudités with Caesar
Mayonnaise; Gorgonzola, Fava Bean, and Purple
Potato Canapés

Crab, Mango, and Mint Nori Rolls

Pernod-Marinated New Zealand Mussels with Chervil Oil; Chicken Negimaki with
Spicy Red Pepper Dipping Sauce; Grape Leaves Stuffed with Prosciutto,
Dried Fruit, and Herbed Rice; Goat Cheese and Onion Tart

Caramelized Chestnuts

A TRADITIONAL THANKSGIVING

Caramelized Chestnuts, p. 90

Roasted Red Pepper and Garlic Dip with Fennel Crudités, p. 108

•

Roast Turkey with White-Wine Gravy, p. 150   Herb and Bacon Corn-Bread Stuffing, p. 151

Cranberry Kumquat Compote, p. 192

Brussels Sprouts and Roasted Red Onions, p. 170

Bourbon Sweet-Potato Purée with Buttered Pecans, p. 178

Creamed Turnips, p. 179

Peter Michael Chardonnay Mon Plaisir '95
St. Francis Merlot '94

•

Pumpkin Pie "Pumpkin", p. 210

Dried-Fruit Tart with Brandied Crème Anglaise, p. 206

Cossart Gordon 15-Year-Old Bual Madeira

•

Serves 8

Roast Turkey; Brussels Sprouts and Roasted Red Onions;
Cranberry Kumquat Compote; Bourbon Sweet-Potato
Purée with Buttered Pecans; Herb and Bacon
Corn-Bread Stuffing; Creamed Turnips

Dried-Fruit Tart with Brandied Crème Anglaise

Pumpkin Pie "Pumpkin"

Spinach and Lentil Salad

A PACIFIC NORTHWEST THANKSGIVING

Warm Spiked Cider, p. 229

Crisp Wild Rice Griddlecakes with Golden Caviar and Sour Cream, p. 99

•

Spinach and Lentil Salad with Oregon Blue Cheese and Tart Cherry Vinaigrette, p. 188

Chateau Ste. Michelle Columbia Valley Chardonnay '95

•

Cedar Planked Salmon with Maple Glaze and Mustard Mashed Potatoes, p. 124

Sautéed Fresh Chanterelles, p. 173   *Cracked Black Pepper Cream Biscuits, p. 112*

Ponzi Vineyards Reserve Pinot Noir '95

•

Roasted Pears with Hazelnut Syrup and Candied Hazelnuts, p. 220

Chateau Ste. Michelle Horse Heaven Vineyard
Late Harvest Reserve Riesling '95

•

Serves 6

Roasted Pears with Hazelnut Syrup

Cedar Planked Salmon with Maple Glaze and Mustard
Mashed Potatoes; Sautéed Fresh Chanterelles; Cracked
Black Pepper Cream Biscuits

73

Seeded Crisps

COME A CAROLING

Seeded Crisps, p. 113

Cranberry Hot Toddies, p. 230

•

Beef en Croûte with Coriander Walnut Filling, p. 130

Scalloped Fennel and Potatoes, p. 172

Haricots Verts and Red Peppers with Almonds, p. 169

Château Jonquèyres '95

•

Chocolate Coconut Squares, p. 205

Sugared Anise Rosettes, p. 201

Caramel Lollipops, p. 222

A Selection of Late-Harvest Dessert Wines
Ports   Madeiras

•

Serves 16

Sugared Anise Rosettes;
Chocolate Coconut Squares

Beef en Crôute with Coriander Walnut Filling; Haricots Verts and
Red Peppers with Almonds; Scalloped Fennel and Potatoes

Shrimp, Endive, and Watercress Salad

AN AUSTRIAN CHRISTMAS DINNER

Shrimp, Endive, and Watercress Salad, p. 184

Weingut Franz Prager
Riesling Smaragd "Ried Steinriegl" '95

•

Roast Goose with Port Gravy, p. 148

Sausage, Apple, and Rye-Bread Stuffing, p. 148

Mushroom Ragout with Paprika, p. 173

Carrot Marjoram Purée, p. 169

Spiced Red Cabbage, p. 170

Domaine Chave Hermitage '94

•

Chocolate Orange Dobostorte, p. 196

Taylor 20-Year-Old Tawny Port

•

Serves 8

Roast Goose with Port Gravy; Spiced Red Cabbage; Mushroom Ragout with
Paprika; Carrot Marjoram Purée; Sausage, Apple, and Rye-Bread Stuffing

Chocolate Orange Dobostorte

Chilled Minted Cucumber Honeydew Soup

LESS IS MORE

A VEGETARIAN MENU

Chilled Minted Cucumber Honeydew Soup, p. 120

•

Roasted Peppers Stuffed with Chick-Pea and Eggplant Purée and Mushrooms, p. 174

Mesclun Salad with Celery and Croutons, p. 188

•

Serves 4

Each serving about 497 calories
and 10 grams fat (19% of calories from fat)

Peach and Passion-Fruit Phyllo Tart

LESS IS MORE

EASE INTO AUTUMN

Veal Scallops with Squash, Tomatoes, and Roasted-Garlic Basil Sauce, p. 134

Lemon Wild Rice, p. 168

•

Peach and Passion-Fruit Phyllo Tarts, p. 211

•

Serves 4

Each serving about 489 calories
and 10.5 grams fat (19% of calories from fat)

Veal Scallops with Squash, Tomatoes,
and Roasted-Garlic Basil Sauce; Lemon Wild Rice

Cider and Calvados Gelée with Champagne Grapes

LESS IS MORE

HAVE YOUR STEAK...

Poached Filets Mignons with Horseradish Sauce, p. 132

Butternut Squash, Turnip, and Green-Bean Quinoa, p. 166

•

Cider and Calvados Gelées with Champagne Grapes, p. 228

•

Serves 4

Each serving about 497 calories
and 11.6 grams fat (21% of calories from fat)

Poached Filets Mignons with Horseradish Sauce;
Butternut Squash, Turnip, and Green-Bean Quinoa

A RECIPE
COMPENDIUM

With a year's worth of *Gourmet*'s best recipes in hand, the possibilities seem endless: quick weeknight dishes, fancy weekend splurges, easy snacks, luscious desserts, and more. In addition to all the recipes that make up our menus, hundreds of other favorites, culled from *Gourmet*'s food columns, are included. In all, this collection brings together over 400 recipes from 1997.

Because time is always tight these days, we've included nearly 200 recipes that can be made in 45 minutes or less. Plenty of dishes from our Quick Kitchen column make satisfying "meals-in-one," like Sausage and White Bean "Cassoulet" or Curried Lamb Patties with Radish Raita. Many options are perfect for special occasions too. Try Red Snapper Papillotes with Lemon and Thyme accompanied by Vegetable Couscous with Black Olives for a streamlined, elegant little meal. (This year we've made it even easier to find all the quick recipes—they're indicated by a clock symbol (○) throughout the book *and* in the General Index.)

Recipes from our Last Touch column offer familiar dishes with inventive twists. If you're craving something a bit more sophisticated than a hamburger, grill one Indonesian-style with peanut sauce, or make turkey burgers with basil mayonnaise. Seasonal favorites also come in exciting variations. A long-simmered, spicy Louisiana gumbo, whether Beef Filé or Goose and Tasso, warms up any winter table; and sweet-and-sour fruit preparations, like Plum Chutney and Plum Crisp, make great totable treats for fall picnics.

For intensely flavorful dishes without lots of calories and fat—like Cannellini and Lentil Soup with Caramelized Onions or Peppered Pork Loin with Beet and Leek Purée—choose recipes from our Less Is More column. (To find them, look for the feather symbol (✒) throughout the book *and* in the General Index.) And, for the first time ever, we've even included some irresistible readers' offerings from our Sugar and Spice column: Cinnamon Sweet Rolls and Pulled Turkey Barbecue are just a few of our favorites that soon will be yours.

Gourmet's recipes make any occasion special and delicious. Come enjoy the remarkable variety as you peruse the following chapters.

APPETIZERS

Salted Almonds ◔

1 cup blanched whole almonds
1 teaspoon unsalted butter
1 teaspoon coarse kosher or fine sea salt

Preheat oven to 350° F.

In a baking pan spread almonds in one layer and toast in middle of oven until golden, about 12 minutes. Toss almonds with butter and salt until coated well and butter is melted. Makes 1 cup.

For this recipe you will need 4 mini-muffin pans, each containing twelve 1¾- by 1-inch cups. (You could use 2 pans and make shells in 2 batches.)

Brie and Saffron Phyllo Tartlets

six 17- by 12-inch *phyllo* sheets, thawed if
    frozen, stacked between 2 sheets wax
    paper and covered with a kitchen towel
3 tablespoons unsalted butter, melted
1 cup heavy cream
½ teaspoon saffron threads
3 large egg yolks
10 ounces Brie, rind discarded and cheese
    cut into ⅓-inch cubes

Preheat oven to 350° F.

On a work surface arrange 1 *phyllo* sheet with a long side facing you and brush lightly with some butter. Top with a second *phyllo* sheet and brush lightly with butter. Top with a third *phyllo* sheet and cut stacked *phyllo* lengthwise into 4 strips and crosswise into 6 strips to make twenty-four 3-inch squares. With scissors cut off corners of squares to form octagons and cover with plastic wrap.

Line each of 24 mini-muffin cups with 1 *phyllo* octagon, letting edges curl naturally, and bake in middle of oven until golden brown, about 10 minutes. Carefully transfer shells in cups to racks to cool completely. Make 24 more octagons with remaining 3 *phyllo* sheets and butter in same manner. *Shells may be made 1 week ahead and kept in muffin pans, wrapped in plastic wrap, at room temperature or 1 month ahead and frozen.*

In a small saucepan simmer cream with saffron until reduced to about ¾ cup and cool slightly. Whisk in yolks and season with salt and pepper. Divide Brie among shells and spoon 2 teaspoons saffron cream into each shell. Bake tartlets in 2 batches in middle of oven about 8 minutes, or until filling is puffed. Cool tartlets in pans on racks 5 minutes and carefully lift out onto racks to cool completely. Serve tartlets warm or at room temperature. Makes 48 hors d'oeuvres.

Caramelized Chestnuts ◔

1 cup confectioners' sugar
1 tablespoon salt
a 1-pound jar vacuum-packed whole chestnuts*
    (not canned)
about 4 cups vegetable oil for deep-frying

*available at specialty foods shops and some
    supermarkets

Preheat oven to 325° F.

Into a large bowl sift together confectioners' sugar and salt. In a shallow baking pan arrange chestnuts in one layer and bake in upper third of oven 6 to 8 minutes, or until hot and outsides are dry. Add hot chestnuts to sugar mixture, tossing gently to coat, and put a rack over baking pan. In a 3-quart saucepan heat 1½ inches oil over moderate heat until a deep-fat thermometer registers 350° F. Working in batches of 8, fry chestnuts 1 to 2 minutes, or until brown and crisp. With a slotted spoon transfer chestnuts as fried to rack. Return oil to 350° F. between batches and carefully skim caramelized sugar from surface of oil as necessary. *Chestnuts are best served immediately but may be made 1 hour ahead and kept, uncovered, at room temperature.* Makes about 3 cups.

PHOTO ON PAGE 66

Chicken Negimaki with Spicy Red Pepper Dipping Sauce

For chicken negimaki
8 small boneless skinless chicken breast
    halves (about 2½ pounds total)
2 bunches scallions
1 garlic clove
¼ cup soy sauce
2 tablespoons seasoned rice vinegar
2 teaspoons Asian sesame oil
For red pepper dipping sauce
1 red bell pepper
¾ cup distilled white vinegar
½ cup sugar
½ teaspoon dried hot red pepper flakes

⅓ cup black* or white sesame seeds
3 tablespoons vegetable oil
about sixty-five 6-inch wooden skewers

*available at Asian markets and some specialty
    foods shops and supermarkets and by mail
    order from Uwajimaya, tel. (800) 889-1928
    or (206) 624-6248

Make negimaki:
Remove "tenders" (small fillet strips containing white tendon on underside of each breast half) from chicken if necessary. Pound breast halves ½ inch thick between 2 sheets of plastic wrap. On a work surface arrange 1 breast half, smooth side down, with a long side facing you and put 1 scallion (or 2 if very thin) lengthwise on chicken. Roll chicken around scallion and tie with kitchen string at 1-inch intervals. Trim scallion flush with chicken. Make 7 more rolls in same manner.

Mince garlic and in a shallow baking dish just large enough to hold rolls in one layer stir together garlic, soy sauce, rice vinegar, and sesame oil. Add rolls, turning them to coat. *Marinate negimaki, covered and chilled, at least 4 hours and up to 1 day.*
Make sauce:

Coarsely chop bell pepper and in a blender purée with white vinegar. Transfer mixture to a small saucepan and stir in sugar, red pepper flakes, and salt to taste. Simmer sauce 5 minutes and cool. *Sauce may be made 1 week ahead and chilled in an airtight container.*

Spread sesame seeds on a sheet of wax paper. Remove *negimaki* from marinade, letting excess drip off, and roll in sesame seeds to coat. In a large skillet heat 2 tablespoons vegetable oil over moderate heat until hot but not smoking and cook *negimaki* in 2 batches, turning them occasionally, until cooked through, about 10 minutes, adding remaining tablespoon vegetable oil to skillet as necessary. Transfer *negimaki* as cooked to a cutting board and cut crosswise into ½-inch-thick slices, discarding string.

Push skewers through sesame-seed-coated edge of slices. Serve *negimaki* warm or at room temperature with sauce. Makes about 65 hors d'oeuvres.

PHOTO ON PAGE 65

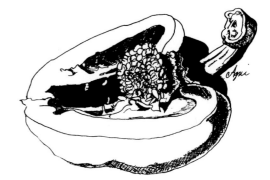

To make these tarts, two tart pans, 13½ by 4 by 1 inches, with removable rims are ideal; however, you could also use one 11- by 1-inch round tart pan with a removable rim.

Goat Cheese and Onion Tarts

For pastry dough
1¼ sticks (10 tablespoons) cold unsalted butter
2 cups all-purpose flour
½ teaspoon salt
2 to 4 tablespoons ice water

3 onions (about 1½ pounds total)
2 tablespoons olive oil
pie weights or raw rice for weighting shells
10 ounces soft mild goat cheese (about 1 heaping cup), softened
1 stick (½ cup) unsalted butter, softened
¾ cup sour cream
3 large eggs
1 teaspoon fresh thyme leaves

Make dough:
Cut butter into bits and in a bowl with a pastry blender or in a food processor blend or pulse together with flour and salt until mixture resembles coarse meal. Add 2 tablespoons ice water and toss with a fork or pulse until incorporated. Add enough remaining ice water, 1 tablespoon at a time, tossing with fork or pulsing to incorporate, to form a dough. On a work surface smear dough with heel of hand in 3 or 4 forward motions to make dough easier to work with. Divide dough in half and pat each half into a rectangle, about 6 by 3 inches. *Chill dough*

rectangles, wrapped separately in plastic wrap, at least 1 hour and up to 1 week.

Thinly slice onions and in a large skillet cook with salt to taste in oil, covered, over moderate heat, stirring occasionally, 10 minutes, or until softened. Cook onions, uncovered, stirring, until golden and any liquid in skillet is evaporated.

Preheat oven to 375° F.

On a lightly floured surface roll out 1 dough rectangle into a 16- by 6-inch rectangle and fit it into a tart pan, 13½ by 4 by 1 inches, with a removable fluted rim. Roll a rolling pin over pastry to trim it flush with top of rim and prick bottom of shell in several places with a fork. Make 1 more tart shell in another tart pan in same manner.

Line shells with foil and fill with pie weights or raw rice. Bake shells in middle of oven 10 minutes. Carefully remove foil and weights or rice and bake shells until pale golden, about 5 minutes more.

While shells are baking, whisk together goat cheese, butter, and sour cream until smooth and whisk in eggs until combined well. Season custard with salt and pepper.

Spread onions evenly in shells and pour custard over onions. Sprinkle thyme over custard and bake tarts in middle of oven 20 minutes, or until puffed and golden. Cool tarts in pans on racks (filling will deflate). *Tarts may be made 2 days ahead, cooled completely in pans, and chilled, covered, in pans. Reheat tarts in pans, uncovered, in a 350° F. oven about 15 minutes to crisp crusts. Remove rims from tart pans.*

Cut tarts crosswise into ¾-inch-wide slices to make about 32 hors d'oeuvres and, if desired, halve slices crosswise to make about 64 hors d'oeuvres. Serve tarts warm or at room temperature. Makes about 32 large or 64 small hors d'oeuvres.

PHOTO ON PAGE 65

Chorizo and Potato Empanaditas
(Sausage and Potato Mini-Turnovers)

For filling
1 large boiling potato (about ½ pound)
½ pound fresh Mexican *chorizo** (spicy
   pork sausage)
1 teaspoon dried oregano (preferably
   Mexican), crumbled
For dough
2 cups *masa harina**
1¼ cups warm water

vegetable oil for deep-frying

Accompaniment: guacamole (page 108)
   or fresh tomato salsa (page 193)

*available at Latino markets, some specialty
   foods shops, and supermarkets. Tortilla presses
   are available by mail order from Williams-
   Sonoma, (800) 541-2233.

Make filling:
Peel potato and cut into ¼-inch dice. In a saucepan of boiling salted water cook potato 3 minutes, or
until just cooked through, and drain in a colander.

Remove casings from *chorizo* and crumble or
finely chop meat. In a heavy skillet cook *chorizo*
over moderate heat, stirring, 5 minutes. Add potato,
oregano, and salt to taste and cook, stirring, 5
minutes. Cool filling completely. *Filling may be
kept, covered, chilled 2 days or frozen 2 weeks.*
Make dough:
Line 2 baking sheets with plastic wrap.

In a large bowl stir together *masa harina* and
warm water until a dough forms. Pinch off small
pieces of dough and shape into about forty 1-inch
balls. Transfer balls to a baking sheet and cover with
more plastic wrap.

From a plastic bag cut two 5-inch squares and use
one to line lower half of a tortilla press (see above
source). Put a ball of dough in tortilla press and top
with second square of plastic. Close tortilla press,
pushing gently on lever to flatten dough just to a 2½-
inch round. (Alternatively, flatten dough between
squares of plastic using a rolling pin.) Remove top
plastic square and put a rounded teaspoon filling in

center of round. Fold round over filling to form a
half moon, using plastic underneath to support
dough if necessary, and pinch edges together to seal.
Transfer turnover to other baking sheet. Make more
turnovers in same manner, reusing plastic squares,
and put on baking sheets. *Turnovers may be prepared up to this point and kept, covered with plastic
wrap, chilled 1 day or frozen 1 week. Thaw turnovers
1 hour before proceeding.*

In a large saucepan heat 1 inch oil until it registers
375° F. on a deep-fat thermometer and fry turnovers
in batches of 8 to 10 until golden, 2 to 3 minutes,
transferring with a slotted spoon to paper towels to
drain and making sure oil returns to 375° F. before
adding next batch.

Serve *empanaditas* immediately with guacamole
or salsa. Makes about 40 hors d'oeuvres.

PHOTO ON PAGE 47

Piquant Crab on Jícama Wedges ◌

a 2-pound *jícama**
2 tablespoons fresh lime juice,
   or to taste
½ pound jumbo lump crab meat
about 2 cups fresh tomato salsa
   (page 193)

Garnish: about 40 fresh coriander leaves

*available seasonally at Latino markets
   and some specialty foods shops and
   supermarkets

Peel *jícama* and cut crosswise into ¼-inch-thick
rounds. Cut each round into 6 or 8 wedges. In a
sealable plastic bag toss wedges with 1 tablespoon
lime juice to coat. *Wedges may be made 1 day ahead
and chilled in bag.*

Pick over crab meat, removing cartilage, and
shred meat. *Crab meat may be prepared 1 day ahead
and chilled, covered.* In a bowl combine crab meat,
salsa, remaining lime juice, and salt to taste.

Top each *jícama* wedge with 1 tablespoon crab
meat mixture and a coriander leaf. Makes about 40
hors d'oeuvres.

PHOTO ON PAGE 46

Fresh Figs with Rosemary Goat Cheese ☺

11 ounces soft mild goat cheese at room
temperature (about 1¼ cups)
½ cup heavy cream
2 teaspoons finely chopped fresh rosemary
leaves, or to taste
1 tablespoon honey
1 pound fresh figs

In a bowl whisk together all ingredients except figs until smooth and season with salt and pepper. *Rosemary goat cheese may be made 1 day ahead and chilled, covered. Bring goat cheese to cool room temperature before serving.*

Mound goat cheese in center of a platter. Halve figs and arrange around goat cheese for dipping. Makes about 1¾ cups rosemary goat cheese.

PHOTO ON PAGE 50

Crab, Mango, and Mint Nori Rolls

½ firm-ripe mango
1 pound jumbo lump crab meat
2 tablespoons fresh lime juice
1½ tablespoons packed light brown sugar
2 tablespoons *wasabi* powder* (Japanese
horseradish powder) or *wasabi* paste*
ten 8- by 7½-inch sheets toasted *nori**
(dried laver)
1 cup packed fresh mint leaves

*available at Asian markets and some specialty
foods shops and supermarkets and by mail
order from Uwajimaya, (800) 889-1928.
Bamboo *sushi* mat is also available from
these sources.

Cut skin from mango and cut flesh into julienne strips. Pick over crab meat to remove any bits of cartilage and shell and in a bowl stir together with lime juice, brown sugar, and salt to taste. If using *wasabi* powder, in a small bowl stir together with 2 teaspoons water and let stand, covered, 10 minutes to make *wasabi* paste.

Cut *nori* sheets in half lengthwise. On a work surface put a *sushi* mat with bamboo strips of mat parallel to front of work surface. (Alternatively, use a 9-inch square of heavy-duty foil as a mat.) Put 1 *nori* piece on mat with a short side lined up with edge of mat that is closest to you. Spread ¼ teaspoon *wasabi* paste across bottom edge of *nori* and top with 5 or 6 mint leaves so that some stick out on each side. Top mint leaves evenly with a heaping tablespoon crab mixture and 2 or 3 mango strips. Beginning with a short side and using mat as a guide, roll up *nori* tightly (use mat to help tighten roll). Seal seam with a little water and with a sharp knife cut roll crosswise into 3 pieces. Make more rolls in same manner. *Nori rolls may be made 3 hours ahead and chilled, covered.* Makes about 60 hors d'oeuvres.

PHOTO ON PAGE 64

Grape Leaves Stuffed with Prosciutto, Dried Fruit, and Herbed Rice

a 1-pound jar brine-packed grape leaves*
½ cup pine nuts
1 onion
6 ounces thinly sliced prosciutto
½ cup golden raisins
¼ cup packed fresh dill leaves
¼ cup packed fresh flat-leafed parsley leaves
2 cups water
½ teaspoon salt
1 cup long-grain rice
4 tablespoons olive oil
⅓ cup dried currants
6 tablespoons fresh lemon juice
about 2½ cups chicken broth

*available at specialty foods shops and some
supermarkets

Rinse grape leaves in several changes of cold water and in a large saucepan of boiling water blanch 3 minutes. In a colander drain leaves and refresh under cold water. Drain leaves well.

Toast pine nuts golden and chop separately onion, prosciutto, raisins, dill, and parsley. In a saucepan bring 2 cups water to a boil with salt and stir in rice. Cook rice, covered, over moderately low heat until water is absorbed, 17 to 20 minutes, and transfer to a large bowl. In a heavy skillet cook onion in

2 tablespoons oil over moderate heat, stirring, until tender and golden and stir into rice with pine nuts, prosciutto, raisins, dill, parsley, currants, 3 tablespoons lemon juice, and salt and pepper to taste until combined well.

Arrange 1 grape leaf, smooth side down, on a kitchen towel. Trim stem flush with leaf (if leaf is large, trim to 5½ inches across), reserving stem and any trimmings. Spoon about 1 tablespoon filling onto leaf near stem end and roll up filling tightly in leaf, folding in sides and squeezing roll to pack filling. (Roll should be about 3½ inches long.) Make more rolls in same manner.

In a saucepan heat broth just to a simmer and keep warm, covered. Line bottom of a 3-quart heavy saucepan with reserved stems and trimmings and any remaining grape leaves and arrange rolls, seam sides down, close together in layers over leaves, seasoning each layer with salt. Drizzle remaining 2 tablespoons oil and remaining 3 tablespoons lemon juice over rolls and cover with an inverted heatproof plate slightly smaller than diameter of pan, pressing down lightly. Add just enough broth to come up to rim of plate and bring to a boil. Reduce heat to low and cook rolls, covered with plate and a lid, 50 minutes, or until leaves are tender and most of liquid is absorbed.

Remove pan from heat and cool rolls, covered. Using plate to hold back rolls, pour off remaining liquid and transfer rolls to another plate, discarding stems, trimmings, and grape leaves. *Stuffed grape leaves may be made 5 days ahead and chilled, covered.*

Halve rolls diagonally and serve at room temperature or chilled. Makes about 80 hors d'oeuvres.

PHOTO ON PAGE 65

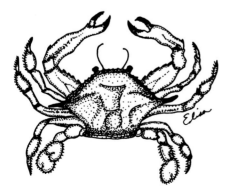

Pernod-Marinated New Zealand Mussels with Chervil Oil

2 garlic cloves
½ cup plus 2 tablespoons olive oil
¼ cup water
6 pounds mussels (preferably New Zealand green)
3 tablespoons Pernod or other anise-flavored liqueur
½ cup packed fresh chervil sprigs or fresh basil leaves
¼ cup packed fresh flat-leafed parsley leaves
¼ teaspoon salt

Garnish: about 60 small fresh chervil sprigs or tiny basil leaves

Mince 1 garlic clove and in a large skillet cook in 2 tablespoons oil over moderate heat, stirring, until golden. Add water and half of mussels and steam mussels, covered, stirring once or twice, 2 to 5 minutes, transferring them as they open with a slotted spoon to a large bowl. (Discard any mussels that are unopened after 5 minutes.) In liquid remaining in skillet steam remaining mussels in same manner and transfer to bowl.

Pour liquid remaining in skillet through a fine sieve into a small bowl and stir in liqueur to make marinade.

When mussels are cool enough to handle, remove from shells. Clean and reserve 1 half shell from each mussel. Add mussels to marinade, tossing to coat, and season with salt. *Marinate mussels, covered with plastic wrap and chilled, at least 3 hours and up to 1 day. Chill reserved shells in a sealable plastic bag.*

Thinly slice remaining garlic clove and in a small saucepan cook in remaining ½ cup oil over moderate heat, stirring, until golden. Discard garlic with slotted spoon and in a blender blend oil, chervil or basil, parsley, and salt until herbs are finely chopped. *Chervil oil may be made 1 week ahead and chilled in an airtight container. Bring oil to room temperature before using.*

Arrange reserved mussel shells on plates and spoon about ½ teaspoon chervil oil into each shell. Add mussels and garnish with chervil or basil. Makes about 60 hors d'oeuvres.

PHOTO ON PAGE 65

Miniature Olive Focaccias with Marinated Peppers

For tomato paste
¼ cup dried tomatoes in oil, drained,
    reserving 1 tablespoon oil
¼ cup pine nuts, toasted golden
3 tablespoons freshly grated Parmesan
For marinated peppers
2 red bell peppers, quick-roasted and
    peeled (procedure follows)
2 yellow bell peppers, quick-roasted
    and peeled (procedure follows)
2 garlic cloves, minced
⅓ cup extra-virgin olive oil
½ tablespoon fresh thyme leaves

1 recipe olive *focaccia* dough (page 97)
2 tablespoons fresh thyme leaves

Make tomato paste:

In a small food processor purée dried tomatoes, reserved tablespoon oil, pine nuts, and Parmesan until smooth. *Tomato paste may be made 1 week ahead and chilled, covered.*

Prepare peppers:

Cut roasted peppers into 1-inch-long thin strips. In a small bowl stir together peppers, garlic, oil, and thyme and season with salt and pepper. *Marinate peppers at room temperature, covered, at least 3 hours. Peppers may be prepared 1 week ahead and chilled, covered.*

Preheat oven to 375° F. and lightly oil 2 large baking sheets.

On a lightly floured surface with a floured rolling pin roll out dough into a 16-inch round (⅛ inch thick). Cut out 36 rounds with a 1½-inch round cutter and arrange 1 inch apart on baking sheets. Spoon about ¾ teaspoon tomato paste onto each round and top with about 1 tablespoon marinated peppers. Sprinkle hors d'oeuvres with thyme.

Bake hors d'oeuvres in batches in middle of oven 16 minutes, or until rounds are pale golden, and cool on a rack. *Hors d'oeuvres may be made 1 day ahead, cooled completely, and chilled, covered, or 1 month ahead and frozen. Bring hors d'oeuvres to room temperature and heat in a 300° F. oven 10 minutes before serving.* Makes 36 hors d'oeuvres.

*To Quick-Roast and Peel Bell Peppers
or Chilies* ◐

Gas stove method:

Lay peppers, on their sides, on racks of burners (preferably 1 to a burner) and turn flame on high. Char peppers, turning them with tongs, until skins are blackened, 6 to 8 minutes.

Transfer peppers to a bowl and let stand, covered with plastic wrap, until cool enough to handle. Peel peppers (wear rubber gloves when handling chilies). Cut off tops and discard seeds and ribs.

Broiler method:

Preheat broiler.

Quarter peppers lengthwise, discarding stems, seeds, and ribs (wear rubber gloves when handling chilies). Put peppers, skin sides up, on rack of a broiler pan and broil about 2 inches from heat until skins are blistered and charred, 8 to 12 minutes.

Transfer peppers to a small bowl and let stand, covered with plastic wrap, until cool enough to handle. Peel peppers.

Olive Focaccia Dough

¾ cup warm water (105°–115° F.)
1½ teaspoons active dry yeast
½ teaspoon sugar
2¼ to 2½ cups all-purpose flour
1 teaspoon salt
⅛ teaspoon freshly ground black pepper
2 tablespoons olive oil
3 tablespoons chopped pitted Kalamata olives

In bowl of a standing electric mixer fitted with dough hook stir together water, yeast, and sugar and let stand 5 minutes, or until foamy. Stir in 2¼ cups flour, salt, pepper, oil, and olives and knead dough, scraping down dough hook occasionally and adding enough of remaining ¼ cup flour to form a soft, slightly sticky dough, about 3 minutes.

Transfer dough to a lightly oiled bowl, turning to coat, and let rise, covered with plastic wrap, in a warm place until doubled in bulk, about 45 minutes. *Dough may be made 1 day ahead and chilled in bowl, covered with plastic wrap.*

Asian Pork Crêpes

½ pound pork tenderloin, trimmed of excess fat
1 tablespoon vegetable oil
3 tablespoons hoisin sauce*
1 tablespoon honey
8 chive-ginger crêpes (recipe follows)
¼ cup Asian plum sauce*
4 radishes, cut into thin strips
10 chives, cut diagonally into 1-inch-long pieces
2 scallions, cut into 1-inch-long pieces and pieces
    cut into thin strips

*available at Asian markets and most
    supermarkets

Pat pork dry with paper towels and season with salt and pepper. In an ovenproof skillet heat oil over moderately high heat until hot but not smoking and brown pork on all sides. Roast pork in skillet in middle of oven until a meat thermometer registers 155° F., about 20 minutes.

Transfer pork to a board and cool completely. Cut pork into 1-inch-long strips and put in a small bowl.

Add hoisin sauce and honey, stirring to combine, and season with salt and pepper.

Brush 1 crêpe lightly with plum sauce and cut into 4 wedges. Arrange 3 or 4 pork strips on each wedge parallel to 1 cut edge and top with 6 radish strips, 4 chive pieces, and some scallion strips. Roll up crêpe around filling into a cone, tucking in pointed end as rolling. Make 31 more hors d'oeuvres with remaining crêpes, plum sauce, pork, and vegetables in same manner. Makes 32 hors d'oeuvres.

PHOTO ON PAGE 17

Chive-Ginger Crêpes

½ cup all-purpose flour
¼ teaspoon salt
1 large egg
⅓ cup milk
½ cup club soda or seltzer (from a new bottle)
2 teaspoons vegetable oil
½ teaspoon grated peeled fresh gingerroot
freshly ground black pepper to taste
¼ cup chopped fresh chives
½ stick (¼ cup) unsalted butter, melted

In a blender or food processor blend all crêpe ingredients except chives and butter until smooth and transfer to a bowl. *Let batter stand at room temperature, covered, 1 hour. Batter may be made 1 day ahead and chilled, covered.*

Add chives to batter and stir well. Heat a 6-inch non-stick skillet over moderate heat until hot. Brush skillet lightly with some butter and remove from heat. Half fill a ¼-cup measure with batter and pour into skillet, tilting skillet quickly to cover bottom.

Cook crêpe until underside is golden and top appears almost dry, about 30 seconds. Turn crêpe over with a thin spatula and cook until underside is golden, 15 to 20 seconds more. Slide crêpe onto a kitchen towel and cool. Make more crêpes with remaining batter in same manner, brushing skillet lightly with butter for each crêpe and stacking cooked crêpes on another kitchen towel after they cool. *Crêpes may be made 1 day ahead and chilled, stacked between sheets of wax paper and wrapped well in plastic wrap. Bring crêpes to room temperature before using.* Makes about 10 crêpes.

Tempura Shrimp Nori Rolls

For dipping sauce
¼ cup soy sauce
2 tablespoons honey
2 tablespoons fresh lime juice
1 teaspoon grated peeled fresh gingerroot
2 tablespoons chopped fresh coriander sprigs
For shrimp paste
¾ pound shrimp (about 30 medium), shelled
    and deveined
2 tablespoons egg white (from about
    1 large egg)
2 tablespoons heavy cream
1 tablespoon fresh lime juice
½ teaspoon grated peeled fresh gingerroot
2 teaspoons cornstarch
For tempura batter
1 large egg yolk
1 cup all-purpose flour
1 cup ice water
¼ cup cornstarch
1 teaspoon salt
freshly ground black pepper to taste

four 8- by 7½-inch sheets toasted nori*
    (dried laver)
1 scallion, quartered lengthwise
½ large carrot, cut lengthwise into
    thin strips
½ red bell pepper, cut into thin strips
¼ cup chopped fresh coriander sprigs
vegetable oil for deep-frying

*available at Japanese markets and some
    supermarkets and by mail order from
    Uwajimaya, tel. (800) 889-1928

Make sauce:
In a bowl stir together soy sauce, honey, lime juice, and gingerroot until combined well. Sauce may be made 3 days ahead and chilled, covered. Bring sauce to room temperature before serving. Stir in coriander.

Make shrimp paste:
In a food processor pulse shrimp paste ingredients together until they just form a smooth paste. Shrimp paste may be made 1 day ahead and chilled, covered.

Make batter:
In a blender blend batter ingredients until smooth. Transfer batter to a shallow bowl.

Assemble nori rolls:
On a work surface arrange 1 nori sheet, shiny side down, with a long side facing you. Spread ½ cup shrimp paste across lower two thirds of nori and brush top third of nori with sauce. Arrange 1 scallion quarter on shrimp paste across bottom edge and top with 3 carrot strips.

Top carrot evenly with one fourth bell pepper strips and sprinkle with 1 tablespoon coriander. Beginning with edge closest to you, roll up nori tightly and trim ends if necessary. Make 3 more rolls with remaining nori, shrimp paste, sauce, vegetables, and coriander in same manner. Rolls may be assembled 1 day ahead and chilled, covered. Bring rolls to room temperature before proceeding.

In a deep heavy skillet heat 3 inches oil to 375° F. on a deep-fat thermometer. Dip 1 roll in batter to coat completely. Transfer roll to hot oil with 2 pairs of metal tongs and fry until golden, about 4 minutes. Transfer roll to paper towels to drain and fry remaining 3 rolls in same manner, making sure oil returns to 375° F. before adding next roll.

Cut rolls diagonally into ½-inch-thick slices and serve warm or at room temperature with dipping sauce. Makes about 32 hors d'oeuvres.

PHOTO ON PAGE 17

Batter-Fried Zucchini Spears with Basil ☺

¾ cup all-purpose flour
¾ cup beer
¾ teaspoon salt
2 medium zucchini (about ¾ pound total)
12 fresh basil leaves
about 3 cups vegetable oil for deep-frying

In a bowl whisk together flour, beer, and salt and season with pepper.

Halve zucchini crosswise. Cut each half into 6 spears and put, skin side down, on a cutting board. With a sharp thin knife cut a lengthwise slit about ½ inch deep along top edge of each spear. Halve basil leaves lengthwise and, using dull side of a small knife, push a half leaf into slit of each spear.

In an 8-inch heavy saucepan or deep skillet heat 1 inch oil over moderate heat until it registers 375° F. on a deep-fat thermometer.

Working in batches of 6, coat spears in batter, letting excess drip off, and fry until deep golden, about 2 minutes, transferring with metal tongs to paper towels to drain. Serves 2 generously as an hors d'oeuvre or a side dish.

*Crisp Wild Rice Griddlecakes with
Golden Caviar and Sour Cream*

½ cup wild rice
2 cups water
1 large egg
⅓ cup chopped fresh chives
2 tablespoons vegetable oil
¼ cup sour cream
2 ounces caviar (preferably golden whitefish*)

Garnish: whole fresh chives

*available fresh at some specialty foods shops
  or pasteurized in jars at supermarkets

In a fine sieve rinse rice under cold running water and drain. In a small heavy saucepan bring 2 cups water to a boil and stir in rice. Simmer rice, uncovered, until just tender but grains are not open, about 40 minutes. Drain rice in sieve and rinse under cold running water. Drain rice well and transfer to a bowl. *Rice may be made 1 day ahead and chilled, covered. Bring rice to room temperature before proceeding.*

Lightly beat egg and stir into rice with chives and salt and pepper to taste.

In a large non-stick skillet heat 1 tablespoon oil over moderately high heat until hot but not smoking. Drop heaping teaspoons rice mixture into skillet without crowding and cook, flattening griddlecakes slightly with a spatula (griddlecakes should be about 1½ to 2 inches in diameter), until golden brown, about 1½ minutes on each side. Transfer griddlecakes as cooked to paper towels to drain and season with salt and pepper. Make more griddlecakes in same manner with remaining rice mixture and oil.

Cool griddlecakes slightly and top with sour cream and caviar. Garnish griddlecakes with chives. Makes about 24 griddlecakes.

Lemon-Vodka Cherry Tomatoes with Dill

4 pints firm vine-ripened cherry tomatoes
⅓ cup lemon-flavored or plain vodka
3 tablespoons white-wine vinegar
1 tablespoon sugar
2 tablespoons small fresh dill leaves
freshly ground black pepper to taste
1 firm lemon

Cut a small shallow X in stem end of each tomato and have ready a bowl of ice and cold water. In a saucepan of boiling water blanch tomatoes, 3 at a time, 2 to 3 seconds and immediately transfer with a slotted spoon to ice water to stop cooking. (Tomatoes should still be firm, but skins should slip off easily.)

In a bowl stir together vodka, vinegar, and sugar until sugar is dissolved. Peel tomatoes and add to vodka mixture with dill, pepper, and salt to taste, tossing gently. *Marinate tomatoes, covered and chilled, at least 30 minutes and up to 1 hour.*

With a citrus zester cut 2 tablespoons zest in strips from lemon. (Alternatively, cut a 3- by 1-inch piece zest from lemon with a vegetable peeler and cut crosswise into thin strips.)

Just before serving, gently toss tomatoes with a rubber spatula and sprinkle with zest. Serve tomatoes with small forks or wooden picks. Makes about 80 hors d'oeuvres.

For this recipe you will need three mini-muffin pans, each containing twelve 1¾- by 1-inch cups.

Individual Yorkshire Puddings with Rare Roast Beef

For Yorkshire pudding batter
1 cup plus 2 tablespoons milk
2 large eggs
1 large egg yolk
1 cup all-purpose flour
1 teaspoon salt
freshly ground black pepper to taste

¾ cup vegetable oil
¾ cup sour cream
1 tablespoon plus 1 teaspoon drained bottled
  horseradish
1 teaspoon chopped fresh flat-leafed parsley
  leaves
½ pound cooked rare roast beef, sliced ⅜ inch
  thick and slices cut into 1-inch pieces

Garnish: 36 small fresh flat-leafed parsley leaves

Make batter:
In a blender blend batter ingredients until smooth and transfer to a small bowl. Let batter stand, covered, 1 hour.
Preheat oven to 425° F.
Put 2 mini-muffin pans on 1 baking sheet and put a third pan on another baking sheet. Spoon 1 teaspoon oil into each cup. Put first baking sheet in middle of oven 3 minutes to heat oil in cups. Working quickly, pour 2 teaspoons batter into hot oil in each cup and bake in middle of oven 18 minutes, or until pudding shells are golden and puffed. Remove shells from cups with tongs and cool on racks. Repeat procedure with other baking sheet. Shells may be made 3 days ahead and chilled, covered, or 1 month ahead and frozen in airtight containers. Bring shells to room temperature and recrisp in a 300° F. oven 10 minutes.
In a bowl stir together sour cream, horseradish, and parsley and transfer to a small pastry bag fitted with ⅛-inch plain tip.
Fold a few beef slices into each shell and pipe 1

teaspoon horseradish cream onto each pudding. Garnish puddings with parsley leaves. Makes 36 hors d'oeuvres.

SWEDISH HORS D'OEUVRES

Grilled Swedish Meatball Kebabs

about twenty-eight 10-inch bamboo skewers
For Swedish meatballs
¾ pound ground chuck
¾ pound ground pork
1¼ cups fine fresh bread crumbs
1 large egg
½ cup finely chopped onion
½ teaspoon ground allspice
1 teaspoon salt, or to taste
freshly ground black pepper to taste
For mustard sauce
⅓ cup Dijon mustard
⅓ cup packed brown sugar
3 tablespoons cider vinegar
3 tablespoons vegetable oil
2 tablespoons finely chopped fresh parsley leaves

2 medium yellow squash
1 onion
2 yellow bell peppers
1 pint vine-ripened yellow cherry tomatoes

Accompaniment: pickled cucumbers (recipe
  follows)

In a large dish soak bamboo skewers in warm water to cover 30 minutes.
Make meatballs:
In a large bowl with your hands blend together all meatball ingredients until just combined well (do not overmix). Form mixture into 1¼-inch balls and arrange on a tray. Meatballs may be prepared up to this point 1 day ahead and chilled, covered.
Make sauce:
In a bowl whisk together all sauce ingredients until brown sugar is dissolved. Sauce may be made 1 day ahead and chilled, covered.

Halve squash lengthwise and cut crosswise into ½-inch-thick pieces. Quarter onion and cut onion and bell peppers into 1-inch pieces. Thread 2 meatballs alternately with assorted cut vegetables and tomatoes onto each skewer. *Kebabs may be assembled 8 hours ahead and chilled, covered.*

Prepare grill.

Grill kebabs on an oiled rack set 5 to 6 inches over glowing coals, turning kebabs frequently, 10 minutes. Brush kebabs with sauce and grill, turning them and brushing frequently with sauce, until meatballs are cooked through, about 5 to 10 minutes more. (Alternatively, kebabs may be broiled under a preheated broiler about 3 inches from heat.) Discard any remaining sauce.

Serve kebabs with pickled cucumbers. Makes about 28 kebabs, serving 10 to 12 as part of a buffet.

PHOTO ON PAGE 38

Pickled Cucumbers ☉+

1 English cucumber
½ cup white-wine vinegar
3 tablespoons sugar
1 tablespoon finely chopped fresh mint leaves
1 tablespoon finely chopped fresh parsley leaves
½ teaspoon salt
¼ teaspoon freshly ground black pepper

Cut cucumber crosswise into very thin slices (preferably using a manual slicer). In a bowl whisk together remaining ingredients until sugar is dissolved and add cucumber, tossing to coat. *Marinate cucumbers, covered and chilled, stirring occasionally, 4 hours.* Serves 10 to 12 as part of a buffet.

PHOTO ON PAGE 38

Herring Canapés ☉

¾ pound small boiling potatoes (preferably new)
3 pickled *matjes* herring fillets* (about 6 ounces)
about ½ cup sour cream
1 hard-boiled large egg, chopped fine
¼ cup chopped drained canned beets (about 1)
1 scallion (white and pale green parts only),
    chopped fine

*available at specialty foods shops and by mail order from Murray's Sturgeon Shop, tel. (212) 724-2650

In a saucepan cover potatoes with salted cold water by 1 inch and simmer until just tender, 10 to 15 minutes. Drain potatoes in a colander and cool completely. Cut potatoes crosswise into ¼-inch-thick slices.

Rinse herring under cold water and pat dry with paper towels. Cut fillets diagonally into ½-inch-thick slices.

Assemble canapés:

Arrange a herring slice on each potato slice. Top each canapé with about ½ teaspoon sour cream. Top half of canapés with egg and half with beet. Sprinkle canapés with scallion. Makes about 34 canapés, serving 10 to 12 as part of a buffet.

PHOTO ON PAGE 36

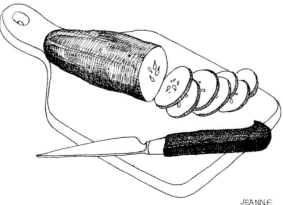

JEANNE

Matjes Herring with Red Onion and Dill ◐+

10 pickled *matjes* herring fillets* (about
  1½ pounds)
2 medium red onions,
  chopped fine
1 cup finely chopped fresh dill sprigs
¼ cup red-wine vinegar
freshly ground black pepper to taste
½ cup vegetable oil

Accompaniment: boiled small potatoes
  (preferably new)

*available at specialty foods shops and by mail
  order from Murray's Sturgeon Shop,
  tel. (212) 724-2650

Rinse herring fillets under cold water and pat dry
with paper towels. Cut fillets crosswise into ¾-inch
pieces.

In a 1-quart glass or ceramic crock or bowl arrange some herring in one layer. Top herring with a
layer of some onions and sprinkle with some dill.
Layer remaining herring, onions, and dill in same
manner.

In a small bowl whisk together vinegar, pepper,
and salt to taste and add oil in a stream, whisking
until emulsified. Pour dressing over herring mixture.
*Chill herring mixture, covered, stirring occasionally,
at least 8 hours and up to 2 days.*

Serve herring with potatoes. Serves 10 to 12 as
part of a buffet.

PHOTO ON PAGE 38

Smörgåstårta
Savory Sandwich Torte

For egg salad filling
8 hard-boiled large eggs, chopped fine
⅔ cup mayonnaise
2 scallions (white and pale green parts only),
  chopped fine
1 teaspoon drained capers, chopped
For smoked salmon filling
10 ounces smoked salmon, chopped fine
1½ cups *crème fraîche**
1 teaspoon fresh lemon juice

For cream cheese filling
¾ cup whipped cream cheese
½ stick (¼ cup) unsalted butter,
  softened
3 tablespoons mixed finely chopped fresh herbs
  such as parsley, dill, and chives
40 slices very thin firm white sandwich bread
  (from two 1-pound loaves)
For herb topping
⅓ cup finely chopped fresh parsley leaves
⅓ cup finely chopped fresh dill sprigs
⅓ cup finely chopped fresh chives

*available at specialty foods shops and many
  supermarkets

Make fillings:
In 3 separate bowls combine all ingredients for
each filling, stirring each together until combined
well. Season each filling with salt and pepper.

Stack 4 bread slices together and with a serrated
knife trim crusts from bread. Stack and trim remaining 36 bread slices in same manner.

On a baking sheet lined with parchment paper or
wax paper arrange 8 bread slices side by side in 2
rows of 4 slices each to form a rectangle. Top rectangle with half of egg salad filling, spreading
evenly, and cover with 8 more bread slices in same
manner, pressing gently on top and sides to form an
even layer.

Top second layer of bread with half of salmon
filling, spreading evenly, and cover with 8 bread
slices in same manner to form an even layer.

Top third layer of bread with all of cream cheese
filling, spreading evenly, and cover with 8 bread
slices in same manner to form an even layer.

Make layers with remaining salmon filling, remaining 8 bread slices, and remaining egg salad filling
in same manner, ending with egg salad. *Chill torte,
covered with plastic wrap, at least 12 hours and up
to 2 days.*
Make topping:
In a bowl stir together herbs until combined well.

Trim sides of torte and sprinkle topping over egg
salad layer.

Serve torte cut into small pieces. Serves 10 to 12
as part of a buffet.

PHOTO ON PAGE 38

Shrimp Tart

For pumpernickel crust
9 ounces dense pumpernickel* (about eight
    4-inch square slices; preferably Wild's
    multigrain Danish)
5 tablespoons unsalted butter, melted and cooled
For shrimp filling
1¼ pounds medium shrimp (about 36)
3 tablespoons golden or red lumpfish caviar**
    (from a 2-ounce jar)
2 cups sour cream
½ cup mayonnaise
½ cup heavy cream
2 teaspoons unflavored gelatin
3 tablespoons fresh lemon juice
1 tablespoon water
1 tablespoon finely chopped fresh chives
freshly ground white pepper to taste

Garnish: coarsely chopped fresh chives

*available at Scandinavian stores and some
    specialty foods shops and by mail order from
    Schaller and Weber, tel. (800) 847-4115
**available at supermarkets and by mail order
    from T. Marzetti Co., tel. (614) 846-2232

Make crust:
Preheat oven to 350° F. and lightly oil rim of a
12-inch tart pan with a removable fluted rim.

Tear pumpernickel into pieces and in a food
processor pulse until coarse crumbs form. In a bowl
stir together bread crumbs and butter until combined
well and press onto bottom of tart pan. Bake crust in
middle of oven 15 minutes, or until golden brown,
and cool in pan on a rack.

Make filling:
Shell shrimp and if desired devein. In a saucepan
of boiling salted water cook shrimp until just cooked
through, about 1 minute, and drain in a colander.
Rinse shrimp under cold water and pat dry. Coarsely
chop shrimp.

If using red lumpfish caviar, in a fine sieve rinse
and drain well. In a large bowl stir together shrimp,
caviar, sour cream, mayonnaise, and heavy cream.

In a small saucepan sprinkle gelatin over lemon
juice and water and let stand 1 minute to soften. Heat

gelatin mixture over low heat, stirring, until gelatin
is dissolved. Cool mixture slightly and stir into
shrimp and caviar mixture with chives, white pepper,
and salt to taste.

Pour filling into crust, spreading evenly. *Chill
tart, loosely covered with plastic wrap, at least 6
hours, or until filling is set, and up to 1 day.*

Garnish tart with chives. Serves 10 to 12 as part
of a buffet.

PHOTO ON PAGE 38

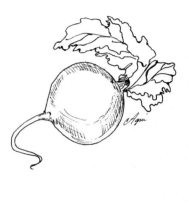

CANAPÉS

Radish Canapés ◐

12 large radishes (about ¾ pound)
8 ounces cream cheese, softened
1 tablespoon finely chopped fresh parsley leaves
1 teaspoon finely chopped fresh chives
1 tablespoon fresh lemon juice
kosher salt to taste
8 slices pumpernickel or rye bread, crusts
    discarded, each slice cut into 4 triangles
    and toasted

Into a bowl finely shred 8 radishes and squeeze
out excess liquid. In another bowl stir together cream
cheese, herbs, and lemon juice. Stir in grated
radishes and salt and pepper to taste. *Radish mixture
may be made 1 day ahead and chilled, covered.*

Just before serving, spread radish mixture on
toasts. Thinly slice remaining 4 radishes and arrange
a few slices decoratively on each canapé. Sprinkle
canapés with salt to taste. Makes 32 canapés.

Crostini with Garlic Pea Purée and Roasted Asparagus

1 head garlic, unpeeled
2 tablespoons olive oil plus additional for brushing bread
1 *baguette*, cut diagonally into ½-inch-thick slices
a 10-ounce package frozen peas, cooked and drained
1 bunch thin asparagus (about ¾ pound), trimmed and cut into 1½-inch pieces
2 tablespoons sesame seeds

Preheat oven to 400° F.

Cut ½ inch off top of garlic head and put head on a sheet of foil. Drizzle 1 tablespoon oil over garlic and wrap tightly in foil. Roast garlic in middle of oven until very soft, 40 to 50 minutes, and cool.

While garlic is cooling, arrange *baguette* slices in one layer on a large baking sheet and brush lightly on each side with additional oil. Toast slices in middle of oven until crisp and pale golden, 5 to 10 minutes, and transfer to a rack.

Squeeze roasted garlic from head into a food processor and add peas and salt and pepper to taste. Blend pea mixture until coarsely puréed. On baking sheet toss asparagus pieces with remaining tablespoon oil and sesame seeds and arrange in one layer. Roast asparagus in middle of oven, stirring occasionally, until tender, about 10 minutes.

Spread toasts with pea purée and divide asparagus among them. Makes about 30 *crostini*.

Smoked Bocconcini and Tomato-Olive Salsa Canapés

1 *baguette* (about 16 inches long and 1½ inches in diameter)
about 3 tablespoons extra-virgin olive oil
For tomato-olive salsa
6 plum tomatoes (about 1½ pounds)
½ cup Kalamata or other brine-cured black olives
½ cup packed fresh flat-leafed parsley leaves
1 shallot
1 tablespoon fresh lemon juice
2 tablespoons extra-virgin olive oil
freshly ground black pepper to taste

2 large garlic cloves
¾ pound smoked *bocconcini** (small mozzarella balls) or other smoked or unsmoked mozzarella

Garnish: about 60 small fresh flat-leafed parsley leaves

*available at specialty foods shops

Preheat oven to 325° F.

Cut *baguette* crosswise into ¼-inch-thick slices and arrange in one layer on a large baking sheet. Lightly brush slices with oil and season with salt. Toast slices in middle of oven 15 minutes, or until golden, and transfer to a rack to cool completely. *Toasts may be made 4 days ahead and kept in a sealable plastic bag at room temperature.*

Make salsa:

Seed tomatoes and cut into ¼-inch dice. Pit and chop olives. Finely chop parsley leaves and shallot. In a bowl stir together all salsa ingredients and salt to taste.

Lightly rub toasts with garlic cloves. If using *bocconcini*, cut into ¼-inch-thick slices. If using other mozzarella, cut into slices and quarter.

To assemble canapés:

Top each toast with a mozzarella slice and some salsa and garnish with parsley. *Canapés may be made 1 hour ahead and chilled, covered.*

Serve canapés at room temperature. Makes about 60 canapés.

Crisp Potato Canapés with Caviar

2 large russet (baking) potatoes (each about 10 ounces)
vegetable oil for deep-frying
2 tablespoons sour cream
1 ounce beluga or sevruga caviar*

Garnish: fresh chives, cut into ½-inch-long pieces

*available at specialty foods shops and some fish markets

In a 2-quart saucepan bring 1 quart salted water to a boil.

Cut potatoes crosswise into 1-inch-thick slices. Put slices flat on a cutting board and cut each slice into the largest possible rectangle, discarding excess. Halve each rectangle crosswise to form 2 cubes, each about 1 inch.

Simmer potatoes 5 minutes, or until just tender, and drain. Pat potatoes dry thoroughly. With a small melon-ball cutter or knife, scoop out an indentation about ⅓ inch deep in 1 side of each potato cube. *Potatoes may be prepared up to this point 1 day ahead and chilled in an airtight container.*

In a heavy saucepan heat 1½ inches oil over moderate heat until a deep-fat thermometer registers 350° F. Fry potatoes until golden, 3 to 5 minutes, and transfer with a slotted spoon to paper towels to drain. *Potatoes may be fried 8 hours ahead and kept, covered loosely, at room temperature. Recrisp potatoes in a 375° F. oven 5 minutes.*

Fill indentation in each potato cube with sour cream and top with caviar. Garnish canapés with chives. Makes 8 to 10 canapés, serving 2.

PHOTO ON PAGE 12

Gorgonzola, Fava Bean, and Purple Potato Canapés

⅓ cup walnuts
1 tablespoon olive oil
¾ cup shelled fresh fava beans* or lima beans
    (about ¾ pound in pods)
10 small purple potatoes* or small red potatoes
    (each about 2 inches in diameter; about
    1½ pounds)
6 ounces Gorgonzola cheese, softened
6 ounces cream cheese (about ¾ cup), softened

*available at specialty produce markets and some
    specialty foods shops

Finely chop walnuts. In a small heavy skillet cook walnuts in oil over moderate heat, stirring, until golden and transfer with a slotted spoon to paper towels to drain.

Have ready a bowl of ice and cold water. In a kettle of boiling salted water blanch beans 1 minute and immediately transfer with slotted spoon to ice water to stop cooking. Drain beans and gently peel away outer skins.

Return kettle of water to a boil and cut potatoes into ¼-inch-thick rounds. Cook potatoes 8 minutes, or until just tender, and transfer with slotted spoon to ice water to stop cooking. Drain potatoes in a colander and pat dry with paper towels.

In a small bowl stir together Gorgonzola and cream cheese until combined well. *Canapé ingredients may be prepared up to this point 2 days ahead. Keep toasted walnuts in an airtight container at room temperature. Chill beans and potatoes separately in sealable plastic bags and chill Gorgonzola cream, covered with plastic wrap.*

To assemble canapés:

Spread about 1 teaspoon Gorgonzola cream on each potato slice and top each canapé with a bean, pressing down gently. Sprinkle canapés with walnuts. *Canapés may be assembled 6 hours ahead and chilled, covered.* Makes about 60 canapés.

PHOTO ON PAGE 62

Prosciutto, Asian Pear, and Date Canapés with Mint

2 medium Asian pears* (about 1 pound total)
20 pitted dates (preferably Medjool)
7 tablespoons reduced-fat cream cheese such as Neufchâtel (about 3½ ounces)
3 ounces thinly sliced prosciutto
40 small fresh mint leaves

*available at specialty produce markets and many supermarkets

On a cutting board hold 1 Asian pear, stem side up, and cut down through pear just to right of stem, cutting off largest piece of fruit possible and avoiding core. Turn pear so cut side faces you and cut again in same manner. Cut off remaining 2 sides of pear in same manner and discard core. Put 1 piece, cut side down, on cutting board and cut into ¼-inch-thick slices. Cut remaining pieces of pear in same manner. Repeat procedure with remaining pear. (Yield is about forty ¼-inch-thick slices.)

Halve each date lengthwise and fill indentation in each half with ½ teaspoon cream cheese. Cut prosciutto into 3- by ¾-inch strips. Top a pear slice with a mint leaf and top mint leaf with a date half, filling side down. Fold a piece of prosciutto lengthwise in half and wrap crosswise over pear and date, tucking ends underneath. Make more canapés in same manner. Makes about 40 canapés.

Each canapé about 34 calories, 1 gram fat (26% of calories from fat)

DIPS AND SPREADS

Exotic Mushroom Pâté

For mushroom pâté
1½ cups chicken broth
1 cup dried *porcini* mushrooms* (about 1 ounce)
1 stick (½ cup) unsalted butter
¾ cup minced shallot
2 garlic cloves, minced
¼ cup dry Sherry

¾ pound fresh *shiitake* mushrooms, stems discarded and caps sliced thin (about 4½ cups)
¾ pound fresh oyster mushrooms, stems discarded and caps sliced thin (about 4½ cups)
1 cup heavy cream
4 large eggs
¼ cup whole almonds, toasted golden and ground fine
2 teaspoons chopped fresh thyme leaves
¼ cup chopped fresh flat-leafed parsley leaves
⅓ cup fine fresh bread crumbs
1½ tablespoons fresh lemon juice
2 teaspoons salt
½ teaspoon freshly ground black pepper
For mushroom topping
2 tablespoons unsalted butter
1 tablespoon olive oil
1 cup fresh *shiitake* mushrooms, stems discarded and caps quartered
1 cup fresh oyster mushrooms, stems discarded and caps quartered
¾ cup whole almonds, toasted golden and chopped coarse
¼ cup fresh flat-leafed parsley leaves

Accompaniment: assorted toasts or crackers

*available at specialty foods shops and some supermarkets

Make pâté:
Butter a 2-quart terrine, 12 by 3 by 2¾ inches. Line terrine with wax paper and butter paper.

In a small saucepan bring broth to a boil and remove pan from heat. Soak *porcini* in hot broth 30 minutes, or until softened. Remove *porcini*, squeezing out excess liquid, and reserve soaking liquid. Rinse *porcini* to remove any grit and pat dry. Chop *porcini* and put in a large bowl. Strain reserved soaking liquid through a fine sieve lined with a coffee filter or dampened paper towel into another small saucepan. Simmer soaking liquid over moderate heat until reduced to about ¼ cup and return to bowl with *porcini*.

Preheat oven to 350° F.

In a large non-stick skillet heat 2 tablespoons butter over moderate heat until foam subsides and cook shallot and garlic, stirring, until softened, about

6 minutes. Add Sherry and cook, stirring, 1 minute. Transfer shallot mixture to a blender. In skillet heat 2 tablespoons butter over moderately high heat until foam subsides and sauté *shiitake* and oyster mushrooms in batches, stirring, about 2 minutes. Add remaining ½ stick butter, cut into pieces, as necessary. Add 2 cups sautéed mushrooms to shallot mixture in blender and add remaining sautéed mushrooms to *porcini* mixture.

Add cream, eggs, and almonds to mixture in blender and purée about 1 minute, or until very smooth. Add purée to *porcini* mixture and stir in remaining pâté ingredients until combined well.

Pour mixture into terrine and cover with foil. Put terrine in a large baking pan and add enough water to baking pan to reach halfway up sides of terrine. Bake pâté in middle of oven 1 hour and 10 minutes. (Pâté will not be completely set in center.) Remove terrine from baking pan and cool completely on a rack. *Chill pâté in terrine, covered, at least 6 hours and up to 5 days. Bring pâté to room temperature before unmolding.*

Make topping:

In a skillet heat butter and oil over moderately high heat until foam subsides and sauté mushrooms and almonds, stirring, until mushrooms are tender. Transfer mixture to a bowl and cool. Add parsley and season with salt and pepper, tossing well.

To unmold pâté, run a thin knife around edge of terrine and dip terrine into a bowl of hot water 10 seconds. Invert a large plate over terrine and invert pâté onto plate.

Mound topping on top of pâté and serve with toasts or crackers. Serves 30 as an hors d'oeuvre.

PHOTO ON PAGE 17

Chunky Clam and Bacon Dip with Pita Toasts ◐

¼ pound bacon (about 8 slices), chopped
two 6½-ounce cans minced clams
8 ounces cream cheese, softened
¼ cup sour cream
⅓ cup finely chopped red bell pepper
3 scallions, chopped fine
2 tablespoons finely chopped fresh basil leaves
1 teaspoon drained bottled horseradish
1 teaspoon fresh lemon juice, or to taste

¾ teaspoon Worcestershire sauce
Tabasco to taste

Accompaniment: pita toasts (recipe follows) or
    potato chips

In a skillet cook bacon over moderate heat, stirring, until golden and crisp and transfer with a slotted spoon to paper towels to drain.

In a large sieve set over a bowl drain clams, reserving clam juice, and in another bowl whisk together cream cheese and sour cream. Whisk 2 tablespoons reserved clam juice into cream cheese mixture with clams, bacon, and remaining ingredients reserving some bacon, bell pepper, scallions, and basil in a small bowl for garnish. *Dip may be made 1 day ahead and chilled, covered. Bring dip to room temperature before serving.*

Garnish dip with reserved bacon mixture and serve with toasts or chips. Makes about 2 cups dip.

PHOTO ON PAGE 40

Pita Toasts ◐

four 6-inch pita loaves
about ¼ cup olive oil
coarse kosher salt if desired

Preheat oven to 375° F.

Halve pitas horizontally to form 8 rounds and lightly brush rough sides with oil. Season pitas with salt and cut each round into 6 wedges.

Arrange wedges in one layer on 2 baking sheets and bake in upper and lower thirds of oven, switching position of sheets halfway through baking, 10 to 15 minutes, or until golden and crisp. Cool toasts. *Toasts may be made 1 day ahead and kept in an airtight container at room temperature.* Makes 48 toasts.

Guacamole ⊙

3 ripe avocados
2 fresh *serrano* chilies*
3 tablespoons finely chopped white onion
coarse salt to taste

*available at Latino markets, specialty foods
   shops, and some supermarkets

Halve and pit avocados. Scoop flesh into a bowl.
Wearing rubber gloves, finely chop chilies, including seeds if desired, and add to avocados with onion
and salt. Mash avocado mixture with a fork.
*Guacamole may be made 2 hours ahead and chilled,
its surface covered with plastic wrap.* Makes about
1½ cups.

PHOTO ON PAGE 47

Smoked Salmon, Cucumber, and Dill Mousse

1 pound smoked salmon* (preferably unsliced),
   skinned, pin bones removed, and fish cut into
   ¼-inch dice (about 2 cups)
2 cups ¼-inch dice seeded English cucumber
¼ cup chopped fresh dill sprigs
⅓ cup chopped red onion, soaked in ice water
   5 minutes, drained, and patted dry
2¼ cups sour cream
3 tablespoons fresh lemon juice
1 tablespoon freshly grated lemon zest
2 tablespoons cold water
2½ teaspoons (1 envelope) unflavored gelatin

Garnish: thin cucumber ribbons made by
   cutting 1 large English cucumber
   lengthwise with a vegetable peeler
Accompaniment: assorted toasts and/or crackers

*available at fish markets and some specialty
   foods shops

Lightly oil an 8- by 2-inch round cake pan and
line with plastic wrap.

Spread 1¼ cups salmon evenly in cake pan. In a
bowl stir together remaining salmon, cucumber, dill,
onion, sour cream, lemon juice, and zest until combined well.

Put cold water in a small heatproof cup and
sprinkle gelatin over it. Set cup in a saucepan and
add enough water to pan to reach halfway up side of
cup. Heat gelatin mixture over low heat until gelatin
is dissolved and stir into salmon mixture. Season
mixture with salt and pepper and spoon over salmon
in cake pan. *Chill mousse, covered with plastic
wrap, at least 6 hours and up to 3 days.*

To unmold mousse, invert a large plate over cake
pan and invert mousse onto plate. Lift off cake pan
and peel off plastic wrap.

Garnish mousse with cucumber ribbons and serve
with toasts. Serves 30 as an hors d'oeuvre.

PHOTO ON PAGE 17

Roasted Red Pepper and
Garlic Dip with Fennel Crudités

4 medium fennel bulbs (sometimes
   called anise; about 3 pounds total)
For dip
1 red bell pepper
1 small head garlic
½ teaspoon cumin seeds
½ teaspoon caraway seeds
½ cup sour cream
1 tablespoon olive oil
¾ teaspoon salt, or to taste
a pinch cayenne,
   or to taste

Trim fennel stalks flush with bulbs and discard
any tough outer layers. Cut bulbs lengthwise into
⅛-inch-thick slices and, if desired, halve slices
lengthwise. Transfer fennel to a bowl of ice and cold
water. *Chill fennel at least 30 minutes, or until crisp,
and up to 3 hours.*

Preheat oven to 450° F.
While fennel is chilling, make dip:
Quarter bell pepper lengthwise and discard stems,
seeds, and ribs. In a shallow baking pan arrange
quarters skin sides up. Separate garlic cloves,
leaving skins intact, and wrap together in foil. Add
garlic package to pan with bell pepper and bake in
upper third of oven 20 minutes. When cool enough
to handle, peel pepper and transfer to a blender.
Remove garlic from foil and squeeze pulp into
blender.

In a small heavy skillet dry-roast cumin and caraway seeds over moderate heat, stirring, until fragrant and a few shades darker, about 1 minute, being careful not to burn them. In a cleaned electric coffee/spice grinder grind seeds to a powder and add to pepper mixture with remaining dip ingredients. Purée mixture until smooth. *Dip may be made 5 days ahead and chilled, covered.*

Drain fennel in a colander and pat dry.

Serve dip with fennel crudités. Serves 8 as an hors d'oeuvre.

Curried Chicken Liver Pâté ☉

½ stick (¼ cup) cold unsalted butter
¼ cup chopped onion
5 ounces chicken livers (about ½ cup), rinsed, patted dry, and chopped coarse
¾ teaspoon curry powder
½ teaspoon paprika
½ teaspoon salt
1 tablespoon brandy

Accompaniments:
crackers
fresh pear slices

In a 9-inch skillet heat 1 tablespoon butter over moderate heat until foam subsides and cook onion and chicken livers with curry powder, paprika, and salt, stirring, 1 minute. Cover skillet and cook mixture, stirring occasionally, 8 minutes more, or until livers are just cooked through. Add brandy and cook, stirring, 1 minute.

Remove skillet from heat and in a food processor purée mixture with remaining 3 tablespoons butter, cut into pieces, until smooth. Transfer pâté to a ¾-cup ramekin and smooth top. *Pâté may be served immediately (texture will be mousse-like) or chilled, its surface covered with plastic wrap, at least 2 hours and up to 5 days. Bring pâté to room temperature before serving.*

Serve pâté with crackers and pears. Serves 2 as an hors d'oeuvre.

Pimiento Cheese

3 large garlic cloves
1 cup pecans
a 4-ounce jar pimientos
12 ounces extra-sharp Cheddar
1 tablespoon olive oil
4 ounces cream cheese, softened
¼ cup mayonnaise
½ cup finely chopped fresh flat-leafed parsley leaves
Tabasco to taste

Accompaniment: crackers

Preheat oven to 350° F.

Crush 2 garlic cloves with the flat side of a large knife and mince remaining garlic clove. Chop pecans. Drain pimientos and rinse well. Pat pimientos dry between paper towels and chop. Coarsely grate Cheddar.

In an ovenproof heavy skillet cook crushed garlic in oil over moderately low heat, stirring, until pale golden. Discard garlic with a slotted spoon and stir pecans into oil. Cook pecans over moderate heat, stirring, 1 minute and transfer skillet to oven. Toast pecans, stirring occasionally, until golden, about 5 minutes, and cool.

In a bowl stir together cream cheese, mayonnaise, and minced garlic. Stir in remaining ingredients and salt and pepper to taste until combined well. *Pack spread into a crock (or crocks) and chill, covered with plastic wrap, at least 1 day and up to 4.*

Let spread stand at room temperature 30 minutes and serve with crackers. Makes about 3½ cups.

Wearing rubber gloves, seed and devein *jalapeños*, reserving ¼ teaspoon seeds. Cut chilies into pieces and in a blender purée with reserved chili seeds, coriander, fennel, and cumin seeds, and water until smooth.

Thinly slice shallots. In a skillet heat oil over moderate heat until hot but not smoking and cook shallots, stirring occasionally, until golden. With a slotted spoon transfer shallots to paper towels to drain and season with salt. In oil remaining in skillet cook chili purée, stirring frequently, until liquid evaporates, about 3 minutes, and cool completely.

Chop separately mint, parsley, and peanuts and in a bowl stir together with yogurt, chili purée, lime zest and juice, and salt and pepper to taste. *Dip may be made 2 days ahead and chilled, covered. Chill shallots separately in an airtight container.*

Top dip with shallots and serve with chips and vegetables. Makes about 2½ cups dip.

PHOTO ON PAGE 44

Spicy Yogurt Dip with Chips and Vegetables ☺

2 cups plain yogurt
4 fresh *jalapeño* chilies
1½ tablespoons coriander seeds
2 teaspoons fennel seeds
1 teaspoon cumin seeds
¼ cup water
2 shallots
3 tablespoons vegetable oil
½ cup fresh mint leaves
½ cup fresh flat-leafed parsley leaves
¼ cup dry-roasted peanuts
1 teaspoon finely grated fresh lime zest
1 tablespoon fresh lime juice

Accompaniments:
potato chips
assorted raw vegetables such as cherry
    tomatoes, trimmed radishes, cucumber
    spears, celery sticks

In a cheesecloth-lined sieve set over a bowl drain yogurt, chilled, 1 hour. Discard liquid.

Asparagus Crudités with Mayonnaise Verte ☺

1½ pounds thin asparagus, trimmed
½ cup packed fresh flat-leafed parsley leaves
2 tablespoons extra-virgin olive oil
2 tablespoons *verjus** (juice of unripe fruits)
    or 1 tablespoon fresh lemon juice
1 teaspoon Dijon mustard, or to taste
½ cup mayonnaise

*available at some specialty foods shops and
    by mail order from Dean & DeLuca,
    tel. (212) 226-6800, ext. 268

Have ready a large bowl of ice and cold water. In a large saucepan of boiling salted water blanch asparagus 1 minute and transfer with tongs to ice water to stop cooking. Drain asparagus well in a colander and pat dry. *Asparagus may be blanched 1 day ahead and chilled in a sealable plastic bag.*

Wash and dry parsley and in a blender purée with oil, *verjus* or lemon juice, and mustard until smooth. In a bowl stir purée into mayonnaise and season with salt and pepper.

Serve mayonnaise with asparagus for dipping. Serves 4.

PHOTO ON PAGE 29

Snap Bean and Radish Crudités with Caesar Mayonnaise ☺

For Caesar mayonnaise
½ cup packed fresh flat-leafed parsley leaves
2 teaspoons minced garlic
¼ teaspoon salt
1 cup mayonnaise
1 cup freshly grated Parmesan (about 3 ounces)
1 teaspoon mashed drained anchovy fillet
3 tablespoons fresh lemon juice
freshly ground black pepper to taste

1 pound green beans
1 pound wax beans
1 pound purple beans*
6 bunches assorted red and white radishes
   with tops*

*available at specialty produce markets and some
   specialty foods shops

Make Caesar mayonnaise:
Chop parsley and mash garlic to a paste with salt. In a bowl stir together parsley, garlic paste, and remaining mayonnaise ingredients and season with salt if necessary. *Mayonnaise may be made 1 week ahead and chilled, covered.*

Trim beans and have ready a large bowl of ice and cold water. In a large kettle of boiling salted water blanch green beans and wax beans separately 2 minutes, or until colors brighten but beans are still crisp, transferring to ice water to stop cooking. (Do not blanch purple beans or they will lose their color.) Drain beans and pat dry. *Green and wax beans may be blanched 1 day ahead and chilled in sealable plastic bags.*

Trim radishes, leaving some small green leaves attached.

Serve beans and radishes with mayonnaise. Serves 20 generously.

PHOTO ON PAGE 62

BREADS

Sage, Bacon and Cheddar Biscuits ◌

2 cups all-purpose flour
2 teaspoons baking powder
2 teaspoons sugar
¾ teaspoon baking soda
½ teaspoon salt
2 tablespoons finely chopped fresh sage leaves
5 tablespoons cold unsalted butter, cut into pieces
5 bacon slices, cooked crisp and chopped
¾ cup grated Cheddar
¾ cup well-shaken buttermilk

Preheat oven to 450° F. and grease a large baking sheet.

Into a bowl sift together flour, baking powder, sugar, baking soda, and salt. Stir in sage and with fingertips blend in butter until mixture resembles meal. Stir in bacon and Cheddar. Add buttermilk and stir until mixture just forms a dough. Gather dough into a ball and on a lightly floured surface knead gently 8 times. Pat out dough into a 6- by 5-inch rectangle. Cut dough into 9 rectangles and arrange about 1 inch apart on baking sheet. Bake biscuits in middle of oven 15 minutes. Makes 9 biscuits.

Cracked Black Pepper Cream Biscuits ◌

3 cups cake flour (not self-rising)
1 tablespoon baking powder
1 tablespoon sugar
2 tablespoons coarsely ground black pepper
1 teaspoon table salt
1¼ cups heavy cream
2 tablespoons unsalted butter
¼ teaspoon coarse salt

Preheat oven to 425° F. and lightly grease a large baking sheet.

Into a bowl sift together flour and baking powder. With a fork stir in sugar, 1½ tablespoons pepper, and table salt. Add cream and stir to form a

soft dough. On a lightly floured surface with floured hands knead dough gently 8 times.

Melt butter and cool.

Pat out dough into a 9-inch square (about ½ inch thick). With a rectangular cutter (about 2¾ by 1¾ inches) dipped in flour or with a sharp knife cut out as many rectangles as possible. Dip tops of biscuits in butter and arrange, buttered sides up, ½ inch apart on baking sheet. Gather scraps into a ball. Pat out dough and make more biscuits in same manner. Sprinkle biscuits with coarse salt and remaining ½ tablespoon pepper.

Bake biscuits in middle of oven until golden and cooked through, about 15 minutes. *Biscuits may be made 6 hours ahead and cooled completely before being kept, wrapped well, at room temperature. Just before serving, reheat biscuits in a 350° F. oven until just warm, about 5 minutes.* Makes about 16 biscuits.

PHOTO ON PAGE 72

Cheddar Corn Bread ◌

½ cup yellow cornmeal
½ cup all-purpose flour
1 tablespoon sugar
½ teaspoon salt
¾ teaspoon baking soda
1 teaspoon baking powder
2 tablespoons unsalted butter, cut into pieces
1 cup well-shaken buttermilk
1 large egg
2 ounces grated Cheddar (about ½ cup)

Preheat oven to 400° F.

Into a large bowl sift together cornmeal, flour, sugar, salt, baking soda, and baking powder. Put butter in a well-seasoned 8-inch cast-iron skillet or a 1-quart baking dish and heat in middle of oven until melted. Swirl skillet or baking dish to coat bottom and sides with butter and pour excess into another large bowl.

Whisk buttermilk and egg into bowl with butter. Stir buttermilk mixture and Cheddar into cornmeal mixture until just combined. Pour batter into hot skillet or baking dish and bake 20 minutes, or until a tester inserted in center comes out clean.

Cool corn bread in skillet or baking dish on a rack 10 minutes. *Corn bread may be made 1 day ahead and cooled to room temperature before being chilled, wrapped in foil.* Cut corn bread into 8 wedges. *Reheat corn bread, covered with a paper towel to retain moisture, in a microwave oven 30 seconds on high.*

PHOTO ON PAGE 26

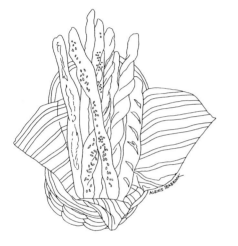

Seeded Crisps ☺

½ cup white sesame seeds
¼ cup black sesame seeds*
2 tablespoons poppy seeds
2 tablespoons mustard seeds
1 tablespoon coarse kosher salt
¾ teaspoon cayenne
6 tablespoons water
2 tablespoons cornstarch
1 quart vegetable oil for deep-frying
40 won ton wrappers*

*available at Asian markets and some specialty foods shops and supermarkets

In a small shallow bowl stir together seeds, salt, and cayenne. In a small bowl stir together water and cornstarch until combined well.

In a 3-quart heavy kettle heat oil over moderate heat until a deep-fat thermometer registers 360° F. Working quickly (do not let oil overheat), brush one side of each of 2 won ton wrappers with cornstarch mixture and gently press coated sides into seed mixture. Shake off any excess seeds from wrappers and fry wrappers, turning them over once, until golden, 8 to 10 seconds total. (Some seeds will fall off during frying.) With tongs transfer crisps as fried to brown paper or paper towels to drain. Make more crisps, 2 at a time, in same manner. *Seeded crisps may be made 3 days ahead and kept in an airtight container at room temperature. Before serving, "recrisp" crisps in a 225° F. oven 10 to 15 minutes.* Makes 40 crisps.

PHOTO ON PAGE 74

Molasses Corn Bread

1¼ cups all-purpose flour
2½ teaspoons baking powder
¾ teaspoon salt
¼ teaspoon baking soda
1¼ cups yellow cornmeal
3 tablespoons sugar
1¼ cups milk
¼ cup unsulfured molasses
1 large egg
1¼ sticks (10 tablespoons) unsalted butter, softened

Preheat oven to 400° F. and butter a loaf pan, 9 by 5 by 3 inches.

Into a large bowl sift together flour, baking powder, salt, and baking soda and whisk in cornmeal and sugar until combined well. In a small bowl whisk together milk, molasses, and egg until just combined. Add butter to flour mixture and with an electric mixer beat until mixture resembles fine crumbs. Beat in milk mixture until just combined.

Pour batter into pan and bake in middle of oven 35 minutes, or until a tester comes out clean. Cool corn bread in pan on a rack 10 minutes and turn out onto rack to cool completely. *Corn bread may be made 2 days ahead and kept, wrapped in plastic wrap, in a cool, dry place.*

PHOTO ON PAGE 54

Cinnamon and Currant Sweet Rolls

For dough
two ¼-ounce packages (5 teaspoons total)
   active dry yeast
½ cup warm water (105°–115° F.)
1 cup plus 1 tablespoon sugar
7 to 8 cups all-purpose flour
½ teaspoon salt
½ stick (¼ cup) unsalted butter, melted and cooled
¾ cup milk, heated to lukewarm
½ cup sour cream
4 large eggs, beaten lightly
For filling
1 cup dried currants or raisins
½ cup sugar
1 teaspoon cinnamon

Make dough:

In a small bowl combine yeast, water, and 1 tablespoon sugar and let stand until foamy, about 5 minutes. In a large bowl whisk together remaining cup sugar, 4 cups flour, and salt and add yeast mixture, butter, milk, sour cream, and eggs, stirring until combined well. Stir in 3 cups flour and turn dough out onto a lightly floured surface. Knead dough 8 to 10 minutes, adding enough of remaining cup flour to form a soft but slightly sticky dough. Form dough into a ball and transfer to a buttered bowl, turning to coat dough completely with butter. *Let dough rise in a warm place, covered with a kitchen towel, until doubled in bulk, about 1 hour.*

Prepare filling while dough is rising:

In a small heatproof bowl combine currants or raisins with boiling water to cover and let stand 20 minutes. Drain currants or raisins well. In a small bowl stir together sugar and cinnamon.

Butter two 13- by 9-inch baking pans.

Punch down dough and turn out onto lightly floured surface. Divide dough into 4 pieces. Roll out 1 piece of dough into a 10-inch round (about ¼ inch thick) and cut into 12 wedges. Sprinkle each wedge with about 1 teaspoon currants and about ½ teaspoon cinnamon sugar.

Beginning with outer, curved edge, roll up each wedge toward tip and curve ends gently to form a crescent. Transfer crescents, tips down, to a baking pan and form more crescents with remaining dough and filling in same manner. (Crescents should be arranged in 3 rows of 8 in each pan for a total of 48.) Cover each pan with a kitchen towel. *Let crescents rise in a warm place until almost doubled in bulk, about 1 hour.*

Preheat oven to 350° F.

Bake rolls in middle of oven 20 minutes, or until golden brown. Serve rolls warm. Makes 48 rolls.

Cider-Glazed Mini Apple Muffins ☺

¼ cup walnuts
½ Granny Smith or Golden Delicious apple
1 cup all-purpose flour
1½ teaspoons baking powder
½ teaspoon cinnamon
¼ teaspoon salt
3 tablespoons unsalted butter
¼ cup packed brown sugar
2 tablespoons unfiltered apple cider
1 large egg
For cider glaze
2 cups unfiltered apple cider
2 tablespoons granulated sugar

Preheat oven to 400° F. and grease a mini-muffin pan containing twelve 1¾- by 1-inch cups.

Lightly toast walnuts and chop fine. Core and peel apple and cut into ¼-inch dice. Into a bowl sift together flour, baking powder, cinnamon, and salt. In a saucepan melt butter and stir in brown sugar. Remove pan from heat. Whisk cider and egg into butter mixture until smooth and add to flour mixture, stirring until combined well. Stir in walnuts and apple. Divide batter among muffin cups and bake 15 minutes, or until golden.

Make glaze while muffins are baking:

In a 2-quart saucepan boil cider 15 minutes, or until reduced to about ½ cup, and pour through a sieve lined with 4 layers of cheesecloth to remove sediment. Return cider to cleaned pan and add sugar. Simmer mixture, stirring, until syrupy, about 5 minutes.

While muffins are still warm, with a wooden pick make several holes in top of each muffin. Brush warm cider glaze over muffins several times until absorbed. Makes 12 mini muffins.

Chive Pepper Popovers

1 cup milk
1 cup minus 2 tablespoons all-purpose flour
1 tablespoon vegetable oil
½ teaspoon salt
2 large eggs
⅓ cup chopped fresh chives
¼ teaspoon freshly ground black pepper

Generously grease six ⅔-cup popover cups or nine ½-cup muffin cups.

In a large bowl with an electric mixer combine milk, flour, oil, and salt and beat mixture on high speed 1 minute. Add eggs 1 at a time, beating 20 seconds after each addition, and beat in chives and pepper.

Divide batter among cups and put in middle of a cold oven. Set oven at 425° F. and bake popovers 35 to 40 minutes, or until puffed and golden brown. Makes 6 large or 9 medium popovers.

Pecan Blue Cheese Crackers

1½ cups pecan halves
1 large egg
1 stick (½ cup) unsalted butter, softened
½ pound Saga blue cheese, softened
1 cup all-purpose flour

In a preheated 350° F. oven toast ½ cup pecans, about 7 minutes, and cool. Finely chop toasted pecans and separate egg. In a bowl with a fork cream butter and Saga until smooth. Add egg yolk, stirring until combined well. Add flour and chopped pecans and stir until mixture just forms a dough.

Halve dough and on separate sheets of wax paper form each half into a 12- by 1¼-inch log, using wax paper as a guide. *Freeze logs, wrapped in wax paper, just until firm, about 30 minutes.*

Preheat oven to 375° F. and lightly grease 2 large baking sheets.

Cut logs crosswise into ¼-inch-thick slices and arrange slices about ½ inch apart on baking sheets. Top each cracker with a remaining pecan half, pressing slightly into dough. Lightly beat egg white and brush tops of crackers, including pecans, with it. Bake crackers in batches, if necessary, in upper and lower thirds of oven, switching position of sheets halfway through baking, until golden brown, about 12 minutes total. With a spatula transfer crackers to paper towels to blot and transfer to a rack to cool. Each log makes about 45 crackers.

Caraway Currant Scones ◗

1 cup all-purpose flour
2½ teaspoons baking powder
¼ teaspoon salt
2 teaspoons sugar
2½ tablespoons cold unsalted butter, cut into bits,
    plus ½ tablespoon melted unsalted butter
6 tablespoons well-shaken buttermilk
2 tablespoons dried currants
½ teaspoon crushed caraway seeds,
    toasted lightly

Preheat oven to 400° F. and lightly grease a baking sheet.

Into a large bowl sift together flour, baking powder, salt, and 1 teaspoon sugar. Blend in cold butter with fingertips until mixture resembles coarse meal. Stir in buttermilk, currants, and caraway seeds until mixture just forms a dough.

On a lightly floured surface knead dough gently about 10 times and flatten into a 1½-inch-thick disk. Brush disk with melted butter and sprinkle with remaining teaspoon sugar. Cut dough into quarters with a sharp knife and arrange scones 2 inches apart on baking sheet.

Bake scones in middle of oven 18 minutes, or until pale golden, and cool on a rack. Serve scones warm or at room temperature. Makes 4 scones.

If you need only one focaccia, freeze the other for later use. Focaccia keeps, frozen, 2 weeks.

Thyme Focaccia and Parmesan Focaccia

two ¼-ounce packages (5 teaspoons) active
    dry yeast
1 teaspoon sugar
2 cups warm water (105°–115° F.)
1 tablespoon table salt
about 5½ cups all-purpose flour
⅓ cup olive oil
2 teaspoons minced fresh thyme leaves
2 tablespoons cornmeal
½ cup coarsely grated Parmesan
coarse salt for sprinkling
freshly ground black pepper for sprinkling

In a standing electric mixer fitted with paddle attachment beat together yeast, sugar, and water and let stand 5 minutes, or until foamy. In a bowl stir together table salt and 5 cups flour. Stir olive oil into yeast mixture. With motor on low speed, gradually add flour mixture to yeast mixture. With dough hook knead dough 2 minutes, or until soft and slightly sticky.

Transfer dough to a floured surface and knead in enough remaining flour to form a soft but not sticky dough. Form dough into a ball and put in an oiled large bowl, turning to coat. Cover bowl with a kitchen towel and let dough rise in a warm place until doubled in bulk, about 45 minutes.

Transfer dough to a lightly floured surface and divide in half. Knead thyme into one half and knead plain half 1 minute. Form each half into an oval and invert bowl over them. Let dough rest 5 minutes for easier rolling.

Preheat oven to 450° F.

Oil two 13- by 9-inch baking pans and sprinkle each with 1 tablespoon cornmeal. On lightly floured surface with a floured rolling pin roll out dough halves into 13- by 9-inch rectangles and fit into pans. Cover each pan with a kitchen towel and let dough rise in a warm place until doubled in bulk, about 20 minutes.

Sprinkle plain dough with Parmesan and sprinkle both doughs with coarse salt and pepper. With lightly oiled fingertips make indentations, about ½ inch deep and 1 inch apart, all over dough rectangles and bake in middle of oven 12 minutes, or until golden. Remove *focaccie* from pans and cool on racks. Makes 1 thyme *focaccia* and 1 Parmesan *focaccia*.

SOUPS

Chilled Avocado Cucumber Soup ☺

½ medium cucumber
1 ripe small California avocado
1 scallion
1 garlic clove
2 tablespoons fresh coriander leaves
2 tablespoons fresh lemon juice
½ cup plain yogurt
½ cup cold water
½ cup ice cubes

Garnish: 2 fresh coriander sprigs

Peel cucumber and cut into 4 pieces. Quarter avocado, removing pit, and peel. Cut scallion into large pieces. In a blender purée all ingredients until smooth and season with salt and pepper.

Serve soup garnished with coriander. Serves 2.

Cannellini and Lentil Soup with Caramelized Onions

¾ cup dried *cannellini* beans (about 5 ounces),
    picked over
12 cups water
¾ cup dried lentils, picked over
⅓ cup bulgur
⅓ cup long-grain white rice
2 teaspoons ground coriander
1 teaspoon ground cinnamon
2 medium onions, halved lengthwise and
    sliced thin
2 tablespoons olive oil
2 teaspoons salt
cayenne to taste
½ cup packed fresh parsley leaves, minced

In a 4-quart heavy saucepan simmer *cannellini* beans in water 10 minutes. Stir in lentils, bulgur, rice, coriander, and cinnamon and simmer until *cannellini* are very tender and lentils fall apart, about 45 minutes. (Old beans may take longer to cook.)

Preheat oven to 450° F.

In a shallow baking pan toss together onions, oil, salt, and cayenne and roast in middle of oven, stirring occasionally, until golden brown, about 20 minutes. Stir onions and parsley into soup and simmer 1 minute. Makes about 9 cups, serving 4 as a main course.

🍃 Each serving about 429 calories, 8.25 grams fat
(17% of calories from fat)

Adzuki Bean Miso Soup

4 cups water
2 vegetable bouillon cubes (0.75 ounce total)
3 cups cooked dried adzuki beans* (procedure
    on page 118) or rinsed and drained canned
    adzuki beans* (about two 15-ounce cans)
2 teaspoons vegetable oil
3 medium carrots, cut diagonally into
    1/16-inch-thick slices
¼ cup white *miso* (fermented bean paste)
4 scallions, sliced thin

*available at natural foods stores and some
    specialty foods shops and Asian markets

In a 4-quart saucepan bring water to a boil and add bouillon cubes, stirring until dissolved. Add beans and simmer, stirring occasionally, 15 minutes.

In a heavy skillet heat oil over moderately high heat until it just begins to smoke and stir-fry carrots until crisp-tender, about 3 minutes. Stir fried carrots into soup.

In a small bowl stir together *miso* and ½ cup hot broth until combined well and stir into soup. Bring soup just to a boil, stirring occasionally, and stir in scallions and freshly ground black pepper to taste. Makes about 9½ cups, serving 4 as a main course.

🍃 Each serving about 431 calories, 4 grams fat
(8% of calories from fat)

To Cook Dried Beans

½ cup dried beans, picked over
1 teaspoon salt
4 cups water

In a saucepan simmer beans with salt in water, covered, until tender, 45 minutes to 1 hour, and remove pan from heat. (Old beans may take longer to cook, and chick-peas may take up to 1½ hours.) Cool beans in cooking liquid and drain. *Beans may be made 1 day ahead and chilled, covered.* Makes about 1½ cups.

Beef Goulash Soup

6 medium onions, chopped coarse
½ stick (¼ cup) unsalted butter
2 pounds boneless beef shin, cut into
　　½-inch cubes
¼ cup all-purpose flour
4 teaspoons paprika (preferably sweet
　　Hungarian*)
1 teaspoon caraway seeds
¼ teaspoon dried marjoram
3 tablespoons wine vinegar
12 cups beef broth
6 medium boiling potatoes
　　(about 2 pounds)

Accompaniment: crusty sourdough bread

*available at specialty foods shops and
　　many supermarkets

In a 5- to 6-quart kettle cook onions in 2 tablespoons butter over moderate heat, stirring, until pale golden and transfer to a bowl. In another bowl toss beef with flour until coated evenly. In kettle heat remaining 2 tablespoons butter over moderately high heat until foam subsides and cook beef, stirring occasionally, until no longer pink. Stir in onions, paprika, caraway seeds, marjoram, vinegar, broth, and salt and pepper to taste and simmer, covered, 45 minutes. Peel potatoes and cut into ½-inch cubes. Add potatoes to soup and simmer, covered, 20 minutes more, or until potatoes are tender. Makes about 18 cups.

Carrot Cumin Soup with Toasted Pecans ◎

For soup
1 medium onion, chopped (about ¾ cup)
2 tablespoons unsalted butter
2 to 3 large carrots, sliced thin (about 1¾ cups)
½ teaspoon ground cumin
½ teaspoon salt, or to taste
2 cups water
For pecans
2 tablespoons pecans, chopped coarse
1 teaspoon unsalted butter

Preheat oven to 350° F.
Make soup:
In a saucepan cook onion in butter over moderate heat, stirring, until softened. Add carrots, cumin, and salt and cook, stirring, 1 minute. Add water and simmer mixture, covered, 25 minutes, or until carrots are very tender.
Prepare pecans while carrot soup is simmering:
On a baking sheet toast pecans in middle of oven 8 minutes, or until fragrant and 1 shade darker. Toss pecans with butter and salt to taste.
In a blender purée soup until smooth.
Divide soup between 2 soup bowls and top with pecans. Makes 2¼ cups, serving 2.

Cauliflower Fennel Soup ☉

1 small head cauliflower
1 large garlic clove, chopped
¾ teaspoon fennel seeds
2½ cups water
½ cup heavy cream

Cut cauliflower into 2-inch pieces, discarding outer leaves and core. In a 2- to 3-quart heavy saucepan simmer cauliflower with garlic and fennel seeds in water, covered, until cauliflower is very tender, about 10 minutes. Cool mixture 15 minutes and in a blender purée in batches, transferring to a bowl. In pan stir together purée, cream, and salt and pepper to taste and heat soup over moderate heat, stirring occasionally, until heated through. Makes about 4½ cups.

Chinese Chicken Noodle Soup with Spinach and Garlic Chives

a 3½- to 4-pound chicken
8 thin slices fresh gingerroot
1 bunch scallions, cut crosswise into thirds
10 cups water
¾ cup Chinese rice wine or medium-dry Sherry
2 ounces dried rice-stick noodles*
    (rice vermicelli)
½ pound fresh spinach, coarse stems discarded
    and leaves washed, drained, and chopped
    coarse (about 4 packed cups)
¾ cup thinly sliced fresh garlic chives* or
    regular fresh chives

*available at Asian markets and some specialty
    foods shops and supermarkets

With a cleaver or heavy chef's knife cut chicken into large pieces. Cut chicken through bones into 2-inch pieces. In a large kettle of boiling water blanch chicken 1 minute. In a colander drain chicken and rinse under cold water.

With flat side of cleaver or knife lightly smash gingerroot and scallions. In cleaned kettle bring 10 cups water to a boil with chicken, gingerroot, scallions, and rice wine or Sherry and simmer, uncovered, skimming froth occasionally, 2 hours.

Pour broth through colander lined with a triple thickness of cheesecloth into a large heatproof bowl, reserving chicken for another use. *Broth may be made 3 days ahead, cooled completely, uncovered, and chilled, covered.*

In cleaned kettle bring broth to a boil. Add noodles and boil, stirring occasionally, 2 minutes. Stir in spinach and simmer, stirring once or twice, until spinach turns bright green and is just tender, about 3 minutes. Stir in chives and salt and pepper to taste and simmer 1 minute. Makes about 8 cups.

PHOTO ON PAGE 18

Velvety Lemon Chicken Soup ☉

1 lemon
2 chicken breast halves with skin and
    bones (about ¾ pound)
2¾ cups chicken broth
10 snow pea pods
2 tablespoons unsalted butter
2 tablespoons all-purpose flour
¼ cup heavy cream
2 tablespoons minced fresh flat-leafed
    parsley leaves

With a vegetable peeler remove two 2-inch-long strips zest from lemon and squeeze 1 teaspoon juice into a small cup. In a small saucepan simmer chicken and zest in broth, covered, 20 minutes, or until chicken is just cooked through. Transfer chicken to a bowl and pour broth through a sieve into a 4-cup measuring cup. Chill chicken until it is cool.

While chicken is cooling, trim snow peas and cut diagonally into thin slivers.

In a 2-quart saucepan heat butter over moderately low heat until foam subsides and stir in flour. Cook *roux*, stirring constantly, 2 minutes. Add broth and cream in a stream, whisking, and simmer, whisking, 2 minutes, or until soup thickens slightly. Remove pan from heat.

When chicken is cool enough to handle, discard skin and bones and cut chicken into thin strips. Add chicken and snow peas to soup and simmer, stirring occasionally, 1 minute, or until peas are crisp-tender. Stir in lemon juice, parsley, and salt and pepper to taste. Makes about 4½ cups, serving 2.

Corn Chowder with Basil

7 ears fresh corn
9 cups water
a 19-ounce container silken tofu
⅔ cup packed fresh basil leaves
1 cup thinly sliced scallion greens

Garnish: fresh basil sprigs
Accompaniment: bottled *jalapeño* pepper sauce

Shuck corn and, working over a 6- to 8-quart kettle, cut off kernels, reserving cobs. In kettle simmer corn, cobs, water, and salt and pepper to taste, uncovered, until corn is tender, 10 to 20 minutes. Carefully pour off liquid from tofu. Discard cobs and transfer half of corn mixture to a bowl. In a blender in batches purée tofu with corn mixture from bowl until smooth, transferring to kettle. Finely chop basil and stir into chowder with scallion greens and salt to taste. Heat chowder over moderate heat, stirring, until heated through.

Garnish chowder with basil sprigs and serve with *jalapeño* sauce. Makes about 10 cups, serving 4 as a main-course soup.

Each serving about 286 calories, 6 grams fat
(18% of calories from fat)

PHOTO ON PAGE 6

Chilled Minted Cucumber Honeydew Soup ◖+

1 English cucumber
2 cups honeydew pieces
   (from about ¼ medium melon)
8 ounces plain nonfat yogurt
¼ cup fresh mint leaves
2 tablespoons fresh lime juice

Garnish: 4 fresh mint leaves

Cut cucumber into 1-inch pieces. In a bowl combine cucumber and honeydew pieces, yogurt, mint leaves, and lime juice.

In a blender purée mixture in batches 30 seconds, pouring mixture as puréed through a sieve into a bowl, and season soup with salt and pepper. *Chill soup, covered, at least 2 hours and up to 6.*

Serve soup garnished with mint. Makes about 5 cups, serving 4.

Each serving about 73.5 calories, 0.28 gram fat
(3% of calories from fat)

PHOTO ON PAGE 82

Leek and Potato Soup ◖

1 medium boiling potato (about ½ pound)
1 garlic clove, minced
½ medium onion, chopped fine
1 tablespoon unsalted butter
2 medium leeks (white parts only), halved
   lengthwise, sliced thin crosswise, and
   washed well
2½ cups chicken broth
3 tablespoons heavy cream
2 tablespoons chopped fresh flat-leafed
   parsley leaves

Peel potato and dice fine. In a 3½- to 4-quart saucepan cook garlic and onion in butter over moderately low heat, stirring, until onion is softened. Add potato and leeks and cook, stirring occasionally, 2 minutes. Stir in broth and simmer, uncovered, 15 minutes, or until potato is very tender.

If desired, in a blender purée soup in batches until very smooth (use caution when blending hot liquids), transferring to another saucepan. Stir in cream, parsley, and salt and pepper to taste and heat over moderate heat, stirring occasionally, until hot. Serves 2 generously.

Curried Potato and Leek Soup with Spinach ◖

2 medium leeks (white and pale green parts only)
1 medium boiling potato such as Yukon Gold
1 tablespoon unsalted butter
½ teaspoon curry powder
2 cups water
1 cup packed spinach leaves
½ cup milk

Halve leeks lengthwise and cut enough crosswise into ¼-inch pieces to measure 2 cups. In a bowl of cold water wash leeks well and lift from water into a sieve to drain. Peel potato and cut enough into ¼-inch pieces to measure 1 cup.

In a 1½-quart saucepan cook leeks and potato in butter with curry powder over moderate heat, stirring, 5 minutes. Stir in 2 cups water and simmer, uncovered, 20 minutes.

While soup is cooking, cut spinach into thin strips. In a blender purée soup until completely smooth (use caution when blending hot liquids) and return to pan. Add milk and salt and pepper to taste and bring to a simmer. Remove pan from heat and stir in spinach. Serves 2 generously.

Scallion Chive Soup ◌

½ cup coarsely shredded zucchini
⅓ cup chopped shallots (about 2)
1 garlic clove, minced
1 teaspoon olive oil
2 teaspoons unsalted butter
1 cup chopped scallions (about
   1 bunch)
½ cup chopped fresh chives
2 cups chicken broth
½ cup water

Accompaniment: Parmesan puffs (recipe follows)

In a saucepan cook zucchini, shallots, and garlic in oil and butter over moderately low heat, stirring occasionally, until shallots are tender, about 5

minutes. Add scallions and all but 2 tablespoons chives and cook, stirring, until scallions are softened, about 2 minutes. Stir in broth and water and simmer 2 minutes.

In a blender purée mixture (use caution when blending hot liquids). Pour soup through a fine sieve into cleaned pan, pressing hard on solids and discarding them. Heat soup over moderate heat, stirring, until hot and season with salt and pepper. Stir in remaining 2 tablespoons chives.

Serve soup with Parmesan puffs. Makes about 3 cups, serving 2.

Parmesan Puffs ◌

2 large egg whites
1 cup freshly grated Parmesan
a pinch cayenne
vegetable oil for deep-frying

Put whites in a large bowl and let stand at room temperature 15 minutes. With an electric mixer beat whites until they hold stiff peaks and with a metal spoon thoroughly fold in Parmesan and cayenne. Roll mixture into about twenty ¾-inch balls.

In a 3-quart heavy kettle heat 1 inch oil to 375° F. Working in batches, fry balls, turning them, until golden, about 2 minutes, transferring to paper towels to drain. Serve Parmesan puffs warm as an accompaniment to soup or as an hors d'oeuvre. Makes about 20 Parmesan puffs.

*Chilled Tarragon Tomato Soup with
Vegetable Confetti*

For tarragon tomato soup
3 pounds vine-ripened tomatoes
   (about 8 medium)
2 teaspoons balsamic vinegar, or to taste
1 teaspoon sugar, or to taste
1 teaspoon fresh lemon juice, or to taste
1½ cups ice water

1 tablespoon finely chopped fresh tarragon leaves
8 vine-ripened yellow cherry tomatoes
¼ cup finely chopped zucchini
¼ cup finely chopped red onion

Accompaniment: baguette toasts
   (recipe follows)

Make soup:
Chop tomatoes and in a food processor purée with
vinegar, sugar, and lemon juice until smooth. Pour
purée through a sieve into a bowl, pressing hard on
solids. Discard solids. Stir in ice water and salt and
pepper to taste. *Soup may be made 1 day ahead and
chilled, covered. Reseason soup before serving.*

Stir tarragon into soup and thinly slice cherry
tomatoes.

Serve soup sprinkled with tomatoes, zucchini, and
onion, and with *baguette* toasts on the side. Makes
about 6 cups.

PHOTO ON PAGE 51

Baguette Toasts ☺

1 *baguette*
2 tablespoons extra-virgin olive oil

Preheat oven to 400° F.

Diagonally cut twenty-four ⅛-inch-thick slices
from *baguette* and arrange in one layer on baking
sheets. Brush tops of slices with oil and sprinkle
with salt and pepper to taste. Toast slices in middle
and upper thirds of oven until golden brown, about
5 minutes, and cool on racks. *Toasts may be made
2 days ahead and kept in an airtight container at
room temperature.*

FISH AND SHELLFISH

Honey and Soy Glazed Salmon ☺

2 tablespoons honey
2 tablespoons soy sauce
1½ tablespoons fresh lime juice
2 teaspoons Dijon mustard
1 tablespoon water
2 teaspoons vegetable oil
two 6-ounce pieces salmon fillet

In a small bowl whisk together honey, soy sauce, lime juice, mustard, and water. In a small non-stick skillet heat oil over moderately high heat until hot but not smoking and cook salmon 2 to 3 minutes on each side, or until golden and just cooked through. Transfer salmon to 2 plates. Add honey glaze to skillet and simmer, stirring, 1 minute. Pour glaze over salmon. Serves 2.

Red Snapper Papillotes with Lemon and Thyme ☺

2 sheets 12-inch-wide heavy-duty foil
    (each about 15 inches long)
two 6-ounce red snapper fillets, pin bones
    removed
2 tablespoons extra-virgin olive oil
freshly ground black pepper
2 teaspoons fresh lemon juice
½ teaspoon chopped fresh thyme leaves
6 very thin lemon slices (about ¹⁄₁₆ inch thick)

Accompaniment if desired: vegetable couscous
    with black olives (page 159)

Preheat oven to 500° F. and heat a baking sheet in lower third of oven 5 minutes.
Fold each sheet of foil in half crosswise to crease, and then unfold.

On a plate coat red snapper fillets with oil and sprinkle with pepper and salt to taste. On each sheet of foil put 1 fillet to one side of crease and sprinkle with 1 teaspoon lemon juice, ¼ teaspoon thyme, and half of any oil remaining on plate. Top each fillet with 3 lemon slices.

Working with 1 foil package (*papillote*) at a time, fold left half of foil over fillet. Starting at 1 corner of crease, fold edge of foil over in triangles, following a semicircular path around fillet (each fold should overlap previous one), smoothing out folds as you go and tucking last fold under, until *papillote* is completely sealed. Put *papillotes* on hot baking sheet and bake in middle of oven 5 minutes.

Serve *papillotes* with couscous. Serves 2.

Halibut in Spiced Court Bouillon ☺

¾ cup dry white wine
5 cups water
1 onion, chopped
1 carrot, chopped
1 celery rib, chopped
1½ teaspoons ground coriander seeds
1 teaspoon black pepper
a pinch ground cloves
1 teaspoon salt
1 tablespoon olive oil
two 6-ounce pieces halibut fillet
2 teaspoons chopped fresh coriander leaves

Garnish: lemon wedges

In a 4- to 6-quart heavy saucepan bring wine and water to a boil with onion, carrot, celery, spices, and salt and simmer *court bouillon* 20 minutes. Add oil and halibut fillets and poach fish at a bare simmer, covered, until just cooked through, 5 to 6 minutes. Transfer fish with a slotted spatula to 2 plates. Spoon *court bouillon* over fish. Sprinkle fish with fresh coriander and garnish with lemon wedges. Serves 2.

Broiled Bluefish Fillets with Fennel Mayonnaise ◌

two 8-ounce skinless bluefish or mackerel fillets
For fennel mayonnaise
1 teaspoon fennel seeds
1 large garlic clove
½ teaspoon salt
2 tablespoons mayonnaise
½ tablespoon fresh lemon juice

Preheat broiler and oil a shallow baking pan large enough to hold fillets in one layer.
Make fennel mayonnaise:
In a dry small skillet toast fennel seeds over moderate heat, stirring, until fragrant. Mince fennel seeds and garlic clove with salt and in a small bowl stir together with mayonnaise, lemon juice, and pepper to taste.

Arrange fillets in baking pan and spread fennel mayonnaise evenly over tops. Broil fillets 3 inches from heat until just cooked through, about 7 minutes. Serves 2.

Open-Faced Pickled Mackerel and Apple Sandwiches ◌

½ pound fresh mackerel fillets (preferably Boston)
½ cup water
¼ cup white-wine vinegar
¼ cup sugar
2½ teaspoons salt
1 teaspoon pickling spices
¼ cup cream cheese (about 2 ounces), softened
2 tablespoons sour cream
1 tablespoon chopped fresh chives
2 slices rye bread
½ crisp apple such as Braeburn or McIntosh

Garnish: chopped fresh chives

Trim any excess skin from fish and with tweezers remove any small bones.

In a saucepan just large enough to hold fillets in one layer bring water and vinegar to a boil with sugar, salt, and pickling spices and simmer 1 minute. Add fish to pickling liquid and cover with a heat-proof plate slightly smaller than diameter of pan,

weighting plate with a can to prevent fish from curling. Cook fish at a bare simmer 4 minutes, or until just cooked through, and transfer fish and pickling liquid to a glass dish. *Chill mixture in freezer 20 minutes.*

In a small bowl whisk together cream cheese and sour cream until smooth and whisk in chives and salt and pepper to taste. Lightly toast bread. Core apple and slice thin.

Spread toast with chive cream and arrange apple slices over cream. Drain mackerel and top each toast with half of fish. (Alternatively, chop apples and flake fish. Stir together apple, fish, and chive cream and spread on toasts.)

Garnish open-faced sandwiches with chives. Serves 2.

Plank cooking is a Native American technique that imparts a subtle smoky flavor to fish, meat, poultry, and vegetables. We recommend using a plank of untreated Western red cedar made specifically for cooking purposes.

Cedar Planked Salmon with Maple Glaze and Mustard Mashed Potatoes

1 cup pure maple syrup
2 tablespoons finely grated peeled fresh gingerroot
4 tablespoons fresh lemon juice
3 tablespoons soy sauce
1½ teaspoons minced garlic
an untreated cedar plank* (about 17 by 10½ inches) if desired
a 2½-pound center-cut salmon fillet with skin
greens from 1 bunch scallions

Accompaniment: mustard mashed potatoes (recipe follows)

*available by mail order from Chinook Planks, tel. (800) 765-4408

In a small heavy saucepan simmer maple syrup, gingerroot, 3 tablespoons lemon juice, soy sauce, garlic, and salt and pepper to taste until reduced to about 1 cup, about 30 minutes, and let cool. *Maple glaze may be made 2 days ahead and chilled, covered. Bring maple glaze to room temperature before proceeding.*

Preheat oven to 350° F. If using cedar plank, lightly oil and heat in middle of oven 15 minutes; or lightly oil a shallow baking pan.

Arrange scallion greens in one layer on plank or in baking pan to form a bed for fish.

In another small saucepan heat half of glaze over low heat until heated through to use as a sauce. Stir in remaining tablespoon lemon juice. Remove pan from heat and keep sauce warm, covered.

Put salmon, skin side down, on scallion greens and brush with remaining glaze. Season salmon with salt and pepper and roast in middle of oven until just cooked through, about 20 minutes if using baking pan or about 35 minutes if using plank.

Cut salmon crosswise into 6 pieces. On each of 6 plates arrange salmon and scallion greens on a bed of mashed potatoes. Drizzle salmon with warm sauce. Serves 6.

PHOTO ON PAGE 72

Mustard Mashed Potatoes

3 pounds Yukon Gold potatoes
1½ cups milk
¾ stick (6 tablespoons) unsalted butter
3 tablespoons whole-grain or coarse-grain mustard

In a 5-quart kettle cover potatoes with cold salted water by 2 inches and simmer until tender, 35 to 45 minutes. While potatoes are simmering, in a small saucepan heat milk with butter over moderate heat until butter is melted. Remove pan from heat and keep milk mixture warm, covered.

In a colander drain potatoes and cool just until they can be handled. Peel potatoes, transferring to a large bowl. Add mustard, salt and pepper to taste, and three fourths hot milk mixture and with a potato masher mash potatoes until smooth, adding more milk mixture if necessary to make them creamy. *Potatoes may be made 1 day ahead and cooled completely before being chilled in a buttered ovenproof dish, covered. Bring potatoes to room temperature before reheating, covered.* Serves 6.

Smoked Salmon, Horseradish Sour Cream, and Cucumber Lavash Sandwiches ☺

1 English cucumber
1 small red onion
½ cup sour cream
1½ tablespoons chopped drained capers
2 teaspoons drained bottled horseradish
a 16- to 18-inch round, very thin, pliable *lavash* *
　such as Damascus mountain shepherd bread
6 thin slices smoked salmon (about 6 ounces total)
16 fresh chives
1 cup watercress sprigs

Garnish: watercress sprigs and fresh chives

*available at Middle Eastern markets, some
　supermarkets, and by mail order from
　Damascus Bakeries, tel. (718) 855-1456

Halve and seed cucumber. Cut cucumber into sixteen 5- by ¼-inch-thick sticks. Halve onion lengthwise and cut crosswise into thin slices.

In a small bowl stir together sour cream, capers, horseradish, and salt and pepper to taste.

Quarter *lavash* and spread 1 side of each quarter evenly with 1 tablespoon sour cream mixture, leaving a ½-inch border all around. On each quarter arrange about 1½ slices salmon in one layer over sour cream mixture and spread 1 tablespoon sour cream mixture evenly over salmon. On each quarter arrange 4 cucumber sticks, about 3 onion slices, 4 chives, and one fourth watercress parallel to 1 cut edge and season with salt and pepper. Tightly roll up each lavash around filling into a cone and wrap individually in wax paper and plastic wrap. *Sandwiches may be made 6 hours ahead and chilled, wrapped in plastic wrap.*

Garnish sandwiches with watercress and chives. Makes 4 small sandwiches.

PHOTO ON PAGE 58

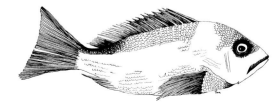

*Grilled Tuna and Roasted Pepper Sandwiches
on Thyme Focaccia*

2 pounds ½-inch-thick tuna steaks or four
    6-ounce cans oil-packed tuna
2 tablespoons fresh lemon juice
1 teaspoon minced fresh thyme leaves
¼ cup plus 2 tablespoons extra-virgin olive oil
2 cups fresh flat-leafed parsley leaves
¾ cup sliced red onion (about 1)
1 thyme *focaccia* (page 116)
3 large red bell peppers, roasted and peeled
    (procedure on page 96)
2 tablespoons drained capers

If using tuna steaks, prepare grill.

Season tuna steaks with salt and pepper and grill on an oiled rack set 5 to 6 inches over glowing coals 3 to 4 minutes on each side, or until just cooked through. (Alternatively, steaks may be grilled in a hot well-seasoned ridged grill pan over moderately high heat.) Transfer tuna to a platter and cool. In a large sealable plastic bag combine lemon juice, thyme, and ¼ cup oil and add grilled tuna. *Marinate grilled tuna, chilled, turning bag occasionally, at least 1 hour and up to 1 day.* If using canned tuna, drain tuna and in a bowl stir together with lemon juice, thyme, ¼ cup oil, and salt and pepper to taste.

In a bowl toss together parsley, onion, and remaining 2 tablespoons oil and season with salt and pepper. Pat roasted peppers dry. Halve *focaccia* horizontally and layer one half with peppers, tuna, capers, and parsley salad. Top sandwich with remaining *focaccia* half, pressing gently, and cut lengthwise in half and crosswise into thirds to make 6 sandwiches. Cut sandwiches in half diagonally and wrap tightly in plastic wrap. *Chill sandwiches at least 1 hour and up to 1 day.* Makes 6 sandwiches.

PHOTO ON PAGE 44

SHELLFISH

*Camarones Adobados a la Parrilla
(Grilled Shrimp with Ancho Pasilla Sauce)*

about 16 bamboo skewers

2 pounds large shrimp (about 48)
½ cup *ancho pasilla* sauce
    (recipe follows)

Accompaniments:
warm tortillas (procedure on page 127)
additional *ancho pasilla* sauce
chopped avocado
chopped white onion

Soak skewers in water at least 30 minutes and up to several hours.

Shell and devein shrimp. Holding 2 skewers parallel and slightly apart, thread 6 shrimp onto them (this will facilitate turning them on the grill). Thread remaining shrimp onto pairs of skewers in same manner. Brush both sides of shrimp with *ancho pasilla* sauce and discard any remaining sauce. *Marinate shrimp, covered and chilled, at least 30 minutes and up to 6 hours.*

Prepare grill.

Grill shrimp on a well-oiled rack set 5 to 6 inches over glowing coals 2 minutes on each side, or until just cooked through. (Alternatively, shrimp may be broiled on rack of a broiler pan under a preheated broiler about 3 inches from heat 3 to 4 minutes on each side.)

Remove shrimp from bamboo skewers and serve with accompaniments. Makes enough filling for 16 to 24 tacos.

PHOTO ON PAGE 48

Ancho Pasilla Sauce ☺

3 dried *ancho* chilies* (about 2 ounces)
4 dried *pasilla* chilies* (about 1½ ounces)
1½ cups fresh orange juice
3 garlic cloves
2 tablespoons olive oil
¾ teaspoon salt

*available at Latino markets, specialty foods
    shops, and some supermarkets, and by mail
    order from Kitchen Market (888) 468-4433

Heat a dry griddle or heavy skillet over moderate heat until hot but not smoking and toast chilies, 1 or

2 at a time, pressing down with tongs, a few seconds on each side to make more pliable. Wearing rubber gloves, remove stems, seeds, and veins. In a blender purée chilies with remaining ingredients until completely smooth. *Sauce may be made 2 days ahead and chilled, covered.* Makes about 2 cups sauce, enough for the preceding recipe, including accompaniment.

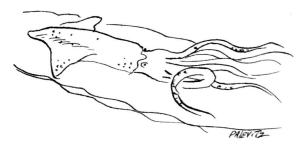

Look for good-quality fresh tortillas, which are available by mail order from Maria and Ricardo's Tortilla Factory, tel. (800) 881-7040 (call on Monday for Friday delivery).

To Warm Tortillas ◯

Wrap stacks of 8 tortillas in foil and chill in sealable plastic bags until ready to heat. *Tortillas may be wrapped and chilled 6 hours ahead.*
Preheat oven to 350° F.
As needed, heat foil packages in oven 12 to 15 minutes, or until hot. Unwrap packages and transfer tortillas to a cloth-lined basket and cover with cloth.

Squid and Bell Pepper Stir-Fry ◯

3 tablespoons sesame seeds
½ large onion
2 red bell peppers
1 yellow bell pepper
2 garlic cloves
6 plum tomatoes
1 pound cleaned small squid
4 tablespoons peanut oil
¼ cup soy sauce
3 tablespoons seasoned rice vinegar
2 teaspoons Asian sesame oil

Accompaniment: cooked rice
    (page 167)
Garnish: fresh parsley leaves

Toast sesame seeds until golden. Cut onion half lengthwise into thin slices. Cut bell peppers into 1-inch pieces and mince garlic. Peel and quarter tomatoes. Seed tomato quarters and halve lengthwise. Cut flaps and tentacles from squid sacs. Cut sacs into ¼-inch-thick strips and cut strips crosswise into ¼-inch-thick rings. Halve tentacles and flaps lengthwise if large. Pat squid dry with paper towels and season with salt and pepper.

Heat a wok or large heavy skillet over high heat until a bead of water dropped on cooking surface evaporates immediately. Add 2 tablespoons peanut oil, swirling wok or skillet to coat evenly, and heat until hot but not smoking. Add onion and stir-fry until softened. Add bell peppers and stir-fry until crisp-tender, about 5 minutes. Add garlic and stir-fry until fragrant, about 30 seconds. Add tomatoes, soy sauce, and vinegar and simmer, stirring, 1 minute. Transfer mixture to a large bowl.

Add 1 tablespoon peanut oil to wok or skillet and heat until just smoking. Stir-fry half of squid until just opaque, about 30 seconds, and transfer with juices to bowl of vegetables. Add remaining tablespoon peanut oil to wok or skillet and stir-fry remaining squid, transferring to bowl. Return squid-vegetable mixture to wok or skillet and stir-fry until heated. Season stir-fry with salt and pepper and stir in sesame oil.

Serve stir-fry over rice, sprinkled with sesame seeds and garnished with parsley. Serves 4.

Chili Lime Shrimp with Avocado and Coriander ☺

¾ pound large shrimp (about 14)
1 garlic clove
1 tablespoon packed brown sugar
3 tablespoons soy sauce
1 teaspoon chili powder
2 teaspoons fresh lime juice
¼ teaspoon dried hot red pepper flakes
4 teaspoons olive oil
1 firm-ripe California avocado
2 teaspoons fresh lemon juice
2 tablespoons coarsely chopped fresh
   coriander leaves

Shell and devein shrimp and mince garlic. In a bowl stir together garlic, brown sugar, soy sauce, chili powder, lime juice, red pepper flakes, and 2 teaspoons oil and add shrimp, tossing to coat. *Marinate shrimp 15 minutes.*

Preheat broiler.

Pit and peel avocado and cut into 1-inch pieces. Drain shrimp and arrange on rack of a broiler pan in one layer. Broil shrimp about 4 inches from heat 2 minutes and with tongs turn shrimp over. Broil shrimp 2 minutes more, or until just cooked through, and transfer to another bowl. Add avocado, lemon juice, coriander, remaining 2 teaspoons oil, and salt and pepper to taste and gently toss to coat. Serves 2.

Thai-Inspired Shrimp Stir-Fry ☺

half of a 4-inch-long fresh red chili
¼ cup seasoned rice vinegar
¼ cup sugar
a 1-inch piece fresh lemongrass*
2 teaspoons minced garlic
2 teaspoons minced peeled fresh
   gingerroot
1 pound large shrimp (16 to 20)
3 medium carrots
2 medium zucchini
½ English cucumber
3 scallions
¼ cup packed fresh coriander leaves
¼ cup salted peanuts (about 1 ounce)
3 tablespoons peanut oil

Accompaniment: cooked rice (page 167)
Garnish: fresh mint leaves cut into
   thin strips, fresh coriander leaves,
   and lime wedges

*available at Asian markets and some specialty
   foods shops and by mail order from Adriana's
   Caravan, tel. (800) 316-0820

Wearing rubber gloves, cut chili crosswise into thin slices and in a small saucepan stir together with vinegar and sugar. Bring mixture to a boil and simmer 30 seconds. Remove chili vinegar from heat.

Remove and discard tough outer layer of lemongrass if necessary and finely chop enough to measure 1 teaspoon. In a small bowl stir together lemongrass, garlic, and gingerroot. Peel shrimp and devein if desired. Pat shrimp dry with paper towels and season with salt and pepper. Add shrimp to lemongrass mixture, stirring to coat well, and marinate at room temperature 15 minutes.

While shrimp are marinating, diagonally cut carrots into ⅛-inch-thick slices. Halve zucchini lengthwise and diagonally cut halves into ⅛-inch-thick slices. Halve cucumber lengthwise and seed. Diagonally cut cucumber halves into thin slices. Diagonally cut scallions into thin slices. Chop coriander and coarsely chop peanuts.

Heat a wok or large heavy skillet over high heat until a bead of water dropped on cooking surface evaporates immediately. Add 1 tablespoon oil, swirling wok or skillet to coat evenly, and heat until hot but not smoking. Add carrots and stir-fry until barely crisp-tender, about 3 minutes. Add zucchini and stir-fry until crisp-tender, about 2 minutes. Transfer vegetables to a large bowl.

Add 1 tablespoon oil to wok or skillet and heat until just smoking. Stir-fry half of shrimp until just cooked through, about 3 minutes, and transfer to bowl of vegetables. Add remaining tablespoon oil and stir-fry remaining shrimp in same manner.

Return shrimp-vegetable mixture to wok or skillet and stir-fry until combined and heated through. Add chili vinegar, cucumber, scallions, coriander, peanuts, and salt and pepper to taste and stir to combine.

Serve stir-fry over rice in bowls, garnished with mint, coriander, and lime wedges. Serves 4.

Baked Oysters in Jackets with Bacon Cognac Butter

For bacon Cognac butter
1½ slices lean bacon (about 1 ounce),
   chopped fine
1 tablespoon minced shallot
1½ tablespoons Cognac
2 tablespoons unsalted butter, softened
1½ teaspoons minced fresh flat-leafed parsley
   leaves

6 spinach leaves, tough stems discarded
6 oysters on the half shell
coarse sea or kosher salt for filling roasting pan
   and plates

Prepare butter:
In a heavy skillet cook bacon over moderate heat, stirring occasionally, until golden and add shallot. Cook mixture, stirring, until shallot is softened. Stir in Cognac and cool mixture to room temperature. In a small bowl stir together bacon mixture, butter, and parsley. *Butter may be prepared 3 days ahead, formed into a 3-inch-long log, and chilled, wrapped well in plastic wrap.*

Preheat oven to 425° F.

In a steamer set over ½ inch simmering water steam spinach, covered, until just wilted, about 1 minute. Gently rinse spinach under cold water to stop cooking and pat each leaf dry.

Loosen each oyster from shell with a small knife if necessary and wrap in a spinach leaf. Return oysters to shells and top with butter. In a small roasting pan spread coarse salt ¼ inch deep and nestle shells in salt to keep them level. *Oysters may be prepared up to this point 8 hours ahead and chilled, covered.* Bake oysters in middle of oven until plump and butter is sizzling, about 10 minutes.

Spread coarse salt ¼ inch deep on each of 2 plates and nestle oysters in salt. Makes 6 baked oysters, serving 2 as an hors d'oeuvre.

PHOTO ON PAGE 12

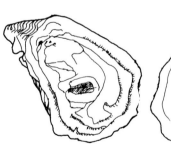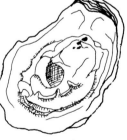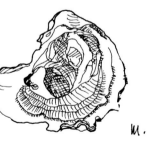

M. Shields

129

MEAT

Tenderloin roasts vary in shape, size, and weight. For this recipe it's important that the tenderloin be of uniform shape and size. If you can't find a whole tenderloin, 2 center-cut pieces will work. (We cut our whole one in half in order to brown it.)

Beef en Croûte with Coriander Walnut Filling

a trimmed 4½- to 5-pound beef tenderloin roast
  (about 16 inches long and 3 inches in diameter)
1 tablespoon vegetable oil
1 large egg
1 tablespoon water
sour cream pastry dough (recipe follows)
coriander walnut filling (page 131)

Trim tenderloin if necessary and pat dry. Halve tenderloin crosswise and season with salt and pepper. In a large heavy skillet heat oil over moderately high heat until just smoking and brown beef, 1 piece at a time, on all sides, about 2 minutes total for each piece of beef, transferring to a platter.

Make an egg wash by lightly beating egg with water. On a lightly floured surface with a floured rolling pin roll out dough into a 19- by 15-inch rectangle (slightly less than ¼ inch thick). Cut a 1-inch strip of dough from a shorter end (leaving an 18- by 15-inch rectangle) and reserve strip. Arrange rectangle lengthwise on a baking sheet or tray (about 17½ by 12½ inches), letting excess dough hang over. Spread one third filling lengthwise down middle of rectangle, forming a 16- by 2-inch strip. Arrange beef pieces end to end lengthwise on filling and spread remaining filling on top of beef. Brush edges of dough with some egg wash. Fold up long sides of dough to enclose beef completely and seal edge. Fold ends of dough over wrapped beef and seal edges. Invert a large baking sheet onto wrapped beef and invert beef onto sheet so that pastry is seam side down. Brush crust evenly with some egg wash. Cut out holly leaves and berries from reserved pastry strip and arrange on crust, gently pressing to make them adhere. Brush decorations with some egg wash and with a sharp knife make small steam vents every 3 inches on top of crust. *Chill beef en croûte, loosely covered, at least 1 hour and up to 6.*

Preheat oven to 400° F.

Bake beef *en croûte* in middle of oven 45 minutes, or until pastry is golden brown and a thermometer inserted diagonally 2 inches into center of beef registers 115° F. Let beef stand on sheet on a rack 25 minutes. Beef will continue to cook as it stands, reaching 125° F. (medium-rare). Serves 16.

PHOTO ON PAGE 77

Sour Cream Pastry Dough ◐+

2½ sticks (1¼ cups) cold unsalted butter
3¼ cups all-purpose flour
1 teaspoon salt
1¼ cups well-chilled sour cream
4 to 6 tablespoons ice water

Cut butter into ½-inch cubes.
To blend by hand:

In a bowl with your fingertips or a pastry blender blend together flour, butter, and salt until most of mixture resembles coarse meal with remainder in small (roughly pea-size) lumps. Stir in sour cream with a fork just until incorporated. Drizzle 4 tablespoons ice water over mixture and gently stir just until incorporated. Test mixture by gently squeezing a small handful: When it has proper texture it should hold together without crumbling apart. If necessary, add enough remaining water, 1 tablespoon at a time, stirring until incorporated and testing, to give mixture proper texture. (If you overwork mixture or add too much water, pastry will be tough.)

To blend in a food processor:

In a food processor pulse together flour, butter, and salt until most of mixture resembles coarse meal with remainder in small (roughly pea-size) lumps. Add sour cream and pulse just until incorporated. Drizzle 4 tablespoons water over mixture and pulse just until incorporated. Test mixture by gently squeezing a small handful: When it has proper texture it should hold together without crumbling apart. If necessary, add enough remaining water, 1 tablespoon at a time, pulsing until incorporated and testing, to give mixture proper texture. (If you overwork mixture or add too much water, pastry will be tough.)

To form dough after blending by either method:

Turn mixture out onto a work surface and divide into 4 portions. With heel of hand smear each portion once in a forward motion to help distribute fat. Gather dough together and form it, rotating it on work surface, into a disk. *Chill dough, wrapped in plastic wrap, until firm, at least 1 hour, and up to 1 day.* Makes enough pastry dough to wrap a 5-pound beef tenderloin roast.

Coriander Walnut Filling

2 cups walnuts
4 garlic cloves
two ¾-pound bunches spinach
3 cups packed fresh coriander sprigs
2 cups packed fresh flat-leafed parsley sprigs
1 cup fine fresh bread crumbs
¼ cup honey
2 large egg whites
1½ teaspoons salt
1 teaspoon ground cumin
1 teaspoon ground coriander seeds
¼ teaspoon freshly ground black pepper

Preheat oven to 350° F.

In a baking pan toast walnuts in one layer in middle of oven 10 to 15 minutes, or until lightly colored, and cool completely. Mince garlic and discard stems from spinach.

Have ready a large bowl of ice and cold water. In a 3-quart kettle half filled with boiling salted water blanch spinach 20 seconds and with a slotted skimmer transfer to ice water bath to stop cooking. Return water to a boil and blanch fresh coriander and parsley 5 seconds. Drain herbs in a colander and transfer to ice water to stop cooking. Drain spinach and herbs in colander and squeeze in small handfuls until as dry as possible.

In a food processor pulse walnuts just until finely ground. Add garlic, spinach mixture, and remaining ingredients and pulse just until smooth. *Filling may be made 2 days ahead and chilled, covered.* Makes about 3½ cups.

Grilled Porterhouse Steaks

three 1½-inch-thick porterhouse steaks
    (each about 2 to 2¼ pounds)
3 tablespoons mixed whole peppercorns
1½ teaspoons coarse kosher salt

Prepare grill.

Let steaks stand at room temperature 30 minutes. With a mortar and pestle or bottom of a heavy skillet coarsely crush peppercorns and in a small bowl combine with salt. Pat steaks dry and rub seasoning onto both sides of steaks, pressing to adhere.

Grill steaks on an oiled rack set 5 to 6 inches over glowing coals 7 to 9 minutes on each side, or until an instant-read thermometer registers 125° F. for medium-rare. (Alternatively, steaks may be broiled on rack of a broiler pan under a preheated broiler about 4 inches from heat.) Transfer steaks to a platter and let stand 10 minutes.

Serve steaks sliced. Serves 6.

PHOTO ON PAGE 42

Poached Filets Mignons with Horseradish Sauce ◔

four 4-ounce fully trimmed center-cut filets
   mignons
1 cup veal *demiglace**
1 cup water
2 tablespoons Dijon mustard
2 tablespoons bottled horseradish

Accompaniment: butternut squash, turnip, and
   green-bean quinoa (page 166)

*available at some butchers and by mail order
   from Citarella, tel. (800) 588-0383

Season filets with salt and pepper.

In a 2-quart saucepan heat *demiglace* and water
just to a simmer and add steak. Add some boiling
water to mixture if necessary to make enough liquid
to just cover steak. Poach steak at a bare simmer
(meat will toughen if liquid is allowed to boil),
without turning, 8 minutes and remove from broth.
Boil broth over high heat until reduced to about ½
cup and stir in Dijon mustard and horseradish. Keep
horseradish sauce warm over low heat and halve
steaks horizontally.

Mound quinoa mixture on 1 side of 4 large
plates and arrange 2 slices steak alongside. Spoon
sauce over steak. Serves 4.

🥘 Each serving of steak with vegetable quinoa:
325 calories, 11 grams fat
(30% of calories from fat)

PHOTO ON PAGE 87

Filets Mignons on Jerusalem Artichoke Purée

1 pound Jerusalem artichokes*
   (sunchokes)
2 cups skim milk
1 teaspoon salt
1 tablespoon drained bottled horseradish,
   or to taste
vegetable-oil cooking spray
six 4-ounce filets mignons

Accompaniment: roasted balsamic red onions
   (page 174)

*available at specialty produce markets and
   some supermarkets

Peel Jerusalem artichokes and cut into 1-inch
pieces. In a stainless-steel or enameled saucepan
simmer artichokes in milk and water to cover by 1
inch until tender, about 20 minutes. (Milk will help
prevent artichokes from discoloring.) In a blender
purée artichokes with cooking liquid, salt, pepper to
taste, and horseradish (use caution when blending
hot liquids). Keep purée warm in pan, covered.

Preheat oven to 450° F. Lightly coat a non-stick
skillet and shallow baking pan with vegetable-oil
cooking spray.

Pat filets mignons dry and season with salt and
pepper. Heat skillet over moderately high heat until
hot but not smoking and brown steaks. Transfer
steaks to baking pan and roast in middle of oven
until a meat thermometer registers 130° F. for
medium-rare, about 10 minutes.

Spoon some purée onto 6 plates and top with
onions and steaks. Serve remaining purée on side.
Serves 6.

🥘 Each serving, including ⅓ cup onions,
about 254 calories, 7 grams fat
(26% of calories from fat)

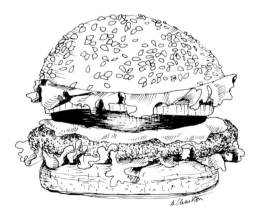

Indonesian-Style Burgers with Peanut Sauce ◯

6 tablespoons creamy peanut butter
3 tablespoons sour cream
2 tablespoons fresh lime juice
4 teaspoons soy sauce
1¼ pounds ground chuck
2 tablespoons chopped fresh coriander
2 teaspoons grated peeled fresh
  gingerroot
½ teaspoon dried hot red pepper flakes
4 sesame buns
4 soft-leafed lettuce leaves

In a small bowl stir together peanut butter, sour cream, 1 tablespoon lime juice, and 2 teaspoons soy sauce until combined. In a large bowl blend together ground chuck, remaining 2 teaspoons soy sauce, remaining tablespoon lime juice, coriander, gingerroot, red pepper flakes, and salt and pepper to taste until just combined. Form mixture into four 1-inch-thick patties and cook (procedure follows). Toast sesame buns. Transfer burgers to buns and top with peanut sauce and lettuce. Serves 4.

To Form and Grill Burgers ◯

Prepare grill.
When forming patties, handle meat as little as possible for a juicier burger. Grill burgers on an oiled rack set 5 to 6 inches over glowing coals about 4½ minutes on each side for well-done meat. (Alternatively, burgers may be cooked in a hot well-seasoned cast-iron skillet or ridged grill pan.)

Roast Beef, Basil, and Spicy Tomato Chutney
Lavash Sandwiches

a 16- to 18-inch round, very thin, pliable
  *lavash** such as Damascus mountain
  shepherd bread
½ cup spicy tomato chutney (recipe follows)
  or bottled tomato chutney
6 large thin slices rare roast beef (about
  ¼ pound total)
16 fresh basil leaves
8 arugula leaves

Garnish: arugula and fresh basil leaves
Accompaniment: spicy tomato chutney
  (recipe follows) or bottled tomato chutney

*available at Middle Eastern markets, specialty
  foods shops, and some supermarkets and by
  mail order from Damascus Bakeries,
  tel. (718) 855-1456

Quarter *lavash* and spread 1 side of each quarter evenly with 1 tablespoon chutney, leaving a ½-inch border all around. On each quarter arrange about 1½ slices roast beef in one layer over chutney and season with salt and pepper. Spread 1 tablespoon chutney evenly over roast beef and top with basil, arugula, and salt and pepper to taste. Tightly roll up each *lavash* around filling into a cone and wrap cones individually in wax paper and plastic wrap. *Sandwiches may be made 6 hours ahead and chilled, wrapped in plastic wrap.*
Garnish sandwiches with arugula and basil and serve with chutney. Makes 4 small sandwiches.

PHOTO ON PAGE 58

Spicy Tomato Chutney

1 pound vine-ripened tomatoes
1 red bell pepper
½ cup red-wine vinegar
¾ cup cider vinegar
¾ cup sugar
1 teaspoon salt
2 teaspoons mustard seeds
½ teaspoon freshly ground black pepper
½ teaspoon dried hot red pepper flakes
¾ cup chopped scallion greens

Chop tomatoes and bell pepper.
In a medium saucepan bring vinegars to a boil with sugar, salt, mustard seeds, black pepper, and red pepper flakes, stirring occasionally, and stir in tomatoes, bell pepper, and scallions. Simmer mixture, uncovered, stirring occasionally (stir more frequently toward end of cooking), about 1¼ hours, or until thickened and reduced to about 1½ cups. Cool chutney completely. *Chutney keeps, covered and chilled, 2 weeks.* Makes about 1½ cups.

Arrachera con Ajo y Limón a la Parrilla ◐+
(Grilled Garlic-Marinated Skirt Steak with Lime)

3 pounds skirt steak (about 3 long steaks)
3 tablespoons finely chopped garlic
3 tablespoons olive oil
coarse salt to taste
3 tablespoons fresh lime juice,
    or to taste

Accompaniments:
warm tortillas (page 127)
poblano strips with onions and cream (page 171)
    or grilled spring onions (page 174)
fresh tomato salsa (page 193)

If necessary, trim steaks, leaving some fat. In a shallow dish rub steaks with garlic and oil. *Marinate steaks, covered and chilled, at least 30 minutes and up to 1 day.*
    Prepare grill.
    Season steaks generously with coarse salt and grill on a rack set 5 to 6 inches over glowing coals 2 to 3 minutes on each side for medium-rare. (Alternatively, steaks may be broiled on rack of a broiler pan under a preheated broiler 3 inches from heat about 4 minutes on each side.) Transfer steaks to a board and drizzle with lime juice. Let steaks stand, uncovered, 5 to 10 minutes and with a sharp knife cut diagonally across grain into thin slices.
    Serve steak with accompaniments. Makes enough filling for about 24 tacos.

PHOTO ON PAGE 48

Beef Filé Gumbo

2 tablespoons vegetable oil
6 pounds cross-cut sections beef shanks
2½ pounds beef short ribs (sometimes called
    Flanken), cut into 1-rib pieces if necessary
2 onions, chopped
3 large red bell peppers,
    chopped
12 cups water
4 cups beef broth
6 garlic cloves, minced
cayenne to taste
3 tablespoons filé powder*

Accompaniment: Cajun-style white rice
    (page 167)

*available at some specialty foods shops and
    by mail order from Mo Hotta–Mo Betta,
    tel. (800) 462-3220

In a heavy skillet (preferably cast-iron) heat oil over moderately high heat until hot but not smoking. Pat shanks and short ribs dry and season with salt and pepper. Brown shanks and short ribs in oil in batches, without crowding, transferring to a 9½- to 10-quart heavy kettle. In fat remaining in skillet cook onions and bell peppers over moderate heat, stirring occasionally, until vegetables are softened.
    To beef in kettle add water, beef broth, and onion mixture and bring to a boil, stirring occasionally. Simmer mixture, uncovered, until shanks are very tender, about 2½ hours, and stir in garlic and cayenne. With a narrow knife ease any marrow remaining in shank bones into mixture and discard shank and short rib bones. *Beef mixture may be prepared up to this point 3 days ahead, cooled completely, uncovered, and chilled, covered.*
    Skim fat from beef mixture. Reheat mixture if previously chilled. Bring beef mixture to a bare simmer and stir in filé powder. Cook gumbo over moderately low heat, stirring occasionally, 5 minutes. (Do not let gumbo boil with filé powder; it will become stringy.)
    Serve gumbo ladled over Cajun-style white rice in large soup plates. Makes about 22 cups, serving 10 to 12 as a main course.

VEAL

*Veal Scallops with Squash, Tomatoes,
    and Roasted-Garlic Basil Sauce* ◐

vegetable-oil cooking spray
4 plum tomatoes
¾ pound baby pattypan squash
2 tablespoons fresh lemon juice
1 teaspoon Dijon mustard
2 teaspoons extra-virgin olive oil
1 pound veal scallops (each about ⅛ inch thick)

Accompaniment: roasted-garlic basil sauce (recipe follows)

Preheat broiler and lightly spray a baking sheet with vegetable oil.

Cut plum tomatoes lengthwise into ¼-inch-thick slices and arrange in one layer on sheet. Season tomatoes with salt and pepper and broil 3 inches from heat until edges are browned, about 15 minutes.

While tomatoes are broiling, in a saucepan of boiling salted water cook squash until crisp-tender, about 4 minutes. Drain squash in a colander and season with salt and pepper. Keep tomatoes and squash warm.

In a cup stir together lemon juice, mustard, and oil. If veal scallops are too thick, put each veal scallop between 2 sheets of plastic wrap and with a rolling pin or smooth side of a meat pounder, gently flatten veal to ⅛ inch thick. Pat veal scallops dry and brush one side of each with lemon mixture. Season veal with salt.

In a well-seasoned ridged grill pan cook veal scallops in batches over moderately high heat about 1 minute on each side, or until cooked through.

If scallops are large, cut in half diagonally. Serve veal with tomatoes, squash, and sauce. Serves 4.

🖛 Each serving of veal, vegetables, and sauce
about 207 calories, 6.9 grams fat
(30% of calories from fat)

PHOTO ON PAGE 85

Roasted-Garlic Basil Sauce ◔

4 large garlic cloves
1 medium zucchini
¾ cup packed fresh basil leaves
¼ cup packed fresh flat-leafed parsley leaves
½ cup water
2 teaspoons fresh lemon juice

Preheat oven to 425° F.
Wrap garlic cloves tightly in foil. Cut zucchini into ¼-inch-thick slices and season with salt and pepper. Put foil-wrapped garlic and zucchini on a baking sheet and roast in middle of oven until garlic is tender and zucchini is pale golden, about 15 minutes. Unwrap garlic and cool.

Have ready a bowl of ice water. In a saucepan of boiling water blanch basil and parsley 10 seconds and drain in a sieve. Refresh herbs in ice water to stop cooking and drain in sieve. *Sauce ingredients may be prepared up to this point 1 day ahead and kept separately, covered and chilled.*

In a blender blend garlic, zucchini, herbs, water, and lemon juice until smooth, about 1 minute, and season with salt and pepper. Makes about ¾ cup.

🖛 Each 3 tablespoon serving about
14 calories, 0 grams fat

Veal Scallops with Mushrooms and Rosemary ☉

½ pound white mushrooms
¾ pound veal scallops (each about
    ⅛ inch thick)
1 teaspoon chopped fresh rosemary leaves
1 tablespoon unsalted butter
1 tablespoon vegetable oil
¼ cup dry white wine
¼ cup heavy cream

Thinly slice mushrooms. If veal scallops are too thick, with smooth side of a meat pounder pound thin between sheets of plastic wrap. Pat veal dry with paper towels and season with salt and pepper.

In a large heavy skillet cook mushrooms and rosemary in butter over high heat, stirring, until liquid mushrooms give off is evaporated and mushrooms are lightly browned, about 7 minutes. Transfer mushroom mixture to a plate. Add 1½ teaspoons oil to skillet and heat until hot but not smoking. Add half of veal to skillet and sear over high heat, 1 to 2 minutes on each side or until lightly browned and cooked through. Transfer veal to a small platter and cook remaining veal in remaining 1½ teaspoons oil in same manner. Add wine carefully to skillet and deglaze, scraping up brown bits. Add cream, mushroom mixture, and salt and pepper to taste and simmer 1 minute.

Pour mushroom mixture over veal. Serves 2.

*Sautéed Veal with Roasted Pepper and
Anchovy Sauce* ☉

For sauce
1 red bell pepper
1 garlic clove
4 flat anchovy fillets
a pinch cayenne
3 tablespoons olive oil
freshly ground black pepper to taste

all-purpose flour for dredging veal
two ¼-inch-thick veal cutlets (about
    10 ounces total), flattened between
    sheets of plastic wrap
1 tablespoon vegetable oil
1 tablespoon unsalted butter

Make sauce:
Preheat broiler.
Quarter bell pepper lengthwise, discarding stem, seeds, and ribs. Put pepper, skin side up, on rack of a broiler pan and broil about 2 inches from heat until skin is blistered and charred, 8 to 12 minutes.

Transfer bell pepper to a bowl and let stand, covered, until cool enough to handle. Peel pepper.

In a blender purée roasted pepper with remaining sauce ingredients until smooth and add salt to taste. *Sauce may be made 4 days ahead and chilled, covered.* Transfer sauce to a sauceboat.

Put flour in a shallow dish. Pat veal cutlets dry and season with salt and pepper. Dredge cutlets in flour, shaking off excess. In a 12-inch non-stick skillet heat oil and butter over moderately high heat until foam subsides and sauté cutlets 1 minute on each side, or until golden and just cooked through.

Serve veal with sauce. Serves 2.

PORK

If making the roasted celery root, it may be baked along with the pork loin, but should go into the oven about 30 minutes before the loin does. Transfer the celery root to the lower third of the oven after 30 minutes so that the loin can be put in the upper third.

Pork Loin with Morel Stuffing

1½ ounces small dried morels* (about 1½ cups)
2 cups boiling-hot water
2 tablespoons extra-virgin olive oil
½ cup chopped shallot
1 garlic clove, minced
¾ cup fine fresh bread crumbs
¼ cup chopped fresh parsley leaves
a 3- to 3½-pound center-cut boneless pork loin
    (about 3½ inches thick)
2 tablespoons fresh lime juice
2 cups rich veal stock** or *demiglace***

Accompaniment if desired: roasted celery root
    (page 172)

*available at specialty foods shops and
   by mail order from Comptoir Exotique,
   tel. (888) 547-5471 (toll free)
**available at specialty foods shops and some
   supermarkets and by mail order from
   D'Artagnan, tel. (800) 327-8246 or
   (201) 792-0748

In a small bowl soak morels in boiling-hot water
30 minutes and transfer with a slotted spoon to paper
towels to drain. Pour soaking liquid through a sieve
lined with a dampened coffee filter or paper towel
into a small saucepan and simmer until reduced to
about ⅓ cup, about 10 minutes. Add one third morels
and reserve. Finely chop remaining morels. *Morels
may be prepared up to this point 1 day ahead and
chilled, covered.*

Preheat oven to 375° F.

In a large skillet heat 1½ tablespoons oil over
moderately high heat until hot but not smoking and
sauté shallot and garlic until softened. Transfer
mixture to a bowl and stir in chopped morels, bread
crumbs, parsley, and salt and pepper to taste. *Morel
stuffing may be made 1 day ahead and chilled,
covered. Bring stuffing to room temperature before
proceeding.*

To make a hole for stuffing that runs through
center of pork loin, pat loin dry and, beginning in
middle of one end, with a long, thin, sharp knife
make a lengthwise incision toward center of loin.
Repeat procedure starting from opposite end of loin
(to complete hole running through middle). With
handle of a wooden spoon or your fingers open up
incision to create a 1½-inch-wide opening. Working
from both ends of loin, pack stuffing into opening,
pushing toward center. Season outside of loin with
salt and pepper.

In skillet heat remaining ½ tablespoon oil over
high heat until hot and just smoking and brown loin
on all sides, about 1½ minutes total. Transfer loin to
a flameproof roasting pan and roast in middle of
oven about 1 hour, or until a meat thermometer
inserted in center of meat (but to the side of stuffing)
registers 155° F. Transfer loin to a cutting board and
let stand 10 minutes.

While loin is standing, add lime juice to roasting
pan and deglaze on top of stove over moderate heat,
scraping up brown bits. Add stock or *demiglace* and

reserved morel liquid with morels and simmer sauce,
stirring occasionally, 5 minutes.

Slice pork loin and serve with sauce and celery
root. Serves 6.

PHOTO ON PAGE 24

Grilled Jerk Pork Chops

¼ cup chopped onion
1 teaspoon dried thyme, crumbled
1 teaspoon sugar
1 teaspoon salt
½ teaspoon black pepper
½ teaspoon cayenne
½ teaspoon ground allspice
⅛ teaspoon freshly grated nutmeg
⅛ teaspoon cinnamon
two ½-inch-thick rib pork chops
   (each about 4 ounces)

Prepare grill.

Mince and mash onion to a coarse paste with
thyme, sugar, salt, and spices. Pat pork chops dry
and rub all over with jerk paste. Grill pork on an
oiled rack set 5 to 6 inches over glowing coals 4
minutes on each side, or until just cooked through.
(Alternatively, pork may be grilled in a hot well-
seasoned ridged grill pan over moderately high
heat.) Serves 2.

Pork Chops with Spicy Citrus Marinade ☺

½ cup fresh orange juice
1 teaspoon freshly ground black pepper
¼ teaspoon chili powder
¼ teaspoon paprika
a pinch cayenne, or to taste
two 1-inch-thick rib or loin pork chops
    (about ½ pound each)
2 tablespoons chopped fresh coriander leaves

In a shallow baking dish whisk together orange juice, black pepper, chili powder, paprika, cayenne, and salt to taste. Add pork to marinade, turning to coat, and marinate at room temperature 20 minutes.

In a non-stick skillet cook pork in marinade, covered, over moderately high heat 6 minutes on each side, or until just cooked through. Sprinkle pork with coriander. Serves 2.

Five-Spice Pork and Green Bean Stir-Fry

a ¾-pound piece well-trimmed boneless pork loin
For sauce
3 garlic cloves
2 teaspoons minced peeled fresh gingerroot
⅔ cup water
¼ cup soy sauce
¼ cup mango chutney such as Major Grey's
1 teaspoon Chinese five-spice powder*
½ teaspoon *sambal oelek** (Indonesian chili paste)

1 medium red onion
½ pound green beans
a ¾-pound piece green cabbage (about
    ½ medium head)
¼ cup packed fresh coriander leaves
4½ tablespoons peanut oil
½ pound fresh bean sprouts (about 2 cups)
1 cup snow-pea shoots* or *daikon*
    (Asian radish) sprouts*
2 teaspoons Asian sesame oil

Accompaniment: cooked rice (page 167)

*available at Asian markets, specialty produce
    markets, and some supermarkets

Freeze pork, wrapped in plastic wrap, until firm, 30 minutes, to facilitate slicing. Cut pork crosswise into ⅛-inch-thick slices and season with salt and pepper.

Make sauce:
Mince garlic and in a small bowl stir together with remaining sauce ingredients until combined.

Halve onion lengthwise and cut into thin slices. Diagonally cut beans into 1½-inch pieces. Core cabbage and cut into 1-inch pieces. Chop coriander.

Heat a wok or large heavy skillet over high heat until a bead of water dropped on cooking surface evaporates immediately. Add 1½ tablespoons peanut oil, swirling wok or skillet to coat evenly, and heat until hot but not smoking. Add onion and stir-fry until slightly softened. Add beans and stir-fry until crisp-tender, about 4 minutes. Transfer mixture to a large bowl. Add 1 tablespoon peanut oil to wok or skillet and stir-fry cabbage until crisp-tender, about 2 minutes. Add bean sprouts and stir-fry until sprouts are slightly wilted, about 30 seconds. Transfer cabbage mixture to bowl.

Add 1 tablespoon peanut oil to wok or skillet and heat until just smoking. Stir-fry half of pork, separating slices, until browned and transfer to bowl. Add remaining tablespoon peanut oil and stir-fry remaining pork, transferring to bowl.

Add sauce to wok or skillet and bring to a boil, stirring. Return pork-vegetable mixture to wok or skillet and stir-fry until heated through. Stir in coriander, snow-pea shoots or *daikon* sprouts, sesame oil, and salt and pepper to taste.

Serve stir-fry over rice. Serves 4.

Peppered Pork Loin with Beet and Leek Purée

4 medium leeks (white and pale green parts only)
4 medium beets (about 1 pound total), trimmed
1 tablespoon fresh lemon juice
2 teaspoons balsamic vinegar, or to taste
vegetable-oil cooking spray
a 1½-pound pork loin
2 teaspoons coarsely ground black pepper
1 pound small boiling potatoes, scrubbed

In a saucepan bring salted water to a boil for leeks.

Trim and coarsely chop leeks. Wash leeks and drain in a colander. In saucepan of salted boiling water cook leeks until tender, about 4 minutes, and transfer with a slotted spoon to a blender, reserving cooking liquid.

Trim beet stems to 1 inch if necessary and scrub beets. In a saucepan cover beets with salted water by 1 inch and simmer, covered, 35 to 45 minutes, or until tender. Reserve 1½ cups cooking liquid. Drain beets in colander and cool just until they can be handled. Slip off beet skins and cut each beet into quarters.

Add beets and reserved beet cooking liquid to leeks and purée with salt and pepper to taste. In cleaned pan heat purée, lemon juice, and vinegar over low heat, stirring and adding water if necessary to reach desired consistency, until hot. Keep sauce warm, covered.

Preheat oven to 450° F. Lightly coat a non-stick skillet and a shallow baking pan with vegetable-oil cooking spray.

Pat pork dry and sprinkle 1 side with pepper and salt to taste. In skillet brown pork, seasoned side down first, over moderately high heat. Transfer pork, seasoned side up, to baking pan and roast in middle of oven 20 minutes, or until a meat thermometer registers 155° F.

While pork is roasting, boil potatoes in reserved leek cooking liquid until tender, about 7 minutes, and drain.

Let pork stand, covered with foil, 10 minutes and cut into ¼-inch-thick slices.

Quarter potatoes and serve with pork. Drizzle some sauce around pork and serve remainder on the side. Serves 6.

Each serving about 299 calories, 9 grams fat (26% of calories from fat)

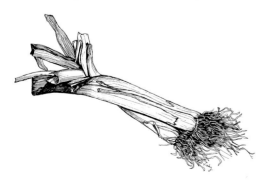

Sausage and White Bean "Cassoulet"

4 sweet Italian sausage links (about 10 ounces total), skins pricked all over with a fork
1 teaspoon olive oil
2 medium onions, halved and sliced thin lengthwise (about 1½ cups)
2 garlic cloves, chopped fine
1½ teaspoons mixed chopped fresh herbs such as rosemary, thyme, and/or sage or ¾ teaspoon mixed dried herbs, crumbled
1 bay leaf
½ cup chopped scallion greens or fresh parsley leaves
a 14½-ounce can diced tomatoes including juice
a 19-ounce can white beans such as *cannellini*, navy, or Great Northern, drained and rinsed
For topping
1 tablespoon olive oil
2 slices firm white sandwich bread, crusts discarded, cut into ¼-inch dice
1 small garlic clove, chopped fine
2 tablespoons finely chopped fresh parsley leaves

In a medium skillet cook sausages in oil over moderate heat, turning them, until browned on all sides and cooked through, about 8 minutes, and transfer to paper towels to drain.

In fat remaining in skillet cook onions and garlic, stirring, until golden and stir in herbs (including bay leaf), scallions or parsley, tomatoes with juice, and salt and pepper to taste. Boil mixture, stirring, 5 minutes. Cut sausage into ¼-inch-thick slices. Add sausage and beans to tomato mixture and cook, stirring, until heated through. Discard bay leaf and keep "cassoulet" warm, covered.

Make topping:

In a small skillet heat oil over moderately high heat until hot but not smoking and sauté bread until pale golden. Stir in garlic, parsley, and salt and pepper to taste and sauté, stirring, 1 minute.

Transfer "cassoulet" to a 1-quart serving dish and cover evenly with topping. Serves 2.

LAMB

Roast Lamb Loin Persillade

¼ cup plus 2 tablespoons packed fresh parsley
　leaves, chopped
3 tablespoons extra-virgin olive oil
2 garlic cloves, minced, plus 1 teaspoon
　chopped garlic
½ teaspoon finely grated fresh lemon zest
¼ teaspoon salt
1 boneless lamb loin (one side only; about
　1½ pounds), rolled and tied by butcher
½ teaspoon fresh lemon juice

In a blender purée 2 tablespoons parsley, oil, 1 teaspoon chopped garlic, zest, and salt until parsley is finely chopped. *Persillade sauce may be made 1 day ahead and chilled, covered.*

Preheat oven to 425° F.

Untie and unroll lamb. Season inside of lamb with salt and pepper and sprinkle with remaining parsley and minced garlic. Reroll lamb and retie with kitchen string. Season outside of lamb with salt and pepper. Put lamb on a rack in a roasting pan and roast in middle of oven 30 to 40 minutes, or until a meat thermometer registers 125° F. for medium-rare or 130° F. for medium. Transfer lamb to a cutting board and let stand 10 minutes.

In a small saucepan heat sauce over moderate heat until hot and just before serving stir in lemon juice. Slice lamb about ½ inch thick.

Divide sauce between 2 plates and top with lamb. Serves 2 generously.

PHOTO ON PAGE 14

Lemon-Garlic Lamb Chops

1 garlic clove
2 lamb shoulder chops (each
　about ¾ inch thick)
1 tablespoon olive oil
1 tablespoon fresh lemon juice
2 tablespoons water

Chop garlic. Pat lamb dry and season with salt and pepper. In a 10-inch heavy skillet heat oil over moderately high heat until hot but not smoking and sear lamb 3 minutes. Turn lamb over and sear 2 minutes more for medium-rare. Transfer lamb to 2 plates. Add garlic, lemon juice, and water to skillet and deglaze over high heat, stirring and scraping up brown bits, 1 minute.

Pour sauce over lamb. Serves 2.

Curried Lamb Patties with Radish Raita

For radish raita
⅓ cup plain yogurt
2 tablespoons diced radish
1 teaspoon diced red onion
1 teaspoon fresh lime juice
For lamb patties
¾ pound ground lamb
3 tablespoons chopped red onion
1½ tablespoons Major Grey's mango chutney
3 tablespoons chopped fresh coriander
¼ teaspoon ground cumin
¼ teaspoon ground coriander seeds
⅛ teaspoon paprika
1 tablespoon vegetable oil

Make raita:
In a small bowl stir together all *raita* ingredients and season with salt and pepper.

Make patties:
In a large bowl mix together all patty ingredients except oil until combined well and season with salt and pepper. Form mixture into 4 patties about 1 inch thick. In a large heavy skillet heat oil over moderately high heat until hot but not smoking and cook patties until just cooked through, about 3½ minutes on each side.

Serve lamb patties with *raita.* Serves 2.

Lamb and Shiitake Mushroom Stir-Fry �𝕆+

1 pound boneless leg of lamb
2 tablespoons cornstarch
For sauce
¾ cup chicken broth
3 tablespoons honey
2 tablespoons soy sauce
2 tablespoons oyster sauce
¾ teaspoon dried hot red pepper flakes

½ pound eggplant (about 1 small)
3 celery ribs
3 garlic cloves
½ pound fresh *shiitake* mushrooms
½ pound small white mushrooms
1 bunch watercress
4 tablespoons peanut oil

Accompaniment: cooked rice (page 167)

Freeze lamb, wrapped in plastic wrap, until firm, 30 minutes, to facilitate slicing. Trim lamb well and cut into ⅛-inch-thick slices. Halve lamb slices crosswise. In a large bowl toss lamb with cornstarch until coated well and season with salt and pepper.
Make sauce:
In a bowl stir together sauce ingredients until combined well.

Cut eggplant into 1-inch cubes. Diagonally cut celery into ¼-inch-thick slices and mince garlic. Discard stems from *shiitakes* and halve caps (quarter if large). Halve white mushrooms lengthwise. Discard tough stems from watercress.

Heat a wok or large heavy skillet over high heat until a bead of water dropped on cooking surface evaporates immediately. Add 2 tablespoons oil, swirling wok or skillet to coat evenly, and heat until hot but not smoking. Add eggplant and stir-fry until golden and tender, about 4 minutes. Add celery and stir-fry until crisp-tender, about 2 minutes. Add garlic and mushrooms and stir-fry until mushrooms are tender, about 2 minutes. Transfer mixture to a large bowl.

Add 1 tablespoon oil to wok or skillet and heat until just smoking. Add half of lamb and stir-fry, separating slices, until browned. Transfer lamb to

bowl. Add remaining tablespoon oil and stir-fry remaining lamb, transferring to bowl.

Add sauce to wok or skillet and bring to a boil, stirring. Return lamb-vegetable mixture to wok or skillet and stir-fry until combined and heated through. Stir in watercress and season stir-fry with salt and pepper.

Serve stir-fry over rice. Serves 4.

Lamb Stew

2 pounds boneless lamb shoulder, trimmed
    and cut into 1-inch cubes
3 tablespoons all-purpose flour seasoned
    with salt and pepper
2 tablespoons vegetable oil
1 large onion, chopped fine
6 large garlic cloves, chopped fine
4 carrots, cut crosswise into ½-inch pieces
4 celery ribs, cut crosswise into ½-inch pieces
2 tablespoons packed brown sugar
1 teaspoon dried thyme, crumbled
1 teaspoon ground cumin
1 teaspoon paprika
½ teaspoon ground cinnamon
¼ teaspoon ground cloves
¼ teaspoon cayenne, or to taste
1 tablespoon green peppercorns if desired
1½ cups dry red wine
3 cups beef broth

Accompaniment: couscous or egg noodles

In a bowl toss lamb with seasoned flour until well-coated. In a 4- to 6-quart heavy saucepan heat 1 tablespoon oil over moderately high heat until hot but not smoking and brown lamb in 2 batches, transferring to another bowl. In pan cook onion and garlic in remaining tablespoon oil over moderate heat, stirring, until softened. Add carrots, celery, brown sugar, thyme, spices, and salt and pepper to taste and cook, stirring, 1 minute. Add wine, broth, and lamb. Simmer stew over low heat, partially covered, stirring occasionally, 2½ hours, or until thickened and lamb is very tender.

Serve stew over couscous or noodles. Serves 4.

POULTRY

Lavender and Thyme Roasted Poussins

2 teaspoons dried untreated lavender flowers*
   if desired
¾ stick (6 tablespoons) unsalted butter, softened
1 teaspoon fresh thyme leaves, minced
¼ teaspoon finely grated fresh lemon zest
4 *poussins*** (young chickens; about 1 pound
   each) or 4 small Cornish hens (about
   1¼ pounds each)
1 small lemon, halved
¼ cup Sauternes

Garnish: lavender and thyme leaves

*available by mail order from Dean & DeLuca,
   tel. (212) 226-6800, ext. 268
**available from butchers and by mail order
   from D'Artagnan, tel. (800) 327-8246 or
   (201) 792-0748

With a mortar and pestle coarsely crush lavender and in a small bowl stir together with butter, thyme, zest, and salt and pepper to taste until combined well. Spoon mixture onto a sheet of plastic wrap and form into a 4-inch-long log. *Chill compound butter, wrapped well in plastic wrap, until firm, at least 30 minutes, and up to 3 days.*

Preheat oven to 475° F.

Discard gizzards from birds and trim necks flush with bodies if necessary. Rinse birds inside and out and pat dry. Starting at neck end of each bird, slide fingers between meat and skin to loosen skin (be careful not to tear skin). Cut butter into sixteen ¼-inch-thick slices and gently push 4 slices under skin of each bird, putting 1 slice over each breast half and thigh. Tie legs of each bird together with kitchen string and secure wings to sides with wooden picks or bamboo skewers.

Arrange birds in a flameproof roasting pan large enough to hold them without crowding. Gently rub birds with lemon halves, squeezing juice over them, and season with salt and pepper. Roast birds in middle of oven 30 minutes (for *poussins*) to 45 minutes (for Cornish hens), or until an instant-read thermometer inserted in thickest part of a thigh (be careful not to touch bone) registers 170° F.

Transfer birds to a platter and loosely cover with foil to keep warm. Add Sauternes to roasting pan and deglaze over moderate heat, scraping up brown bits. Transfer *jus* to a small saucepan. Skim fat from *jus* and simmer until reduced to about ½ cup.

Garnish birds with herbs and serve with *jus*. Serves 4.

PHOTO ON PAGE 30

Pollo en Pipián Verde
(Chicken in Pumpkin-Seed Sauce)

a 3½-pound chicken plus 1 whole chicken breast
1 head garlic, unpeeled
½ large white onion
6 long sprigs fresh coriander
½ teaspoon salt
6 black peppercorns
3 allspice berries
For pumpkin-seed sauce
1½ cups hulled green pumpkin seeds*
   (about 7 ounces)
2 tablespoons sesame seeds
½ teaspoon cumin seeds
4 allspice berries
3 cloves
6 black peppercorns
1 pound fresh tomatillos* or a 28-ounce can
   tomatillos*
6 fresh *serrano* chilies*
½ large white onion
4 garlic cloves
½ cup packed coarsely chopped fresh coriander

142

2 teaspoons salt
¼ cup lard or vegetable oil
3 cups stock from cooking chicken
1 fresh *poblano* chili*

*available at Latino markets, specialty foods
   shops, and some supermarkets

Garnish: chopped toasted hulled pumpkin
   seeds and chopped fresh coriander
Accompaniment: warm tortillas (procedure
   on page 127)

Rinse chicken and cut garlic head in half
crosswise. In a 6-quart kettle cover chicken, garlic
halves, onion, coriander, salt, peppercorns, and
allspice with water and simmer, covered, 1 hour, or
until chicken is tender. Transfer chicken to a bowl to
cool and reserve stock.

Shred chicken, discarding skin and bones. Pour
reserved stock through a fine sieve into a bowl,
pressing garlic pulp through sieve. Measure 3 cups
stock for sauce and reserve remainder for another
use. *Chicken and stock may be made 1 day ahead
and cooled completely, uncovered, before being
chilled separately, covered. (Stock keeps, frozen, 1
month.)*

Make sauce:

Heat a large heavy skillet over moderate heat until
hot and toast pumpkin seeds, stirring constantly,
until they have expanded and begin to pop, 3 to 5
minutes. Transfer seeds to a plate to cool. In skillet

heat sesame and cumin seeds, allspice, cloves, and
peppercorns, stirring, until fragrant, about 1 minute,
and transfer to plate. When seeds and spices are
cool, in an electric spice/coffee grinder grind
mixture in 4 batches to a powder.

If using fresh tomatillos, discard husks and rinse
with warm water to remove stickiness. Stem *serrano*
chilies. In a saucepan simmer fresh tomatillos and
serranos in salted water to cover 10 minutes. If
using canned tomatillos, drain them and leave
serranos uncooked. Transfer tomatillos and *serranos*
(use a slotted spoon if simmered) to a blender and
purée with onion, garlic, ¼ cup coriander, and salt
until completely smooth.

In a 5-quart heavy kettle simmer tomatillo purée
in lard or oil, stirring frequently, 10 minutes. Add
2½ cups stock and stir in powdered pumpkin-seed
mixture. Simmer sauce, stirring occasionally, 15
minutes, or until slightly thickened. *Sauce may be
prepared up to this point 1 day ahead and cooled
completely, uncovered, before being chilled,
covered.*

Roast and peel *poblano* chili (procedure on page
96). In blender purée *poblano* with remaining ½ cup
chicken stock and remaining ¼ cup coriander until
completely smooth. Stir *poblano* purée and chicken
into sauce and heat on top of stove or in a 350° F.
oven until chicken is heated through.

Garnish chicken with pumpkin seeds and
coriander and serve with tortillas. Makes enough
filling for about 32 tacos.

PHOTO ON PAGE 47

Chicken and Beef Satés ○

eight 10-inch wooden skewers
½ cup heavy cream
1 teaspoon curry powder
¼ teaspoon turmeric
¾ teaspoon ground cumin
¼ teaspoon cayenne
¾ teaspoon salt
1 small onion, chopped
2 garlic cloves, minced
1 small whole boneless skinless chicken breast
   (about 6 ounces)
1 small rib-eye steak (about 6 ounces), trimmed

In a baking pan soak skewers in warm water 20 minutes. While skewers are soaking, in a blender blend cream, spices, salt, onion, and garlic. Cut chicken and beef crosswise into ¼-inch-thick strips and in a bowl toss with cream mixture. Marinate chicken and beef, covered, at room temperature 15 minutes.

Preheat broiler.

Thread some chicken and beef strips lengthwise, without bunching, onto each skewer (using three fourths of skewer) and discard any remaining marinade. Broil *satés* on well-oiled rack of a broiler pan as close to heat as possible, turning once, 2 to 3 minutes on each side, or until just cooked through. Serves 2 as a main course.

Grilled Chicken Breast Stuffed with Prosciutto and Basil ○

2 prosciutto slices
1 teaspoon coarse-grained mustard
8 fresh basil leaves
¼ cup freshly grated mozzarella
1 skinless boneless whole chicken breast,
   halved (about 1 pound)

Prepare grill.

On a work surface spread prosciutto slices evenly with mustard. Top slices with basil leaves and sprinkle evenly with mozzarella. Starting with a short end roll up each prosciutto slice.

Pat chicken dry and put on a work surface, skinned sides down. Remove "tender" (fillet strip located on either side of where breast bone was) from each breast half, keeping rest of chicken breast intact, and reserve tenders for another use. (There should be 1 tender from each breast half.)

To form a long thin pocket in chicken for prosciutto roll: Put chicken breast halves on cutting board and, beginning at thicker end of breast half, horizontally insert a thin sharp knife three fourths of the way through center of each. Open cut to create a 1-inch-wide pocket in each half. Fit a prosciutto roll into each pocket and season chicken with salt and pepper.

Grill chicken on a lightly oiled rack set 5 to 6 inches over glowing coals until cooked through, about 5 minutes on each side. (Alternatively, chicken may be grilled in a hot well-seasoned ridged grill pan over moderately high heat.) Serves 2.

Deviled Drumsticks

6 tablespoons fresh lemon juice
4 tablespoons Tabasco
24 chicken drumsticks (about 5½ pounds)
For bread-crumb coating
¾ stick (6 tablespoons) unsalted butter
⅓ cup packed fresh parsley leaves
1½ cups fine dry bread crumbs
1½ teaspoons salt
2 tablespoons paprika
¼ teaspoon cayenne

Divide lemon juice, Tabasco, and drumsticks between 2 large sealable plastic bags and seal bags. Shake bags to coat drumsticks with Tabasco mixture. *Chill drumsticks in one layer, turning bags occasionally, 1 hour.*

Preheat oven to 425° F. and grease 2 large shallow baking pans.

Make coating:

In a small saucepan melt butter. Finely chop parsley and in a bowl stir together with remaining coating ingredients.

Drain drumsticks in a colander and arrange, without crowding, in baking pans. Brush each drumstick on all sides with melted butter and roll in coating, pressing crumbs gently to adhere and returning to pan.

Bake drumsticks in upper and lower thirds of oven, switching position of pans halfway through baking, 40 minutes total, or until cooked through and golden brown. *Drumsticks may be made 1 day ahead and cooled before being chilled in an airtight container.*

Serve drumsticks hot or at room temperature. Serves 8.

PHOTO ON PAGE 54

If anchos or similar dried chilies are not readily available, substitute one roasted and peeled red bell pepper and ¼ teaspoon dried hot red pepper flakes when puréeing.

Chicken Cashew Chili

For chili purée
2 dried *ancho* chilies* (see note above)
¼ cup cashews, raw or roasted
1 cup chicken broth

2 whole chicken legs plus ½ chicken breast
   (about 1½ pounds total)
2 tablespoons olive oil
1 large onion, chopped coarse
3 garlic cloves, chopped fine
1 tablespoon ground cumin
1 teaspoon chili powder
1 teaspoon salt
3 tablespoons chopped fresh coriander sprigs
a 14½-ounce can diced tomatoes with juice
½ cup cashews, raw or roasted
½ ounce fine-quality bittersweet chocolate (not
   unsweetened) or semisweet chocolate
1 cup canned kidney beans, rinsed and drained

*available at specialty foods shops, some
   supermarkets, and by mail order from Chile
   Today–Hot Tamale, Inc., tel. (800) 468-7377

Make chili purée:
Heat a small heavy skillet over moderate heat until hot and toast chilies, 1 at a time, pressing down with tongs, a few seconds on each side to make more pliable. Wearing rubber gloves, seed and devein chilies. In a blender purée chilies with cashews and broth until smooth.

Cut legs into drumstick and thigh portions. Remove excess fat from chicken and pat chicken dry.

In a large heavy saucepan heat oil over moderate heat until hot but not smoking and cook onion and garlic, stirring, until softened. Add cumin, chili powder, and salt and cook, stirring, 1 minute. Add chicken and stir to coat with onion mixture. Stir in chili purée, 2 tablespoons coriander, and tomatoes with juice and simmer, covered, stirring occasionally to avoid sticking, 45 minutes, or until chicken legs are cooked through.

Remove pan from heat and transfer chicken to a bowl. With 2 forks shred meat, discarding bones and skin. Return chicken to pan and stir in cashews, remaining tablespoon coriander, chocolate, and beans. Cook chili over moderate heat, stirring, until heated through and chocolate is melted. *Chili may be made 2 days ahead and cooled completely, uncovered, before being chilled, covered.* Serves 2 generously.

PHOTO ON PAGE 26

Fried Chicken Drumsticks with Cumin Salt ☺

1 cup well-shaken buttermilk
1 tablespoon ground cumin
6 chicken drumsticks
1 cup all-purpose flour
1 teaspoon salt
½ teaspoon black pepper
4 cups vegetable oil

In a large sealable plastic bag combine buttermilk and ½ tablespoon cumin. Add drumsticks and seal bag, pressing out excess air. Marinate drumsticks at room temperature 15 minutes. In another plastic bag combine flour and salt and pepper to taste. In a small cup stir together remaining ½ tablespoon cumin, 1 teaspoon salt, and ½ teaspoon pepper.

In a 5-quart kettle (preferably cast-iron) heat oil. Just before oil reaches 345° F. on a deep-fat thermometer drain half of drumsticks. Add drumsticks to bag with flour mixture and shake to coat, knocking off excess. Using tongs, lower floured drumsticks carefully into hot oil. Fry drumsticks, turning occasionally and regulating heat to keep oil at a constant 345° F., until mahogany-colored and cooked through, about 12 minutes. Transfer fried drumsticks with tongs to a rack set over paper towels to drain and season while hot with half of cumin salt. Prepare remaining drumsticks in same manner. Serves 2.

Chicken, Sausage, and Okra Gumbo

1 tablespoon vegetable oil
2 pounds smoked pork sausage or
    pork-and-beef sausage such as
    kielbasa, cut into ¼-inch-thick
    slices
8 chicken thighs
8 chicken drumsticks
two 10-ounce boxes frozen whole okra,
    rinsed to separate okra and cut into
    ¼-inch-thick rounds
2 large onions, chopped
3 celery ribs, chopped
8 cups chicken broth
8 cups water
1 cup thinly sliced scallion greens
    (about 1 bunch)

Accompaniments:
Cajun-style white rice (page 167)
bottled hot sauce such as Tabasco

In a heavy skillet (preferably cast-iron) heat oil over moderately high heat until hot but not smoking and brown sausage in batches, without crowding, transferring to paper towels to drain. Pat chicken dry and season with salt and pepper. Brown chicken in fat remaining in skillet in batches, without crowding, transferring to paper towels to drain.

Pour off all but about 1 tablespoon fat from skillet and cook okra rounds over moderate heat, stirring occasionally, until golden. Add onions and celery and cook, stirring occasionally, until celery is softened.

In a 9½- to 10-quart heavy kettle bring broth and water to a boil. Stir in okra mixture and chicken and simmer, stirring occasionally, until chicken is cooked through and gumbo is thickened, about 30 minutes. Add sausage, scallions, and salt and pepper to taste and simmer, stirring occasionally, 5 minutes. *Gumbo may be made 3 days ahead, cooled completely, uncovered, and chilled, covered.*

Serve gumbo ladled over rice in large soup plates. Serve hot sauce on the side. Makes about 20 cups not including chicken, serving 10 to 12 as a main course.

Crisp-Skinned Roast Duck with Mock Mandarin Pancakes

two 5- to 6-pound Long Island (Pekin) ducks*,
    thawed if frozen
1 cup boiling water
¼ cup honey
1 tablespoon rice vinegar

Accompaniments:
scallion brushes (procedure
    follows)
hoisin sauce
mock Mandarin pancakes
    (page 147)

*available fresh from butchers and by mail order
    from D'Artagnan, tel. (800) 327-8246 or (201)
    792-0748, or frozen at some supermarkets

Rinse ducks inside and out and pat dry. Remove excess fat from cavities and truss ducks. On a metal rack set in a large roasting pan arrange ducks, breast sides up and several inches apart. *Let ducks dry, uncovered and chilled, 3 days.*

In a small bowl stir together boiling water, honey, and vinegar and cool to room temperature. Brush ducks with some honey mixture, keeping them chilled, and brush again every 20 minutes for 1 hour. Let ducks dry at room temperature 30 minutes.

Preheat oven to 350° F.

Pierce skin of ducks all over with a fork to allow fat to drain and help skin become crisp. Roast ducks in middle of oven until mahogany brown and a meat thermometer inserted in fleshy part of a thigh registers 180° F., about 1 hour and 15 minutes. Let ducks stand 10 minutes. Discard string and carefully pour out juices from cavities.

Cut around entire breast of each duck with a sharp paring knife and carefully peel off crisp skin in large pieces. Cut skin into 2½- by 1-inch strips. Cut away and discard any fat on breast meat and remove breast meat from bone. Slice breast meat diagonally into ¼-inch-thick slices and arrange on a platter with crisp skin. Remove legs from ducks and arrange on another platter. Duck meat may be reheated and skin recrisped in a 350° F. oven just until hot.

To assemble pancakes:

Using a scallion brush spread some hoisin sauce on a pancake (whole or half) and top with the scallion brush, some breast meat, and some crisp skin. Roll up pancake to enclose filling. Make more pancakes with remaining scallion brushes, hoisin sauce, breast meat, and crisp skin in same manner.

Serve duck legs on the side. Serves 6.

PHOTO ON PAGE 19

If serving the mock pancakes halved, 48 scallion brushes (one for each half) will be necessary for rolling inside the pancakes. If leaving the pancakes whole, 24 scallion brushes will be needed.

To Make Scallion Brushes ◔+

24 or 48 thin scallions

Trim roots and green parts from scallions, leaving about 2½ inches of stalk. Fringe ends of scallions by cutting slits about ½ inch deep all around both ends of each stalk, leaving about 1 inch of solid scallion in center, and spread fringed ends gently. Put scallions in a bowl of ice and cold water. *Chill scallions 2 hours, or until fringed ends have curled.*

Drain scallions well. Makes 24 or 48 scallion brushes.

Mock Mandarin Pancakes ◔

twenty-four 6- to 8-inch flour tortillas*
¼ cup Asian sesame oil

*available from Maria and Ricardo's Tortilla
    Factory, tel. (800) 881-7040

Preheat oven to 350° F.

Brush one side of each tortilla with some oil and stack on a large sheet of foil. Wrap tortillas loosely in the foil and heat on middle rack of oven until warm, about 10 minutes.

Serve pancakes whole or halved. Makes 24 whole pancakes.

Roast Goose with Port Gravy

a 12-pound goose* (with neck and giblets,
    reserve liver for another use)
3 onions
2 celery ribs
about 3 bread slices (any type)
2 carrots
1 cup boiling water
1 cup dry white wine
¼ cup Tawny Port
⅓ cup all-purpose flour
3 cups chicken broth

Garnish: fresh flat-leafed parsley sprigs

*available by special order from some butchers
    and by mail order from D'Artagnan,
    tel. (800) 327-8246

Preheat oven to 425° F.

Discard loose fat from goose. With a cleaver or heavy knife cut goose neck into 2-inch pieces. Quarter 1 onion and quarter celery crosswise. Rinse goose inside and out and pat dry. Pierce skin of goose all over with a fork to allow fat to drain and help skin to become crisp. Season goose with salt and pepper and loosely pack neck cavity with enough bread to fill out cavity (this will prevent cavity skin from collapsing during roasting). Fold neck skin under body and fasten with a small skewer. Fill body cavity with quartered onion and celery and tie legs together loosely with kitchen string (or insert legs through slit in lower skin flap if provided).

Cut remaining 2 onions and carrots into 2-inch pieces. Transfer goose, breast side up, to a rack set in a flameproof roasting pan at least 2 inches deep (do not use a non-stick pan) and scatter onion and carrot pieces, neck pieces, and giblets in pan. Roast goose in middle of oven 30 minutes. Reduce temperature to 325° F. and carefully pour boiling water over goose (juices may splatter). Roast goose, skimming off fat (save fat for another use) and basting with pan juices using a metal bulb baster every 20 minutes, 2 to 2½ hours more, or until a meat thermometer inserted in fleshy part of thigh registers 175° F. and juices run clear when thigh is pierced with a skewer. Transfer goose to a heated platter. Remove skewer and discard string. Keep goose warm, loosely covered with foil.

With a slotted spoon discard vegetables, neck pieces, and giblets from pan. Spoon off fat from pan juices and reserve. On top of stove deglaze pan with white wine and Port over moderately high heat, scraping up brown bits, and boil mixture until reduced by about half. In a 2½- to 3-quart heavy saucepan whisk together ¼ cup reserved fat (save remainder for another use) and flour and cook *roux* over moderately low heat, whisking, 3 minutes. Add Port mixture and broth in a stream, whisking to prevent lumps, and bring gravy to a boil, whisking constantly. Simmer gravy, whisking frequently, 5 minutes, or until thickened. Season gravy with salt and pepper. Transfer gravy to a heated sauceboat.

Garnish goose with parsley. Serves 8.

PHOTO ON PAGE 78

L. Charlton

Sausage, Apple, and Rye-Bread Stuffing

12 light rye bread slices (about 1 pound)
1 pound smoked *kielbasa* (not low-fat)
2 onions
2 celery ribs
1 large garlic clove
1 stick (½ cup) unsalted butter
2 Granny Smith apples
1 cup packed fresh flat-leafed parsley leaves
2 cups chicken broth

Preheat oven to 375° F. and butter a 3- to 4-quart shallow baking dish.

Cut rye bread into ½-inch cubes. In 2 shallow baking pans arrange bread in one layer and toast in upper and lower thirds of oven until golden, 10 to 15 minutes.

Quarter *kielbasa* lengthwise and cut crosswise into ¼-inch-thick pieces. Chop onions and celery and mince garlic. In a large heavy skillet brown *kielbasa* over moderate heat, stirring occasionally, and transfer with a slotted spoon to paper towels to drain. To skillet add 6 tablespoons butter (do not discard any fat in skillet) and cook onions, celery, and garlic over moderately low heat, stirring, until celery is crisp-tender.

Finely chop apples. Stir apples into vegetable mixture and cook, stirring occasionally, until apple is softened. Mince parsley. In a large bowl toss together bread, *kielbasa*, vegetable mixture, parsley, broth, and salt and pepper to taste and transfer to baking dish. *Stuffing may be made 1 day ahead and cooled completely before being chilled, covered.*

Dot stuffing with remaining 2 tablespoons butter and bake, uncovered, in middle of oven until golden, about 30 minutes. (Stuffing may be baked while making gravy for roast goose; recipe precedes.) Serves 8.

PHOTO ON PAGE 78

There will be a large amount of rendered goose fat left over from this gumbo. The French often use the fat to coat potatoes for roasting. Rendered goose fat keeps, covered and chilled, 3 months. Two 8-pound ducks can be substituted for the goose if desired.

Goose and Tasso Gumbo

a 12- to 15-pound goose*, thawed if frozen
  and cut into large serving pieces,
  including neck and heart
½ cup bread flour
2 onions, chopped
1 green bell pepper, chopped
3 celery ribs, chopped
½ pound tasso** (Cajun-cured smoked pork)
  or fine-quality ham, cut into ¼-inch pieces
  (about 2 cups)

two 28- to 32-ounce cans whole tomatoes
  including juice
3 quarts water
1 cup thinly sliced scallion greens
  (about 1 bunch)
cayenne to taste

Accompaniment: Cajun-style white rice
  (page 167)

*available at some butcher shops and by mail
  order from D'Artagnan, tel. (800) 327-8246
  or (201) 792-0748
**available at some specialty foods shops and
  by mail order from The Art of Food, Kajun
  Kitchens Way, tel. (800) 535-9901

Pat goose dry and prick all over with a fork. Season goose with salt and pepper. In a large heavy skillet (preferably cast-iron) brown goose in batches, without crowding, pouring off all but 2 tablespoons fat into a large heatproof bowl after each batch and reserving fat in bowl. Transfer goose as browned to a heavy 12-quart kettle.

In skillet cook ⅓ cup reserved goose fat and bread flour over moderately low heat, stirring constantly with a flat-edged metal or wooden spatula, until *roux* is the dark reddish-brown color of chestnut shells, about 45 minutes. (Alternatively, make microwave brown *roux*, procedure on page 150, and transfer to skillet.) Stir in onions, bell pepper, and celery and cook, stirring occasionally, until vegetables are softened.

While *roux* is cooking bring goose, tasso or ham, tomatoes with juice, and water to a boil. Add *roux* mixture by large spoonfuls, stirring well after each addition, and simmer gumbo, covered, stirring occasionally, until goose is very tender, about 1½ hours. Transfer goose with tongs to a large bowl and cool until it can be handled. Discard skin and bones and shred goose meat. Stir meat into gumbo with scallions, cayenne, and salt to taste. *Gumbo may be made 3 days ahead, cooled completely, uncovered, and chilled, covered.* Skim fat from gumbo. Reheat mixture if previously chilled.

Serve gumbo ladled over rice in large soup plates. Makes about 24 cups, serving 10 to 12 as a main course.

The following microwave recipe was tested in an 800-watt oven. Cooking times will vary from one manufacturer's product to another, depending on power and size configuration. Refer to the manufacturers' instructions and treat the times given in our recipe as guidelines.

Microwave Brown Roux ◔

⅓ cup vegetable oil or rendered fat such as
    leftover goose fat
½ cup bread flour

In a 1-quart microwave-safe measuring cup or soufflé dish whisk together vegetable oil or rendered fat and flour until combined well. Microwave *roux*, uncovered, at high power (100%), whisking at 2-minute intervals, 8 minutes. If *roux* is not the dark reddish-brown color of chestnut shells, microwave at high power, whisking and checking color at 1-minute intervals, until *roux* reaches desired color. *Roux may be made 1 week ahead, cooled completely, and chilled, covered. Reheat roux before using.* Makes about ½ cup.

Roast Turkey with White-Wine Gravy

a 12- to 14-pound turkey (reserving neck and
    giblets, but excluding liver, for making stock)
1 stick (½ cup) unsalted butter
8 sprigs mixed fresh herbs such as thyme, sage,
    rosemary, and/or marjoram
1½ cups water
For gravy
1 large onion
1½ cups dry white wine
4 cups turkey giblet stock (recipe follows) plus
    additional for thinning gravy
⅓ cup all-purpose flour

Garnish: large bouquet of mixed fresh herb sprigs
Accompaniment if desired: herb and bacon corn-
    bread stuffing (page 151)

Preheat oven to 325° F.
Rinse turkey inside and out and pat dry. Fold neck skin under body and fasten with a small skewer.

Using small skewers secure wings to body. Transfer turkey to a rack set in a roasting pan and melt butter. Brush inside of turkey with some butter and season with salt and pepper. Put herb sprigs inside body cavity. Brush outside of turkey with remaining butter and season with salt and pepper. Loosely tie drumsticks together with kitchen string. Roast turkey in middle of oven 1 hour.

Add water to pan and roast turkey, basting every 20 minutes, 2 hours more, or until a meat thermometer inserted in fleshy part of a thigh registers 175° F. and juices run clear when thigh is pierced. Transfer turkey to a heated platter and reserve juices in pan. Remove skewers and discard string. Let turkey stand 30 minutes.

While turkey is standing, make gravy:
Finely chop onion. Skim fat from reserved pan juices and reserve ½ cup fat (for sautéing onions, below, and for stuffing, page 151). On top of stove deglaze pan with wine over moderately high heat, scraping up brown bits, and boil mixture until reduced to about ½ cup. Add 4 cups stock and bring to a simmer. Pour wine mixture through a sieve into a saucepan.

In a large heavy skillet sauté onion in ¼ cup reserved fat over moderately high heat, stirring frequently, until browned, about 15 minutes. Stir in flour and cook *roux* over moderately low heat, whisking, 3 minutes. Bring wine mixture to a simmer. Add hot wine mixture to *roux* in a fast stream, whisking constantly to prevent lumps, and simmer, whisking occasionally, 10 minutes. Whisk in additional stock to thin gravy to desired consistency. Season gravy with salt and pepper and transfer to a heated sauceboat.

Garnish turkey with herb bouquet and serve with gravy. Serves 8.

PHOTO ON PAGE 67

Turkey Giblet Stock

1 celery rib
1 carrot
1 onion
5 cups chicken broth
6 cups water
neck and giblets (excluding liver)
    from a 12- to 14-pound turkey
1 bay leaf
8 sprigs mixed fresh herbs such as
    thyme, sage, rosemary, and/or
    marjoram
1 teaspoon black peppercorns

Coarsely chop celery and carrot and quarter onion. In a large deep saucepan bring broth and water to a boil with celery, carrot, onion, neck, and giblets, skimming froth. Add remaining ingredients and cook, uncovered, at a bare simmer 2 hours, or until liquid is reduced to about 6 cups. Pour stock through a fine sieve into a bowl. *Stock may be made 2 days ahead and cooled completely, uncovered, before being chilled or frozen in an airtight container.* Makes about 6 cups.

Herb and Bacon Corn-Bread Stuffing

2 loaves corn bread
    (recipe follows)
6 large celery ribs
1 pound onions (about 2 large)
1 pound sliced bacon
½ cup chopped mixed fresh herbs
    such as thyme, sage, rosemary,
    and/or marjoram or 2 tablespoons
    mixed dried herbs,
    crumbled
1 cup turkey giblet stock (recipe
    precedes) or chicken broth
¼ cup reserved fat from roast turkey
    (page 150) or melted butter

Preheat oven to 325° F. and butter a 4-quart baking dish.

Cut corn bread into ½-inch cubes and dry in 2 large shallow baking pans in oven 20 minutes. Remove corn bread from oven and leave oven at 325° F.

Coarsely chop separately celery, onions, and bacon.

In a large deep skillet sauté bacon over moderately high heat, stirring, until browned, about 10 minutes. Add celery and onions and cook, stirring, until vegetables are softened, about 5 minutes. Add herbs and salt and pepper to taste and cook, stirring, 1 minute.

In a large bowl toss together corn bread and bacon mixture and transfer to baking dish. *Stuffing may be prepared up to this point 1 day ahead and cooled completely before being chilled, covered.*

Drizzle stock or broth over stuffing and bake, covered, 1 hour. Drizzle reserved fat or butter over stuffing and bake (while turkey is standing, recipe page 150), uncovered, in upper third of oven 30 minutes more, or until top is golden. Makes about 16 cups, serving 8 with leftovers.

PHOTO ON PAGE 67

Corn Bread

2 cups all-purpose flour
2 tablespoons baking powder
1 teaspoon salt
2 cups yellow cornmeal
½ cup sugar
2 cups milk
2 large eggs
2 sticks (1 cup) unsalted butter,
    softened

Preheat oven to 400° F. and butter two loaf pans, 9 by 5 by 3 inches.

Into a large bowl sift together flour, baking powder, and salt and whisk in cornmeal and sugar until combined well. In a bowl whisk together milk and eggs until just combined. Add butter to flour mixture and with an electric mixer beat until mixture resembles coarse meal. Beat in egg mixture until just combined (batter will be thin).

Pour batter into pans and bake in middle of oven until golden and a tester comes out clean, about 50 minutes. Cool corn bread in pans on a rack 10 minutes and turn out onto rack to cool completely. *Corn bread may be wrapped in plastic wrap and kept in a cool, dry place 2 days or frozen 2 weeks.* Makes 2 loaves.

Pulled Turkey Barbecue

2 large onions
1 large garlic clove
2 cups cider vinegar
½ stick (¼ cup) unsalted butter
½ cup ketchup
3 tablespoons Worcestershire sauce
2 tablespoons Tabasco plus additional to taste
1 tablespoon salt
1 tablespoon freshly ground black pepper
a 4½- to 5-pound turkey breast, skin discarded

Accompaniment: soft sandwich rolls, toasted
 lightly if desired

Finely chop onions and mince garlic.

In a 6-quart heavy saucepan combine onions, garlic, vinegar, butter, ketchup, Worcestershire sauce, 2 tablespoons Tabasco, salt, and pepper and simmer, covered, stirring occasionally, 15 minutes. Add turkey breast, cavity side down, and cook at a bare simmer, covered, 2½ hours. Transfer breast to a cutting board, reserving sauce, and cool until it can be handled. Shred turkey meat, discarding bones, and stir meat into reserved sauce. Simmer barbecue, covered, over low heat, stirring occasionally, 1½ hours more and season with salt, pepper, and additional Tabasco.

Serve barbecue on rolls. Makes about 8 cups.

Turkey Burgers ☺

½ cup mayonnaise
3 tablespoons chopped fresh basil leaves
10 Kalamata olives
1¼ pounds ground turkey
2 tablespoons chopped dried tomatoes
 packed in oil
¾ teaspoon chopped fresh thyme leaves
4 sesame buns
1½ cups packed arugula

In a small bowl stir together mayonnaise and basil. Pit and chop olives. In a large bowl blend together olives, turkey, tomatoes, thyme, and salt and pepper to taste. Form mixture into four 1-inch-thick patties and cook (procedure on page 133, making sure burgers are cooked through). Toast sesame buns. Transfer burgers to buns and top with basil mayonnaise and arugula. Serves 4.

Warm Turkey, Tomatillo, and Smoked Mozzarella Pita Sandwiches ☺

2 pita loaves with pockets
6 fresh tomatillos* (about ½ pound total)
1 fresh *jalapeño* chili, seeded and chopped
 (wear rubber gloves)
1 garlic clove, chopped
6 ounces thinly sliced cooked turkey breast
half a 7-ounce jar roasted red pepper, rinsed
 and patted dry
2 ounces smoked mozzarella, cut into 6 slices
¼ cup fresh coriander, washed, dried, and
 chopped
1 teaspoon olive oil

*available at specialty produce markets and
 many supermarkets

Preheat oven to 350° F.
Split pita loaves horizontally to create 4 rounds.
Discard husks from tomatillos and rinse under warm water. Chop tomatillos and in a blender purée with *jalapeño*, garlic, and salt and pepper to taste until smooth. In a small saucepan cook purée over moderate heat, stirring, until thickened, about 4 minutes.

Spread one-fourth tomatillo purée on rough side of each pita round. Arrange 2 pita rounds on a baking sheet and top evenly with turkey, roasted pepper, mozzarella, and coriander. Top with remaining pita rounds, tomatillo sides down. Brush tops of sandwiches with oil and season with salt and pepper. Bake sandwiches in middle of oven 10 minutes, or until cheese is slightly melted and tops of pitas are golden brown.

Cut sandwiches into wedges if desired. Serves 2.

BREAKFAST, BRUNCH, AND CHEESE DISHES

Although these are called fritters, they more closely resemble pancakes.

Corn Fritters ○

3 bacon slices
3 ears corn
1 large egg
3 tablespoons all-purpose flour
1½ tablespoons sugar
1 teaspoon baking powder
½ teaspoon salt
freshly ground black pepper to taste

Accompaniment: pure maple syrup or sliced
   tomatoes

In a heavy skillet cook bacon over moderately low heat until crisp. Transfer bacon to paper towels to drain and reserve bacon fat in a heatproof bowl. Crumble bacon.

Working in a large bowl and using the largest holes of a 4-sided grater, grate enough corn to measure ½ cup. Lightly beat egg and add to corn. Stir in flour, sugar, baking powder, salt, and pepper until combined well.

In skillet heat 1 tablespoon reserved bacon fat over moderate heat. Working in 2 batches, form fritters by dropping ⅛-cup measures of batter for each into skillet and cook until golden brown, 1 to 2 minutes on each side.

Serve fritters warm with bacon and syrup or tomatoes. Makes about 6 fritters.

Herbed Yellow Pepper Scrambled Eggs with Chive Sour Cream on Brioche ○

2 small brioches* (about 4 by 3 inches) or four
   ½-inch-thick slices from a brioche loaf*
5 large eggs, beaten lightly
1½ teaspoons chopped fresh chives

¼ teaspoon finely chopped fresh
   tarragon leaves
1 tablespoon unsalted butter
1 yellow bell pepper, cut into
   ¼-inch dice
2 tablespoons sour cream
freshly ground black pepper

Accompaniment: chive sour cream
   (recipe follows)

*available at specialty bakeries and some
   specialty foods shops

Preheat oven to 350° F.

If using small brioches, cut off tops (about 1 inch). On a baking sheet arrange tops and bottoms of brioche, cut sides up, or slices from loaf in one layer. Toast brioche in middle of oven until golden.

While brioche is toasting, in a bowl lightly whisk together eggs, chives, and tarragon. In a non-stick skillet heat butter over moderate heat until foam subsides and cook bell pepper, stirring, until softened. Add eggs and cook, stirring, until just cooked through, about 3 minutes. Stir in sour cream and pepper and salt to taste and cook, stirring, just until heated through.

Divide brioche and eggs between 2 plates and top with chive sour cream. Serves 2.

PHOTO ON PAGE 21

Chive Sour Cream ○

2 teaspoons chopped fresh chives
¼ cup sour cream
freshly ground black pepper

In a bowl whisk together chives, sour cream, and pepper and salt to taste. *Chive sour cream may be made 1 day ahead and chilled, covered.* Makes about ¼ cup.

Broiled Brown-Sugar Apples with Bacon

2 McIntosh apples (about ¾ pound total)
3 tablespoons packed light brown sugar
¼ pound sliced bacon (about 4 slices), cooked
  until crisp and chopped

Preheat broiler and lightly grease a broiler pan or 15½- by 10½-inch jelly-roll pan.

Cut apples crosswise into ⅓-inch-thick slices. Cut out core from middle of each slice and stack slices to reform whole apples. Arrange slices from 1 apple in one layer in pan, keeping slices in order, and sprinkle with half of brown sugar. Broil sugared apple slices 4 to 6 inches from heat 2 minutes, or until barely tender and sugar is caramelized. Transfer broiled slices in one layer to a tray. In cleaned lightly greased pan broil remaining apple slices with remaining brown sugar in same manner.

Preheat oven to 350° F. and grease a small shallow baking pan.

Arrange bottom slice of each apple in baking pan and sprinkle with some bacon. Stack remaining apple slices in order on top, sprinkling layers with bacon and ending with top slices of apples, to form 2 whole apples. *Apples may be prepared up to this point 1 day ahead and chilled in baking pan, covered. Bring apples to room temperature before proceeding.*

Reheat apples, uncovered, in oven until hot, about 15 minutes. Serves 2.

PHOTO ON PAGE 21

*Fried Eggs, Prosciutto, and Arugula
with Cheese Sauce* ☺

For cheese sauce
1 tablespoon unsalted butter
1 tablespoon all-purpose flour
1 cup whole milk
1 tablespoon heavy cream
½ cup coarsely grated Gruyère or
  Swiss cheese (about 2 ounces)
a small pinch freshly grated nutmeg

2 English muffins
1 teaspoon olive oil
3 cups packed trimmed arugula

4 thin slices prosciutto
1 tablespoon unsalted butter
4 large eggs

Make sauce:
In a small saucepan heat butter over moderately low heat until foam subsides and stir in flour. Cook *roux,* stirring constantly, 2 minutes. Add milk and cream in a stream, whisking, and simmer, whisking, 2 minutes, or until sauce thickens slightly. Remove pan from heat and stir in cheese, nutmeg, and salt and pepper to taste until cheese is melted. Keep sauce warm, covered, over very low heat.

Split and toast muffins. Put 2 muffin halves on each of 2 plates. In a non-stick skillet heat oil over moderately high heat until hot but not smoking and sauté arugula with salt to taste, stirring, until just wilted. Divide arugula among muffin halves and top with prosciutto.

In same skillet heat butter over moderate heat until foam subsides and crack eggs, 1 at a time, into a small bowl, adding them as they are cracked to skillet. Season eggs with salt and pepper and cook 2 minutes, or until whites are set on bottom but still runny on top. With a spatula gently turn each egg over and cook 2 minutes more, or until yolks are just set. With spatula gently transfer eggs to prosciutto and top with cheese sauce. Serves 2.

Banana Pecan Cornmeal Pancakes ☺

1 very ripe medium banana (about ½ pound)
½ cup plus 1 tablespoon all-purpose flour
1 tablespoon baking powder
1 tablespoon sugar
½ teaspoon salt
⅓ cup yellow cornmeal
¾ cup milk
1 large egg
⅓ cup pecans, toasted lightly and chopped
vegetable oil for brushing griddle

Accompaniment: pure maple syrup, heated

Chop banana and in a blender blend with all remaining pancake ingredients except pecans and oil. Transfer batter to a bowl and stir in pecans.

154

Heat a griddle over moderate heat until hot enough to make a drop of water scatter over surface and brush with oil. Working in batches, drop scant ¼-cup measures of batter onto hot griddle to form pancakes about 4 inches in diameter and cook until bubbles appear on surface and undersides are golden brown, about 1 minute. Flip pancakes with a metal spatula and cook until undersides are golden brown and pancakes are cooked through, about 1 minute.

Serve pancakes with maple syrup. Makes about 10 pancakes.

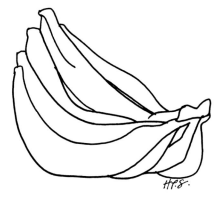

Raspberry Chocolate-Chip Pancakes ☺

½ stick (¼ cup) unsalted butter
¾ cup plus 3 tablespoons milk
1 large egg
1 cup all-purpose flour
2 teaspoons baking powder
¼ teaspoon salt
1 cup picked-over raspberries
½ cup semisweet chocolate chips

Accompaniment: pure maple syrup, heated

In a small saucepan melt 2 tablespoons butter over moderately low heat, stirring. Stir in milk and heat until just warm. Remove pan from heat. In a bowl whisk together milk mixture and egg. Into another bowl sift together flour, baking powder, and salt and stir in egg mixture until just combined. Gently stir in raspberries and chocolate chips.

Preheat oven to 200° F.

Heat a griddle over moderate heat until hot enough to make a drop of water scatter over surface.

Add 1 teaspoon butter and with a metal spatula spread over griddle. Working in batches, drop ¼-cup measures of batter onto griddle to form pancakes about 4 inches in diameter and cook until bubbles appear on surface and undersides are golden brown, about 2 minutes. Flip pancakes with spatula and cook until undersides are golden brown and pancakes are cooked through. Transfer pancakes as cooked to an ovenproof platter and keep warm, uncovered, in oven. Make more pancakes with remaining butter and batter in same manner.

Serve pancakes with syrup. Makes about 10 pancakes, serving 2 generously.

PHOTO ON PAGE 88

Spiced Two-Grain Pancakes ☺

1 cup milk
1 large egg
½ stick (¼ cup) unsalted butter, melted
  and cooled
1 cup old-fashioned oats
¼ cup plus 1 tablespoon packed brown sugar
¾ cup all-purpose flour
¼ cup toasted wheat germ
1 teaspoon baking soda
1¼ teaspoons ground ginger
1¼ teaspoons ground cinnamon
a scant ½ teaspoon ground cloves
1 teaspoon salt
vegetable oil for brushing griddle

Accompaniment: pure maple syrup, heated

In a blender blend all pancake ingredients except oil until just combined.

Heat a griddle over moderate heat until hot enough to make a drop of water scatter over surface and brush with oil. Working in batches, drop scant ¼-cup measures of batter onto hot griddle to form pancakes about 4 inches in diameter and cook until bubbles appear on surface and undersides are brown, about 2 minutes. Flip pancakes with a metal spatula and cook until undersides are golden brown and pancakes are cooked through, about 2 minutes.

Serve pancakes with maple syrup. Makes about 14 pancakes.

Bacon Buttermilk Waffles with Blackberry Syrup ☺

6 bacon slices
1 cup all-purpose flour
1 tablespoon sugar
1 teaspoon baking powder
¼ teaspoon baking soda
¼ teaspoon salt
1 cup well-shaken buttermilk
1 large egg
For blackberry syrup
½ cup picked-over blackberries
½ cup pure maple syrup

Garnish: ½ cup blackberries

Preheat a well-seasoned or non-stick Belgian or standard waffle iron. Preheat oven to 200° F.

Finely chop bacon and in a skillet cook over moderate heat, stirring, until crisp. Into a large bowl sift together flour, sugar, baking powder, baking soda, and salt and stir in buttermilk, egg, and bacon including bacon fat (about ¼ cup) until smooth (batter will be very thick).

Make syrup:

Halve berries lengthwise. In a small saucepan simmer berries with syrup over moderately low heat 1 minute.

Spoon batter into waffle iron (using 1 cup batter for two 4-inch square Belgian waffles or four 4-inch square standard waffles), spreading evenly, and cook according to manufacturer's instructions. Transfer waffles to a baking sheet and keep warm, uncovered, in middle of oven. Make more waffles with remaining batter in same manner.

Serve waffles with blackberry syrup and garnish with blackberries. Makes 4 Belgian or 8 standard waffles, serving 2 generously.

Cornmeal Buttermilk Waffles ☺

1 cup sifted all-purpose flour (sift before measuring)
¾ cup yellow cornmeal
2 teaspoons baking powder
1 teaspoon baking soda
¼ teaspoon salt
¼ cup wheat germ

3 large eggs
2 cups well-shaken buttermilk
6 tablespoons vegetable oil plus additional for brushing waffle iron

Accompaniment: pure maple syrup

Into a large bowl sift together flour, cornmeal, baking powder, baking soda, and salt. Repeat sifting 2 times and stir in wheat germ.

In another large bowl whisk together eggs, buttermilk, and 6 tablespoons oil. Add flour mixture all at once and whisk just until combined.

Preheat a waffle iron and preheat oven to 200° F.

Brush waffle iron lightly with additional oil. Spoon batter into waffle iron, using ¼ cup batter for each 4-inch square standard waffle and spreading batter evenly, and cook according to manufacturer's instructions. Transfer waffle to a baking sheet and keep warm, uncovered, in middle of oven. Make more waffles with remaining batter in same manner, brushing waffle iron with more oil before adding each batch.

Serve waffles with warm maple syrup. Makes about 16 waffles.

Smoked Salmon on Cream Cheese Toasts with Chives ☺

3 slices firm white sandwich bread, toasted
3 tablespoons cream cheese, softened
6 thin slices smoked salmon (about 6 ounces total)
1 tablespoon chopped fresh chives
1 teaspoon finely chopped red onion
4 lemon wedges

Accompaniment if desired: slivered endive salad (page 188)

Spread one side of toasts with cream cheese and top with salmon, wrapping salmon ends under toasts. Sprinkle salmon with chives and red onion and halve toasts diagonally.

Divide toasts and lemon wedges between 2 plates and serve with endive salad. Serves 2.

Preheat broiler.

Put tortillas on a large baking sheet and brush tops with oil. Broil tortillas on a rack set 2 to 4 inches from heat until pale golden. Turn tortillas over and broil until other sides are pale golden. Sprinkle tortillas evenly with Monterey Jack and broil until cheese is melted and bubbling. Spread avocado mixture evenly over 2 tortillas and top each with 1 of remaining tortillas, cheese side down, to make 2 *quesadillas*. Transfer *quesadillas* to a cutting board and cut each into 4 wedges.

Top each wedge with a heaping teaspoon of sour cream mixture and garnish with coriander sprigs. Serves 2 as a first course or a light main course.

Avocado Quesadillas ◌

2 vine-ripened tomatoes
1 firm-ripe California avocado
1 tablespoon chopped red onion
2 teaspoons fresh lemon juice
¼ teaspoon Tabasco
¼ cup sour cream
3 tablespoons chopped fresh coriander
four 6- to 7-inch flour tortillas
½ teaspoon vegetable oil
1⅓ cups coarsely grated Monterey Jack

Garnish: fresh coriander sprigs

Seed tomatoes and cut into ¼-inch dice. Quarter avocado, removing pit, and peel. Cut avocado into ¼-inch dice. In a small bowl stir together tomatoes, avocado, onion, lemon juice, and Tabasco and season with salt and pepper. In another small bowl stir together sour cream, coriander, and salt and pepper to taste.

Prosciutto, Mozzarella, and Olive Sandwiches on Parmesan Focaccia ◌+

1 large plum tomato
3 tablespoons black olive paste*
¼ cup chopped fresh basil leaves
1 pound fresh mozzarella*
4 cups trimmed arugula
2 tablespoons extra-virgin olive oil
1 Parmesan *focaccia* (page 116)
½ pound thinly sliced prosciutto

*available at Italian markets and specialty foods shops

Seed tomato and chop fine. In a bowl stir together tomato, olive paste, and basil. Cut mozzarella into thin slices. Coarsely chop arugula and in a bowl toss with oil and salt and pepper to taste.

Halve *focaccia* horizontally and spread bottom half with olive mixture. Top olive mixture with mozzarella, prosciutto, arugula, and remaining *focaccia* half. Press *focaccia* gently and cut lengthwise in half and crosswise into thirds to make 6 sandwiches. Cut sandwiches diagonally in half and wrap tightly in plastic wrap. *Chill sandwiches at least 1 hour and up to 1 day.* Makes 6 sandwiches.

PHOTO ON PAGE 44

PASTA AND GRAINS

Thai-Style Fusilli With Eggplant and Shiitake ☺

6 ounces *fusilli* (long spiral spaghetti)
1 small eggplant (about ½ pound)
¼ pound fresh *shiitake* mushrooms
1 bunch scallions
6 vine-ripened cherry tomatoes
¼ fresh *jalapeño* chili
1 tablespoon chopped peeled fresh
   gingerroot
2 teaspoons chopped garlic
2 tablespoons vegetable oil
½ cup well-stirred canned unsweetened
   coconut milk
⅓ cup coarsely chopped fresh basil leaves

Fill a 4-quart kettle three-fourths full with salted water and bring to a boil for cooking *fusilli*.

Cut eggplant into ½-inch cubes and transfer to a colander set over a bowl. Sprinkle eggplant lightly with salt and let drain 10 minutes. While eggplant is draining, discard stems from mushrooms and cut caps into ¾-inch pieces. Cut scallions diagonally into thin slices. Quarter tomatoes and chop *jalapeño* including seeds (wear rubber gloves). Rinse eggplant and squeeze dry, discarding any liquid in bowl.

   Boil *fusilli* until *al dente*.

   While *fusilli* is boiling, in a large non-stick skillet cook gingerroot and garlic in oil over moderately high heat, stirring, until fragrant, about 30 seconds. Add eggplant and mushrooms and sauté, stirring constantly, until softened, 3 to 4 minutes. Add scallions and sauté, stirring, until eggplant is tender, about 2 minutes. Stir in coconut milk, tomatoes, *jalapeño*, basil, and salt and pepper to taste and cook just until heated through, about 30 seconds.

   Drain *fusilli* in a colander and in a bowl toss with sauce. Serves 2.

Orecchiette with Sausage and Red Pepper Sauce

For sauce
1½ pounds sweet Italian sausage
1 tablespoon olive oil
2 red bell peppers, chopped coarse
3 large garlic cloves, chopped fine
a 28- to 32-ounce can whole tomatoes
   including juice

1½ pounds fresh semolina *orecchiette* (recipe
   follows) or 1¼ pounds dried *orecchiette**

*available at specialty foods shops and some
   supermarkets

Make sauce:
Remove sausage meat from casings. In a large heavy skillet heat oil over moderately high heat until hot but not smoking and cook sausage, stirring to break up lumps, until golden. Transfer sausage with a slotted spoon to a plate and pour off all but about 3 tablespoons fat from skillet. Add bell peppers and garlic to skillet with salt and pepper to taste and cook over moderate heat, stirring, until bell peppers are softened, about 5 minutes.

   In a blender or food processor coarsely purée tomatoes with juice and stir into bell pepper mixture with sausage. Simmer sauce, covered, stirring occasionally, 15 minutes. *Sauce may be made ahead, cooled completely, uncovered, and chilled, covered, 1 day or frozen 1 month.*

In an 8-quart kettle bring 7 quarts salted water to a boil. Cook *orecchiette* until *al dente* (about 6 minutes for fresh, longer for dried) and drain in a colander. In a heated large bowl immediately toss pasta with sauce. Serves 6 as a main course.

Fresh Semolina Orecchiette

2 cups semolina*
2 cups unbleached all-purpose flour
1 cup lukewarm water

*available at specialty foods shops and
　by mail order from Dean & DeLuca,
　tel. (800) 221-7714

In a large bowl stir together semolina and flour and form a well in center. Add water and a generous pinch salt to well and with a fork gradually incorporate semolina mixture until a dough is formed (some of mixture will not be incorporated). On a work surface knead dough, incorporating more semolina mixture from bowl as necessary and discarding any hard clumps, until smooth and elastic, about 8 minutes. Divide dough into 8 pieces and wrap separately in plastic wrap.

Line each of 2 trays with a dry kitchen towel and dust your hands with some semolina mixture. Remove plastic wrap from 1 piece of dough and roll between your hands to create a rope 3 to 4 feet long and ½ inch wide. Put rope on a work surface and with a sharp knife cut into ½-inch pieces, separating pieces as cut so they are no longer touching. Lightly toss cut pieces with a little semolina mixture.

Put each cut piece of dough, a cut side down, in palm of 1 hand and form a depression by pressing thumb of other hand into dough and twisting slightly. Arrange *orecchiette* on kitchen-towel-lined tray. Make more *orecchiette* with remaining 7 pieces of dough in same manner, transferring to kitchen-towel-lined trays. *Orecchiette may be made 2 days ahead and chilled on towel-lined trays, covered with plastic wrap.* Makes about 1½ pounds.

Couscous with Red Onion and Chives ⊙

¾ cup chopped red onion
¾ teaspoon olive oil
1 tablespoon balsamic vinegar
⅓ cup couscous
½ cup boiling water
2 tablespoons chopped fresh chives

In a saucepan cook onion in oil over moderately low heat, stirring, until softened. Add vinegar and cook 1 minute. Remove pan from heat and stir in couscous, boiling water, and salt and pepper to taste. Let couscous mixture stand, covered, 5 minutes. Fluff couscous with a fork and stir in chives. Serves 2 as a side dish.

Vegetable Couscous with Black Olives ⊙

1 cup water
½ teaspoon salt
2 tablespoons extra-virgin olive oil
⅔ cup couscous
1 small onion, chopped
　(about ⅓ cup)
1 large garlic clove, chopped fine
1 plum tomato, seeded and cut into
　½-inch dice
½ small zucchini, cut into ¼-inch dice
3 Kalamata or other brine-cured black
　olives, pitted and cut into slivers
1 tablespoon chopped fresh flat-leafed
　parsley leaves
freshly ground black pepper to taste

In a small saucepan bring water, salt, and 1 tablespoon oil to a boil and stir in couscous. Remove pan from heat and let couscous stand, covered, 5 minutes.

While couscous is standing, in a skillet sauté onion, garlic, tomato, and zucchini with salt to taste in remaining tablespoon oil over moderately high heat, stirring, until vegetables are tender, 3 to 4 minutes. Stir in olives, parsley, and pepper and remove skillet from heat.

Fluff couscous with a fork and stir into vegetables. Serves 2 as a side dish.

Zucchini Couscous ◌

1½ pounds zucchini (about 3 large)
1 tablespoon olive oil
½ teaspoon ground cumin
1 cup boiling water
⅔ cup couscous

Cut zucchini into ¼-inch dice. In a large non-stick skillet cook zucchini in oil with cumin and salt and pepper to taste over moderate heat, stirring, until just tender, about 5 minutes. Add water and bring to a boil. Stir in couscous and remove skillet from heat. Let mixture stand, covered, 5 minutes. Fluff couscous with a fork. Serves 4 as a side dish.

Pasta with Bolognese Sauce

For sauce
2 tablespoons olive oil
2 tablespoons unsalted butter
1 small onion, chopped fine
1 carrot, chopped fine
1 celery rib, chopped fine
½ pound ground chuck
½ pound ground pork
1 cup milk
freshly grated nutmeg to taste
1 cup dry white wine
a 28- to 32-ounce can whole tomatoes
    including juice

1¼ pounds dried pasta such as *tagliatelle, penne, rigatoni, fusilli,* or *orecchiette,* or 1½ pounds fresh semolina *orecchiette* (page 159)

Make sauce:
In a large heavy saucepan heat oil and butter over moderately high heat until foam subsides and sauté onion, carrot, and celery, stirring, 2 minutes. Add beef and pork and cook, stirring, 2 minutes, or until meat is no longer pink. Season mixture with salt and pepper. Add milk and nutmeg and cook, stirring, until most of milk is evaporated, about 10 minutes. Add wine and cook, stirring occasionally, until liquid is evaporated, about 10 minutes.

In a blender or food processor coarsely purée

tomatoes with juice and stir into sauce. Cook sauce at a bare simmer, uncovered, stirring occasionally, 1 hour and 15 minutes (sauce will be thickened) and season with salt and pepper. *Sauce may be made ahead and cooled, uncovered, before being chilled, covered, 2 days or frozen 1 month.*

In an 8-quart kettle bring 7 quarts salted water to a boil. Cook pasta until *al dente* (about 6 minutes for fresh, longer for dried) and drain in a colander. In a heated large bowl immediately toss pasta with sauce. Serves 6 as a main course.

Tomato and Fennel Orzo ◌

½ cup *orzo* (rice-shaped pasta)
1 tablespoon olive oil
1 tablespoon unsalted butter
½ cup finely chopped fennel bulb
¼ cup finely chopped onion
3 plum tomatoes, chopped fine
¾ teaspoon finely chopped fresh tarragon leaves
    or ⅛ teaspoon dried tarragon, crumbled

Bring a saucepan of salted water to a boil for *orzo.*
In a heavy skillet heat olive oil and butter over moderate heat until hot but not smoking and cook fennel, onion, tomatoes, and tarragon until fennel is tender, about 5 minutes. Season mixture with salt and pepper and keep warm, covered.

Cook *orzo* in boiling water until *al dente* and drain in a colander. In a bowl stir together *orzo,* fennel mixture, and salt and pepper to taste. Serves 2 as a side dish.

Pasta with Butternut Squash and Spinach ☾

6 ounces *cavatappi* or other spiral-shaped
    pasta
1 small butternut squash (about 1 pound)
5 cups packed spinach leaves (about 1 bunch)
2 garlic cloves
1 tablespoon olive oil
2 teaspoons fresh lemon juice
½ cup freshly grated Parmesan (about
    1½ ounces)

Fill a 4-quart kettle three fourths full with salted water and bring to a boil for cooking pasta.

Quarter, seed, and peel squash. Cut squash into ½-inch cubes. Coarsely chop spinach and mince garlic cloves.

In a large heavy skillet heat oil over moderately high heat until hot but not smoking and sauté squash with salt to taste, stirring occasionally, until almost tender, about 7 minutes.

While squash is cooking, cook pasta in boiling water until *al dente*. Reserve ½ cup cooking water and drain pasta in a colander.

Add spinach and garlic to skillet with squash and cook over moderately high heat, stirring, until any liquid is evaporated. Add pasta and reserved cooking water and bring to a boil. Season pasta with lemon juice and salt and pepper. Remove skillet from heat and toss pasta with Parmesan. Serves 2.

Pasta Paella with Clams and Spicy Sausage ☾

1 medium zucchini
4 plum tomatoes
1 medium onion
2 garlic cloves
2 tablespoons olive oil
6 ounces *fideos* (Spanish dried coiled vermicelli
    noodles) or 6 ounces thin spaghetti broken
    into 2-inch pieces
¼ pound hot Italian sausage links
1¼ cups water
¾ cup dry white wine
12 small (less than 2 inches in diameter)
    hard-shelled clams such as littlenecks
1 tablespoon chopped fresh parsley leaves

Cut zucchini and tomatoes into ½-inch pieces and keep vegetables separate. Chop onion and mince garlic.

In a heavy kettle heat oil over moderately high heat until hot but not smoking and sauté uncooked pasta, turning occasionally, until golden, about 2 minutes. With a slotted spoon transfer pasta to a bowl. In oil remaining in kettle sauté zucchini with salt to taste, stirring occasionally, until browned, about 3 minutes, and transfer to another bowl. Squeeze sausage from casings into kettle and add onion and garlic. Sauté mixture, stirring and breaking up sausage, until browned, about 5 minutes. Add tomatoes, water, and wine and bring to a boil. Add pasta and clams and boil, uncovered, stirring occasionally, 8 minutes, or until clams are opened and pasta is *al dente*. (Discard any unopened clams.) Stir in zucchini and parsley and cook until heated through. Serves 2.

Penne with Fried Sardines, Capers, and Parsley ☾

½ pound *penne* or *ziti*
1 cup fresh flat-leafed parsley leaves,
    chopped fine
1 small red onion, chopped fine
2 tablespoons drained capers,
    chopped fine
1 tablespoon fresh lemon juice
2 tablespoons extra-virgin olive oil
vegetable oil for frying
a 3¾-ounce can brisling sardines, drained
    on paper towels

Bring a kettle of salted water to a boil. Cook pasta until *al dente* and drain well in a colander. In a bowl toss together pasta, parsley, onion, capers, and salt and pepper to taste. Drizzle mixture with lemon juice and olive oil and toss to combine.

In a 9- to 10-inch heavy deep skillet heat ½ inch vegetable oil over high heat until hot but not smoking and gently lower half of sardines with a slotted spoon into oil. Fry sardines until crisp and golden, about 1 minute, and transfer with slotted spoon to paper towels to drain. Fry and drain remaining sardines in same manner. Add sardines to pasta and toss to combine. Serves 2.

Penne with Herbed Zucchini and Goat Cheese ◎

6 ounces *penne* or other tubular pasta
3 medium zucchini
1 large garlic clove
2 teaspoons mixed fresh herbs such as rosemary,
    thyme, oregano, and marjoram leaves
2 ounces (¼ cup) soft mild goat cheese
1 tablespoon olive oil

Fill a 4-quart kettle three-fourths full with salted water and bring water to a boil for pasta.

Halve zucchini lengthwise and cut crosswise into ¼-inch-thick slices. Thinly slice garlic lengthwise and finely chop herbs. Crumble goat cheese.

In a heavy skillet heat oil over moderately high heat until hot but not smoking and sauté zucchini, stirring, until browned and just tender. Stir in garlic and herbs and sauté, stirring, 1 minute.

Cook pasta in boiling water until *al dente* and reserve 1 cup cooking water. Drain pasta in a colander and in a bowl toss with zucchini mixture, cheese, ¼ cup reserved cooking water, and salt and pepper to taste, adding additional reserved cooking water if necessary. Serves 2.

Penne with Swiss Chard ◎

6 ounces *penne* or other tubular pasta
1½ pounds Swiss chard
¼ teaspoon dried hot red pepper flakes
1 small onion
2 teaspoons unsalted butter
¼ cup heavy cream
¼ teaspoon freshly grated nutmeg
2 tablespoons freshly grated Parmesan

Fill a 4-quart kettle three-fourths full with salted water and bring to a boil for pasta.

Chop Swiss chard into ¼-inch-wide pieces and finely chop separately red pepper flakes and onion. In a 12-inch heavy skillet cook onion in butter over moderate heat, stirring occasionally, until golden brown, about 5 minutes. Add Swiss chard and cook, stirring, 15 minutes, or until tender.

While Swiss chard mixture is cooking, cook pasta in boiling water until *al dente* and drain in a colander. Add pasta to Swiss chard mixture with red pepper flakes, cream, and nutmeg and cook, stirring, 1 minute. Remove skillet from heat and stir in Parmesan and salt and pepper to taste. Serves 2.

Trenette with Rabbit and Shiitake Mushroom Sauce

For sauce
¾ pound fresh *shiitake* mushrooms, stems
    discarded
a 2-pound rabbit, thawed if frozen, cut into
    serving pieces and liver chopped and
    reserved if desired
all-purpose flour for dredging
3 tablespoons olive oil
5 ounces *pancetta** or bacon, chopped coarse
1 large onion, chopped
2 large garlic cloves, chopped, plus 1 small
    head garlic, left unpeeled and whole
¼ cup white-wine vinegar
½ cup dry white wine
2 cups beef broth
1 cup water
2 tablespoons finely chopped mixed fresh herbs
    such as sage, rosemary, and thyme leaves

¾ pound fresh *trenette* (ruffle-edged egg noodles;
    recipe follows) or ¾ pound dried *trenette*

Garnish: finely chopped fresh parsley leaves

*available at specialty foods shops

Make sauce:
Preheat oven to 325° F.

Cut mushrooms into ¼-inch-thick slices. Pat rabbit and reserved liver dry. Season rabbit with salt and pepper and dredge it in flour, shaking off excess.

In a large heavy ovenproof skillet heat oil over moderately high heat until hot but not smoking and brown rabbit on all sides. Transfer rabbit to a plate and in skillet sauté *pancetta* or bacon, stirring, until golden. Add onion and chopped garlic and sauté, stirring, until onion is golden. Add vinegar and wine and deglaze skillet, scraping up brown bits. Simmer onion mixture until liquid is evaporated, about 5 minutes. Cut off and discard top ¼ inch of head of garlic, exposing cloves, and add head to onion mixture with broth, water, and herbs. Bring mixture to a simmer and season with salt and pepper. Stir in mushrooms and rabbit and braise, covered, in middle of oven 1 hour, or until meat is tender.

Transfer rabbit to a plate and cool slightly. Remove garlic head and squeeze softened cloves into sauce, discarding skins. Mash garlic with a fork and stir sauce well.

Using 2 forks shred meat, discarding bones, and stir into sauce with reserved liver if using. Simmer sauce over moderate heat 10 minutes and season with salt and pepper. *Sauce may be made 1 day ahead and cooled, uncovered, before being chilled, covered.*

In an 8-quart kettle bring 7 quarts salted water to a boil. Cook pasta until *al dente* (about 2 minutes for fresh, longer for dried) and drain in a colander. In a heated large bowl immediately toss pasta with sauce and garnish with parsley. Serves 4 to 6.

Fresh Trenette

food-processor pasta dough (recipe follows),
    rolled out (procedure opposite)
all-purpose flour for tossing

Line a tray with a dry kitchen towel. Arrange first rolled-out pasta sheet, which will have dried slightly but should still be soft, on a work surface and cut lengthwise at about ½-inch intervals, alternately using a plain pastry wheel and a fluted pastry wheel. (Each ribbon of *trenette* should have 1 straight side and 1 fluted side.) Toss *trenette* generously with flour. Form pasta loosely into a nest and arrange on kitchen-towel-lined tray. Make more *trenette* with remaining dough in same manner. *Trenette may be*

made 1 day ahead and chilled on towel-lined tray, covered loosely with plastic wrap. Makes about ¾ pound pasta.

This pasta dough may instead be mixed by hand, following the instructions in the first paragraph of the recipe for semolina orecchiette (page 159).

Food-Processor Pasta Dough ◐

2 cups unbleached all-purpose flour plus
    additional for kneading
3 large eggs
1 teaspoon water
1 teaspoon olive oil
1 teaspoon salt

In a food processor blend all ingredients except additional flour until mixture just begins to form a ball. On a lightly floured surface knead dough, incorporating additional flour as necessary, until smooth and elastic, about 8 minutes. *Dough is best used immediately but may be made 1 day ahead and chilled, wrapped in plastic wrap. Makes about ¾ pound pasta dough.*

To Roll Pasta Dough

food-processor pasta dough (recipe precedes)
all-purpose flour for dusting

Set smooth rollers of a pasta machine at widest setting. Cut dough into 4 pieces and wrap 3 of them separately in plastic wrap. Flatten unwrapped piece of dough into a rectangle and feed through rollers. Fold rectangle in half and feed through rollers 8 or 9 more times, folding in half each time and dusting with flour as necessary to prevent sticking.

Turn dial down to next (narrower) setting and feed dough through rollers without folding. Continue to feed dough through, without folding, making space between rollers narrower each time, until narrowest setting is reached. Halve sheet crosswise and arrange on a dry kitchen towel, letting pasta hang over edge of work surface. Roll out remaining dough in same manner. Cut dough while still soft.

*Butternut Squash, Sage, and Goat Cheese Ravioli
with Hazelnut Brown-Butter Sauce*

For filling
a 2-pound butternut squash, halved lengthwise
    and seeded
1 medium onion, chopped
    (about 1½ cups)
1½ teaspoons ground sage
1 tablespoon unsalted butter
1 garlic clove, minced
3 ounces aged goat cheese such as Coach Farm,
    grated (about ⅔ cup)

60 won ton wrappers*, thawed if frozen
1 stick (½ cup) unsalted butter
⅓ cup hazelnuts, toasted lightly and skinned
    (procedure follows) and chopped coarse

*available at Asian markets and specialty foods
    shops

Preheat oven to 425° F. and lightly grease a
baking sheet.
Make filling:
Put squash halves, flesh sides down, on baking
sheet and roast in middle of oven 30 minutes, or
until flesh is very tender. When squash is cool
enough to handle, scoop out flesh into a bowl and
discard skin. Mash squash with a fork until smooth.

While squash is roasting, in a skillet cook onion
and sage in butter with salt and pepper to taste over
moderate heat, stirring, 5 minutes, or until onion is
golden brown. Stir in garlic and cook, stirring, 1
minute.

Cool onion mixture slightly and add to squash.
Add goat cheese and stir to combine well.

In a 6-quart kettle bring 5 quarts salted water to a
gentle boil for ravioli.

Put 1 won ton wrapper on a lightly floured
surface, keeping remaining wrappers in plastic wrap,
and mound 1 tablespoon filling in center. Lightly
brush edges of wrapper with water and put a second
wrapper over first, pressing down around filling to
force out air and seal edges well. If desired, trim
excess dough with a round cutter or sharp knife.
Transfer ravioli to a dry kitchen towel. Make more
ravioli with remaining wrappers and filling in same
manner, transferring as formed to towel and turning
occasionally to dry slightly.

In skillet cook butter with hazelnuts over
moderate heat until butter begins to brown, about 3
minutes, and immediately remove from heat (nuts
will continue to cook). Season hazelnut butter with
salt and pepper and keep warm, covered.

Cook ravioli in 3 batches in gently boiling water 6
minutes, or until they rise to surface and are tender
(do not let water boil vigorously once ravioli have
been added). Carefully transfer ravioli as cooked
with a slotted spoon to a large shallow baking pan
and add enough cooking water to reach ½ inch up
side of pan. Keep ravioli warm, covered.

Transfer ravioli with a slotted spoon (letting
excess cooking liquid drip off) to 6 plates and top
with hazelnut brown-butter sauce. Makes 30 ravioli,
serving 6 generously.

To Toast and Skin Hazelnuts ☺

Preheat oven to 350° F.

In a baking pan toast hazelnuts in one layer in middle of oven 10 to 15 minutes, or until colored lightly and skins blister. Wrap nuts in a kitchen towel and let steam 1 minute. Rub nuts in towel to remove loose skins (do not worry about skins that do not come off) and cool.

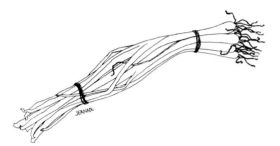

Spaghetti with Shrimp and Arugula ☺

8 ounces spaghetti
2 tablespoons extra-virgin olive oil
1 garlic clove, minced
2 tablespoons chopped fresh flat-leafed parsley
   leaves
1 teaspoon freshly grated lemon zest
freshly ground black pepper
½ pound large shrimp (about 10), shelled and
   deveined
2 tablespoons dry white wine
2 cups chopped arugula (about 1 bunch)

In a 5-quart kettle bring 4 quarts salted water to a boil for spaghetti.

In a large bowl stir together 1 tablespoon oil, garlic, parsley, zest, and pepper and salt to taste.

Cook spaghetti in boiling water until *al dente* and drain in a colander. Immediately add pasta to parsley mixture and toss until combined well. Season pasta with pepper and salt and cover.

In a large non-stick skillet heat remaining tablespoon oil over moderate heat until hot but not smoking and cook shrimp, stirring, until cooked

through, about 2 minutes. Add wine and cook, stirring, 30 seconds. Add shrimp to pasta. Add arugula and toss until combined well. Serves 2.

Open Shrimp Ravioli with Lime Ginger Butter ☺

6 won ton wrappers
⅓ cup finely chopped shallot
¼ teaspoon grated peeled fresh gingerroot
½ cup dry white wine
2 tablespoons cold unsalted butter, cut into pieces
½ teaspoon freshly grated lime zest
½ teaspoon fresh lime juice, or to taste
1 tablespoon olive oil
½ pound large shrimp (about 10), shelled and
   halved lengthwise
1 carrot, cut into ¼-inch dice
2 scallions, cut diagonally into ½-inch pieces

Garnish: 1 scallion green, sliced thin lengthwise

Bring a large saucepan of salted water to a boil for won ton wrappers.

In a small saucepan cook shallot and gingerroot in wine until wine is reduced to about 1 tablespoon. Remove pan from heat and whisk butter into sauce, 1 piece at a time, adding each new piece before previous one has melted completely. (Sauce should not become hot enough to liquefy.) Whisk in zest, juice, and salt and pepper to taste and keep sauce warm, covered.

In a large heavy skillet heat oil over moderately high heat until hot but not smoking and sauté shrimp, carrot, and scallions with salt and pepper to taste, stirring, about 2 minutes, or until shrimp is just cooked through and vegetables are tender. Keep shrimp mixture warm, covered.

Add won tons to boiling water and cook, stirring gently, until *al dente*, about 3 minutes. Drain won tons in a colander.

Immediately spoon a scant tablespoon sauce on each of 2 plates. On each plate stack 1 won ton, one fourth of the shrimp mixture, and another scant tablespoon sauce. Stack remaining ingredients on top in same manner, ending each stack with a won ton.

Garnish each serving with some scallion green. Serves 2 as a main course.

Bulgur Pilaf with Carrot and Scallion ☺

1 medium carrot, minced
1 tablespoon olive oil
1 cup water
¾ cup bulgur*
¼ teaspoon salt
2 scallions, sliced thin

*available at natural foods stores and many
 supermarkets

In a small heavy saucepan cook carrot in oil over moderate heat, stirring, until softened and transfer to a bowl.

In pan stir together water, bulgur, and salt and bring to a boil. Cook mixture, covered, over low heat 12 minutes, or until liquid is absorbed. Remove pan from heat and let bulgur stand, covered, 5 minutes. Stir in carrot, scallions, and salt and pepper to taste. Serves 2.

Butternut Squash, Turnip, and Green-Bean Quinoa ☺

⅔ cup quinoa,* preferably
 Ancient Harvest brand
1⅓ cups water
½ teaspoon salt
1 medium turnip
1 large garlic clove
4 scallions
2 ounces green beans
1 cup ⅓-inch cubes butternut squash

*available at natural foods stores and specialty
 foods shops and by mail order from Healthy
 Trader, tel. (800) 636-2584

In a sieve rinse quinoa under cold running water until water runs clear.

In a small saucepan bring water to a boil with quinoa and salt and simmer mixture, covered, over moderately low heat until just cooked through, 5 to

10 minutes. Drain quinoa in sieve (do not rinse) and spread out on a plate to cool.

Peel turnip and cut into ⅓-inch cubes. Mince garlic. Slice scallions thin on the diagonal and cut beans into ⅓-inch pieces.

In a steamer set over 1 inch boiling water combine squash, turnip, and garlic and steam vegetables, covered, 7 minutes, or until almost tender. Add beans, quinoa, and salt and pepper to taste and steam 3 minutes, or until beans are crisp-tender. Transfer mixture to a bowl and toss with scallions. Serves 4.

 Each serving: 143 calories, 2 grams fat
(11% of calories from fat)

PHOTO ON PAGE 87

Rice with Dill, Walnuts, and Golden Raisins ☺

1½ cups water
¼ teaspoon salt
¾ cup long-grain rice
¼ cup walnuts
¼ cup fresh dill leaves
¼ cup golden raisins
½ teaspoon finely grated fresh lemon zest
1 tablespoon white-wine vinegar
½ tablespoon olive oil

In a saucepan with a tight-fitting lid bring water to a boil with salt. Stir in rice and cook, covered, over low heat 20 minutes, or until water is absorbed and rice is tender.

While rice is cooking, lightly toast walnuts and chop coarse. Chop dill.

Fluff rice with a fork and stir in walnuts, dill, raisins, zest, vinegar, oil, and salt and pepper to taste. Serves 2.

Mushroom Rice ☺

½ cup long-grain rice
1 cup water
½ teaspoon salt
½ pound mushrooms
2 scallions
1 tablespoon unsalted butter
¼ cup dry white wine

In a 1½-quart heavy saucepan bring rice and water with salt to a boil. Stir rice once and cook, covered, over moderately low heat 15 minutes. Remove pan from heat and let rice stand, covered, 5 minutes.

While rice is cooking, cut mushrooms into ¼-inch-thick slices and chop scallions. In a skillet heat butter over moderately high heat until foam subsides and sauté mushrooms with salt to taste until golden and any liquid mushrooms give off is evaporated. Add wine and simmer, stirring occasionally, until wine is evaporated.

Fluff rice with a fork and stir in mushrooms and scallions. Serves 2.

Cajun-Style White Rice ☉

2 cups white rice
3 cups water
½ teaspoon salt

In a 3-quart heavy saucepan wash rice in several changes of water, pouring off each change of water carefully, until water is almost clear. Drain rice in a sieve and return to pan. Add 3 cups water and salt and bring to a boil, uncovered, without stirring. Boil mixture until surface of rice is covered with steam holes and grains on top appear dry, 8 to 10 minutes. Reduce heat to low and cook rice, covered, without stirring, 15 minutes. Remove pan from heat and let rice stand, covered, 5 minutes. Fluff rice with a fork. Makes about 6 cups.

Cooked Rice ☉

5 cups cold water
2½ cups long-grain white rice (not converted)

In a 5-quart heavy kettle bring water with rice to a boil over moderately high heat and boil mixture, uncovered and undisturbed, until water has evaporated and steam holes appear on surface of rice, about 8 minutes. Reduce heat to low and cook rice, covered and undisturbed, 15 minutes. Fluff rice with a fork. Serves 4.

Jasmine Rice Pilaf with Mustard Seeds ☉

1 shallot, sliced thin
1 tablespoon olive oil
1½ teaspoons mustard seeds
½ cup jasmine or long-grain white rice
1 teaspoon salt
1 cup water
¼ cup thinly sliced scallion greens

In a 1½-quart heavy saucepan cook shallot in oil over moderately low heat, stirring occasionally, until softened. Add mustard seeds and cook, stirring occasionally, 1 minute. Stir in rice, salt, and water and bring to a boil. Stir rice once and cook, covered, over very low heat 15 minutes. Remove pan from heat and let pilaf stand, covered, 5 minutes. Fluff pilaf with a fork and stir in scallions. Serves 2.

Lemon Wild Rice

⅓ cup wild rice
3½ cups water
½ medium onion
¾ cup long-grain white rice
3 tablespoons chopped fresh flat-leafed parsley
    leaves
1 teaspoon finely grated fresh lemon zest

Rinse wild rice under cold running water and drain in a sieve. In a 1-quart heavy saucepan bring wild rice and 2 cups water to a boil and simmer, covered, 40 minutes, or until rice is tender.

While wild rice is simmering, finely chop medium onion. After wild rice has been simmering 20 minutes, in a 3-quart heavy saucepan bring white rice, chopped onion, and remaining 1½ cups water to a boil and simmer, covered, 13 minutes. Remove white rice from heat and let stand, covered, 5 minutes. Drain wild rice in sieve and in a large bowl combine with white rice. Stir in chopped parsley and grated zest with a fork, fluffing rice, and season with salt and pepper. Serves 4.

☞ Each serving about 115 calories, 3 grams fat
(23% of calories from fat)

PHOTO ON PAGE 85

VEGETABLES AND BEANS

Lemony Green Beans ☺

6 ounces green beans
½ teaspoon finely grated fresh lemon zest
2 teaspoons extra-virgin olive oil

Trim beans and in a large saucepan of boiling salted water cook until crisp-tender, 3 to 5 minutes. Drain beans well in a colander and in a bowl toss with zest, oil, and salt and pepper to taste. Serves 2.

Haricots Verts and Red Peppers with Almonds ☺

1 cup sliced almonds
7 red bell peppers (about
    3½ pounds)
2 tablespoons olive oil
2½ pounds *haricots verts* (French thin
    green beans) or regular green beans

Preheat oven to 350° F.
In a baking pan toast almonds in one layer in middle of oven 10 to 15 minutes, or until lightly colored. Cut bell peppers into 2-inch-long strips. In a 12-inch heavy skillet heat 1 tablespoon oil over moderate heat until hot but not smoking and cook half of peppers, stirring frequently, until crisp-tender, about 12 minutes. Transfer cooked peppers to a serving bowl. Cook remaining peppers in remaining tablespoon oil in same manner and transfer to bowl.
In a 4-quart kettle half filled with boiling salted water cook beans until crisp-tender, about 3 minutes for *haricots verts* or about 6 minutes for regular green beans. Drain beans in a colander and transfer to bowl. Toss vegetables with almonds and salt and pepper to taste. Serves 16.

PHOTO ON PAGE 76

Brussels Sprouts with Golden Onion ☺

10 ounces Brussels sprouts (about 2½ cups)
1 small onion, sliced thin
1 tablespoon unsalted butter
2½ teaspoons Dijon mustard (preferably
    coarse-grained)
1 teaspoon water

Trim Brussels sprouts and quarter lengthwise. In a large saucepan of boiling salted water boil sprouts 5 minutes, or until just tender, and drain in a colander. In pan cook onion in butter over moderate heat, stirring occasionally, until golden. Add sprouts and cook, stirring, 1 minute. In a small bowl stir together mustard and water and stir into sprouts with salt and pepper to taste. Serves 2.

Carrot Marjoram Purée ☺

2 pounds carrots
⅔ cup long-grain rice
3 tablespoons unsalted butter, softened
2 teaspoons fresh marjoram leaves or
    1¼ teaspoons dried marjoram, crumbled

Garnish: fresh marjoram leaves

Peel carrots and cut into ½-inch pieces. Fill a 7- to 8-quart kettle three fourths full with salted water and bring to a boil. Add carrots and rice and cook, stirring until water returns to a boil, until carrots are very tender, about 30 minutes. Drain mixture well in a large sieve. In a food processor purée half of carrot mixture with half of butter until smooth and transfer to a bowl. Purée remaining carrot mixture and butter in same manner and transfer to bowl. Season purée with salt and pepper and stir in marjoram. *Purée may be made 2 days ahead and cooled completely before being chilled, covered.*
Serve purée garnished with marjoram. Serves 8.

PHOTO ON PAGE 78

Brussels Sprouts and Roasted Red Onions

4 pounds medium red onions (about 9)
1 tablespoon olive oil
1¼ pounds Brussels sprouts
1½ tablespoons Dijon mustard
¼ cup water
3 tablespoons unsalted butter

Preheat oven to 425° F.

Trim onions, keeping root ends intact, and cut each lengthwise into 6 wedges, keeping wedges intact. In a large bowl toss onions with oil and salt and pepper to taste. In 2 shallow baking pans arrange onions in one layer and roast in upper and lower thirds of oven 20 minutes. Carefully turn onions over and switch position of pans. Roast onions 20 minutes more, or until just tender and some edges are golden brown.

Trim Brussels sprouts and have ready a large bowl of ice and cold water. In a large saucepan of boiling salted water cook sprouts until just tender, 8 to 10 minutes, and drain in colander. Transfer sprouts to ice water to stop cooking and drain in colander. *Vegetables may be prepared up to this point 1 day ahead and chilled separately, covered.*

In a small bowl stir together mustard and water. In a 12-inch heavy skillet cook onions and sprouts in butter over moderately high heat, stirring, until heated through and stir in mustard mixture and salt and pepper to taste. Serves 8 generously.

PHOTO ON PAGE 67

Gingered Red Cabbage and Carrots

¼ pound carrots (about 2 medium)
½ pound red cabbage
2 teaspoons unsalted butter
½ teaspoon minced peeled fresh gingerroot
1 teaspoon soy sauce
½ teaspoon sugar

Separately cut carrots and cabbage into julienne strips. In a saucepan of boiling salted water cook carrots 2 minutes, or until just crisp-tender, and transfer with a slotted spoon to a bowl. Cook cabbage in boiling water 1 minute, or until just tender, and drain in a sieve.

In a skillet melt butter over moderately high heat until foam subsides and in it sauté gingerroot, stirring, 30 seconds. Add carrots, cabbage, soy sauce, and sugar and sauté, stirring, 2 minutes. Serves 2.

Spiced Red Cabbage

1 medium head red cabbage
    (about 2½ pounds)
2 tablespoons vegetable oil
3 tablespoons sugar
1 cup dry red wine
¼ cup red-wine vinegar
1 bay leaf
a 4-inch cinnamon stick
2 whole cloves

Quarter and core red cabbage and cut into ¼-inch-thick shreds. In a 7- to 8-quart heavy kettle cook cabbage in oil over moderate heat, stirring occasionally, 5 minutes. Stir in remaining ingredients and simmer, covered, stirring occasionally, until cabbage is tender, about 20 minutes. Discard cloves and, if desired, bay leaf and cinnamon stick. Season cabbage with salt and pepper. *Cabbage may be made 3 days ahead and chilled, covered.* Serves 8.

PHOTO ON PAGE 78

Wilted Cabbage with Carrots and Bacon ☉

4 bacon slices, cut into ½-inch pieces
1 garlic clove, minced
¼ medium onion, sliced thin
3½ cups thinly sliced cabbage
    (about ¾ pound)
2 carrots, grated coarse
¼ cup chopped fresh flat-leafed parsley leaves

In a large non-stick skillet cook bacon over moderate heat until crisp and transfer with a slotted spoon to paper towels to drain. In fat remaining in skillet cook garlic and onion over moderately low heat, stirring, until onion is softened. Add cabbage and carrots and cook, stirring, over moderate heat until crisp-tender, about 5 minutes. Stir in bacon and parsley and season with salt and pepper. Serves 2.

*Roasted Cauliflower with Coriander
and Cumin Seeds* ☉

a small head cauliflower
    (about 1 pound)
1½ tablespoons olive oil
¼ teaspoon cumin seeds
¼ teaspoon ground coriander

Preheat oven to 450° F.
Cut cauliflower into 1-inch flowerets and in a roasting pan or ovenproof skillet toss with remaining ingredients. Roast mixture in oven 25 minutes, or until cauliflower is just tender. Serves 2.

Rajas con Crema ☉
(Poblano Strips with Onions and Cream)

2 pounds fresh *poblano* chilies* (about 8)
1 medium white onion (about 8 ounces)
3 tablespoons vegetable oil
⅓ cup *crème fraîche* or heavy cream

*available at Latino markets, specialty foods
    shops, and some supermarkets

Roast and peel chilies (procedure on page 96). Wearing rubber gloves, cut chilies into ⅓-inch-thick strips. Halve onion lengthwise and cut each half lengthwise into ¼-inch-thick slices.
In a heavy skillet cook onion in oil over moderately low heat, stirring frequently, until softened, about 5 minutes. Add chilies and salt to taste and cook, stirring, 5 minutes. Add *crème fraîche* or cream and cook, stirring, 2 minutes. *Rajas may be made 1 day ahead and chilled, covered.* Reheat *rajas* before serving. Makes enough *rajas* to serve as an accompaniment for 32 tacos.

PHOTO ON PAGE 48

Indian-Spiced Eggplant ☉

1 teaspoon ground coriander seeds
½ teaspoon ground cumin
½ teaspoon ground turmeric
¼ teaspoon ground cloves
¼ teaspoon ground cinnamon
¼ teaspoon ground cardamom
¾ cup water
1 tablespoon sugar
1 tablespoon red-wine vinegar
1 small eggplant (about ¾ pound)
2 tablespoons unsalted butter
1 teaspoon salt
2 tablespoons chopped fresh coriander
    sprigs

In a small bowl combine all spices and in a measuring cup stir together water, sugar, and vinegar. Cut eggplant into 2-inch pieces.
In a large heavy non-stick skillet heat butter over moderate heat until foam subsides and cook spices, stirring, until fragrant, about 1 minute. Add eggplant and salt and toss to coat with spice mixture. Stir vinegar mixture and add to eggplant mixture. Simmer mixture, covered, without stirring, 10 minutes, or until eggplant is just tender. Uncover skillet and cook eggplant mixture at a rapid simmer, without stirring, until most of liquid is evaporated and eggplant is slightly charred (but not burned) on bottom, about 15 minutes.
Remove skillet from heat and let eggplant stand, covered, 5 minutes.
Serve eggplant sprinkled with fresh coriander. Serves 2.

Roasted Celery Root

4 pounds (about 3) celery root
  (sometimes called celeriac)
⅓ cup vegetable oil
2 teaspoons salt

Preheat oven to 425° F.

Trim and peel celery root and cut into 1-inch pieces. In a large roasting pan toss celery root with oil and salt and roast in middle of oven 30 minutes. Stir celery root and reduce temperature to 375° F. Roast celery root, stirring after 30 minutes, 1 hour more. Serves 6.

PHOTO ON PAGE 24

Scalloped Fennel and Potatoes

5 garlic cloves
5 cups heavy cream
3 cups chicken broth
3 tablespoons all-purpose flour
1 tablespoon salt
¼ teaspoon freshly grated nutmeg
¼ teaspoon freshly ground black pepper
3 pounds fennel bulbs (sometimes called
  anise, about 3 large)
4 pounds yellow-fleshed potatoes such as
  Yukon Gold
1 stick (½ cup) unsalted butter

Preheat oven to 400° F. and lightly butter two 3-quart gratin dishes (about 15 by 10 by 2 inches).

Mince garlic and in a large bowl whisk together with 4 cups cream, broth, flour, salt, nutmeg, and pepper.

Trim fennel stalks flush with bulbs, reserving stalks for another use, and cut bulbs crosswise into ¼-inch-thick slices. Divide fennel into 4 equal portions. Peel potatoes and with a *mandoline* or other manual slicer cut crosswise into ⅛-inch-thick slices. Divide potatoes into 6 equal portions. In 1 gratin dish arrange 1 portion potatoes, spreading evenly, and top with 1 portion fennel slices. Top fennel with a second portion potatoes, spreading evenly. Season layer with salt and pepper and top with a second portion fennel. Pour half of cream mixture over fennel and top with a third portion

potatoes, overlapping them. Press down on potatoes to temporarily submerge them in cream mixture.

Repeat layering in second gratin dish.

Melt butter. Brush top of gratins with all of butter and bake in upper and lower thirds of oven 30 minutes. Remove gratin dishes from oven and pour ½ cup remaining cream evenly over each top potato layer. Season scalloped vegetables with salt and pepper and bake, switching position of dishes in oven, 30 minutes more, or until tops are golden and potatoes are tender. *Scalloped vegetables may be baked 1 day ahead and cooled completely before being chilled, covered. Bring scalloped vegetables to room temperature and reheat, covered.* Serves 16.

PHOTO ON PAGE 76

Sautéed Kale with Bacon and Vinegar

1 large bunch kale (about ¾ pound)
2 bacon slices, chopped
2 teaspoons cider vinegar,
  or to taste

Cut stems and center ribs away from kale leaves and coarsely tear leaves. In a large heavy saucepan of boiling salted water cook leaves 5 minutes and drain well in a colander. In pan cook bacon over moderate heat, stirring, until crisp. Pour off all but about 1 tablespoon fat from pan. Add kale to bacon and sauté over moderately high heat, stirring, until heated through. Toss kale with vinegar and season with salt and pepper. Serves 2.

Grilled Endive with Orange Vinaigrette

1 navel orange
1½ teaspoons white-wine vinegar
1 tablespoon plus 2 teaspoons olive oil
2 Belgian endives

Prepare grill.

With a vegetable peeler remove two 1¼- by ½-inch strips zest from orange and cut lengthwise into very thin strips. Squeeze enough juice from orange to measure 1 tablespoon. In a bowl whisk together zest, orange juice, vinegar, 1 tablespoon oil, and salt and pepper to taste until combined well.

Halve endives lengthwise, keeping halves from separating into leaves, and brush all over with remaining 2 teaspoons oil. Season endives with salt and pepper and grill, cut sides down, on a rack set 5 to 6 inches over glowing coals 6 minutes. Turn endives and grill until just tender, 6 minutes more. (Alternatively, endives may be grilled in a hot well-seasoned ridged grill pan over moderately high heat.)

Serve endives drizzled with vinaigrette. Serves 2.

Mushroom Ragout with Paprika ☺

1½ pounds fresh white mushrooms
1 pound fresh exotic mushrooms such as
    porcini*, chanterelles*, or Portobellos
½ pound shallots
¾ stick (6 tablespoons) unsalted butter
2 tablespoons Cognac
⅔ cup chicken broth
⅔ cup heavy cream
1 tablespoon paprika (preferably mild
    Hungarian)
½ cup packed fresh flat-leafed parsley leaves
⅔ cup sour cream

*available from specialty produce markets and
    by mail order from Comptoir Exotique,
    tel. (888) 547-5471 (toll free)

Cut white mushrooms lengthwise into ½-inch wedges and chop exotic mushrooms. Finely chop shallots.

In a deep 12-inch heavy skillet cook shallots in butter over moderately low heat, stirring, until softened. Add Cognac and cook over moderate heat,

stirring, 1 minute. Stir in mushrooms and cook, stirring occasionally, 2 minutes. Add broth, heavy cream, paprika, and salt and pepper to taste and simmer, stirring occasionally, until liquid is reduced to about 1½ cups, 12 to 15 minutes. *Ragout may be made up to this point 1 day ahead and cooled completely before being chilled, covered. Reheat ragout before proceeding.* Mince parsley. Remove skillet from heat and stir in parsley and sour cream. Heat ragout over moderate heat, stirring, until hot (do not let boil). Serves 8.

PHOTO ON PAGE 78

Sautéed Fresh Chanterelles ☺

1¼ pounds fresh chanterelles* or Portobellos
2 tablespoons unsalted butter
1 tablespoon olive oil
¼ cup dry white wine
3 tablespoons coarsely chopped fresh
    flat-leafed parsley leaves
fresh lemon juice to taste

*available by mail order from Comptoir
    Exotique, tel. (888) 547-5471 (toll free)

Halve chanterelles lengthwise or cut Portobellos into ½-inch-thick slices. In a large non-stick skillet melt butter with oil over moderately high heat until foam subsides and sauté mushrooms, stirring, with salt and pepper to taste until barely tender, about 2 minutes. Add wine and cook, stirring, until liquid is evaporated and mushrooms are tender, about 5 minutes. In a bowl toss mushrooms with parsley and lemon juice. Serves 6.

PHOTO ON PAGE 72

Sautéed Okra with Tomato and Corn ☽

½ pound fresh okra
1 medium vine-ripened tomato
1 small onion
1 ear corn
1½ tablespoons vegetable oil
½ cup water
½ teaspoon Worcestershire sauce

Cut okra into ½-inch-thick rounds. Peel and chop tomato. Cut onion into thin slices and cut corn from cob. In a heavy skillet heat 1 tablespoon oil over moderately high heat until hot but not smoking and sauté okra with salt to taste, stirring occasionally, until browned, about 3 minutes. With a slotted spoon transfer okra to a bowl.

Add remaining ½ tablespoon oil to skillet and sauté onion, stirring, until it begins to soften. Stir in tomato, ½ cup water, and Worcestershire sauce and simmer, stirring occasionally, 3 minutes. Add corn and simmer until corn is crisp-tender and sauce is thickened, about 3 minutes. Stir in okra with salt and pepper to taste and cook until heated through. Serves 2.

Cebollitas Asadas ☽
(Grilled Spring Onions)

40 spring onions (green onions) or large
    scallions (about 8 bunches)
2 tablespoons vegetable oil
coarse salt to taste
1 lime, cut into 4 wedges

Garnish: lime wedges

Prepare grill.
Trim roots and ends from onions or scallions, leaving about 8 inches of stalk. *Onions or scallions may be prepared up to this point 6 hours ahead and chilled in a sealed plastic bag.*

In a sealable plastic bag or large bowl toss onions or scallions with oil and salt. Grill onions or scallions on a rack set 5 to 6 inches over glowing coals, turning them with tongs 3 or 4 times, 5 to 7 minutes, or until softened and lightly charred. (Alternatively, onions or scallions may be broiled on rack of a broiler pan about 3 inches from heat, turning them with tongs 2 or 3 times, 10 to 12 minutes.)

Transfer onions or scallions to a platter and squeeze 4 lime wedges over them. Garnish platter with additional lime wedges. Makes 40 grilled onions.

PHOTO ON PAGE 47

Roasted Balsamic Red Onions

vegetable-oil cooking spray
1½ pounds red onions (about 3 medium),
    each cut into 8 wedges
2 tablespoons balsamic vinegar

Preheat oven to 450° F. and lightly coat a shallow baking pan with cooking spray.

Arrange onions in one layer in pan and roast in middle of oven, stirring occasionally, until golden brown and just tender, about 15 minutes. Drizzle vinegar over onions and roast onions until most of vinegar is evaporated, about 3 minutes. Season onions with salt and pepper and keep warm, covered. Makes about 2 cups, serving 6.

🍃 Each serving about 41 calories,
0 grams fat

Roasted Peppers Stuffed with Chick-Pea and Eggplant Purée and Mushrooms

6 ounces fresh *shiitake* mushrooms
6 ounces button mushrooms
1 pound mixed vine-ripened red and yellow
    cherry tomatoes
1 tablespoon extra-virgin olive oil
1 shallot, sliced thin
1 garlic clove, sliced thin
4 medium yellow bell peppers with stems
    attached
2 cups chick-pea and eggplant purée (recipe
    follows)
1 tablespoon pine nuts

Preheat oven to 425° F.
Trim and quarter mushrooms. Halve tomatoes lengthwise. In a large non-stick skillet heat oil over

moderately high heat until hot but not smoking and sauté shallot, stirring, until softened. Reduce heat to moderate and cook garlic, stirring, until fragrant, about 20 seconds. Add mushrooms and cook, stirring, 2 minutes. Remove skillet from heat. Stir in tomatoes and season with salt and pepper.

Halve bell peppers lengthwise through stems and discard seeds and ribs. Season pepper shells with salt and pepper and in a large baking pan bake in upper third of oven 10 minutes.

Spoon chick-pea and eggplant purée evenly into shells, smoothing tops. Mound mushroom mixture onto center of purée and sprinkle with pine nuts. Bake stuffed peppers in upper third of oven until heated through, about 15 minutes. (Alternatively, grill pepper shells, skin sides up, on an oiled rack set 5 to 6 inches over glowing coals 7 to 10 minutes, or until slightly charred. Transfer shells to a work surface and stuff them as above. Grill stuffed peppers, covered, until heated through, about 5 minutes.) Serves 4 as a main course.

☛ Each serving about 345 calories, 7 grams fat
(18% of calories from fat)

PHOTO ON PAGE 83

Chick-Pea and Eggplant Purée ☉+

¾ pound eggplant (about 1 small)
2 tablespoons coarse kosher salt
1 cup rinsed and drained canned chick-peas
2 garlic cloves, minced
¼ cup packed fresh flat-leafed parsley
    leaves
¼ cup packed fresh basil leaves
1½ tablespoons fresh lime juice
2 tablespoons water

Cut eggplant into ¾-inch-thick slices and sprinkle both sides with coarse salt. Arrange eggplant in a large colander set over a bowl and let stand 30 minutes to drain.

Preheat broiler.

Rinse eggplant slices and pat dry with paper towels. Broil eggplant on a rack of a broiler pan about 4 inches from heat until deep golden, about 6 minutes on each side. When eggplant is cool enough to handle, peel off skins, scraping all flesh from skins and discarding them.

In a food processor pulse eggplant with remaining ingredients until just puréed and season with salt and black pepper. *Purée may be made 3 days ahead and chilled, covered.* Makes about 2¼ cups.

☛ Each serving about 217 calories, 3.8 grams fat
(3% of calories from fat)

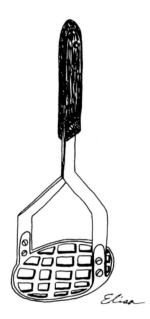

Basic Mashed Potatoes ☉

2 pounds russet (baking) or red potatoes
3 tablespoons unsalted butter
¾ to 1 cup milk

Peel potatoes and cut into 2-inch pieces. (If using red potatoes, it is not necessary to peel them.) In a large heavy saucepan simmer potatoes in salted water to cover by 1 inch 10 minutes, or until tender, and drain in a colander. In pan or a bowl combine potatoes, butter, and ¾ cup milk. With a potato masher mash potatoes until smooth, adding more milk if necessary to make creamy. In pan reheat potatoes over moderately low heat, stirring, and season with salt and pepper. Serves 4.

Cabbage and Bacon Mashed Potatoes ☺

3 bacon slices, chopped
1¼ pounds cabbage (about ½ small head),
    cut into ½-inch pieces
½ cup water
basic mashed potatoes (page 175)

In a large skillet cook bacon over moderate heat until crisp and with a slotted spoon transfer to paper towels to drain. Add cabbage to bacon fat in skillet and cook, stirring occasionally, until golden, about 15 minutes. Add water and simmer until evaporated and cabbage is tender. Add bacon and season with salt and pepper. Stir mixture into potatoes. Serves 4 generously.

Chili Mashed Potatoes ☺

2 large dried mild chilies such as *guajillo**,
    *ancho**, or *mulatto**
¾ to 1 cup milk
basic mashed potatoes (page 175), prepared
    without milk

*available at specialty foods shops and some
    supermarkets and by mail order from Chile
    Today–Hot Tamale, tel. (800) 468-7377

Heat a heavy skillet over moderate heat until hot and toast chilies, 1 at a time, pressing down with tongs, a few seconds on each side to make more pliable. Wearing rubber gloves, seed and devein chilies and coarsely chop. In a small saucepan bring chilies and ¾ cup milk just to a simmer and in a blender purée until smooth (use caution when blending hot liquids). Stir mixture into potatoes, adding more milk if necessary to make creamy. Serves 4.

Roasted Garlic Mashed Potatoes

¼ cup garlic cloves (about 6), unpeeled
basic mashed potatoes (page 175)

Preheat oven to 400° F.
Arrange garlic in one layer on a double thickness of foil and wrap tightly. Roast garlic in middle of oven 45 minutes, or until very soft. Unwrap garlic and cool slightly. Peel cloves and with a potato masher mash into potatoes until creamy. Serves 4.

Parmesan-Potato-Stuffed Roasted Onions

2 yellow onions (each about 3 inches in
    diameter), unpeeled
olive oil for brushing onions
8 ounces red potatoes (about 2 medium)
1 tablespoon dry white wine
1 tablespoon water
2 tablespoons heavy cream
1 tablespoon unsalted butter
2 tablespoons freshly grated Parmesan

Preheat oven to 375° F.
Trim root ends flush with onions (so they will stand upright). Cut off tops of onions 1 inch from pointed blossom end and reserve. In a small flame-proof baking pan stand onions upright and replace reserved tops. Brush onions with oil and roast in middle of oven 1 hour and 15 minutes, or until centers are just knife-tender.

While onions are roasting, in a saucepan boil potatoes in water to cover 15 minutes, or until tender, and drain in a colander. Cool potatoes until they can just be handled and peel. Return potatoes to pan.

Transfer onions to a work surface to cool and add wine, water, and cream to baking pan. On top

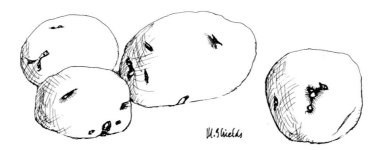

of stove cook cream mixture over moderate heat, stirring until brown bits scraped from bottom of baking pan are just dissolved and add to potatoes.

Leaving outermost layer of each onion inside skin, carefully scoop remaining layers out of onion shells with a small spoon and chop. In a small skillet sauté chopped onion in butter over moderately high heat until golden and add to potato mixture.

Increase oven temperature to 425° F.

Mash potato mixture with a potato masher until potatoes are coarsely mashed and liquid is incorporated and force through a food mill fitted with fine disk into a bowl. Stir in Parmesan and season with salt and pepper. Spoon potato mixture into onion shells and replace tops. *Onions may be prepared up to this point 1 day ahead and chilled, covered.*

In a baking pan roast onions in middle of oven until heated through, 15 to 25 minutes. Serves 2.

PHOTO ON PAGE 14

Herbed Oven-Browned Potatoes ◎

¾ pound boiling potatoes (2 to 3 medium)
1 tablespoon mixed chopped fresh herbs
    such as thyme, rosemary, and/or oregano
    or 1 teaspoon mixed dried herbs, crumbled
1 garlic clove, chopped fine
1 tablespoon unsalted butter
freshly ground black pepper

Preheat oven to 450° F.

Cut potatoes into ¼-inch-thick slices and in a saucepan of boiling salted water cook 5 minutes, or until just cooked through. Drain potatoes well in a sieve and transfer to a 6-cup gratin dish (1½-quart) or other shallow baking dish, 11 by 8 by 1½ inches. Toss potatoes immediately with remaining ingredients and pepper and salt to taste and bake in upper third of oven 20 minutes, or until potatoes are pale golden. Serves 2.

Skillet-Crusted Potatoes ◎

2½ pounds small boiling potatoes
3 tablespoons olive oil
1 tablespoon chopped fresh thyme leaves

In a large saucepan cover potatoes with salted cold water by 1 inch and simmer potatoes about 10 to 15 minutes, or until just tender. Drain potatoes in a colander and cool until they can be handled. *Potatoes may be prepared up to this point 1 day ahead and chilled, covered.*

Halve potatoes crosswise. In a 10- to 12-inch non-stick skillet heat 1½ tablespoons oil with ½ tablespoon thyme and salt to taste over moderately high heat until hot but not smoking and add half of potatoes, cut sides down. Cook potatoes, without stirring, until cut sides are golden and crusty, about 5 minutes, and toss potatoes, shaking skillet, to coat with oil.

Transfer cooked potatoes to a serving bowl and cook remaining potatoes with remaining oil and thyme in same manner. Serves 6.

PHOTO ON PAGE 42

Sautéed Radicchio and Fried Kale

1 head *radicchio di Treviso** or
    medium round *radicchio*
1 tablespoon olive oil
vegetable oil for frying
4 kale leaves, tough ribs discarded,
    washed and patted
    completely dry

*available at specialty produce markets

Cut *radicchio* into quarters through root end, cutting away any tough core but keeping quarters intact. In a skillet heat olive oil over moderately high heat until hot but not smoking and sauté *radicchio*, turning it occasionally, 5 minutes, or until tender. Season *radicchio* with salt and pepper and keep warm, covered.

While *radicchio* is cooking, in a deep heavy skillet heat ½ inch vegetable oil over moderate heat until hot but not smoking (about 350° F. on a deep-fat thermometer) and fry kale leaves, 1 at a time, turning them once, until crisp, about 15 seconds (kale will cause oil to spatter). Transfer kale as fried with tongs to paper towels to drain and season with salt. Serve kale with *radicchio*. Serves 2.

PHOTO ON PAGE 14

Creamed Spinach ◔

1 pound fresh spinach, coarse stems
    discarded and leaves chopped coarse
    (about 8 packed cups)
½ small onion, minced (about 3 tablespoons)
1 tablespoon unsalted butter
¼ cup heavy cream
freshly ground black pepper to taste
a pinch freshly grated nutmeg

In a large saucepan of boiling salted water cook spinach 2 minutes and drain in a sieve, using the back of a large spoon to press as much water as possible out of spinach.

In a skillet cook onion in butter over moderate heat, stirring, until softened. Stir in spinach, cream, pepper, nutmeg, and salt to taste and cook until most of cream is absorbed, about 3 minutes. Serves 2.

Sesame Spinach with Ginger and Garlic ◔

1 garlic clove
2 teaspoons sesame seeds
1 tablespoon vegetable oil
1 teaspoon grated peeled fresh gingerroot
6 ounces trimmed fresh spinach
    (about 12 cups)

Mince garlic and in a small dry skillet toast sesame seeds over moderate heat, stirring, until golden. In a heavy 6-quart kettle heat oil over moderate heat until hot but not smoking and cook garlic and gingerroot, stirring, 30 seconds, or until fragrant and golden. Add spinach by handfuls, stirring, and cook until just wilted.

Serve spinach sprinkled with toasted sesame seeds. Serves 2.

Bourbon Sweet-Potato Purée with Buttered Pecans

6 pounds sweet potatoes (about 6 large)
3 tablespoons bourbon
1 stick (½ cup) unsalted butter, softened
2 cups pecan halves (about 8 ounces)
1 teaspoon coarse kosher salt
2 tablespoons packed dark brown sugar

Preheat oven to 425° F.

Prick potatoes with a fork and in a baking pan bake in middle of oven until tender, about 1 hour.

When just cool enough to handle, peel potatoes and transfer half to a food processor. Add bourbon and 6 tablespoons butter and purée 30 seconds. Transfer purée to a large bowl. Purée remaining potatoes in food processor until completely smooth and transfer to bowl. Stir purée until combined well and season with salt and pepper. Transfer purée to a 2-quart gratin dish or other shallow baking dish. *Purée may be made 2 days ahead and chilled, covered. Bring purée to room temperature before proceeding.*

Reduce temperature to 325° F.

In a shallow baking pan spread pecans in one layer and bake in middle of oven until fragrant, about 10 minutes. Toss hot pecans with remaining 2 tablespoons butter and coarse salt. *Pecans may be made 2 days ahead and kept in an airtight container at room temperature.*

Arrange pecans on top of purée and sprinkle with brown sugar. Bake purée in upper third of oven until heated through and pecans are slightly browned, about 30 minutes. Serves 8.

PHOTO ON PAGE 67

Broiled Tomatoes with Olives and Garlic ◔

2 medium vine-ripened tomatoes
    (about ¾ pound)
3 Kalamata or other brine-cured
    black olives
1 large garlic clove
2 tablespoons olive oil
¼ teaspoon salt
¼ teaspoon freshly ground black pepper

Preheat broiler.

Cut tomatoes into ½-inch-thick slices. Oil a shallow baking pan large enough to hold tomatoes in one layer and arrange tomatoes in pan.

Pit olives and chop fine with garlic. In a small bowl stir together olive mixture, oil, salt, and pepper. Brush tomatoes evenly with mixture and broil about 3 inches from heat 8 minutes, or until bubbling. Serves 2.

Gingered Sweet-Potato Purée ☺

2 medium sweet potatoes (about ¾ pound total)
3 tablespoons milk
1 tablespoon unsalted butter
¾ teaspoon grated peeled fresh gingerroot

Peel potatoes and cut into 1-inch pieces. In a small saucepan boil potatoes in salted water to cover 15 minutes, or until very tender, and drain well in a colander.

In a food processor purée hot potatoes with milk, butter, and gingerroot until smooth and season with salt and pepper. Serves 2.

Creamed Turnips

3 pounds medium turnips (about 9)
4 shallots
4 cups milk
½ cup heavy cream
3 tablespoons unsalted butter
1 tablespoon fresh thyme leaves or
    ½ teaspoon dried thyme, crumbled
¾ teaspoon salt
6 black peppercorns
6 whole cloves
2 bay leaves
3 tablespoons all-purpose flour
white pepper
freshly grated nutmeg

Garnish: chopped fresh parsley leaves

Peel and quarter turnips. In a large saucepan of boiling salted water cook turnips until tender, 15 to 20 minutes, and drain in a colander. Chop shallots.

In a heavy saucepan bring milk and cream just to a simmer and keep hot over low heat. In a 4-quart heavy kettle cook shallots in butter over moderately low heat, stirring, until softened. Add thyme, salt, peppercorns, cloves, and bay leaves and cook, stirring, 1 minute. Add flour and cook *roux*, stirring, 3 minutes. Whisk in hot milk mixture all at once and bring to a boil over moderately high heat, whisking constantly to prevent lumps. Reduce heat to moderately low and simmer sauce, whisking occasionally, 15 minutes. Pour sauce through a sieve into a large saucepan and discard solids. Into sauce stir white pepper, nutmeg, and salt to taste. *Turnips and sauce may be made up to this point 1 day ahead and kept separately in bowls, covered and chilled.*

Return sauce to a simmer and add turnips. Cook mixture, covered, over moderately low heat, stirring occasionally, until turnips are heated through.

Garnish turnips with parsley. Serves 8.

PHOTO ON PAGE 67

Zucchini Pancakes ☺+

1½ pounds zucchini
    (about 3 large)
1 teaspoon salt
¼ cup thinly sliced red onion
1 large egg
¾ cup coarse fresh bread crumbs
vegetable oil for brushing skillet

Grate zucchini on the largest holes of a grater into a colander and combine well with salt. Let zucchini drain 30 minutes.

Preheat oven to 200° F.

Using hands, squeeze as much liquid from zucchini as possible. In a bowl stir together zucchini, onion, egg, bread crumbs, and pepper to taste until combined well.

Lightly brush a 12-inch non-stick skillet with oil and heat over moderately high heat until hot but not smoking. Drop four ⅛-cup measures of zucchini mixture into skillet and with a spatula flatten into ¼-inch-thick pancakes. Cook pancakes 2 to 3 minutes on each side, or until golden and cooked through, transferring pancakes to an ovenproof plate. Keep pancakes warm in oven while making more pancakes in same manner. Makes about 8 to 10 pancakes, serving 4 as a side dish.

Grilled Zucchini with Black Olives and Mint ☺

7 Kalamata or other brine-cured black olives
   (about ¼ cup)
1½ pounds zucchini (about 3 large)
1 tablespoon olive oil
3 tablespoons coarsely chopped fresh mint
   leaves
1½ teaspoons fresh lemon juice

Prepare grill.

Pit and thinly slice olives. Cut zucchini diagonally into ¼-inch-thick slices and in a bowl toss with oil and salt and pepper to taste.

Grill zucchini, in batches if necessary, on a rack set 5 to 6 inches over glowing coals 2 to 3 minutes on each side, or until lightly charred and just tender. (Alternatively, zucchini may be grilled in a hot well-seasoned heavy ridged grill pan over moderately high heat.) Transfer zucchini to bowl and toss with olives, mint, and lemon juice. Serves 4.

Gingered Vegetable Stir-Fry ☺

3 tablespoons chicken broth
2 tablespoons Chinese rice wine or
   medium-dry Sherry
1 teaspoon sugar
1 teaspoon cornstarch
1 teaspoon salt
¼ pound fresh *shiitake* mushrooms, stems
   discarded
2 tablespoons vegetable oil
½ pound carrots (about 3 medium), cut into
   julienne strips
½ pound *daikon* (an Asian radish), cut into
   julienne strips (about 2 cups)
½ pound Napa cabbage, sliced thin
   (about 4 cups)
2 large garlic cloves, minced
2 teaspoons minced peeled fresh gingerroot

In a bowl stir together broth, rice wine or Sherry, sugar, cornstarch, and salt until combined well. Cut mushroom caps into ⅛-inch-thick slices.

Heat a wok over high heat until hot. Add oil and heat until it just begins to smoke. Stir-fry carrots 3 minutes. Add *daikon* and stir-fry vegetables 2 minutes. Add mushrooms, cabbage, garlic, and gingerroot and stir-fry 2 minutes, or until carrots are crisp-tender. Stir broth mixture and add to vegetables. Stir-fry vegetables 1 minute. Serves 6.

Minted Spring Vegetables ☺

3 long, thin Asian eggplants (about ¾ pound
   total) or ¾ pound common eggplant
¾ pound yellow squash (about 2 medium)
2 bunches radishes (about 20)
6 tablespoons extra-virgin olive oil
1 large garlic clove, minced
2 tablespoons chopped fresh flat-leafed parsley
   leaves
1½ tablespoons chopped fresh mint leaves
½ teaspoon coarse kosher salt
1 teaspoon fresh lemon juice

Cut Asian eggplants diagonally into ⅓-inch-thick slices or quarter common eggplants lengthwise and then cut diagonally into ⅓-inch-thick slices. Cut yellow squash diagonally into ¼-inch-thick slices. Trim radish tops to ¼ inch and halve large radishes lengthwise.

In a 12-inch non-stick skillet heat 3 tablespoons oil over moderate heat until hot but not smoking and cook half of eggplant until golden on each side. Transfer eggplant to a bowl and cover with foil to keep warm. Cook remaining eggplant with remaining

3 tablespoons oil in same manner and transfer to bowl. In oil remaining in skillet cook garlic, stirring, 30 seconds, and add to bowl with eggplant.

In a steamer set over boiling water steam squash, covered, until crisp-tender, about 2 to 3 minutes. Transfer squash to bowl with eggplant and keep warm. In steamer steam radishes, covered, until crisp-tender but still pink, about 1 to 2 minutes. Transfer radishes to bowl and add parsley and mint. Season vegetables with coarse salt, pepper, and lemon juice and toss to combine. Serves 6.

PHOTO ON PAGE 24

Roasted Ratatouille ◌

1 medium zucchini, halved lengthwise and cut
    crosswise into ½-inch-thick pieces
1 red bell pepper, cut into 1-inch pieces
1 red onion, cut into 1-inch pieces
1 small eggplant (about 1 pound), cut into
    1-inch cubes
2 tablespoons olive oil
¼ cup golden raisins
1½ teaspoons finely grated fresh lemon zest
2 teaspoons fresh lemon juice, or to taste

Preheat oven to 450° F. and lightly grease a large shallow baking pan.

In a large bowl toss vegetables with oil and salt and pepper to taste and arrange in one layer in pan. Roast vegetables, stirring occasionally, until tender and golden brown, about 20 minutes. Stir in raisins and roast 3 minutes more. In a bowl toss *ratatouille* with zest and juice. Serves 2 as a side dish.

Vegetables Printanier

1 pound *haricots verts** (thin French green beans)
1½ cups red pearl onions
¾ pound tiny white potatoes (about ¾ inch in
    diameter) or quartered small red potatoes
½ pound fresh chanterelles**, any tough
    stems discarded
2 tablespoons unsalted butter
1 cup shelled fresh peas (about 1¼ pounds
    in pods)
2 tablespoons chopped fresh chives

*available at specialty produce markets and
    some supermarkets
**available at specialty produce markets and
    by mail order from Comptoir Exotique,
    tel. (888) 547-5471 (toll-free)

Bring a large saucepan of salted water to a boil and have ready a large bowl of ice and cold water. Trim *haricots verts* to 3-inch lengths and blanch in boiling water 2 minutes. Transfer beans with a slotted spoon to ice water to stop cooking and drain in a colander. Transfer beans to a bowl. In same boiling water cook onions 5 minutes and with slotted spoon transfer to colander to drain. When cool enough to handle, peel and halve onions and transfer to bowl. In same boiling water simmer potatoes 7 minutes, or until tender, and drain in colander. *Vegetables may be prepared up to this point 1 day ahead, cooled completely, and chilled in a sealable plastic bag.*

Halve chanterelles if large. In a large heavy skillet heat butter over moderate heat until foam subsides and cook chanterelles with salt to taste, stirring occasionally, 2 minutes, or until just tender. Add peas and cook 2 minutes, or until bright green. Add beans, onions, and potatoes and cook, stirring occasionally, until just heated through. Stir in chives and season with salt and pepper. Serves 4.

PHOTO ON PAGE 30

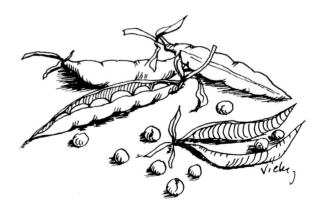

BEANS

Cannellini Beans and Red Peppers with Sage ☺

2 tablespoons olive oil
1 red bell pepper, chopped
1½ tablespoons minced fresh sage leaves
1 garlic clove, minced
a 19-ounce can *cannellini* beans, rinsed and
    drained
1 celery rib, cut crosswise into ¼-inch-thick slices
¾ teaspoon red-wine vinegar

In a large non-stick skillet heat oil over moderate heat until hot but not smoking and cook bell pepper with sage, stirring, until softened. Stir in garlic and cook, stirring, 1 minute. Add remaining ingredients with salt and pepper to taste and heat, stirring, until just heated through. Serves 4 as a side dish.

Chick-Pea Walnut Burgers

a 19-ounce can chick-peas
2 garlic cloves
½ medium onion
1 tablespoon fresh rosemary leaves
¼ cup chopped fresh flat-leafed parsley leaves
½ cup fine fresh bread crumbs
¾ cup walnuts, toasted and chopped
1 large egg
2 tablespoons olive oil
4 sesame buns
4 slices beefsteak tomato
4 slices red onion

In a colander rinse and drain chick-peas. In a food processor pulse garlic, onion, and rosemary until chopped coarse. Add chick-peas, parsley, and bread crumbs and pulse until just combined. Transfer mixture to a bowl and stir in walnuts, egg, and salt and pepper to taste until combined. Form mixture into four 3-inch patties. *Chill patties, covered, at least 1 hour and up to 1 day.*

In a large skillet heat oil over moderate heat until hot but not smoking and cook patties until golden brown, about 4 minutes on each side. Toast sesame buns. Transfer burgers to buns and top with tomato and onion. Serves 4 as a main course.

Frijoles Borrachos
("Drunken" Beans)

1 pound dried pinto beans
1 large white onion
2 tablespoons lard or vegetable oil
2 fresh *epazote* sprigs* (a pungent Mexican
    herb) or 1 teaspoon dried *epazote**,
    crumbled, if desired
1 teaspoon salt
6 bacon slices
2 cups fresh tomato salsa (page 193)
½ cup beer

*available at Latino markets, specialty foods
    shops, and some supermarkets

Pick over beans. *In a large bowl soak beans in cold water to cover by 2 inches for 1 day.*

Drain beans and halve onion. In a 5-quart kettle simmer beans, onion, lard or oil, and *epazote*, if using, in water to cover by 2 inches, covered, 45 minutes, or until beans are almost tender. Add salt and simmer beans until just tender, about 15 minutes more. *Beans may be prepared up to this point 2 days ahead and chilled in cooking liquid, covered.* Drain beans in a colander.

Chop bacon and in a large heavy skillet cook over moderate heat, stirring, until browned. Add beans, salsa, beer, and salt to taste and cook, stirring, until most of liquid evaporates, about 10 minutes. *Beans may be made 2 hours ahead and kept at room temperature. Reheat beans before serving.* Serves 16.

PHOTO ON PAGE 47

SALADS

Corn, Black Bean, and Pita Bread Salad

two 6-inch pita loaves
3 cups cooked black beans (about
    two 1-pound cans)
4 ears fresh corn
1 cup finely chopped red onion
1½ cups finely diced celery
3 tablespoons balsamic vinegar
1 tablespoon extra-virgin olive oil
2 ounces low-fat feta,
    crumbled

Preheat oven to 375° F.

Halve pitas horizontally and sprinkle rough sides with salt and pepper to taste. On a baking sheet toast pitas, rough sides up, in middle of oven until golden, about 5 minutes, and break into bite-size pieces. Rinse and drain beans in a colander.

In a kettle cover corn with water and bring to a boil. Drain corn and when cool enough to handle cut kernels from cobs into a bowl. Add pita pieces, beans, remaining ingredients, and salt and pepper to taste and toss to combine. Serves 4 as a main course.

Each serving about 407 calories, 10 grams fat (22% of calories from fat)

Grilled Shellfish and Potato Salad with Avocado Salsa, Scallion Oil, and Plum Coulis

For scallion oil
2 bunches scallions (about
    ½ pound)
½ cup olive oil

½ pound fingerling potatoes or other
    small boiling potatoes
3 tablespoons olive oil

¾ pound large shrimp (about 12)
¾ pound sea scallops (about 18)
avocado salsa (page 184)
4 cups loosely packed *mesclun* (mixed
    baby greens; about 4 ounces)
plum *coulis* (page 184)

Make scallion oil:
Chop enough scallions (including greens) to measure about 1¼ cups and in a blender purée with oil and salt and pepper to taste until smooth. Pour purée through a fine sieve into a bowl, pressing hard on solids. Discard solids. *Scallion oil may be made 1 day ahead and chilled, covered. Bring oil to room temperature before using.*

In a large saucepan cover potatoes with salted cold water by 1 inch and simmer until just tender, about 7 minutes. In a colander drain potatoes and rinse under cold water to stop cooking. Pat potatoes dry. *Potatoes may be prepared up to this point 1 day ahead and chilled, covered.* Halve potatoes lengthwise. In a bowl toss potatoes with 1 tablespoon olive oil and season with salt and pepper.

Peel and devein shrimp. Remove tough muscle from side of each scallop if necessary. Pat shellfish dry and in a bowl toss with remaining 2 tablespoons olive oil and salt and pepper to taste.

Prepare grill.

Grill potatoes, cut sides down, on an oiled rack set 5 to 6 inches over glowing coals 1 to 2 minutes on each side, or until lightly charred. Grill shrimp and scallops 2 minutes on each side, or until just cooked through and golden brown. (Alternatively, sauté potatoes and shellfish in a lightly oiled non-stick skillet in batches over moderately high heat.)

Spoon salsa onto centers of 6 plates and mound *mesclun* on top. Arrange shellfish and potatoes around salsa and greens. Drizzle shellfish and potatoes with some scallion oil and drizzle greens with some *coulis*. Serve remaining scallion oil and *coulis* on the side. Serves 6.

PHOTO ON PAGE 52

Avocado Salsa ☺

2 large shallots
3 garlic cloves
2 tablespoons chopped fresh coriander
10 medium tomatillos (about ½ pound)
2 firm-ripe California avocados
1 tablespoon fresh lime juice, or to taste

Finely chop shallots and mince garlic. In a bowl toss shallots and garlic with coriander. Discard husks from tomatillos and rinse tomatillos under warm water to remove stickiness. Chop tomatillos and add to shallot mixture, tossing to combine.

Peel and pit avocados and cut into ¾-inch pieces. Add avocados, lime juice, and salt and pepper to taste to tomatillo mixture, gently tossing until just combined. *Salsa may be made 4 hours ahead and chilled, its surface covered with plastic wrap.* Makes about 3 cups.

Plum Coulis ☺

2 ripe large red or purple plums (about ½ pound)
2 tablespoons water
½ teaspoon sugar to sweeten plums
　　if desired
freshly ground black pepper

Pit plums and coarsely chop. In a blender purée plums with water and pour through a fine sieve into a bowl, pressing hard on solids. Discard solids. *Coulis may be made 2 hours ahead and chilled, covered. Bring coulis to cool room temperature before serving.*

Just before serving, add sugar, pepper, and salt to taste. Makes about ⅔ cup.

Shrimp, Endive, and Watercress Salad

For court bouillon
1 onion
3 cups water
1 cup dry white wine
1 bay leaf
2 teaspoons salt
½ teaspoon black peppercorns

32 large shrimp (about 1½ pounds)
1 teaspoon caraway seeds
1 tablespoon white-wine vinegar
¼ teaspoon sugar
3 tablespoons olive oil
2 bunches watercress
3 Belgian endives

Make court bouillon:
In a kettle simmer all *court bouillon* ingredients 30 minutes.

Bring *court bouillon* to a boil and add shrimp. Boil shrimp until just cooked through, about 2 minutes. Drain shrimp in a large sieve set over a bowl and cool completely. Shell shrimp.

With a mortar and pestle or in a cleaned electric coffee/spice grinder finely crush or grind caraway seeds. In a bowl whisk together caraway, vinegar, sugar, and salt and pepper to taste until sugar is dissolved and whisk in oil until emulsified. Add shrimp and toss to coat.

Discard coarse stems from watercress and break remainder into bite-size sprigs. Halve endives and core. Cut endives lengthwise into ¼-inch-thick strips and add with watercress to shrimp mixture, tossing to combine well. Serves 8 as a first course or light entrée.

PHOTO ON PAGE 79

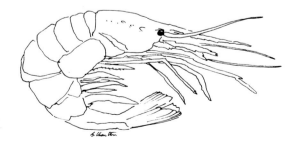

184

Shrimp, Fava Bean, and Asparagus Salad

For dressing
1½ teaspoons honey
1 teaspoon Dijon mustard
¼ cup fresh lime juice
1 tablespoon chopped fresh tarragon
    leaves
⅔ cup extra-virgin olive oil
1 tablespoon finely chopped fresh chives

2 pounds fresh fava beans, shelled
    (about 1 cup)
1 pound thin asparagus, trimmed and cut
    diagonally into 2-inch pieces
1 pound medium shrimp (about 30), shelled
    and deveined
3 cups *mâche** (lamb's-lettuce)
1½ cups *frisée** (French curly endive)

Garnish: 1 tablespoon finely chopped
    fresh chives

*available at specialty produce markets
    and some supermarkets

Make dressing:
In a small bowl whisk together honey, mustard, lime juice, and tarragon. Add olive oil in a stream, whisking until emulsified, and season with salt and pepper. *Dressing may be prepared up to this point 1 day ahead and chilled, covered. Bring dressing to room temperature before proceeding.* Stir in chives.

Have ready a large bowl of ice and cold water. In a large saucepan of boiling salted water cook favas until crisp-tender, about 2½ minutes, and transfer with a slotted spoon to ice water to stop cooking. Drain favas in a colander and gently peel away outer skins. Transfer favas to a large serving bowl.

Have ready another large bowl of ice and cold water. Return water in pan to a boil and cook asparagus until crisp-tender, about 3½ minutes. Transfer asparagus with slotted spoon to ice water to stop cooking. Drain asparagus in colander and pat dry with paper towels.

Return water in pan to a boil and cook shrimp until just cooked through, about 2 minutes. Transfer shrimp with slotted spoon to paper towels to cool.

In bowl with favas, toss together ⅓ cup dressing, asparagus, shrimp, *mâche, frisée,* and salt and pepper to taste. Drizzle salad with some of remaining dressing and garnish with chives. Serves 6 as a first course or light entrée.

PHOTO ON PAGE 23

Grilled Corn and Shrimp Salad

about 12 bamboo skewers
4 ears fresh corn
1 large red bell pepper
1 pound jumbo shrimp (21 to 25)
4 scallions
1 tablespoon fresh lemon juice
2 tablespoons balsamic vinegar
1 tablespoon extra-virgin olive oil
½ pound baby romaine leaves or *mesclun*
    (mixed baby greens)

Prepare grill and soak bamboo skewers in water 30 minutes.

Shuck corn and quarter bell pepper lengthwise. Shell and devein shrimp. Holding 2 skewers parallel and slightly apart, thread 4 shrimp onto each pair of skewers (this will make shrimp easier to turn on grill rack).

Grill corn on a lightly oiled rack set 5 to 6 inches over glowing coals, turning occasionally, until browned and tender, 8 to 10 minutes, and transfer to a large bowl. Grill bell pepper and scallions, turning occasionally, until browned and crisp-tender, about 5 minutes, and transfer to bowl. Grill shrimp until just cooked through, about 1½ minutes on each side, and transfer to bowl.

Cut kernels from cobs into another large bowl. Peel bell pepper and cut into ¼-inch-wide strips. Thinly slice scallions. Add bell pepper, scallions, shrimp, lemon juice, and salt and pepper to taste to corn and toss to combine. In a small bowl whisk together vinegar, oil, and salt and pepper to taste.

Arrange greens on 4 plates and top with corn mixture. Drizzle salads with vinaigrette. Serves 4 as a main course.

Each serving about 279 calories, 7 grams fat
(23% of calories from fat)

Macaroni Salad with Ham and Peas ☺

1 pound elbow macaroni
an 8-ounce piece cooked ham
2 celery ribs
¾ cup packed fresh parsley leaves
1 cup frozen tiny peas
½ cup mayonnaise
3 tablespoons fresh lemon juice
2 tablespoons milk plus additional
    if necessary
½ cup dried currants

Fill a 6-quart kettle three-fourths full with salted water and bring to a boil for macaroni. Cut ham and celery into ¼-inch dice and chop parsley.

Cook macaroni in boiling water 5 minutes, or until just tender (using package instructions as a guide), adding peas to cook for last 2 minutes. In a colander drain macaroni and peas and rinse under cold water. Drain macaroni and peas well.

In a large bowl whisk together mayonnaise and lemon juice and whisk in 2 tablespoons milk. Add macaroni, peas, ham, celery, parsley, currants, and salt and pepper to taste and toss to combine well. *Salad may be made 2 days ahead and chilled, covered. If salad looks dry, toss with additional milk before serving.* Serve salad at room temperature or chilled. Serves 8.

PHOTO ON PAGE 54

![SALADS WITH GREENS]

Arugula Salad with Garlic Balsamic Vinaigrette ☺

For garlic balsamic vinaigrette
2 garlic cloves, or to taste
¼ teaspoon salt
1 tablespoon minced shallot
2 tablespoons balsamic vinegar
¼ cup extra-virgin olive oil

3 bunches arugula (about 1 pound total)
1 pint vine-ripened cherry tomatoes,
    halved
1 carrot, shredded

Make vinaigrette:
Mince garlic and mash to a paste with salt. In a bowl whisk together garlic paste, shallot, and vinegar and add olive oil in a stream, whisking until emulsified. *Vinaigrette may be made 2 days ahead and chilled, covered. Bring vinaigrette to room temperature and whisk well before using.*

Trim arugula and tear leaves in half. In a bowl toss together arugula, tomatoes, and carrot.

Just before serving, drizzle vinaigrette over salad and toss with salt and pepper to taste. Serves 6.

PHOTO ON PAGE 42

Warm Camembert Croûtes with Dandelion Greens and Red Currants

1 tablespoon unsalted butter,
    softened
four ½-inch-thick slices from a *baguette*
1½ tablespoons minced shallot
1 tablespoon white-wine vinegar
1 teaspoon Dijon mustard
3 tablespoons extra-virgin olive oil
½ of an 8-ounce wheel Camembert cheese
5 cups baby dandelion greens* or other baby
    greens such as *mizuna* or arugula
½ cup fresh red currants* if desired

*available at specialty produce markets

Preheat oven to 450° F.
Butter baguette slices on 1 side and on a baking sheet toast in middle of oven 5 minutes, or until pale golden. *Toasts may be made 1 day ahead, cooled completely, and kept in a sealable plastic bag at room temperature.*
Preheat broiler.
In a large bowl whisk together shallot, vinegar, and mustard and add oil in a slow stream, whisking until emulsified. Cut Camembert into 4 wedges. Top each toast with a wedge of Camembert and on baking sheet broil about 4 inches from heat 5 minutes, or until cheese begins to melt. Add greens and currants to vinaigrette, tossing to coat.
Serve salad topped with Camembert *croûtes.* Serves 4.

PHOTO ON PAGE 28

Frisée and Watercress Salad with Jícama and Oranges

2 navel oranges
1 small garlic clove, chopped fine
2 teaspoons soy sauce
1 tablespoon balsamic vinegar
¼ cup extra-virgin olive oil
1 small head *frisée** (French curly endive)
1 small bunch watercress
3 ounces *jícama** (about ¼ small)

*available at specialty produce markets and
    some supermarkets

With a sharp knife cut peel and pith from oranges and cut sections free from membranes. Before discarding membranes squeeze out juice to total ¼ cup for vinaigrette.

In a small bowl whisk together orange juice, garlic, soy sauce, and vinegar. Add oil in a stream, whisking until emulsified, and season with salt and pepper. *Vinaigrette may be made 1 day ahead and chilled, covered.*

Discard any dark green outer leaves from *frisée*. Wash and dry inner leaves and tear into bite-size pieces. Discard coarse stems from watercress and wash and dry remainder. Peel *jícama* and cut into 2- by ⅛-inch sticks (about 1 cup).

In a large sealable plastic bag combine orange sections, *frisée*, watercress, and *jícama*. *Salad may be prepared up to this point 1 day ahead and chilled in plastic bag.*

Just before serving, add vinaigrette to plastic bag and shake to combine. Serves 2 generously.

Mâche, Pomegranate, and Walnut Salad ◔

1 pomegranate
½ teaspoon sugar
½ teaspoon red-wine vinegar
1 tablespoon extra-virgin olive oil
1 cup *mâche* (lamb's lettuce)
2 tablespoons walnut halves, chopped coarse

Halve pomegranate crosswise and reserve 2 tablespoons seeds from 1 half. Juice other pomegranate half with a citrus juicer (about 2 tablespoons juice).

In a very small saucepan simmer juice, sugar, and vinegar until reduced to about 1 tablespoon and cool to room temperature.

Divide juice mixture between 2 salad plates and drizzle with oil. Divide *mâche*, walnuts, and reserved seeds between plates and season with salt and pepper. Serves 2.

PHOTO ON PAGE 13

Boston Lettuce with Radishes and Lemon Dressing ◔

10 radishes
2 heads Boston lettuce
3 tablespoons fresh lemon juice
1 tablespoon minced shallot
2 teaspoons sugar
freshly ground black pepper to taste
½ cup olive oil

Cut radishes into very thin slices (preferably using a manual slicer). Tear large lettuce leaves into bite-size pieces, leaving smaller leaves whole, and in a large bowl toss all lettuce with radishes.

In a small bowl whisk together lemon juice, shallot, sugar, pepper, and salt to taste and add oil in a stream, whisking until emulsified. Drizzle dressing over salad and toss until combined well. Serves 10 to 12 as part of a Swedish Midsummer buffet.

PHOTO ON PAGE 38

Spinach and Lentil Salad with Oregon Blue Cheese
and Tart Cherry Vinaigrette

¾ cup green lentils
7 tablespoons red-wine vinegar
8 bacon slices (about 6 ounces)
¼ cup olive oil
⅓ cup finely chopped shallot
¼ cup water
½ cup dried unsweetened tart cherries*
   (about 3 ounces)
2 tablespoons sugar
3½ cups baby or regular spinach leaves
⅓ cup blue cheese (about 2 ounces), preferably
   Oregon Blue**

*available at specialty foods shops and by
   mail order from Chukar Cherries,
   tel. (800) 624-9544
**available at cheese shops and by mail
   order from Rogue River Valley
   Creamery, tel. (541) 664-2233

In a heavy saucepan cover lentils with water by 2 inches and simmer until just tender but not falling apart, about 15 minutes. Drain lentils well in a sieve. Rinse lentils under cold running water to stop cooking and drain well. In a bowl toss lentils with 2 tablespoons vinegar and salt and pepper to taste. *Lentils may be made 2 days ahead and chilled, covered. Bring lentils to room temperature before proceeding.*

In a skillet cook bacon over moderate heat until crisp and with tongs transfer to paper towels to drain. Crumble bacon.

In cleaned saucepan heat 2 tablespoons oil over moderate heat until hot but not smoking and cook shallot, stirring, until golden brown. Stir in water, cherries, sugar, and remaining 5 tablespoons vinegar and simmer, stirring occasionally, until liquid is reduced by about half, about 10 minutes. Reduce heat to low and whisk in remaining 2 tablespoons oil in a slow stream until emulsified. Season vinaigrette with salt and pepper.

Add half of vinaigrette to lentils and toss well. In another bowl toss spinach with half of lentil mixture, half of bacon, half of blue cheese, remaining vinaigrette, and salt and pepper to taste.

Divide remaining lentil mixture among 6 plates and top with spinach mixture. Sprinkle salads with remaining crumbled bacon and cheese. Serves 6 as a first course.

PHOTO ON PAGE 71

Mesclun Salad with Celery and Croutons ☉

1 cup ¾-inch cubes crusty bread
1 tablespoon balsamic vinegar
2 teaspoons extra-virgin olive oil
½ teaspoon Dijon mustard
3 celery ribs
2 heads Bibb lettuce
4 cups loosely packed *mesclun*
   (mixed baby greens)

Preheat oven to 300° F.

On a baking sheet bake bread cubes in middle of oven until lightly toasted and let cool. In a small bowl whisk together vinegar, oil, and mustard and season with salt and pepper. Cut celery diagonally into ½-inch slices. Tear Bibb lettuce into bite-size pieces. In a large bowl toss all greens, celery, and croutons with dressing and season with salt and pepper. Serves 4.

🍃 Each serving about 79 calories, 3 grams fat
(38% of calories from fat)

Slivered Endive Salad ☉

2 Belgian endives
2 tablespoons sour cream
1½ teaspoons white-wine vinegar
1 teaspoon finely chopped fresh
   tarragon leaves or ¼ teaspoon
   dried tarragon, crumbled,
   or to taste
¼ teaspoon sugar
freshly ground black pepper
   to taste

Trim Belgian endives and separate leaves. Cut leaves lengthwise into thin strips and in a small bowl toss with remaining ingredients and salt to taste. Serves 2.

VEGETABLE SALADS AND SLAWS

Beet and Arugula Salad ◌

½ pound beets without leaves (about 3 medium)
1 small bunch arugula
1 tablespoon white-wine vinegar
¼ cup olive oil

Peel beets and cut into ½-inch wedges. In a steamer set over boiling water steam beets until tender, about 10 minutes, and transfer to a bowl. Discard coarse stems from arugula. Wash arugula well and dry. In a bowl whisk together vinegar and salt and pepper to taste and whisk in oil until emulsified. Pour half of vinaigrette over beets and toss well. To vinaigrette remaining in bowl add arugula and toss well. Arrange beets and arugula on 2 plates. Serves 2.

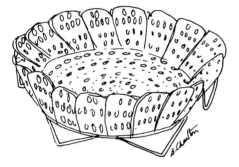

Corn and Tomato Salad with Lemon Thyme and Roasted Poblano Chili

1 fresh *poblano* chili*
1 medium zucchini
2 scallions
5 garlic cloves
¾ pound assorted vine-ripened cherry tomatoes
   (about 1 pint)
2 tablespoons olive oil
4 cups fresh corn (cut from about 8 ears)
2 tablespoons small fresh lemon thyme sprigs
1 tablespoon chopped fresh coriander

*available at Latino markets and some specialty produce markets

Roast and peel *poblano* (procedure on page 96).
Finely chop *poblano* and zucchini and thinly slice scallions. Mince garlic and halve tomatoes. In a large non-stick skillet heat oil over moderately high heat until hot but not smoking and sauté zucchini and corn with salt and pepper to taste, stirring, until corn is golden brown, about 5 minutes. Reduce heat to moderate and stir in *poblano*, scallions, garlic, and thyme. Cook mixture, stirring, 1 minute. Transfer vegetables to a bowl and immediately add tomatoes and coriander, tossing well. Cool corn salad. *Corn salad may be made 1 day ahead and chilled, covered. Bring salad to room temperature before serving.* Serves 4.

PHOTO ON PAGE 58

Dilled Carrot Salad ◌

1 tablespoon vegetable oil
1 tablespoon white-wine vinegar
2 teaspoons Dijon mustard
1 tablespoon chopped fresh dill sprigs
1 teaspoon sugar
1 bunch carrots (about ¾ pound)

In a bowl whisk together all ingredients except carrots and season with salt and pepper. In a food processor fitted with fine-shredding disk or using large holes of a hand grater grate carrots and stir into vinaigrette. Serves 2.

Cucumber Salad with Peanuts ◌

1 English cucumber (about 1 pound)
¼ cup seasoned rice vinegar
1 fresh *jalapeño* chili, or to taste, minced
   (wear rubber gloves)
2 tablespoons finely chopped salted
   peanuts

Seed English cucumber and cut into ¼-inch dice and in a small bowl stir together with remaining ingredients. Season salad with salt and pepper. Serves 2.

189

Pickled Cucumber, Squash, and Red Pepper Salad ◌+

For pickling liquid
3 cups water
1½ cups cider vinegar
6 tablespoons sugar
1½ teaspoons salt
½ teaspoon whole black peppercorns
½ teaspoon coriander seeds
½ teaspoon mustard seeds
¼ teaspoon celery seeds
1 whole clove

3 small yellow squash
1 large cucumber
2 red bell peppers
½ large sweet onion

Make pickling liquid:
In a saucepan simmer pickling liquid ingredients 3 minutes and cool.

Halve squash lengthwise and cut crosswise into ½-inch-thick slices. Halve cucumber lengthwise and cut crosswise into ¼-inch-thick slices. Cut bell peppers lengthwise into ¼-inch-wide strips and cut onion into ¼-inch-thick slices. In a large bowl combine vegetables and pickling liquid. *Chill salad, covered, at least 1 day and up to 4.* Before serving, drain salad. Serves 8.

PHOTO ON PAGE 54

Fennel, Grapefruit, and Prosciutto Salad ◌

2 tablespoons pine nuts
1 tablespoon extra-virgin olive oil
1 tablespoon white-wine vinegar
½ teaspoon Dijon mustard
1 small pink grapefruit
½ fennel bulb (sometimes called anise)
1 small head *radicchio*
¼ pound thinly sliced prosciutto

Finely chop pine nuts and in a small heavy skillet cook in oil over moderate heat, stirring occasionally, until golden. Remove skillet from heat and whisk in vinegar and mustard.

With a sharp knife cut peel and pith from pink grapefruit. Cut fruit sections free from membranes and coarsely chop fruit. Trim fennel stalks flush with bulb and cut bulb lengthwise into very thin slices. Trim and discard core from slices. Thinly slice *radicchio*. In a bowl toss grapefruit, fennel, and *radicchio* with vinaigrette.

Divide prosciutto between 2 plates and top with salad. Serves 2.

Fennel, Grape, and Gorgonzola Salad ◌

1 large fennel bulb (sometimes called anise)
2 tablespoons extra-virgin olive oil
1 tablespoon fresh lemon juice
½ cup halved black grapes, seeded
2 ounces Gorgonzola cheese, crumbled
  (about ½ cup)
1 cup thinly sliced *radicchio*
1 cup thinly sliced romaine

Trim fennel stalks flush with bulb and discard any tough outer layers. Halve bulb lengthwise, discard core, and slice fennel thin. In a bowl toss together fennel, oil, lemon juice, and salt and pepper to taste and let stand 10 minutes. Add halved grapes, Gorgonzola, *radicchio*, and romaine and toss well to combine. Serves 2.

Tomato and Herb Salad ◌

For vinaigrette
¼ cup fresh lime juice
1 teaspoon salt
1 teaspoon sugar
freshly ground black pepper to taste
½ cup extra-virgin olive oil
4 pounds large vine-ripened tomatoes (about 8)
1 cup packed flat-leafed parsley leaves
1 cup packed coriander leaves
½ cup thinly sliced mint leaves
½ cup thinly sliced scallions

Make vinaigrette:
In a small bowl whisk together lime juice, salt, sugar, and pepper and add oil in a stream, whisking.

Cut tomatoes into ½-inch-thick slices and arrange decoratively on a platter. Drizzle tomatoes with about two thirds vinaigrette. In a bowl combine herbs and scallions and toss with remaining vinaigrette.

Mound herb mixture on top of tomato slices. Serves 16.

PHOTO ON PAGE 47

All-American Potato Salad

2½ pounds small boiling potatoes (white, red, or fingerling)
3 tablespoons cider vinegar, or to taste
5 hard-boiled large eggs
¾ cup mayonnaise
2 tablespoons Dijon mustard
½ cup chopped sweet onion
3 large celery ribs

Suggested additions: dill pickle, fresh chives, poppy seeds, crab meat, or corn

In a large saucepan cover potatoes with salted cold water by 1 inch and simmer, covered, until just tender, about 15 to 30 minutes, depending on size of potatoes. In a colander drain potatoes and cool to warm.

With a sharp knife peel warm potatoes and cut into ⅓-inch-thick slices. In a bowl immediately toss potatoes with vinegar. In a bowl mash yolks and stir in mayonnaise, mustard, and onion. Chop whites and celery and gently toss together with potatoes, mayonnaise mixture, and salt and pepper to taste. Serve potato salad chilled or at room temperature. Serves 6.

Zucchini with Sour Cream and Dill ◌+

¾ cup sour cream
½ cup thinly sliced sweet onion
1 tablespoon chopped fresh dill leaves
1 teaspoon sugar
1 pound zucchini (about 2 large)

In a bowl stir together all ingredients except zucchini until combined well. Cut zucchini crosswise into ⅛-inch-thick rounds and toss with sour cream mixture and salt to taste until combined well. *Chill zucchini mixture, covered, at least 1 hour and up to 8.* Serves 4.

Jícama and Red Onion Slaw ◌

1 small *jícama** (about ¾ pound)
1 carrot
¾ cup thinly sliced red onion
1 tablespoon white-wine vinegar
2 teaspoons Dijon mustard
2 tablespoons olive oil

*available at Latino markets, specialty produce markets, and many supermarkets

Peel *jícama* and carrot and with the fine shredding disk of a food processor shred coarse. (Alternatively, peeled vegetables may be cut into fine julienne strips.) Separate onion into rings. In a bowl whisk together vinegar, mustard, and oil until emulsified. Add *jícama*, carrot, onion, and salt and pepper to taste and toss well. Serves 2.

SAUCES

Almond Brown Butter ☺

5 tablespoons unsalted butter
⅓ cup sliced blanched almonds, toasted
1 tablespoon fresh lemon juice

In a small saucepan melt butter over moderately low heat and continue to heat until golden brown with a nutlike fragrance. (Bottom of pan will be covered with brown specks.) Pour butter through a sieve lined with a dampened paper towel into a bowl and discard solids. In a small skillet heat brown butter, almonds, and lemon juice until heated through.

Serve sauce over fish, chicken, rice, or vegetables such as asparagus, broccoli, or green beans. Makes about ½ cup.

Plum Chutney

2½ pounds Italian prune plums
1 cup packed light brown sugar
1 tablespoon minced peeled fresh gingerroot
1 large garlic clove, minced
1 teaspoon salt
1 teaspoon paprika
1 teaspoon ground coriander seeds
1 teaspoon ground allspice
½ cup white-wine vinegar
½ cup fresh lime juice

Sterilize four 8-ounce Mason-type jars (procedure on page 278).

Quarter and pit plums and cut into ¼-inch pieces. In a 2-quart heavy saucepan stir together plums and remaining chutney ingredients and bring to a boil over moderate heat. Lower heat and simmer mixture, stirring occasionally, 15 minutes. Pour chutney into jars. Wipe rims with a dampened cloth and seal jars with lids. Put jars in a water-bath canner or on a rack set in a deep kettle. Cover jars with hot water by 2 inches and boil, covered, 5 minutes. Transfer jars with tongs to a rack and cool completely. Store chutney in a cool, dark place. Makes four 8-ounce jars.

Cranberry Kumquat Compote ☺

¼ pound kumquats (about 10)
a 12-ounce bag fresh or unthawed frozen
    cranberries (about 3½ cups)
1 cup water
1 cup sugar

With a sharp thin knife thinly slice kumquats crosswise, removing seeds. Pick over cranberries. In a small saucepan bring water with sugar to a boil and simmer, stirring until sugar is dissolved, 5 minutes. Add kumquats and simmer 5 minutes. With a slotted spoon transfer kumquats to a bowl. Add cranberries to syrup and simmer 10 minutes. Cool mixture completely. *Cranberry mixture and kumquats may be made 3 days ahead and chilled in separate airtight containers (so kumquats will retain their bright color).*

Just before serving, stir kumquats into cranberry mixture. Makes about 3½ cups.

PHOTO ON PAGE 67

Mixed Olive Relish

2 cups mixed brine-cured black and
    green olives
½ cup drained pimiento-stuffed green olives
⅓ cup finely chopped red onion
2 tablespoons extra-virgin olive oil
1 tablespoon fresh lemon juice, or to taste
1 tablespoon drained capers, chopped
⅓ cup finely chopped fresh flat-leafed
    parsley leaves

Working with several brine-cured olives at a time and using flat side of a large heavy knife, press olives to crush them and remove pits. Coarsely chop all olives and in a bowl toss with onion, oil, lemon juice, and capers. *Relish may be prepared up to this point 2 days ahead and chilled, covered. Bring relish to room temperature before serving.* Stir in parsley. Makes about 2 cups.

PHOTO ON PAGE 42

When making entire ¡Taquiza! menu, quadruple this salsa recipe.

Fresh Tomato Salsa ☺

½ pound plum tomatoes
2 fresh *serrano* chilies*
½ cup finely chopped white onion
¼ cup chopped fresh coriander leaves
1 teaspoon coarse salt, or to taste
3 tablespoons water

*available at Latino markets, some specialty
  foods shops, and some supermarkets

Cut tomatoes in half crosswise and seed if desired. Finely chop tomatoes and transfer with any juices to a bowl. Wearing rubber gloves, finely chop chilies, including seeds. Stir chilies into tomatoes with remaining ingredients. *Salsa may be made 6 hours ahead and chilled, covered.* Makes 2 cups.

PHOTO ON PAGE 48

a.charlton

Blackberry-Raspberry Sauce ☺

½ cup sugar
⅓ cup water
1 cup picked-over blackberries
1 cup picked-over raspberries
1 tablespoon fresh lemon juice

In a small saucepan bring sugar and water to a boil, stirring until sugar is dissolved, and in a blender pulse together with blackberries, raspberries, and lemon juice until berries are chopped. Cool sauce. *Sauce may be made 2 days ahead and chilled, covered.* Makes about 2 cups.

PHOTO ON PAGE 57

Chocolate Sauce ☺

6 ounces fine-quality bittersweet chocolate
  (not unsweetened)
½ stick (¼ cup) unsalted butter
⅓ cup milk

Chop chocolate and cut butter into pieces. In a double boiler or a metal bowl set over a saucepan of barely simmering water melt chocolate and butter, stirring until smooth. Remove top of double boiler or bowl from heat and stir milk into chocolate mixture until combined. *Sauce may be made 3 days ahead and chilled, covered. Reheat sauce over low heat before serving.* Makes about 1½ cups.

PHOTO ON PAGE 56

Marshmallow Sauce ☺

1½ cups Marshmallow Fluff
3 tablespoons water

In a small saucepan heat Marshmallow Fluff and water over moderately low heat, stirring constantly until combined well. Cool sauce. *Sauce may be made 4 hours ahead and kept, covered, at room temperature.* Makes about 1 cup.

PHOTO ON PAGE 56

Almond Praline ○

1 cup sugar
1 cup slivered almonds
  (about 6 ounces)

Line a baking sheet with foil. In a dry heavy saucepan cook sugar over moderately low heat, stirring slowly with a fork (to help sugar melt evenly), until melted and pale golden. Cook caramel, without stirring, swirling pan, until deep golden. Add almonds, stirring until coated well, and cook, stirring, until fragrant, about 1 minute. Working quickly, with a metal spatula spread mixture about ¼ inch thick onto foil and cool until set, about 3 minutes. *Chill praline on foil until hard, about 15 minutes.* Chop praline. *Praline may be made 1 week ahead and kept in an airtight container in a cool, dry place.* Makes about 2 cups.

PHOTO ON PAGE 56

Crystallized Mint Leaves ○+

1 large egg white*
1 tablespoon water
1 cup packed fresh mint leaves
¼ cup superfine granulated sugar

*if egg safety is a problem in your area,
  substitute 2 teaspoons dried egg whites
  (such as Just Whites, available at some
  supermarkets and by mail order from
  New York Cake & Baking Distributors,
  tel. 800-942-2539) reconstituted by stirring
  together with 2 tablespoons water

In a small bowl stir together egg white or reconstituted dried whites and water and brush onto fresh mint leaves to lightly coat both sides. In a bowl toss mint leaves with sugar and transfer to a rack. *Let mint leaves stand about 6 hours, or until dry. Leaves may be made 1 day ahead and kept in an airtight container at room temperature.* Makes about 1½ cups.

PHOTO ON PAGE 57

Chocolate Curls ○

3 ounces fine-quality bittersweet chocolate
  (not unsweetened)
3 ounces fine-quality milk chocolate

Chop bittersweet chocolate and in a double boiler or a small metal bowl set over a saucepan of barely simmering water heat until melted. With a metal spatula spread melted chocolate onto a baking sheet (not non-stick) as thinly and evenly as possible. Cool chocolate until firm to the touch but not hard. (Alternatively, chill melted chocolate on sheet; if it becomes too hard, let it soften slightly at room temperature.) With a pastry scraper or metal spatula held at an angle scrape chocolate slowly from sheet, letting it curl. Carefully transfer curls as formed to a plate lined with waxed paper. Make more curls with milk chocolate in same manner. *Chocolate curls may be made 1 day ahead and chilled, loosely covered.* Makes about 2 cups.

PHOTO ON PAGE 56

Candied Orange and Lemon Zest

2 navel oranges
4 lemons
½ cup sugar
½ cup water

Remove zest from oranges and lemons with a vegetable peeler in long ½-inch-wide pieces and cut pieces lengthwise into julienne strips, reserving orange and lemon zests separately.

In a small saucepan cover orange zest with water and bring to a boil. Simmer zest 5 minutes and drain in a sieve, discarding liquid. Repeat procedure with orange zest 2 more times. In pan bring orange zest, ¼ cup sugar, and ¼ cup water to a boil over moderate heat and simmer until liquid is reduced to a thick syrup. Cool orange zest in syrup. Make candied lemon zest in same manner. *Zests may be made 1 week ahead and chilled in an airtight container.* Makes about ½ cup of each zest.

PHOTO ON PAGE 57

DESSERTS

Chocolate Tangerine Roulade

For cake
6 ounces fine-quality bittersweet chocolate
   (not unsweetened)
5 large eggs, separated
½ cup sugar
1 tablespoon finely grated fresh orange zest
½ teaspoon salt

5 tangerines or 3 navel oranges
1 cup heavy cream
3 tablespoons orange liqueur such as triple sec
Dutch-process cocoa powder for dusting

Make cake:
Preheat oven to 400° F. Butter a 15- by 10½-inch jelly-roll pan and line with wax paper or parchment. Butter and flour paper, knocking out excess flour.

In a metal bowl set over a saucepan of barely simmering water melt chocolate, stirring until smooth, and remove pan from heat.

In a bowl with an electric mixer beat yolks, sugar, zest, and salt until thick, pale, and mixture forms a ribbon when beaters are lifted. Beat in melted chocolate until just combined. In another bowl with cleaned beaters beat whites until they just hold soft peaks. Stir one fourth whites into chocolate mixture to lighten and fold in remaining whites gently but thoroughly. Pour batter into jelly-roll pan, spreading evenly with a spatula, and bake in middle of oven 10 minutes, or until cake is springy to the touch. Cool cake in pan, covered with a dampened kitchen towel.

With a sharp knife cut peel and pith from tangerines or oranges and cut sections free from membranes. In a bowl with an electric mixer beat cream with liqueur until it just holds stiff peaks and fold in fruit sections until just combined.

Assemble roulade:
Put a large sheet of foil (about 20 by 15 inches)

on a work surface and lightly dust with cocoa powder. Invert cake onto foil and gently peel off paper. Spoon cream mixture evenly onto cake. Beginning with a short side and using foil as a guide, roll up *roulade* jelly-roll fashion and transfer to a platter, seam side down.

Dust *roulade* with cocoa powder. *Roulade may be made 1 day ahead and chilled, loosely covered.*

PHOTO ON PAGE 35

Lemon Cupcakes with Lemon Cream ◔

¾ cup cake flour (not self-rising)
½ teaspoon baking powder
⅛ teaspoon salt
2½ teaspoons freshly grated lemon zest
½ stick (¼ cup) unsalted butter, softened
½ cup plus 1 tablespoon sugar
1 tablespoon plus 2 teaspoons fresh lemon juice
2 large eggs
¼ cup plus 1 tablespoon cream cheese
   (about 2 ounces), softened

Preheat oven to 350° F. and line four ½-cup muffin tins with paper liners.

Into a bowl sift together flour, baking powder, and salt and whisk in 2 teaspoons zest. In another bowl with a fork blend butter, ½ cup sugar, and 1 tablespoon plus 1 teaspoon juice until smooth. With a wooden spoon beat in eggs 1 at a time until smooth. Stir butter mixture into flour mixture until batter is combined well.

In a small bowl with a fork stir together cream cheese and remaining ½ teaspoon zest, 1 tablespoon sugar, and 1 teaspoon juice until lemon cream is smooth.

Spoon 3 level tablespoons batter and about 1 tablespoon lemon cream into each paper liner. Spoon remaining batter over lemon cream, smoothing tops. Bake cupcakes in middle of oven 20 minutes, or until golden brown, and transfer to a rack to cool. Makes 4 cupcakes.

To make the very thin layers for this torte, the batter is spread on inverted cake pans. It is important that the batter be spread evenly and that the layers not be overbaked.

Chocolate Orange Dobostorte

For torte layers
6 large eggs
¾ cup sugar
1 teaspoon vanilla
1 cup cake flour (not self-rising)
¼ teaspoon salt
a pinch cream of tartar
For orange glaze
1⅓ cups sweet orange marmalade
    (about 16 ounces)
2 tablespoons Grand Marnier or other
    orange-flavored liqueur

¾ cup hazelnuts (about 3 ounces)
chocolate buttercream (recipe follows)
For caramel
½ cup water
1 cup sugar
¼ teaspoon cream of tartar

Make torte layers:

Preheat oven to 350° F. Invert three 8-inch round cake pans (do not use dark metal or non-stick pans) onto a work surface and butter bottoms (now on top; see illustration) and rounded edges well. Dust pans with flour, knocking off excess.

Separate whites and yolks of eggs into 2 large bowls. With an electric mixer beat together yolks and ½ cup sugar until thick and pale and mixture forms a ribbon when beaters are lifted, about 5 minutes. Beat in vanilla until just combined. Sift together flour and salt over yolk mixture and fold in gently but thoroughly. With cleaned beaters beat whites with a pinch salt until foamy. Add cream of tartar and beat whites until they just hold soft peaks. Gradually beat in remaining ¼ cup sugar, 1 tablespoon at a time, beating whites until they just hold stiff peaks. Stir one third whites into yolk mixture until just combined and fold in remaining whites gently but thoroughly.

Spread ½ cup batter with a rubber spatula or a knife on each of the 3 pan outside bottoms (now the tops) just to edges and bake on same rack in middle of oven until just cooked through and just turning pale golden at edges, about 6½ minutes. Cool layers on pans on racks 1 minute and loosen layers with a long, thin-bladed knife. Carefully transfer layers to racks to cool completely. Cool pans completely and wipe clean with paper towels. Make 6 more layers in same manner, buttering and flouring pans for each batch. (Batter should not stand any longer than necessary because it will begin to lose volume.) *Torte layers may be made 1 day before assembling torte and kept at room temperature, stacked between sheets of wax paper and wrapped in plastic wrap. Carefully remove wax paper before assembling torte.*

Make orange glaze:

In a small saucepan heat marmalade over moderate heat, stirring, until melted and pour through a sieve into a bowl, pressing hard on solids. Stir in liqueur. *Glaze may be made 1 day before assembling torte and chilled, covered.*

In a baking pan toast hazelnuts in one layer in middle of a 350° F. oven 10 to 15 minutes, or until lightly colored and skins are blistered. Wrap nuts in a kitchen towel and let steam 1 minute. Rub nuts in towel to remove loose skins (do not worry about skins that do not come off) and cool. Finely chop nuts.

Assemble torte:

Trim edges of torte layers if necessary so that layers are all the same size and reserve best layer, wrapped in plastic wrap, for caramel top. On a cake stand arrange 1 layer, using a small dab buttercream to anchor it to cake stand, and spread with 3 heaping tablespoons buttercream. Spread a second layer with

2 tablespoons orange glaze and put layer, orange side down, on buttercream-spread layer. Spread top with 3 heaping tablespoons buttercream. Continue to layer remaining torte layers (except reserved layer) in same manner. After spreading eighth layer with buttercream, spread some remaining buttercream around side of torte to coat and chill torte 5 minutes to firm buttercream slightly. Press some hazelnuts on side of torte to cover it and reserve remaining buttercream and nuts. *Torte may be made up to this point 1 day ahead and chilled, covered with an inverted bowl or a cake keeper. Chill reserved torte layer, wrapped in plastic wrap; chill reserved buttercream, covered; keep reserved nuts, covered, at room temperature. Bring torte, reserved torte layer, and buttercream to room temperature before proceeding.*

Put reserved torte layer on a buttered rack set over a sheet of foil and have ready a buttered knife.

Make caramel:

In a 3- to 4-quart heavy saucepan cook water, sugar, and cream of tartar over moderate heat, stirring and washing down sugar crystals clinging to side of pan with a brush dipped in cold water, until sugar is dissolved. Boil syrup, without stirring, until it just turns pale golden and continue to cook, without stirring, swirling pan, until syrup is a deep golden caramel.

Remove pan from heat and when caramel stops boiling immediately pour enough over torte layer to thinly coat. Working very quickly, draw knife through caramel down to torte, marking off 8 wedges, but not cutting through torte. (The lines will make it easier to cut torte without shattering hardened caramel; if caramel becomes too hard, heat knife blade on top of stove to facilitate marking.) Carefully loosen caramel-coated torte layer from rack using knife and transfer to a clean rack to cool completely.

Finish torte:

Arrange caramel-coated layer on top of torte. Fill gap between top 2 torte layers with some reserved buttercream using a small icing spatula or a dinner knife, smoothing it, and press some reserved nuts up around side of torte near top. *Torte may be fully assembled 4 hours ahead and chilled, covered with inverted bowl or cake keeper. Bring torte to room temperature before serving.* Serves 8.

PHOTO ON PAGE 81

Chocolate Buttercream

4 ounces fine-quality bittersweet chocolate
  (not unsweetened)
3 sticks (1½ cups) unsalted butter
6 tablespoons water
¾ cup sugar
3 large egg whites
¼ teaspoon cream of tartar
6 tablespoons unsweetened cocoa powder

Chop bittersweet chocolate. In a metal bowl set over a saucepan of barely simmering water melt chocolate, stirring until smooth, and let cool. Cut butter into pieces and soften to cool room temperature.

In a 1½-quart heavy saucepan bring water and sugar to a boil, stirring until sugar is dissolved. Boil syrup, without stirring, until a candy thermometer registers 248° F.

While syrup is boiling, in a bowl with an electric mixer beat whites with a pinch salt until foamy and beat in cream of tartar. Beat whites until they just hold stiff peaks and beat in hot syrup in a stream (try to avoid pouring onto beaters and side of bowl). Beat mixture at medium speed until *completely* cool, 5 to 10 minutes. Beat in butter, 1 piece at a time, beating until mixture is thickened and smooth. (Buttercream will at first appear very thin and at some point look like it is breaking but, as more butter is beaten in, it will thicken and become glossy and smooth.) Beat in cocoa powder, melted chocolate, and a pinch salt, beating until smooth. *Buttercream may be made 2 days ahead and chilled in an airtight container. Bring buttercream to room temperature and beat before using. (If buttercream is too cold when beaten it will not be glossy and smooth.)* Makes about 3¾ cups.

197

Rhubarb Raspberry Meringue Cake

For meringue layers
4 large egg whites
¼ teaspoon cream of tartar
1 cup sugar
For rhubarb purée
1 pound fresh rhubarb, trimmed and cut
    into ½-inch pieces (3 cups total)
½ cup sugar
1 tablespoon water
2 teaspoons cornstarch

1 cup well-chilled heavy cream
2½ cups picked-over fresh raspberries

Accompaniment: rhubarb raspberry sauce
    (recipe follows)

Make meringue layers:
Let egg whites stand at room temperature 1 hour.
Preheat oven to 250° F. Line 2 baking sheets with parchment paper and draw three 10- by 4½-inch rectangles on parchment (2 on one sheet and 1 on other). Turn parchment over.

In a large bowl with an electric mixer beat whites with cream of tartar and a pinch salt until they hold soft peaks. Gradually add sugar, beating, and beat until meringue holds stiff, glossy peaks.

Transfer meringue to a pastry bag fitted with a ½-inch fluted tip and pipe evenly onto parchment rectangles, filling them in. (Alternatively, divide meringue among parchment rectangles, spreading with a spatula to fill them in.)

Bake meringue layers in upper and lower thirds of oven, switching position of sheets halfway through baking, 1 hour, or until crisp and firm. (If weather is humid, cooking time may be longer.) Cool meringue layers completely on baking sheets in turned-off oven or on a rack and carefully peel off parchment. *Meringue layers may be made 1 day ahead, wrapped well in plastic wrap or sealed in an airtight container, and stored in a cool, dry place.*
Make rhubarb purée:
In a heavy saucepan stir together purée ingredients and simmer, stirring occasionally, until rhubarb is softened, about 12 minutes. Cool mixture slightly and in a blender or food processor purée until smooth (use caution when blending hot mixtures). Transfer purée to a bowl and cool. *Purée may be made 2 days ahead and chilled, covered. Bring purée to room temperature before proceeding.*
Just before serving, assemble cake:
Lightly whip heavy cream.

On a large platter arrange 1 meringue layer and spread evenly with ½ cup rhubarb purée. Spread half of whipped cream evenly over purée and top with ¾ cup raspberries. Repeat procedure with another meringue layer, ½ cup purée, remaining whipped cream, and ¾ cup raspberries. Top with remaining meringue layer.

Garnish cake with remaining cup raspberries and serve with rhubarb raspberry sauce.

PHOTO ON PAGE 25

Rhubarb Raspberry Sauce ☺

½ cup sugar
½ cup water
¾ pound fresh rhubarb, trimmed and cut into
    ¼-inch-thick slices (2 cups total)
1 cup picked-over fresh raspberries, quartered

In a saucepan simmer sugar and water until sugar is dissolved. Add rhubarb and simmer, stirring occasionally, 5 minutes. Transfer mixture to a bowl and cool. Stir in raspberries. *Sauce may be made 1 day ahead and chilled, covered. Bring sauce to room temperature before serving.* Makes 1½ cups.

This cake must be assembled at least 8 hours before serving to allow the layers to absorb juices.

Strawberry Cream Cake

For strawberry filling
2 pounds strawberries (about 3 pints)
⅓ cup sugar
1 tablespoon fresh lemon juice
For custard
3 large egg yolks
¼ cup sugar
1 cup half-and-half
1½ tablespoons cornstarch
1 tablespoon Punsch (Swedish liqueur) if desired
For cake layers
1½ cups cake flour (not self-rising)
1 teaspoon baking powder
½ teaspoon salt
9 large eggs
1¼ cups sugar
½ stick (¼ cup) unsalted butter, melted and cooled
1 teaspoon vanilla
For whipped cream frosting
1½ cups well-chilled heavy cream
2 tablespoons sugar

Garnish: strawberries

Make filling:
Trim and slice strawberries and in a bowl stir together with sugar and lemon juice. *Let strawberry mixture stand at room temperature, stirring occasionally, 4 hours.* In a large sieve set over a bowl drain strawberry mixture and reserve strawberries and liquid separately.

Make custard:
In a saucepan whisk together all custard ingredients except Punsch until combined well. Bring mixture to a boil over moderate heat, whisking constantly, and simmer, whisking constantly, 1 minute. Whisk Punsch (if using) into custard and transfer to a heatproof dish. Cool custard, its surface covered with wax paper. *Chill custard, covered, at least 3 hours, or until cold, and up to 2 days.*

Make cake layers:
Preheat oven to 350° F. Butter two 9- by 2-inch round cake pans and line bottoms with rounds of wax paper. Butter paper and dust pans with flour, knocking out excess flour.

Into a small bowl sift together flour, baking powder, and salt. In bowl of a standing electric mixer combine eggs and sugar and beat, beginning at moderate speed and gradually increasing to high speed, for a total of 9 to 10 minutes, or until very thick and pale and mixture forms a ribbon when beaters are lifted. Transfer egg mixture to a large bowl (for ease of folding).

Sift one third flour mixture over egg mixture and with a large rubber spatula fold in gently but thoroughly. Sift and fold remaining flour mixture into egg mixture in 2 more batches in same manner. Fold in butter and vanilla gently but thoroughly.

Divide batter between pans, smoothing tops, and bake in middle of oven, rotating pans on oven rack after 15 minutes (to ensure even baking), a total of 25 to 30 minutes, or until cake is springy to the touch and a tester comes out clean. Cool cake layers in pans on racks 10 minutes and invert onto racks. Peel off paper and cool completely. *Layers may be made 1 day ahead of cake assembly and kept, wrapped tightly in plastic wrap, at room temperature.*

Assemble cake:
With a long serrated knife halve each cake layer horizontally to make a total of 4 layers. Put 1 cake layer, cut side up, on a serving plate and top with half of reserved strawberry slices, arranging them in an even layer. Drizzle half of reserved strawberry liquid evenly over berries.

Top filling with second cake layer, cut side down. Whisk custard until smooth and spread layer evenly with custard. Top custard with third cake layer, cut side up. Spread layer evenly with remaining strawberries and drizzle with remaining strawberry liquid. Top filling with remaining cake layer, cut side down. *Chill cake, covered with plastic wrap, at least 8 hours and up to 1 day.*

Make frosting:
In a chilled bowl beat cream with sugar until cream just holds stiff peaks.

Spread frosting over top and sides of cake. *Cake may be frosted 4 hours ahead and chilled. Bring cake to cool room temperature before serving.*

Garnish top of cake with strawberries.

PHOTO ON PAGE 39

Walnut Maple Torte with Maple Meringue Frosting

For cake layers
1 cup walnuts
1 cup cake flour (not self-rising)
1½ teaspoons baking powder
1 teaspoon instant espresso powder
1 tablespoon boiling-hot water
1½ sticks (¾ cup) unsalted butter, softened
¾ cup sugar
3 large eggs
1½ tablespoons vegetable oil

6 ounces cream cheese, softened
5 tablespoons pure maple syrup
For meringue frosting
2 large egg whites
1 cup pure maple syrup
¼ teaspoon cream of tartar

Make cake layers:

Preheat oven to 350° F. and butter and flour two 8-inch round cake pans, knocking out excess flour.

On a baking sheet toast walnuts in middle of oven until 1 shade darker, about 8 minutes, and cool. In a food processor grind walnuts fine.

Into a bowl sift together flour, baking powder, and a pinch salt. In a small cup stir together espresso powder and water. In a large bowl with an electric mixer beat together butter and sugar until light and fluffy and add eggs, 1 at a time, beating well after each addition. Beat in flour mixture, espresso, walnuts, and oil until just combined.

Spoon batter into cake pans, smoothing tops, and bake in middle of oven about 25 minutes, or until pale golden and a tester comes out clean. Cool cake layers in pans on a rack 15 minutes. Run a thin knife around edges of pans and invert cake layers onto rack to cool completely.

In a small bowl beat together cream cheese and 2 tablespoons maple syrup until smooth.

Assemble torte:

Arrange 1 cake layer on an ovenproof serving plate and with a pastry brush gently brush top with 1½ tablespoons maple syrup. Spread cream cheese mixture evenly onto layer and top with remaining cake layer. Brush top of torte with remaining 1½ tablespoons maple syrup. *Torte may be prepared up to this point 2 days ahead and chilled, covered. Bring torte to room temperature before proceeding.*

Make frosting:

Let whites stand at room temperature 1 hour. In a 1-quart heavy saucepan bring maple syrup to a boil over moderate heat and simmer until a candy thermometer registers 235° F. (be careful it doesn't bubble over).

While maple syrup is simmering, in bowl of a standing electric mixer beat whites with cream of tartar and a pinch salt until they just hold stiff peaks. Add hot maple syrup in a stream, beating until meringue is thickened and glossy, 1 to 2 minutes.

Preheat broiler.

Immediately frost torte with a narrow metal spatula, mounding extra meringue on top and drawing it up with a fork to form peaks. Broil torte about 4 inches from heat until tops of peaks are pale golden, about 30 seconds. Let torte stand at room temperature 15 minutes before serving.

PHOTO ON PAGE 33

Fallen Chocolate Cake Squares à la Mode with Butterscotch Sauce

9 ounces fine-quality bittersweet chocolate (not unsweetened), chopped
1 stick (½ cup) unsalted butter, cut into pieces
¾ cup sugar
5 large eggs, separated
3 tablespoons all-purpose flour
2 tablespoons unsweetened cocoa powder
1 teaspoon vanilla
¼ teaspoon salt

Accompaniments:
coffee ice cream (preferably super-premium such as Starbucks)
butterscotch sauce (recipe follows)
whipped cream if desired

Preheat oven to 350° F. Butter and flour a 9-inch square baking pan, knocking out excess flour.

In a metal bowl set over a saucepan of barely simmering water melt chocolate and butter, stirring occasionally, until smooth. Remove bowl from heat and whisk ½ cup sugar into chocolate mixture. Add yolks 1 at a time, whisking well after each addition, and whisk in flour, cocoa powder, vanilla, and salt.

In a bowl beat whites until they hold soft peaks and gradually add remaining ¼ cup sugar, beating until whites just hold stiff peaks. Stir one fourth whites into chocolate mixture to lighten and fold in remaining whites gently but thoroughly.

Pour batter into baking pan, spreading evenly, and bake in middle of oven 40 to 45 minutes, or until a tester comes out with moist crumbs adhering. Cool cake in pan on a rack. (Cake will sink as it cools and top crust will crack.) *Cake may be made 1 day ahead and kept, covered, at room temperature.*

Cut cake into 9 squares (crust will shatter) and serve with ice cream, sauce, and whipped cream. Serves 6 generously.

PHOTO ON PAGE 43

Butterscotch Sauce ◐+

1 cup sugar
¼ cup light corn syrup
3 tablespoons water
½ stick (¼ cup) unsalted butter, cut into 4 pieces
1 teaspoon cider vinegar
½ cup heavy cream
2 teaspoons vanilla

In a 1½-quart heavy saucepan bring sugar, corn syrup, and water to a boil over moderate heat, stirring until sugar is dissolved. Boil mixture, without stirring but swirling pan occasionally, until a golden caramel. Remove pan from heat and add butter, vinegar, and a pinch salt, swirling pan until butter is melted. Add cream and vanilla and simmer, stirring, 1 minute (sauce will be a golden brown). Cool sauce to room temperature (sauce will thicken as it cools). *Sauce keeps, covered and chilled, 3 weeks.* Serve sauce warm or at room temperature. Makes 1½ cups.

To make these lacy fried pastries, you will need a rosette iron with decoratively shaped attachments. They are available by mail order from Bridge Kitchenware, tel. (800) 274-3435.

Sugared Anise Rosettes

1 tablespoon anise seeds
1 cup all-purpose flour
½ teaspoon salt
1 cup milk
2 large eggs
2 tablespoons sugar
about 1 quart vegetable oil for deep-frying
confectioners' sugar for dusting

In a cleaned electric coffee/spice grinder finely grind anise seeds. In a bowl whisk together anise, flour, and salt and whisk in milk. In a small bowl whisk together eggs and sugar until combined and whisk egg mixture into flour mixture until just combined. (Overmixing batter will cause blisters on pastries.)

In a 3-quart heavy kettle heat 2 inches oil over moderate heat until a deep-fat thermometer registers 370° F. Put rosette iron in hot oil 20 seconds and carefully lift iron, letting excess oil drip into kettle. Dip bottom and side of oiled iron into batter 3 seconds, being careful not to let batter get onto top of iron. Immerse coated iron in oil and fry until pastry is golden and crisp, about 30 seconds. Lift iron, letting excess oil drip into kettle and, using a fork, loosen fried pastry, letting it drop onto brown paper or paper towels. Turn pastry over and drain on paper. Make more pastries in same manner, returning oil to 370° F. between batches and heating iron in hot oil each time 10 seconds before dipping into batter. *Pastries may be made 2 days ahead and chilled, layered between paper towels, in an airtight container. Before serving, reheat pastries in one layer on a baking sheet in a 225° F. oven 10 minutes.*

Dust pastries with confectioners' sugar. Makes about 40 pastries.

PHOTO ON PAGE 75

To make fortunes for our cookies, cut 3- by ½-inch strips of paper and write or type your own fortunes with non-toxic ink. Because you must work quickly to shape the cookies, it's best to make one at a time. Using more than one baking sheet is also helpful— you won't have to waste time waiting for the baking sheet to cool. A liquid measuring cup or deep heavy bowl is a good tool for shaping the cookies.

Almond Fortune Cookies

1 large egg white
¼ cup all-purpose flour
¼ cup sugar
¼ cup finely chopped sliced almonds
fortunes (see note above)

Preheat oven to 400° F. and butter a large round area (about 6 inches) in middle of a baking sheet.

In a small bowl whisk egg white just until foamy. Add flour, sugar, almonds, and a pinch salt and beat until smooth. Put 2 teaspoons batter on buttered area of baking sheet and with back of measuring spoon spread batter evenly into a round about 3 inches in diameter.

Bake cookie in middle of oven until golden around edge but pale in center, about 5 minutes. Working quickly, with a spatula remove cookie from baking sheet and invert onto a work surface. Put a fortune in middle of cookie and fold cookie in half (see drawing A). Bend pointed edges of cookie toward each other (see drawing B) and hook them onto rim of a liquid measuring cup (see drawing C) or deep heavy bowl to cool completely.

Make more cookies with remaining batter in same manner, letting baking sheet cool before baking next cookie. *Cookies may be made 3 days ahead and kept in an airtight container.* Makes about 8 cookies.

Brandy Snap Twirls

⅓ cup plus 1 tablespoon all-purpose
    flour
¼ teaspoon ground ginger
⅛ teaspoon ground cloves
5 tablespoons unsalted butter
¼ cup sugar
2 tablespoons Lyle's golden syrup*
1 tablespoon water

*available at specialty foods shops
    and some supermarkets

Preheat oven to 375° F. and butter a heavy baking sheet.

Into a small bowl sift together flour, ginger, and cloves. In a small saucepan melt butter with sugar, golden syrup, and water over moderate heat, stirring until smooth. Stir in flour mixture until combined well and let stand off heat 2 minutes. Spoon 1¼ teaspoons batter onto baking sheet and spread into a 6-inch length. Make 2 or 3 more cookies in same manner, keeping them 2 inches apart. Bake cookies in middle of oven 7 to 10 minutes, or until golden brown, and cool on baking sheet on a rack 30 to 45 seconds, or until firm enough to hold their shape but still pliable.

Working quickly, wrap hot cookies, 1 at a time, in a spiral around handle of a wooden spoon. (If cookies become too crisp to remove from baking sheet, return baking sheet to oven 1 minute, or until cookies are heated through and pliable.) Cool cookies 20 seconds and slide off spoon handle. Make more cookies with remaining batter in same manner. *Brandy snap twirls may be made 2 weeks ahead and kept in an airtight container at room temperature.* Makes about 26 cookies.

PHOTO ON PAGE 35

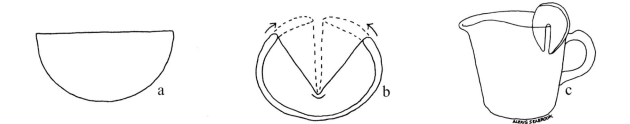

Apricot Almond Shortbreads

For apricot purée
¾ cup dried apricots (about 4 ounces)
1 cup water
¼ cup granulated sugar
For brandied cream
2 tablespoons apricot brandy
2 tablespoons superfine sugar
½ cup well-chilled heavy cream, whipped
    to soft peaks

36 almond shortbread shells (recipe follows)
sifted confectioners' sugar for sprinkling

Garnish: ¼ cup sliced almonds, toasted

Make purée:
In a small heavy saucepan simmer purée ingredients, covered, 10 minutes. In a food processor purée mixture until smooth. *Purée may be made 1 week ahead and chilled, covered.*
Make brandied cream:
In a small bowl fold brandy and sugar into whipped cream and chill, covered.
Transfer purée and brandied cream to separate pastry bags fitted with ¼-inch star tips. Pipe cream into shells until level with tops and pipe a ½-inch-high mound of purée on top.
Sprinkle desserts with confectioners' sugar and garnish with almonds. Makes 36 desserts.

PHOTO ON PAGE 16

Almond Shortbread Shells

1¾ cups all-purpose flour
¾ cup confectioners' sugar
⅓ cup cornstarch
¼ teaspoon salt
⅓ cup blanched whole almonds, toasted and
    ground fine
2 sticks (1 cup) cold unsalted butter, cut into bits
1 teaspoon almond extract

Preheat oven to 350° F. and butter 3 mini-muffin pans, each containing twelve 1¾- by 1-inch cups.
Into a bowl sift together flour, confectioners' sugar, cornstarch, and salt. In a food processor pulse mixture with almonds until combined well. Add butter and almond extract and blend until a dough just forms, about 1 minute.
On a lightly floured surface with floured hands form dough into thirty-six 1-inch balls. Press balls lightly into cups and bake in middle of oven until pale golden, about 15 minutes. Cool shortbreads in cups on racks 2 minutes and with a ¾-inch melon-ball cutter carefully scoop out an indentation about ¼ inch deep in centers. Cool shells completely. Gently loosen sides of shells with a thin knife and carefully remove from cups (shells will be very fragile). *Shells may be made 3 days ahead and kept in an airtight container at room temperature.* Makes 36 shortbread shells.

Apricot, Cornmeal, and Sage Cookies

1 stick (½ cup) unsalted butter, softened well
¾ cup sugar
1 large egg
¾ cup plus 2 tablespoons all-purpose flour
½ teaspoon baking soda
¼ cup chopped dried apricots
2 tablespoons finely chopped fresh sage leaves
½ cup cornmeal
½ teaspoon salt

Preheat oven to 350° F. and lightly grease 2 baking sheets.
In a bowl whisk together butter, sugar, and egg until smooth. Sift in flour and baking soda and add apricots, sage, cornmeal, and salt, stirring until combined.
Drop tablespoons of dough about 1 inch apart onto baking sheets and bake in batches in middle of oven 10 minutes, or until pale golden. Cool cookies on sheets 2 minutes and transfer to a rack to cool. Makes about 18 cookies.

Chocolate-Chunk Cookies with Pecans, Dried Apricots, and Tart Cherries ☾

2½ cups all-purpose flour
1 teaspoon baking soda
½ teaspoon baking powder
1 teaspoon salt
2 sticks (1 cup) unsalted butter, softened
1 cup granulated sugar
½ cup packed light brown sugar
2 large eggs
9 ounces fine-quality bittersweet (not
  unsweetened) or semisweet chocolate
¾ cup quartered dried apricots (about 4½ ounces)
1 cup dried tart cherries (about 5 ounces)
1 cup coarsely chopped pecans (about 4 ounces)

Preheat oven to 375° F.
In a bowl whisk together flour, baking soda, baking powder, and salt. In another bowl with an electric mixer beat together butter and sugars until light and fluffy. Add eggs 1 at a time, beating well after each addition, and beat in flour mixture until just combined.

Chop chocolate into ½-inch pieces and stir into batter with apricots, cherries, and pecans. Working in batches, drop dough by heaping tablespoons about 2 inches apart onto ungreased baking sheets and bake in upper and lower thirds of oven, switching position of sheets halfway through baking, about 12 minutes total, or until golden. Cool cookies on baking sheets on racks 5 minutes and transfer with a spatula to racks to cool. *Cookies keep in airtight containers at room temperature 5 days.* Makes about 34 cookies.

PHOTO ON PAGE 61

Raspberry Linzer Star Bars

2½ cups blanched whole almonds
2 cups confectioners' sugar
2½ sticks (1¼ cups) cold unsalted butter,
  cut into pieces
3¼ cups all-purpose flour
⅔ cup cornstarch
½ teaspoon salt
1 large egg
2½ tablespoons fresh lemon juice

2 cups raspberry jam (about two 12-ounce jars)
about 3 tablespoons milk
about 3 tablespoons granulated sugar

In a food processor finely grind almonds with confectioners' sugar and transfer to a large bowl. In food processor pulse butter with flour until mixture resembles fine crumbs and add to almond mixture with cornstarch and salt, stirring until combined well.

In a small bowl beat together egg and lemon juice until blended and stir into flour mixture until combined well. Work mixture with hands until it forms a dough.

Preheat oven to 350° F.
Pat 1½ cups dough into a disk and chill, wrapped in plastic wrap, 20 minutes. Pat remaining dough evenly into a 17½- by 11-inch jelly-roll pan and spread evenly with jam.

On a lightly floured surface with a floured rolling pin roll out chilled dough ⅛ inch thick and with a ¾- to 1½-inch star-shaped cookie cutter (we used 3 different sizes) cut out as many stars as possible. Reroll scraps and cut out more stars. Arrange stars randomly over jam and carefully brush stars with milk. Sprinkle stars with granulated sugar and bake in middle of oven 30 minutes, or until stars are golden. Cool confection in pan on a rack and cut into 20 bars. Makes 20 cookie bars.

PHOTO ON PAGE 44

Sweet Lemon-Thyme Crisps

3¼ cups all-purpose flour
2 teaspoons baking soda
½ teaspoon salt
4 teaspoons finely chopped fresh lemon thyme
  or regular thyme leaves
2 sticks (1 cup) unsalted butter, softened
1½ cups granulated sugar
2½ tablespoons finely grated fresh lemon zest
1 large egg
3 tablespoons fresh lemon juice
1 tablespoon finely grated peeled fresh gingerroot
confectioners' sugar for dusting

Into a bowl sift together flour, baking soda, and salt and stir in thyme. In a large bowl with an electric mixer beat together butter, granulated sugar, and zest until light and fluffy. Add egg, beating until combined well, and beat in lemon juice and gingerroot. Add flour mixture, beating until just combined.

Halve dough and on separate sheets of wax paper form each half into a 14- by 1½-inch log, using wax paper as a guide. *Freeze logs, wrapped in wax paper and foil, about 20 minutes, or until firm, and up to 3 weeks. If frozen solid, bring logs to cool room temperature for ease of slicing.*

Preheat oven to 350° F.

Cut 1 log diagonally into ¼-inch-thick ovals and halve each slice diagonally. Arrange cookies about 1 inch apart on ungreased baking sheets and bake in batches in upper and lower thirds of oven, switching position of sheets halfway through baking, until golden, about 12 minutes total. Immediately transfer crisps with a spatula to racks to cool. Make more cookies with remaining log if desired. Dust cookies lightly with confectioners' sugar. Each log makes about 60 crisps.

PHOTO ON PAGE 53

Chocolate Coconut Squares

13 small (2-inch) wheatmeal biscuits
    such as Carr's or ten 5- by 2½-inch
    graham crackers
¾ stick (6 tablespoons) unsalted butter
2 cups sweetened flaked coconut
    (about 5 ounces)
¼ teaspoon salt
12 ounces fine-quality bittersweet chocolate
    (not unsweetened)
2 large egg yolks
1 cup heavy cream
confectioners' sugar for dusting

Preheat oven to 350° F.

In a food processor pulse biscuits or crackers until finely ground. Melt butter and in a large bowl stir together with crumbs, coconut, and salt until combined. Firmly press crumb mixture evenly onto bottom of a 9-inch square baking pan and bake in middle of oven until golden, about 15 minutes. Cool crust completely in pan on a rack.

Chop chocolate. In a double boiler or a metal bowl set over a saucepan of barely simmering water melt chocolate, stirring until smooth. Remove top of double boiler or bowl from heat and cool chocolate 15 minutes.

In a small bowl lightly beat yolks. In a saucepan heat cream over moderate heat until it just boils and whisk ½ cup into yolks, whisking constantly. Add mixture to remaining cream and cook over moderate heat, whisking, until an instant-read thermometer registers 160° F. Whisk custard into chocolate until just smooth and pour evenly over crust, smoothing top with a small metal offset spatula or rubber spatula. *Chill confection, covered, at least 4 hours, or until firm.* With a sharp thin knife cut confection into 36 squares. *Squares keep, layered between sheets of wax paper in an airtight container and chilled, 1 week.*

Using star shapes cut out of parchment paper as a stencil, dust squares with confectioners' sugar. Makes 36 squares.

PHOTO ON PAGE 75

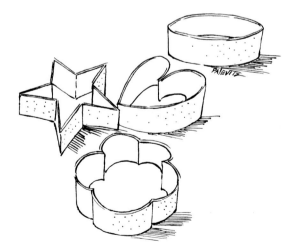

205

Chocolate Walnut Biscotti
with Chocolate Custard Swirls

For chocolate custard
1 tablespoon all-purpose flour
½ teaspoon instant espresso powder
2 large egg yolks
½ cup plus 2 tablespoons water
6 ounces fine-quality bittersweet chocolate
   (not unsweetened), chopped
For candied orange peel
¾ cup water
½ cup granulated sugar
zest of ½ navel orange, removed with a vegetable
   peeler and cut into thin ⅓-inch-long strips
3 tablespoons superfine sugar

about 36 chocolate walnut *biscotti* (recipe
   follows)

Make custard:
In a small saucepan whisk together flour, espresso powder, yolks, water, and a pinch salt until smooth. Bring mixture to a boil over moderate heat, whisking, and simmer, whisking, 30 seconds. Remove pan from heat and whisk chocolate into mixture until melted. Transfer custard to a small bowl to cool. *Chill custard, covered, at least 3 hours and up to 3 days. Bring chocolate custard to room temperature before using.*

Make candied peel:
In a very small heavy saucepan bring water with granulated sugar to a boil over moderate heat. Add zest and simmer, stirring occasionally, 10 minutes. Drain zest in a fine sieve and in a small bowl toss to coat with superfine sugar.

Transfer custard to a pastry bag fitted with ½-inch basket-weave tip and pipe about 1 tablespoon onto each *biscotto.*

Top *biscotti* with candied orange peel. Makes about 36 *biscotti.*

Chocolate Walnut Biscotti

1 cup all-purpose flour
¼ cup unsweetened Dutch-process cocoa
   powder
¾ teaspoon baking powder
½ teaspoon salt
½ stick (¼ cup) unsalted butter,
   softened
¼ cup plus 2 tablespoons sugar
1 large egg
1 tablespoon finely grated fresh orange zest
1 tablespoon fresh orange juice
½ cup chopped walnuts, toasted

Preheat oven to 350° F. and butter a large baking sheet.

In a bowl whisk together flour, cocoa powder, baking powder, and salt. In another bowl with an electric mixer beat together butter and sugar until light and fluffy. Add egg, zest, and orange juice and beat until combined well. Stir in flour mixture until a stiff dough is formed. Stir in walnuts.

On baking sheet with floured hands form dough into two 9-inch-long logs and bake in middle of oven until slightly firm to the touch, about 13 minutes. Cool *biscotti* on baking sheet on a rack 15 minutes. On a cutting board with a serrated knife cut logs diagonally into ½-inch-thick slices. Arrange *biscotti,* a cut side down, on baking sheet and bake until crisp, about 15 minutes. Cool *biscotti* on rack. *Biscotti may be made 1 week ahead and kept in airtight containers, or 1 month ahead and frozen.* Makes about 36 *biscotti.*

PIES AND TARTS

Dried-Fruit Tart with Brandied Crème Anglaise

walnut pastry dough (page 208)
pie weights or raw rice for weighting shell
For dried-fruit mixture
4 cups water
½ cup sugar
1 vanilla bean
1 cup dried apricots (about 6 ounces)
1 cup pitted prunes (about 6 ounces)
½ cup unsweetened dried tart cherries*
   (about 3 ounces)
1 teaspoon unflavored gelatin
1 tablespoon cold water

For crème anglaise
1 cup heavy cream
1 cup syrup reserved from cooking
    dried fruit
vanilla bean reserved from cooking
    dried fruit
4 large egg yolks
½ cup sugar
2 tablespoons brandy

*available at specialty foods shops, many
    supermarkets, and by mail order from
    Chukar Cherries, tel. (800) 624-9544

On a lightly floured surface with a floured rolling
pin roll out dough ⅛ inch thick (about an 11-inch
round). Fit dough into an 8-inch tart pan with a
removable fluted rim and trim edge. With a fork
prick bottom of shell all over. *Chill shell 30 minutes,
or until firm.*
Preheat oven to 375° F.
Line shell with foil and fill with pie weights or
raw rice. Bake shell in middle of oven 20 minutes.
Carefully remove weights or rice and foil and bake
shell until golden, 8 to 10 minutes more. Cool shell
in pan on a rack.

Make dried-fruit mixture:

In a heavy saucepan simmer water with sugar and
vanilla bean, stirring occasionally, until sugar is
dissolved. Halve apricots and add to syrup with prunes
and cherries. Simmer mixture 10 minutes and pour
through a sieve into a 2-cup glass measure (you will
have about 1⅔ cups syrup). Reserve fruit mixture and
vanilla bean.

In a food processor purée ½ cup reserved fruit and
2 tablespoons syrup until smooth. Spread purée
evenly over bottom of tart shell and arrange remaining fruit on top. In a cup sprinkle gelatin over
cold water to soften 1 minute. In a small saucepan
boil ½ cup remaining syrup until reduced to about
¼ cup. Remove pan from heat and add gelatin mixture, stirring until gelatin is dissolved completely,
and with a pastry brush brush glaze on fruit. Reserve
remaining cup syrup for *crème anglaise*.

Make crème anglaise:

Have ready a metal bowl set in a larger bowl of
ice and cold water. In a 2-quart heavy saucepan
combine cream and reserved cup syrup. Split reserved vanilla bean lengthwise and scrape seeds into
pan. Discard vanilla bean. Bring mixture just to a
boil and remove pan from heat. In a bowl with an
electric mixer beat together yolks and sugar until
thick and pale. Add hot cream mixture to yolk mixture in a slow stream, whisking. Transfer mixture
to cleaned pan and cook over moderate heat, stirring constantly with a wooden spoon, until slightly
thickened and a thermometer registers 170° F. (Do
not let custard boil.) Pour custard through a fine
sieve into metal bowl set in bowl of ice water. Cool
crème anglaise completely and stir in brandy. *Crème
anglaise may be made 1 day ahead and chilled, its
surface covered with plastic wrap.*
Serve tart with *crème anglaise*.

PHOTO ON PAGE 68

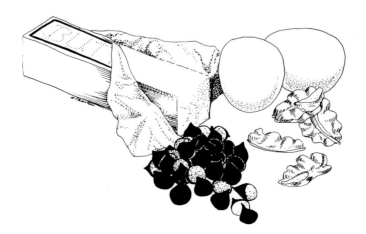

Walnut Pastry Dough ◐+

1 stick (½ cup) unsalted butter
½ cup walnuts (about
   2 ounces)
¼ cup confectioners' sugar
1⅓ cups all-purpose flour
½ teaspoon salt
1 large egg yolk
2 tablespoons ice water

Cut butter into pieces and soften to cool room temperature. In a food processor pulse walnuts until finely ground. Add confectioners' sugar, flour, and salt and pulse until combined. Transfer mixture to a large bowl and add butter.

With your fingertips or a pastry blender blend together flour mixture and butter until most of mixture resembles coarse meal with remainder in small (roughly pea-size) lumps. Stir together yolk and ice water and add to mixture. With a fork toss mixture until liquid is incorporated. Gently form mixture into a ball and on a lightly floured surface smear dough in 3 or 4 forward motions with heel of hand to help distribute fat and make dough easier to work with. Form dough into a ball and flatten to form a disk. *Chill dough, wrapped in plastic wrap, at least 1 hour, or until firm but not hard. Dough keeps, covered and chilled, 1 day or frozen 1 month.* Makes enough walnut pastry dough for an 8- to 10-inch tart shell.

Chocolate Raspberry Bites

For chocolate filling
8 ounces fine-quality bittersweet chocolate
   (not unsweetened)
2 cups heavy cream

½ recipe (24) sweet tartlet shells (recipe
   opposite), removed from baking cups
1 cup picked-over small raspberries
For chocolate glaze
9 ounces fine-quality bittersweet chocolate
   (not unsweetened)
7 tablespoons unsalted butter
1 tablespoon light corn syrup

Make filling:
Chop chocolate and in a heavy saucepan bring cream just to a boil. Reduce heat to low and add chocolate, stirring until mixture is smooth. Transfer filling to a bowl and cool slightly. *Chill filling, its surface covered with plastic wrap, at least 4 hours, or until completely cold, and up to 3 days.*

Put tartlet shells on a tray. With an electric mixer beat filling 30 seconds, or until pale and thickened (do not overbeat or it will become grainy). Transfer filling to a pastry bag fitted with ½-inch plain tip and pipe a small dollop into each shell. Press 2 or 3 raspberries into filling in each shell and pipe more filling 2 inches high into each shell, making sure filling touches insides of shells all the way around (to firmly anchor it). *Chill tartlets until filling is firm, about 1 hour.*

Make glaze:
Chop chocolate and cut butter into pieces. In a double boiler or a metal bowl set over a saucepan of barely simmering water combine all glaze ingredients, stirring until mixture is smooth. Transfer glaze to a small saucepan and cool to barely warm. *Glaze may be made 1 week ahead and chilled, covered. Reheat glaze over low heat to barely warm before proceeding.*

Glaze tartlets:
Holding saucepan at an angle and working quickly, dip top of 1 tartlet into glaze until filling is submerged almost to shell, holding tartlet over glaze a few seconds to let excess glaze drip back into pan. Repeat procedure with remaining tartlets. (Leftover glaze is an excellent sauce for ice-cream.) *Chill tartlets until glaze is set, about 15 minutes. Tartlets may be made 1 day ahead and chilled in airtight containers. Keep tartlets chilled until ready to serve.* Makes 24 tartlets.

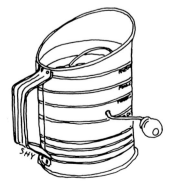

This sweet tartlet shells recipe makes enough shells for both the chocolate raspberry bites (recipe precedes) and the lemon meringue bites (recipe follows). For each of these recipes you will need two mini-muffin pans, each containing twelve 1¾- by 1-inch cups.

Sweet Tartlet Shells

2¼ sticks (1 cup plus 2 tablespoons) cold unsalted butter
3 cups all-purpose flour
¾ cup confectioners' sugar
½ teaspoon salt
3 large egg yolks
3 tablespoons ice water
1 teaspoon vanilla

Cut butter into bits. In a bowl with a pastry blender or in a food processor blend or pulse flour, confectioners' sugar, and salt until combined well and add butter, blending or pulsing until mixture resembles coarse meal. In a small bowl whisk together yolks, ice water, and vanilla until combined well and add to flour mixture, tossing with a fork or pulsing until incorporated. Form dough into a ball and divide into 2 pieces. Form each piece into a ball and flatten to form disks. *Chill disks, wrapped separately in plastic wrap, at least 1 hour and up to 1 week.*

Preheat oven to 400° F.

Form 1 dough disk into twenty-four 1-inch balls, keeping remaining disk wrapped and chilled. Press dough balls into bottoms and up sides of twenty-four ⅛-cup mini-muffin cups (about 1¾ inches across top and 1 inch deep). Trim any overhang with a knife and prick bottoms of shells with a wooden pick. *Chill shells 15 minutes, or until firm.* Bake shells in middle of oven 12 minutes, or until golden, and cool in cups on racks. Gently loosen tartlet shells with a knife. Make tartlet shells with remaining dough in same manner. For chocolate raspberry bites, remove tartlet shells from cups. For lemon meringue bites, do not remove tartlet shells from cups. *Sweet tartlet shells may be made 2 days ahead and kept in an airtight container at room temperature.* Makes 48 tartlet shells.

Lemon Meringue Bites

For lemon curd
¾ stick (6 tablespoons) unsalted butter
1 tablespoon finely grated fresh lemon zest
½ cup fresh lemon juice
½ cup sugar
3 large eggs

½ recipe (24) sweet tartlet shells (recipe precedes) in their baking cups
For meringue
3 large egg whites
½ teaspoon cream of tartar
¾ cup sugar

Make lemon curd:
Cut butter into pieces and in a heavy saucepan cook with zest, lemon juice, and sugar over moderate heat, stirring, until sugar is dissolved and mixture just comes to a simmer. In a bowl whisk together eggs and whisk in lemon mixture until combined well. Transfer lemon curd to pan and heat over moderate heat, whisking constantly, until it just begins to simmer. Pour lemon curd through a fine sieve into a bowl and cool slightly. *Chill lemon curd, its surface covered with plastic wrap, at least 2 hours, or until cold, and up to 3 days.*

Fill tartlet shells in baking cups with lemon curd. *Chill tartlets, covered, 1 hour.*

Preheat oven to 400° F.
Make meringue:
In a large bowl with an electric mixer beat egg whites with a pinch salt until foamy. Add cream of tartar and beat egg whites until they hold soft peaks. Gradually add sugar, beating until meringue holds stiff peaks.

Transfer meringue to a pastry bag fitted with ½-inch plain tip and pipe meringue 2 inches high onto each tartlet, completely covering lemon curd.

Bake tartlets in middle of oven 3 minutes, or until meringue tips are just browned, and cool in cups on racks. *Chill tartlets in airtight containers at least 2 hours, or until cold, and up to 1 day. Keep tartlets chilled until ready to serve.* Makes 24 tartlets.

PHOTO ON PAGE 63

Pumpkin Pie "Pumpkin"

pastry dough (recipe follows)
pie weights or raw rice for weighting shell
For filling
1¾ cups canned solid-pack pumpkin
    (about a 15-ounce can)
½ cup heavy cream
3 large eggs
½ cup packed light brown sugar
1 teaspoon ground cinnamon
¼ teaspoon ground ginger
¼ teaspoon ground allspice
¼ teaspoon freshly grated nutmeg
For topping
1¼ cups well-chilled heavy cream
⅓ cup plus 2 tablespoons superfine
    granulated sugar
1 cup sour cream
1 tablespoon unflavored gelatin (about 1½
    envelopes)
¼ cup cold water
4 large egg whites*

Garnish: ground cinnamon and a 3-inch
    cinnamon stick

*if egg safety is a problem in your area, substitute
    2 tablespoons plus 2 teaspoons powdered egg
    whites (such as Just Whites, available at some
    supermarkets and by mail order from New
    York Cake & Baking Distributors, tel. 800-
    942-2539), reconstituted by stirring in ½ cup
    warm water per package instructions

On a lightly floured surface with a floured rolling pin roll out dough ⅛ inch thick (about a 12-inch round). Fit dough into an 8-inch glass pie plate (measure pie plate across top from inside edge of rim) with a 3-cup capacity and trim edge. Pinch edge up all around to form a continuous ridge and with a fork prick bottom of shell in several places. *Chill shell 30 minutes, or until firm.*

Preheat oven to 375° F.

Line shell with foil and fill with pie weights or raw rice. Bake shell in middle of oven 25 minutes. Carefully remove weights or rice and foil and bake shell until just pale golden, about 10 minutes more.

Reduce temperature to 350° F.
Make filling:

In a bowl whisk together pumpkin, heavy cream, eggs, brown sugar, and spices and pour into shell.

Bake pie in middle of oven 1 hour, or until filling is set but center still trembles slightly. (Filling will continue to set as pie cools.) Transfer pie to a rack and cool completely. *Chill pie, loosely covered, at least 2 hours, or until cold, and up to 1 day. Keep pie chilled until ready to assemble dessert.*

Make topping:

In a chilled bowl with an electric mixer beat heavy cream with 2 tablespoons sugar until it just holds stiff peaks.

In a large bowl lightly whisk sour cream. In a small saucepan sprinkle gelatin over cold water to soften 1 minute. Heat mixture over low heat, stirring, until gelatin is dissolved completely (do not let mixture boil) and whisk into sour cream. Fold one third whipped cream into sour cream mixture until incorporated and fold in remaining whipped cream.

In a bowl with cleaned beaters beat whites on medium speed until they just hold soft peaks. Gradually add remaining ⅓ cup sugar, beating on high speed, until whites just hold stiff, slightly glossy peaks. Fold meringue into cream mixture gently but thoroughly.

Assemble dessert:

Mound topping on chilled pie and, using a cake spatula, smooth into a dome shape that dips in the center to resemble a pumpkin. Make 8 evenly spaced indented ridges from center of dome to edges of pie using pointed end of a church key can opener or tip of a knife to shape pumpkin and with a small offset spatula smooth edges of ridges. *Chill dessert, uncovered, at least 2 hours and up to 1 day.*

Dust dessert with cinnamon and insert cinnamon stick into center for "stem."

PHOTO ON PAGE 69

Pastry Dough ○+

¾ stick (6 tablespoons) cold unsalted butter
1¼ cups all-purpose flour
2 tablespoons cold vegetable shortening
¼ teaspoon salt
2 to 4 tablespoons ice water

Cut butter into ½-inch cubes.

To blend by hand:

In a bowl with your fingertips or a pastry blender blend together flour, butter, shortening, and salt until most of mixture resembles coarse meal with remainder in small (roughly pea-size) lumps. Drizzle 2 tablespoons ice water evenly over mixture and gently stir with a fork until incorporated. Test mixture by gently squeezing a small handful: When it has proper texture it should hold together without crumbling apart. If necessary, add more water, 1 tablespoon at a time, stirring until incorporated, and test mixture again. (Do not overwork or add too much water; pastry will be tough.)

To blend in a food processor:

In a food processor pulse together flour, butter, shortening, and salt until most of mixture resembles coarse meal with remainder in small (roughly pea-size) lumps. Add 2 tablespoons ice water and pulse 2 or 3 times, or just until incorporated. Test mixture by gently squeezing a small handful: When it has the proper texture it should hold together without crumbling apart. If necessary, add more water, 1 tablespoon at a time, pulsing 2 or 3 times after each addition until incorporated, and test mixture again. (Do not overprocess or add too much water; pastry will be tough.)

To form dough after blending by either method:

Turn mixture out onto a work surface and divide into 4 portions. With heel of hand smear each portion once in a forward motion to help distribute fat. Gather dough together and form it, rotating it on work surface, into a disk. *Chill dough, wrapped in plastic wrap, until firm, at least 1 hour, and up to 1 day.* Makes enough dough for a single-crust 9-inch pie or an 11-inch tart.

Peach and Passion-Fruit Phyllo Tarts

For tart shells
three 17- by 12-inch *phyllo* sheets, thawed
    if frozen
1 tablespoon unsalted butter
2 tablespoons crushed *amaretti* (Italian
    almond macaroons)
1½ cups nonfat vanilla yogurt
2 tablespoons sugar
3 firm-ripe peaches
1 passion fruit
1 teaspoon honey

Make shells:
Preheat oven to 425° F.

Stack *phyllo* between 2 sheets of wax paper and cover with a kitchen towel. In a very small saucepan melt butter. On a work surface brush 1 *phyllo* sheet with half of melted butter. Top buttered *phyllo* with a second *phyllo* sheet and brush with remaining butter. Sprinkle *amaretti* crumbs evenly over second *phyllo* sheet and top with remaining *phyllo* sheet. Cut *phyllo* stack into quarters and fit 1 quarter into each of four 3-inch tart pans with removable fluted rims. Fold in pastry overhang to form a shallow crumpled edge.

Bake shells on a baking sheet in middle of oven until golden, about 15 minutes, and cool in pans on a rack. *Shells may be made 1 day ahead and kept in tart pans, loosely covered, in a cool, dry place.*

Line a sieve with a double thickness of cheesecloth or a paper towel and set over a bowl. *Drain yogurt in sieve, covered and chilled, at least 1 hour.* Discard liquid and transfer yogurt to washed and dried bowl. Stir in sugar.

Halve and pit peaches and cut into ½-inch-thick wedges. Transfer wedges to a small bowl. Halve passion fruit and scoop flesh and seeds into bowl. Stir in honey until combined well. *Fruit mixture may be made 2 hours ahead and kept chilled, covered.*

Just before serving, remove shells from pans and divide yogurt among shells, smoothing tops. Top yogurt with fruit mixture. Serves 4.

🍃 Each serving about 168 calories, 3 grams fat
(16% of calories from fat)

PHOTO ON PAGE 84

Raspberry and Lime Custard Tart

For shell
1¼ cups all-purpose flour
¾ stick (6 tablespoons) cold unsalted butter,
    cut into bits
2 tablespoons cold vegetable shortening
¼ teaspoon salt
2 to 4 tablespoons ice water
pie weights or raw rice for weighting shell
For lime custard
½ cup sugar
½ cup heavy cream
3 large eggs
⅓ cup fresh lime juice
4 teaspoons finely grated fresh lime zest

3 cups picked-over raspberries
¼ cup sugar

Make shell:

In a bowl with a pastry blender or in a food processor blend or pulse together flour, butter, shortening, and salt until mixture resembles coarse meal. Add 2 tablespoons ice water and toss or pulse until incorporated. Add enough remaining ice water, 1 tablespoon at a time, tossing with a fork or pulsing to incorporate, to form a dough. On a work surface with heel of hand smear dough in 3 or 4 forward motions to make dough easier to work with. Form dough into a ball and flatten to form a disk. *Chill dough, wrapped in plastic wrap, at least 1 hour and up to 24.*

On a lightly floured surface with a floured rolling pin roll out dough into a 16- by 7-inch rectangle (about ⅛ inch thick). Fit dough into a 13- by 4-inch rectangular tart pan with a removable fluted rim. *Chill shell, covered, 1 hour, or until firm.*

Preheat oven to 400° F.

Line shell with foil and fill with pie weights or raw rice. Bake shell in middle of oven 10 minutes. Remove weights or rice and foil and bake shell until pale golden, about 5 minutes more. Cool shell in pan on a rack. *Shell may be made 2 days ahead and kept in pan, covered, at room temperature.*

Reduce temperature to 250° F. and transfer pan to a baking sheet.

Make custard:

Whisk together custard ingredients.

Pour custard into tart shell. Bake tart on baking sheet in middle of oven 30 minutes and transfer to rack to cool. (Custard will continue to set as tart cools.) *Tart may be prepared up to this point 1 day ahead and chilled, covered.*

In a small saucepan cook 1 cup raspberries and sugar over moderately low heat, mashing with a fork and stirring occasionally, 5 minutes and pour through a fine sieve into a small bowl, pressing hard on solids. Discard solids and cool raspberry mixture. Remove rim of tart pan and transfer tart to a platter. Pour cooked raspberry mixture over custard and arrange remaining 2 cups raspberries on top.

PHOTO ON PAGE 35

FROZEN DESSERTS

Elderflower and Strawberry Bombe

For elderflower ice cream
2 cups heavy cream
1 cup whole milk
2 large eggs
¾ cup sugar
½ cup elderflower concentrate*, or 1 teaspoon
    vanilla stirred into ¼ cup additional milk
For strawberry sorbet
⅔ cup sugar
⅔ cup water
3 cups strawberries, hulled
1 teaspoon fresh lemon juice

Garnish: strawberries, some halved if desired

*available at some specialty foods shops
    and by mail order from Dean & DeLuca,
    tel. (800) 221-7714

Make ice cream:

Have ready a large bowl of ice and cold water. In a saucepan bring cream and milk just to a boil. In a small bowl with an electric mixer beat together eggs and sugar until thick and pale. Add 1 cup hot cream mixture to egg mixture in a slow stream, whisking. Whisk egg mixture into cream mixture in pan and cook over moderate heat, stirring constantly, until thickened slightly, just coats back of spoon, and a candy thermometer registers 170° F. (Do not let custard boil.) Pour custard through a fine sieve into a bowl set in bowl of ice water and stir in elderflower concentrate. Cool custard. *Chill custard, its surface covered with plastic wrap, at least 1 hour and up to 24.* Freeze custard in an ice-cream maker. Transfer ice cream to an airtight container and in freezer harden until firm. *Ice cream may be made 1 week ahead.*

Make sorbet:

In a saucepan bring sugar and water to a boil, stirring until sugar is dissolved. Stir in strawberries and lemon juice and cool 10 minutes. In a food processor purée mixture until very smooth and force through a sieve into a bowl, pressing hard on solids. Discard solids and cool purée. Freeze purée in an ice-cream maker. Transfer sorbet to an airtight container and in freezer harden until firm. *Sorbet may be made 1 week ahead.*

Assemble bombe:

Let ice cream and sorbet stand at room temperature until softened, about 10 minutes. Into a large bowl scoop alternating cup measures of ice cream and sorbet. Make 2 figure-eight swirls with a large metal spoon through ice cream and sorbet and pour into a 7- to 8-cup mold. *Freeze bombe, covered with plastic wrap, at least 4 hours and up to 2 weeks.* To unmold *bombe,* dip mold in a bowl of hot water 1 second and invert *bombe* onto a serving plate.

Garnish *bombe* with strawberries. Serves 8.

PHOTO ON PAGE 35

Blueberry Ice Cream

2 cups picked-over blueberries
¾ cup sugar
⅛ teaspoon salt
1 cup milk
1½ cups heavy cream

In a saucepan bring blueberries, sugar, and salt to a boil over moderate heat, mashing berries and stirring with a fork. Simmer mixture, stirring frequently, 5 minutes and cool slightly. In a blender purée mixture with milk just until smooth and stir in cream. Pour purée through a sieve into a bowl, pressing on solids with back of a spoon. *Chill mixture, covered, at least 2 hours, or until cold, and up to 1 day.*

Freeze mixture in an ice-cream maker. Transfer ice cream to an airtight container and put in freezer to harden. *Ice cream may be made 1 week ahead.* Makes about 1 quart.

PHOTO ON PAGE 55

Chocolate Velvet Ice Cream

6 ounces fine-quality bittersweet chocolate
  (not unsweetened)
1 cup sugar
½ cup unsweetened Dutch-process
  cocoa powder
1½ cups heavy cream
1 cup milk
3 large egg yolks

Chop bittersweet chocolate. In a heavy saucepan whisk together sugar and cocoa powder until combined and whisk in heavy cream and milk. Bring mixture just to a boil, stirring occasionally. In a bowl beat egg yolks until smooth. Add hot cream mixture to egg yolks in a slow stream, whisking, and pour mixture back into saucepan. Cook custard over moderately low heat, stirring constantly, until a thermometer registers 170° F. Remove saucepan from heat and add chopped chocolate, whisking until melted. Pour custard through a sieve into a clean bowl and cool. *Chill custard, its surface covered with plastic wrap, at least 3 hours, or until cold, and up to 1 day.*

Transfer custard to bowl of a standing electric mixer and beat just until thick and fluffy. Freeze custard in an ice-cream maker. Transfer ice cream to an airtight container and put in freezer to harden. *Ice cream may be made 1 week ahead.* Makes about 1 quart.

PHOTO ON PAGE 56

Lemon Meringue Ice Cream

For meringue
2 large egg whites
⅛ teaspoon salt
⅓ cup sugar

1½ cups heavy cream
1 cup milk
¾ cup sugar
4 teaspoons finely grated fresh lemon zest
⅛ teaspoon salt
6 large egg yolks
⅔ cup fresh lemon juice

Make meringue:
Preheat oven to 250° F. and line a baking sheet with parchment paper.

In a bowl with an electric mixer beat whites with salt until they hold soft peaks. Gradually beat in sugar and beat until meringue holds stiff, glossy peaks. Spread meringue ½ inch thick on parchment-lined baking sheet and bake in middle of oven 1 hour, or until firm to the touch. *Turn off oven and let meringue stand 1 hour.* Transfer meringue on parchment to a rack and cool. Peel off parchment and, working over a bowl, break meringue into ½- to 1-inch pieces. *Meringue may be made 3 days ahead and kept in an airtight container in a cool, dry place.*

In a heavy saucepan bring cream, milk, sugar, zest, and salt just to a boil, stirring occasionally. In a bowl beat yolks until smooth. Add hot cream mixture to yolks in a slow stream, whisking, and pour into pan. Cook custard over moderately low heat, stirring constantly, until a thermometer registers 170° F. Pour custard through a sieve into a clean bowl and stir in lemon juice. Cool custard. *Chill custard, its surface covered with plastic wrap, at least 3 hours, or until cold, and up to 1 day.*

Freeze custard in a standard 1-quart ice-cream maker. Transfer ice cream to a bowl and fold in meringue. Transfer ice cream to an airtight container and put in freezer to harden. *Ice cream may be made 1 week ahead. (Meringue bits will stay crisp for about 2 days. Then, the meringue will soften and the ice cream's texture will become more uniform.)* Makes about 1½ quarts.

PHOTO ON PAGE 57

Maple Butter-Pecan Ice Cream

¾ cup pecans
1 tablespoon unsalted butter
2 cups heavy cream
½ cup milk
¾ cup pure maple syrup
⅛ teaspoon salt
3 large egg yolks
½ teaspoon maple extract

Coarsely chop pecans. In a skillet melt butter over moderate heat until foam subsides. Toast pecans in butter, stirring occasionally, until golden and fragrant, about 5 minutes, and sprinkle with salt to taste. Cool pecans and chill in a sealable plastic bag. *Buttered pecans may be made 3 days ahead and chilled.*

In a heavy saucepan bring cream, milk, maple syrup, and salt just to a boil, stirring occasionally. In a bowl beat yolks until smooth. Add hot cream mixture to yolks in a slow stream, whisking, and pour into pan. Cook custard over moderately low heat, stirring constantly, until a thermometer registers 170° F. Pour custard through a sieve into a clean bowl and cool. Stir in extract. *Chill custard, its surface covered with plastic wrap, at least 3 hours, or until cold, and up to 1 day.*

Freeze custard in an ice-cream maker. Transfer ice cream to a bowl and fold in chilled pecans. Transfer ice cream to an airtight container and put in freezer to harden. *Ice cream may be made 1 week ahead.* Makes about 1 quart.

PHOTO ON PAGE 56

Strawberry Ice Cream

¾ pound strawberries (about 1 pint)
8 ounces cream cheese, softened
¾ cup sugar
1 cup milk
1 tablespoon fresh lemon juice
⅛ teaspoon salt
½ cup heavy cream

Coarsely chop strawberries and in a blender purée with all remaining ingredients except cream just until smooth. Stir in cream and freeze mixture in an ice-cream maker. Transfer ice cream to an airtight container and put in freezer to harden. *Ice cream may be made 1 week ahead.* Makes about 1 quart.

PHOTO ON PAGE 57

Frozen Lemon Mousses with Strawberry Mint Sauce

4 foil molds (for taller mousses, procedure
    follows) or ¾-cup ramekins
1¾ teaspoons unflavored gelatin
3 tablespoons cold water
3 large egg yolks
1 teaspoon finely grated fresh lemon zest
½ cup fresh lemon juice
⅔ cup sugar
1 teaspoon vanilla
3 large egg whites*
⅛ teaspoon cream of tartar
½ cup well-chilled heavy cream

Accompaniment: strawberry mint sauce
    (page 216)
Garnish: fresh mint leaves

*if egg safety is a problem in your area, substitute
    2 tablespoons dried egg whites (such as Just
    Whites, available at some supermarkets and
    by mail order from New York Cake & Baking
    Distributors, tel. 800-942-2539) reconstituted
    by stirring in 6 tablespoons warm water per
    package instructions

If using ramekins, line each with plastic wrap, allowing a 2-inch overhang.

In a very small bowl sprinkle gelatin over cold water to soften. In a bowl with a fork beat yolks until smooth. In a saucepan simmer zest, lemon juice, and ⅓ cup sugar over moderate heat, stirring, until sugar is dissolved and whisk half of lemon mixture in a slow stream into yolks. Transfer yolk mixture to remaining lemon mixture and cook over moderate heat, stirring constantly, until thickened and just begins to simmer. Pour mixture through a fine sieve into a large bowl and add gelatin mixture and vanilla, stirring until gelatin is dissolved. Cool lemon mixture to room temperature.

In a bowl with an electric mixer beat together whites (or reconstituted dried egg whites) and cream of tartar until meringue just holds soft peaks. Gradually beat in remaining ⅓ cup sugar until meringue just holds stiff peaks.

In a bowl with electric mixer beat cream until it just holds stiff peaks. Stir one third meringue into lemon mixture to lighten and fold in remaining meringue and whipped cream gently but thoroughly. Spoon mousse into foil molds or lined ramekins. *Chill mousses until set, about 4 hours, and freeze set mousses, covered with plastic wrap, until frozen, about 4 hours, and up to 2 days.*

Assemble desserts:

Spoon some sauce onto 4 dessert plates, tilting plates to coat. If using foil molds, cut tape on cylinders and gently unwrap mousses, arranging 1 on each plate. If using ramekins, remove mousses, using plastic wrap overhang to lift them out, and invert onto plates (gently remove plastic wrap). Garnish desserts with mint. Serves 4.

PHOTO ON PAGE 31

To Make Foil Molds for Mousses ☉

Using foil molds allows for taller, more dramatic shapes than ramekins. Tear off four 12- by 8-inch sheets of foil. Fold each sheet lengthwise into a 12- by 2¼-inch strip (about 3 layers thick) and trim each strip to 10 inches in length. Wrap 1 strip, smooth side in, around base of a bottle or glass that is 2¼ to 2½ inches in diameter and tape overlapping end of strip at top and bottom of cylinder. Gently slide cylinder off bottle or glass. Create 3 more cylinders with remaining foil strips in same manner. On a small baking sheet stand cylinders on 1 end and tape each to baking sheet in 2 places to prevent them from moving while being filled.

Strawberry Mint Sauce ☺

½ cup packed fresh mint leaves
1 pint strawberries, hulled and halved
¼ cup sugar
½ cup water

Chop mint leaves. In a blender purée strawberries, sugar, and water until sugar is dissolved. Transfer purée to a bowl and stir in mint. *Chill mixture, covered, at least 1 hour and up to 24.*

Just before serving, pour sauce through a sieve into a bowl.

Peppermint Chocolate-Chunk Ice Cream

For chocolate chunks
3 ounces fine-quality bittersweet chocolate
   (not unsweetened)
2 ounces individually wrapped red-and-white
   peppermint hard candies (about ⅓ cup)

2 cups heavy cream
½ cup milk
2 tablespoons cornstarch
⅛ teaspoon salt
3 ounces individually wrapped green-and-white,
   clear, or red-and-white peppermint hard
   candies (about ½ cup)
½ teaspoon peppermint extract
1 or 2 drops green food coloring if using clear
   peppermint candies

Make chocolate chunks:
Line a baking sheet with wax paper.

Chop chocolate. In a double boiler or a metal bowl set over a saucepan of barely simmering water melt chocolate, stirring until smooth. Remove top of double boiler or bowl from heat and cool chocolate. Chop mints (largest pieces should be about ¼ inch) and stir into chocolate. Spread chocolate mixture ¼ inch thick on wax-paper-lined baking sheet. *Chill chocolate mixture until firm, about 30 minutes.* Coarsely chop chocolate mixture and chill, wrapped in plastic wrap. *Chocolate chunks may be made 1 week ahead and chilled.*

In a heavy saucepan whisk together cream, milk, cornstarch, and salt until smooth and add mints.

Bring mixture to a boil over moderate heat, stirring constantly, and simmer, stirring constantly, 1 minute, or until mints are dissolved and mixture is thickened. Pour mixture through a sieve into a bowl and cool. Stir in extract and, if using clear mints, food coloring. *Chill mixture, its surface covered with plastic wrap, at least 3 hours, or until cold, and up to 1 day.*

Freeze mixture in an ice-cream maker. Transfer ice cream to a bowl and fold in chilled chocolate chunks. Transfer ice cream to an airtight container and put in freezer to harden. *Ice cream may be made 1 week ahead.* Makes about 1½ pints.

PHOTO ON PAGE 56

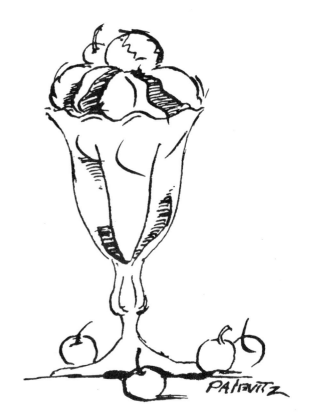

Cactus-Pear Sorbets

8 cactus pears* (also called prickly pears
 or cactus fruits; about 3 pounds total)
1 cup simple syrup (recipe follows)
2 tablespoons fresh lime juice,
 or to taste

*available seasonally at Latino markets,
 specialty produce markets, and by
 mail order from Chef's Produce,
 tel. (213) 624-8909

Line a baking sheet with plastic wrap. Wearing rubber gloves, wash cactus pears and with paper towels rub off any prickly fuzz left on skin. Halve cactus pears lengthwise and with a spoon carefully scoop flesh with seeds into a blender, leaving thick shells intact. Add syrup and lime juice to blender and purée until smooth. Pour cactus-pear purée through a fine sieve into a bowl and discard seeds. Put cactus shells on baking sheet and freeze while making sorbet.

Freeze purée in an ice-cream maker. Scoop sorbet into frozen shells, smoothing surfaces so they are level. *Freeze filled cactus shells at least 6 hours, or until frozen hard. Frozen sorbets in shells may be wrapped individually in plastic wrap and kept in freezer 1 week.* Makes 16 cactus-pear sorbets (about 4 cups sorbet).

PHOTO ON PAGE 49

Simple Syrup ◌

3 cups sugar
3 cups water

In a saucepan bring sugar and water to a boil, stirring, and boil until sugar is completely dissolved. Cool syrup. *Syrup may be made 1 week ahead and chilled, covered.* Makes about 4½ cups.

Lime Sorbets

8 medium limes (about 1½ pounds)
2 cups simple syrup (recipe precedes)
1 cup water

Line a baking sheet with plastic wrap.

Wash limes and halve lengthwise. Working over a bowl to catch juices, with a small sharp knife cut between flesh and pith to loosen flesh and with a spoon scoop out flesh in 1 piece. Into bowl squeeze juice from lime flesh with hands and discard membranes. Scrape any remaining membranes and juice from lime halves into bowl. Pour lime juice through a sieve into a measuring cup to measure 1 cup, discarding membranes. Put lime shells on baking sheet and freeze while making sorbet.

In a bowl stir together 1 cup lime juice, syrup, and water and freeze in an ice-cream maker. Scoop sorbet into frozen shells, smoothing surfaces so they are level. *Freeze filled lime shells at least 6 hours, or until frozen hard. Frozen sorbets in shells may be wrapped individually in plastic wrap and kept in freezer 1 week.* Makes 16 lime sorbets (about 4½ cups sorbet).

PHOTO ON PAGE 49

Mango Sorbets

4 ripe mangoes (about 3½ pounds total)
1 cup simple syrup (recipe opposite)
3 tablespoons fresh lime juice, or to taste

Line a baking sheet with plastic wrap.

Wash and dry mangoes. Using a sharp knife, remove the 2 flat sides of each mango, cutting lengthwise alongside pit and cutting as close to pit as possible so that mango flesh is in 2 large pieces. With a spoon carefully scoop flesh from mango sides into a blender, leaving shells intact. With a knife cut remaining flesh from pit and add to blender. Add syrup and lime juice to blender and purée until smooth. Put mango shells on baking sheet and freeze while making sorbet.

Freeze mango purée in an ice-cream maker. Scoop sorbet into frozen shells, mounding slightly, and smooth surfaces. *Freeze filled mango shells at least 6 hours, or until frozen hard. Frozen sorbets in shells may be wrapped individually in plastic wrap and kept in freezer 1 week.* Makes 8 mango sorbets (about 6 cups sorbet).

PHOTO ON PAGE 49

Fresh Tangerine Sorbet ☽+

3½ cups fresh tangerine juice (from 15 tangerines)
¾ cup superfine sugar

In a bowl stir together juice and sugar until sugar is dissolved. *Chill juice, covered, until cold, about 3 hours.* Freeze juice in an ice-cream maker. *Sorbet may be made 1 week ahead.* Makes about 5 cups.

Litchi Five-Spice Ice Cream

1 cup sugar
1 tablespoon cornstarch
3 large eggs
slightly rounded ¼ teaspoon five-spice powder*
2½ cups milk
1¾ cups drained chilled whole pitted litchis in syrup* (about two 15-ounce cans)
1½ cups chilled heavy cream

*available at Asian markets

In a heatproof bowl whisk together sugar, cornstarch, eggs, five-spice powder, and a pinch salt until combined well. In a heavy saucepan heat milk just to a boil and add in a slow stream to egg mixture, whisking. Transfer custard to pan and bring to a boil over moderate heat, whisking constantly. Boil custard gently, whisking, 1 minute. Remove pan from heat and cool custard, stirring occasionally. *Chill custard, covered, until cold, about 3 hours.*

In a blender purée litchis with ½ cup cream and stir into custard with remaining cup cream. Freeze custard in an ice-cream maker. *Ice cream may be made 1 week ahead.* Makes about 2 quarts.

Minted Blueberries with Lemon Cream ☽

2 tablespoons water
2 tablespoons sugar
½ pint picked-over blueberries
1½ teaspoons chopped fresh mint leaves
½ cup well-chilled heavy cream
1 teaspoon finely grated fresh lemon zest

In a very small saucepan simmer water and 1 tablespoon sugar until sugar is dissolved, about 1 minute, and in a small bowl toss with blueberries and mint. *Chill blueberry mixture, covered, 15 minutes, or until cold.* Divide blueberries between 2 Martini glasses.

In a chilled bowl with an electric mixer beat cream with remaining tablespoon sugar until it just holds stiff peaks and fold in zest. Top blueberries with lemon cream. Serves 2.

Summer-Berry Basil Kissel

1 vanilla bean
½ cup sugar
3 tablespoons cornstarch
¼ teaspoon salt
1¼ cups packed fresh basil sprigs
2 cups sweet Muscat such as Val d'Orbieu St.-Jean-de-Minervois
5 cups picked-over blackberries
4 cups picked-over raspberries
½ teaspoon fresh lemon juice, or to taste

Accompaniment: crème fraîche or sour cream

Split vanilla bean lengthwise and scrape seeds into a bowl, reserving pod for another use. Whisk in sugar, cornstarch, and salt until combined well. Coarsely chop basil.

In a saucepan simmer Muscat and ¾ cup each type of berry 2 minutes. Drain mixture in a sieve set over a bowl, reserving liquid. Transfer cooked berries to a large bowl and stir in remaining fresh berries.

Gradually whisk reserved hot liquid into sugar mixture until smooth. Transfer mixture to pan and stir in basil. Bring mixture to a boil, whisking, and simmer, whisking, 3 minutes. Immediately pour mixture through sieve into berries, discarding basil, and stir until combined well. Stir in lemon juice. Divide *kissel* among 6 bowls. *Chill kissel, covered, at least 2 hours, or until cold, and up to 2 days.*

Serve *kissel* with *crème fraîche* or sour cream. Serves 6.

PHOTO ON PAGE 53

Macerated Grapes in Clove and Cinnamon Syrup ○+

2 pounds red seedless grapes, rinsed
2 cups sugar
4 cups water
1 teaspoon whole cloves
3 cinnamon sticks, halved

Keeping grapes on stems, poke each grape several times with a wooden pick and put in a large heat-proof bowl. In a saucepan stir together remaining ingredients and bring to a boil. Pour hot syrup over red seedless grapes. *Macerate grapes at room temperature, gently turning occasionally, 1 hour. Chill grapes, covered, at least 2 hours and up to 2 days.* Serves 2.

PHOTO ON PAGE 20

Gingered Nectarine Cobbler ○

2 large nectarines (about ¾ pound)
¼ cup sugar
½ teaspoon cornstarch
1 tablespoon fresh lemon juice
1 tablespoon finely chopped crystallized ginger
For biscuit topping
¾ cup all-purpose flour
¾ teaspoon baking powder
¼ teaspoon salt
½ stick (¼ cup) cold unsalted butter
5 tablespoons milk
¾ teaspoon sugar
⅛ teaspoon cinnamon

Preheat oven to 400° F. and butter an 8-inch square baking pan.

Pit nectarines and slice thin. In a bowl stir together sugar and cornstarch and stir in nectarines, lemon juice, and ginger until combined well. Transfer nectarine mixture to pan.

Make topping:

Into a bowl sift together flour, baking powder, and salt. Cut butter into bits and blend into flour mixture until mixture resembles coarse meal. Stir in milk until just combined and drop topping in small mounds over nectarines. In a small cup stir together sugar and cinnamon and sprinkle over dough.

Bake cobbler in middle of oven 20 to 25 minutes, or until top is golden. Serves 2 generously.

Nectarines, Plums, and Blueberries in Lemony Ginger Anise Syrup ○

1 lemon
½ cup water
three ⅓-inch-thick slices fresh gingerroot
4 whole star anise* or 2 tablespoons star anise* pieces
½ cup sugar
1½ teaspoons fresh lemon juice, or to taste
3 firm-ripe nectarines (about ¾ pound)
9 assorted plums (about 1½ pounds)
1 cup picked-over blueberries

*available at Asian markets and specialty foods shops

With a vegetable peeler remove three 3- by ½-inch strips zest from lemon. In a saucepan bring water to a boil with zest, gingerroot, star anise, sugar, and 1 teaspoon lemon juice and simmer, stirring, until sugar is dissolved. Cool syrup and discard star anise and gingerroot. *Syrup may be made 2 days ahead and chilled, covered.*

Halve and pit nectarines and plums. Cut nectarines into wedges. In a bowl toss cut fruit together with blueberries, syrup, and remaining lemon juice. *Mixture may be made 8 hours ahead and chilled, covered.* Serves 4.

PHOTO ON PAGE 61

Fresh Orange Slices with Candied Zest and Pistachios ☽

2 navel oranges
¼ cup sugar
½ cup water
3 tablespoons Grand Marnier or other
    orange-flavored liqueur
20 shelled natural pistachios, chopped
    (about 3 tablespoons)

With a vegetable peeler remove zest from oranges in strips (about 2 by ½ by ¼ inches) and in a small heavy saucepan simmer strips in water to cover 10 minutes.

With a sharp knife cut a slice from top and bottom of each orange to expose flesh and arrange, a cut side down, on a cutting board. Cutting from top to bottom, remove peel and pith. Cut oranges crosswise into ¼-inch-thick slices and arrange on 2 dessert plates.

Drain zest in a sieve and return to pan. Simmer zest with sugar and ½ cup water over moderately low heat 10 minutes, or until zest is translucent and syrup is thickened. Add liqueur and simmer 1 minute.

Arrange candied zest decoratively on and around orange slices and top with syrup. Sprinkle oranges with pistachios. Serves 2.

Caramelized Cardamom Pears with Ice Cream ☽

1 tablespoon unsalted butter
2 tablespoons packed dark brown sugar
2 tablespoons water
¼ teaspoon ground cardamom
1 Bosc pear
1 tablespoon dark rum

Accompaniment: vanilla ice cream

Preheat oven to 450° F.

In a small saucepan melt butter over moderate heat and stir in brown sugar, water, and cardamom until sugar is dissolved. Quarter pear lengthwise and core. Cut each pear quarter in half lengthwise and in an 8-inch square baking pan toss with syrup. Roast pears in middle of oven, turning once, until tender and syrup is caramelized, about 15 minutes.

Transfer pears with a slotted spatula to 2 plates and stir rum into syrup until combined well. Scoop ice cream onto plates and spoon rum syrup over it. Serves 2.

Roasted Pears with Hazelnut Syrup and Candied Hazelnuts

1 cup water
1¼ cups sugar
¾ cup hazelnuts
1 tablespoon unsalted butter
6 firm-ripe Bosc pears (about 2¼ pounds
    total), stems intact
3 tablespoons hazelnut-flavored liqueur
    (preferably Frangelico)
2 tablespoons fresh lemon juice,
    or to taste
1 teaspoon vanilla

In a small heavy saucepan simmer water with 1 cup sugar, stirring until sugar is dissolved. *Syrup may be made up to this point 2 days ahead and cooled completely before being chilled, covered.*

Preheat oven to 350° F. and lightly butter a shallow baking pan.

Coarsely chop hazelnuts. Stir nuts into syrup and simmer 1 minute. With a slotted spoon transfer nuts to baking pan, arranging in one layer, and reserve syrup. Cut butter into pieces. Bake nuts in middle of oven until golden brown, about 15 minutes. Immediately add butter to nuts, tossing to coat and separate, and with a spatula transfer nuts to a plate to cool (nuts will crisp as they cool). *Nuts may be candied 2 days ahead and kept in an airtight container in a cool, dry place. Reserved syrup may be kept, covered and chilled, 2 days.*

Lightly butter a shallow ovenproof kettle or casserole dish (about 12 by 2½ inches). With a sharp knife trim a very thin slice from bottom of each pear to enable pears to stand upright. Dip and roll each pear in reserved syrup to coat completely. Transfer pears as coated to kettle, standing them upright, and sprinkle with remaining ¼ cup sugar. Add liqueur, lemon juice, and vanilla to remaining reserved syrup and pour down side of kettle or casserole.

Roast pears, uncovered, in middle of oven until

undersides are tender when pierced with a knife, about 30 minutes.

Arrange pears on a serving platter. Spoon syrup around pears and sprinkle with candied nuts. Serve pears warm or at room temperature. Serves 6.

PHOTO ON PAGE 73

Poached Pears with Ginger and Port

a 1½-inch piece fresh gingerroot
2 firm-ripe Bartlett, Anjou, or Comice pears
    with stems intact
3 to 4 cups water
½ cup sugar
¼ cup Tawny Port
2 tablespoons fresh lemon juice

Peel gingerroot and slice thin. Cut slices into thin strips and in a saucepan simmer in 1 quart water 10 minutes. Drain gingerroot, discarding water.

In a saucepan just large enough to hold pears lying on their sides bring 3 cups water to a boil with gingerroot, sugar, Port, and lemon juice, stirring until sugar is dissolved.

Peel pears, leaving stems intact, and cut a thin slice from bottom of each if necessary to enable pears to stand upright when served. Arrange pears on their sides in poaching liquid, adding enough of remaining cup water as necessary to just cover. Simmer pears, turning them occasionally, until tender, 20 to 40 minutes (depending on ripeness). Carefully transfer pears with a slotted spoon to a bowl and boil poaching liquid until reduced to about ¾ cup and slightly syrupy. Pour sauce over pears. *Pears may be made 1 day ahead and cooled in sauce before being chilled, covered.* Serve pears warm or chilled. Serves 2.

PHOTO ON PAGE 27

Plum Crisp

For topping
¾ cup sliced almonds
1 stick (½ cup) cold unsalted butter
¾ cup all-purpose flour
¾ cup packed light brown sugar
¾ cup old-fashioned rolled oats
¾ teaspoon cinnamon
½ teaspoon salt
For filling
¾ cup water
4 teaspoons cornstarch
3 pounds Italian prune plums
½ cup sugar

Accompaniment: vanilla ice cream

Preheat oven to 375° F.
Make topping:
On a baking sheet toast almonds until golden, 10 to 15 minutes. (Leave oven on.) Cut butter into bits. In a food processor blend flour, brown sugar, ½ cup oats, cinnamon, salt, and butter until mixture resembles coarse meal. In a bowl stir together flour mixture, remaining ¼ cup oats, and almonds.
Make filling:
In a small bowl stir together water and cornstarch until combined. Halve and pit plums. In a 12-inch skillet cook plums and sugar over moderate heat, stirring, until sugar is melted. Stir in cornstarch mixture and simmer, stirring, 15 minutes, or until mixture is thickened. Transfer plum mixture to a 15-by 9-inch (3-quart) baking dish.

Sprinkle topping over plum filling. Bake mixture in middle of oven 40 to 45 minutes, or until crumb topping is crisp and golden brown, and cool on a rack 10 minutes.

Serve crisp warm with ice cream. Serves 6 to 8.

Strawberry Pistachio Mille-Feuillantines
(Pistachio Wafers Layered with Strawberries and Cream)

For pistachio wafers
½ cup shelled natural pistachios
    (about 2½ ounces)
½ cup granulated sugar
¼ cup all-purpose flour
¼ teaspoon salt
2 large egg whites
5 tablespoons unsalted butter,
    melted
¼ teaspoon vanilla

1 vanilla bean, halved lengthwise
1 cup chilled heavy cream
3 tablespoons granulated sugar
1 pound small strawberries (about
    1 pint), trimmed
confectioners' sugar for dusting

Garnish: 4 small strawberries and chopped
    pistachios

Make wafers:
Preheat oven to 325° F. and spray a heavy or non-stick baking sheet with cooking spray or line with parchment paper.

Rub off loose skins from pistachios and in a food processor grind nuts with granulated sugar. In a bowl whisk together pistachio mixture, flour, and salt and whisk in whites, butter, and vanilla until combined well. Drop rounded teaspoons batter 5 inches apart onto baking sheet and with back of a spoon spread into 3½- to 4-inch rounds. Bake wafers in middle of oven 8 minutes, or until golden.

Working quickly, transfer hot wafers with a thin metal spatula to a rack to cool completely. (If wafers become too crisp to remove from baking sheet, return to oven 1 minute, or until heated through and pliable.) Make more wafers with remaining batter in same manner, spraying or re-lining sheet for each batch. *Wafers may be made 2 days ahead and kept in an airtight container at room temperature.* Makes 16 to 20 wafers.

Into a chilled bowl scrape seeds of vanilla bean and add cream and granulated sugar. With a whisk or an electric mixer beat mixture until it holds stiff peaks. *Whipped cream may be made 2 hours ahead and chilled, covered. Whisk whipped cream briefly before using.*

Just before serving, assemble mille-feuillantines:
Put a wafer in center of each of 4 plates. Spread about 2 tablespoons whipped cream on each wafer, leaving a ¼-inch border, and top with half of strawberries. Put another wafer on top of strawberries and top in same manner with remaining cream and strawberries. Dust 4 wafers with confectioners' sugar and put on top of desserts. Garnish each *mille-feuillantine* with a strawberry and sprinkle plates with pistachios. Serves 4.

PHOTO ON PAGE 6

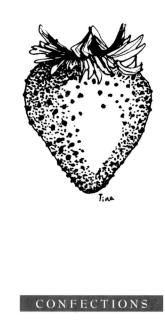

CONFECTIONS

Because caramel hardens so quickly, we made these lollipops in 2 batches, 10 at a time.

Caramel Lollipops

lollipop molds if desired*
vegetable-oil cooking spray
20 lollipop sticks* or short (4-inch)
    wooden skewers
2 cups sugar

1 cup water

⅔ cup light corn syrup

¼ teaspoon orange- or lemon-flavored oil**
    if desired

mixed jellied candies such as jelly beans or
    Jujyfruits, or chocolates such as Sno-Caps
    for decorating

*available by mail order from New York Cake
    and Baking Distributors, tel. (800) 942-2539

**available at specialty foods shops and
    by mail order from Williams-Sonoma,
    tel. (800) 541-2233

Have ready a large bowl of ice and cold water. Lightly spray 10 lollipop molds with cooking spray and, if using skewers, cut off pointed ends with scissors. Put lollipop sticks or skewers in molds. (Alternatively, if not using lollipop molds, lightly spray a sheet of parchment paper with cooking spray and have ready 10 lollipop sticks or skewers.)

In a heavy saucepan bring 1 cup sugar, ½ cup water, ⅓ cup corn syrup, and ⅛ teaspoon flavored oil to a boil over moderate heat, stirring until sugar is dissolved. Boil syrup, without stirring, washing down sugar crystals clinging to side of pan with a brush dipped in cold water, until syrup is pale golden. Continue to cook syrup, without stirring, swirling pan occasionally, until golden.

Remove pan from heat and dip bottom of pan into ice water to stop caramel from cooking further (water will hiss and splatter). Spoon caramel into 10 lollipop molds. (If caramel in pan becomes too hard, heat it again over low heat, without stirring, until spoonable.) If using jellied candies, work quickly to decorate; if using chocolates, cool lollipops about 5 minutes before decorating them. (Alternatively, spoon caramel onto parchment paper to make 10 lollipops. Decorate caramel lollipops in same manner and firmly press 1 end of a lollipop stick or skewer onto each.)

Cool lollipops completely, about 30 minutes, and remove from molds or parchment paper. Make 10 more lollipops in same manner. *Lollipops keep, layered between sheets of wax paper in an airtight container at cool room temperature, 2 weeks.* Makes 20 lollipops.

Triple-Chocolate Hazelnut Truffles

9 ounces fine-quality milk chocolate, chopped

1 cup heavy cream

9 ounces fine-quality white chocolate (use
    Callebaut or Lindt for proper texture), chopped

½ cup hazelnuts, toasted and chopped

4 ounces fine-quality bittersweet chocolate (not
    unsweetened)

Garnish: crystallized violets*

*available at some specialty foods shops
    and by mail order from Dean & DeLuca,
    tel. (800) 221-7714

Lightly oil a 9- by 5-inch loaf pan and line with plastic wrap.

In a double boiler or a small metal bowl set over a saucepan of barely simmering water melt milk chocolate with ½ cup cream, stirring until smooth, and remove double boiler or pan from heat. Spoon mixture into loaf pan and tap pan on counter to level surface. Cool mixture to room temperature and chill, uncovered, 15 minutes.

In cleaned top of double boiler or bowl melt white chocolate with remaining ½ cup cream in same manner. Stir hazelnuts into white chocolate mixture and pour evenly onto chilled milk chocolate layer. *Chill confection, loosely covered, at least 6 hours and up to 1 week.*

Lift confection out of pan and peel off plastic wrap. On a cutting board with a sharp large knife cut confection lengthwise into 6 strips and cut strips crosswise into 11 strips (to make a total of 66 truffles, each about ¾-inch square).

In a double boiler or small metal bowl set over a saucepan of barely simmering water melt bittersweet chocolate, stirring until smooth, and remove double boiler or pan from heat. Cool chocolate 10 minutes. Dip ⅛ inch of white chocolate portion of each truffle into melted chocolate, letting excess chocolate drip off. Top each truffle with a small piece of crystallized violet and chill, uncovered, until firm. *Truffles may be made 2 weeks ahead and chilled in layers separated by wax paper in an airtight container.* Makes 66 truffles.

PHOTO ON PAGE 35

223

Five-Spice Candied Pecans ☽+

¼ cup water
¼ cup sugar
2 teaspoons Chinese five-spice powder*
1 teaspoon salt
2 cups pecan halves

*available at Asian markets and many
  supermarkets

Preheat oven to 375° F. Lightly oil a shallow baking pan and a 12-inch square of foil, keeping pan and foil separate.

In a small heavy saucepan bring water to a boil with sugar, five-spice powder, and salt. Stir in pecans and simmer mixture, stirring, 1 minute. Immediately pour mixture evenly into pan and with a metal spatula spread pecans in one layer. Bake mixture in middle of oven 8 minutes, or until pecans turn mahogany-colored and most of liquid is evaporated. Immediately transfer pecans with metal spatula to foil, keeping them in one layer, and cool completely. (Pecans will continue to crisp as they cool.) Break up any pecans that have stuck together. *Candied pecans keep, in layers separated by wax paper in an airtight container, frozen, 2 weeks.* Makes about 2 cups.

Pecan-Butter Truffles ☽+

2½ cups toasted pecan halves
3 tablespoons superfine granulated sugar
⅓ cup graham cracker crumbs (from about
   three 5- by 2½-inch graham crackers)
1 tablespoon unsalted butter, softened
1 teaspoon vanilla
½ teaspoon cinnamon

Finely chop ½ cup pecans.

In a food processor grind remaining 2 cups pecans with a pinch salt, occasionally scraping down side of bowl, until pecans release their oil and mixture becomes a smooth paste, about 3 minutes. Transfer pecan butter to a bowl and stir in remaining ingredients until combined well.

Form level teaspoons of pecan butter into balls

and roll, no more than 2 at a time, in chopped pecans, pressing pecans gently to make adhere. *Chill truffles, in layers separated by wax paper in an airtight container, at least 1 hour, or until firm, and up to 4 days.* Makes about 40 truffles.

Mint Turkish Delight

four ¼-ounce envelopes unflavored gelatin
   (about 3 tablespoons)
2½ cups cold water
1 cup cornstarch
3 cups granulated sugar
2 cups packed fresh mint leaves, chopped
   coarse
1 drop green food coloring if desired
⅓ cup confectioners' sugar plus additional
   if necessary

Oil an 8-inch square baking pan and line with plastic wrap. Oil plastic wrap.

In a small bowl sprinkle gelatin over ½ cup cold water and let soften. In another small bowl stir together ¾ cup cold water and cornstarch.

In a 4-quart heavy kettle stir together remaining 1¼ cups cold water, granulated sugar, and mint and bring to a boil over moderate heat, stirring until sugar is dissolved. Stir in gelatin and cornstarch mixtures and boil over moderate heat, stirring constantly with a wooden spatula, 10 minutes (mixture will be very thick). Stir in food coloring. Pour mixture into baking pan, smoothing top with spatula, and cool. *Chill confection, loosely covered, until set, about 4 hours.*

Sift 1 tablespoon confectioners' sugar onto a work surface. Invert confection onto sugar and peel off plastic wrap. Cut confection into ¾-inch cubes. Sift remaining confectioners' sugar over cubes and toss to coat. Wrap cubes in parchment paper (do not use wax paper, plastic wrap, or airtight containers because confections will weep) and chill. *Turkish delight may be made 2 weeks ahead and kept chilled, wrapped in parchment paper.*

Just before serving, recoat Turkish delight in additional confectioners' sugar. Makes about 36 confections.

PHOTO ON PAGE 34

Pistachio Rosewater Turkish Delight

½ cup shelled natural pistachios
four ¼-ounce envelopes unflavored gelatin
   (about 3 tablespoons)
2¾ cups cold water
1 cup cornstarch
3 cups granulated sugar
5 teaspoons rosewater*
1 drop red food coloring
   if desired
⅓ cup confectioners' sugar plus additional
   if necessary

*available at specialty foods shops and
   by mail order from Dean & DeLuca,
   tel. (800) 221-7714

Oil an 8-inch square baking pan and line with plastic wrap. Oil plastic wrap.

In a small saucepan of boiling water blanch pistachios 3 minutes and drain in a sieve. Rinse pistachios under cold running water and pat dry. Rub skins off pistachios.

In a small bowl sprinkle gelatin over ½ cup cold water and let soften. In another small bowl stir together ¾ cup cold water and cornstarch.

In a 4-quart heavy kettle stir together remaining 1½ cups cold water, granulated sugar, and rosewater and bring to a boil over moderate heat, stirring until sugar is dissolved. Stir in gelatin and cornstarch mixtures and boil over moderate heat, stirring constantly with a wooden spatula, 10 minutes (mixture will be very thick). Stir in pistachios and food coloring and cook, stirring, 1 minute. Pour mixture into baking pan, smoothing top with spatula, and cool completely. *Chill confection, loosely covered, until set, about 4 hours.*

Sift 1 tablespoon confectioners' sugar onto a work surface. Invert confection onto sugar and peel off plastic wrap. Cut confection into ¾-inch cubes. Sift remaining confectioners' sugar over cubes and toss to coat. Wrap cubes in parchment paper (do not use wax paper, plastic wrap, or airtight containers because confections will weep) and chill. *Turkish delight may be made 2 weeks ahead and kept chilled.*

Just before serving, recoat Turkish delight in additional confectioners' sugar. Makes about 36 confections.

PHOTO ON PAGE 34

GELATINS, CUSTARDS, AND MOUSSES

In this recipe there will be extra mousse and pecan crisps (the recipes will not work if reduced). Both elements are delicious on their own. We would like to give credit to Alice Medrich's innovative method for making egg-safe mousse, as found in her book, Chocolate and the Art of Low-Fat Desserts.

Mocha Mousse with Kumquat Cranberry Sauce and Phyllo Pecan Crisps

For kumquat cranberry sauce
½ cup sugar
½ cup water
¼ cup kumquats (about 6), sliced thin and
    seeded
2 teaspoons Grand Marnier
2 tablespoons fresh or unthawed frozen
    cranberries, sliced thin
For chocolate mousse
¼ cup water
½ cup unsweetened Dutch-process
    cocoa powder
2 teaspoons instant espresso powder
2 large eggs, separated
4 ounces fine-quality bittersweet chocolate
    (not unsweetened)
½ stick (¼ cup) unsalted butter
⅛ teaspoon cream of tartar
6 tablespoons sugar
For espresso cream
⅓ cup well-chilled heavy cream
½ tablespoon sugar
¼ teaspoon instant espresso powder

*Accompaniment: phyllo pecan crisps
    (recipe follows)*

Make sauce:

In a small saucepan simmer sugar, water, and kumquats until reduced to about ⅔ cup and stir in Grand Marnier. Cool sauce to room temperature and stir in cranberries. *Sauce may be made 1 week ahead and chilled, covered.*

Make mousse:

Have ready an instant-read thermometer in a cup of very hot water. In a small bowl stir together ¼ cup water, cocoa powder, espresso powder, and yolks until smooth. In a metal bowl set over a saucepan of simmering water melt bittersweet chocolate and butter, stirring occasionally, until smooth. Stir cocoa mixture into chocolate mixture and cook 1 minute, stirring constantly. Remove bowl from pan and check temperature, tilting bowl to cover thermometer tip by at least 2 inches. If temperature is less than 160° F., rinse thermometer and return to cup. Check temperature every 30 seconds until thermometer registers 160° F. Remove bowl from pan, reserving simmering water over heat, and cool chocolate mixture to room temperature.

Clean thermometer and put in a clean cup of very hot water. In another metal bowl stir together whites, cream of tartar, and sugar with a rubber spatula and put bowl over pan of reserved simmering water. Cook mixture, stirring constantly with rubber spatula (to keep mixture as froth-free as possible), checking temperature in same manner, 30 seconds to 1 minute, or until thermometer registers 160° F., and remove bowl from heat. Beat meringue mixture with an electric mixer until cool and meringue holds stiff peaks.

Gently fold chocolate mixture into meringue until combined well and chill 15 minutes, or until just firm enough to hold its shape when piped. Spoon mousse into a pastry bag fitted with ½-inch star tip and pipe about ½ cup mousse onto each of 2 dessert plates in a mound 2½ inches in diameter and 2 inches high. *Chocolate mousse may be piped onto plates 1 day ahead and chilled, covered loosely with plastic wrap.*

Make espresso cream:

In a large bowl with a whisk or cleaned beaters beat together heavy cream, sugar, and instant espresso powder until cream just holds stiff peaks. *Espresso cream may be made 2 hours ahead and chilled, covered.*

Assemble desserts:

Dollop half of espresso cream on top of each serving of chocolate mousse and lean 2 or 3 pecan crisps against mousse. Spoon kumquat cranberry sauce around desserts. Serves 2.

PHOTO ON PAGE 15

Phyllo Pecan Crisps

⅓ cup pecans
⅓ cup sugar
three 17- by 12-inch *phyllo* sheets, thawed if
    frozen, stacked between 2 sheets wax paper
    and covered with a kitchen towel
3 tablespoons unsalted butter, melted

Preheat oven to 350° F.

In a food processor grind pecans with sugar until
finely chopped. On a piece of parchment paper on a
work surface arrange 1 *phyllo* sheet and brush with
some butter. Sprinkle *phyllo* sheet evenly with half
of pecan sugar and top with a second *phyllo* sheet,
some butter, remaining pecan sugar, and remaining
phyllo sheet, pressing down gently with your fingers
and brushing with some butter. Slide a baking sheet
under parchment and chill *phyllo* 10 minutes.

Transfer *phyllo* with parchment to a cutting board
and with a sharp knife cut stack lengthwise into
2-inch-wide strips, cutting through parchment
and discarding excess. Cut strips and parchment
crosswise into 5-inch-long rectangles, discarding
excess. Cut each rectangle diagonally in half and
transfer triangles on parchment to baking sheet,
separating triangles slightly. Cover triangles directly
with another parchment sheet and bake in lower
third of oven 15 minutes, or until golden. Cool crisps
on baking sheet on a rack. *Crisps keep in an airtight
container at room temperature 1 week.* Makes about
30 crisps.

PHOTO ON PAGE 15

Coconut Caramel Panna Cottas

3½ teaspoons unflavored gelatin (about
    one and one-half ¼-ounce envelopes)
⅓ cup whole milk
¾ cup sugar
a 14½- or 15-ounce can unsweetened coconut
    milk*, well-stirred
1 cup well-stirred canned cream of coconut
    such as Coco Lopez
1 cup heavy cream
3 tablespoons light rum

*available at Asian markets and some specialty
    foods shops and supermarkets

In a small bowl sprinkle gelatin over whole milk
to soften. In a dry heavy saucepan cook sugar over
moderately low heat, stirring slowly with a fork (to
help sugar melt evenly), until melted and pale gold-
en. Cook caramel, without stirring, swirling pan,
until deep golden. Coat bottoms of eight ¾-cup
molds or ramekins with caramel.

In a large saucepan bring coconut milk and cream
of coconut just to a boil, stirring. Remove pan from
heat and add gelatin mixture, stirring until dissolved.
Stir in heavy cream and rum. Cool *panna cotta* 30
minutes. Stir *panna cotta* well and divide among
molds or ramekins. Cool *panna cottas* completely.
*Chill desserts until firm, at least 4 hours, and up to
2 days.*

To unmold *panna cottas*, dip molds or ramekins,
1 at a time, into a bowl of hot water 3 seconds. Run a
thin knife around edges of molds or ramekins and
invert desserts onto a platter. Serves 8.

*Cider and Calvados Gelées with
Champagne Grapes* ○+

1 tablespoon unflavored gelatin (about
    1 envelope plus ½ teaspoon)
¼ cup cold water
3 cups fresh apple cider
¼ cup sugar
2 tablespoons Calvados or other
    apple brandy
1 teaspoon fresh lemon juice

Accompaniment: 4 small bunches Champagne
    grapes (about ¼ pound)

In a small bowl sprinkle gelatin over water to soften 1 minute. In a saucepan combine cider and sugar and bring to a rolling boil. Boil mixture, skimming froth, until reduced to 2 cups. Stir in brandy and lemon juice and pour through a sieve lined with a double thickness of dampened cheesecloth or paper towel into a bowl. Stir gelatin mixture into hot cider mixture, stirring until gelatin is dissolved. Stir mixture well and divide among four ½-cup molds. *Chill gelées until firm, at least 3 hours, and up to 2 days.*

To unmold *gelées*, dip bottoms of molds, 1 at a time, into a bowl of hot water 3 seconds. Run a thin knife around edges of molds and invert *gelées* onto 4 small dessert plates.

Serve *gelées* with small bunches of grapes alongside. Serves 4.

Each serving, including grapes: 172 calories, 1 gram fat
(4% of calories from fat)

PHOTO ON PAGE 86

BEVERAGES

Blueberry Citron "Aquavit" ☺+

½ cup picked-over blueberries
a 750-ml. bottle Absolut Citron vodka

Wash and dry blueberries. Pour off about 2 tablespoons vodka (just enough for a teeny Martini) to make room for blueberries. Put berries in bottle of vodka. *Let vodka stand at room temperature 3 days. Freeze "aquavit" in bottle at least 8 hours, or until ice-cold, and up to 3 days. (Because of its high alcohol content, aquavit will remain liquid.)*

Pour aquavit into a decanter and serve ice-cold. Makes about twenty-four 1-ounce shots.

PHOTO ON PAGE 36

Christer Larsson's Spiced "Aquavit" ☺+

1 navel orange
2 teaspoons fennel seeds
1 teaspoon caraway seeds
3 whole star anise*
a 1-liter bottle Absolut vodka

*available at specialty foods shops and Asian
   markets and by mail order from Adriana's
   Caravan, tel. (800) 316-0820

Wash and dry orange. Beginning at 1 end, with a vegetable peeler carefully remove a long strip of zest in a spiral from half of orange and add with spices to bottle of vodka. *Let vodka stand at room temperature 3 days. Freeze "aquavit" in bottle at least 8 hours, or until ice-cold, and up to 3 days. (Because of its high alcohol content, aquavit will remain liquid.)*

Pour aquavit into a decanter and serve ice-cold. Makes about thirty-three 1-ounce shots.

PHOTO ON PAGE 36

Warm Spiked Cider ☺+

1 lemon
1 navel orange
2 quarts unfiltered apple cider
3 whole star anise* or ⅛ cup star anise pieces
5 whole cloves
2 cinnamon sticks
10 juniper berries**
¼ cup superfine granulated sugar, or to taste
1 cup apple brandy such as Clear Creek,
   or to taste

*available at specialty foods shops and Asian
   markets and by mail order from Adriana's
   Caravan, tel. (800) 316-0820
**available in spice section of most supermarkets

With a vegetable peeler remove four 3-inch-long strips of zest from lemon and two 6-inch-long strips from orange.

In a 3-quart saucepan bring cider to a rolling boil and pour through a sieve lined with a triple layer of cheesecloth or paper towels into a heatproof pitcher. Stir in orange and lemon zests, star anise, cloves, cinnamon sticks, juniper berries, and sugar and steep at room temperature 1 hour. *Cider may be made 1 day ahead and cooled completely before being chilled, covered.*

Just before serving, in a saucepan reheat cider over low heat until just warm. Discard spices and stir in brandy. Makes about 8 cups.

Passion-Fruit Mimosas ○

1 cup chilled Champagne
½ cup chilled passion-fruit nectar* or juice

*available at specialty foods shops and by mail
 order from Balducci's, tel. (800) BALDUCCI

Divide Champagne between 2 glasses and top off
each drink with nectar or juice (3 to 4 tablespoons).
Makes 2 drinks.

PHOTO ON PAGE 21

*We preferred pure cranberry juice in this recipe
but it's possible to substitute the more commonly
available cranberry juice cocktail—simply omit the
sugar called for.*

Cranberry Hot Toddies ○

4 tangerines
⅓ cup whole cloves
3 quarts pure unsweetened cranberry juice*
2 cups sugar, or to taste
3 cups amber rum if desired

*available at natural foods stores and some
 supermarkets

Cut tangerines crosswise into ¼-inch-thick rounds
and remove seeds. Stud rind of each tangerine round
with 4 or 5 cloves. In a large saucepan simmer
cranberry juice, tangerine rounds, and sugar,
covered, 5 minutes and stir in rum.
    Serve toddies with clove-studded tangerine rounds
in heatproof glasses. Makes about 16 cups.

French 75 Cocktails ○

3 ounces gin
3 ounces fresh lemon juice
4 teaspoons superfine granulated sugar
1½ cups ice cubes
1 cup chilled Champagne

In a cocktail shaker combine gin, lemon juice,
sugar, and ice cubes and shake to chill. Strain cocktails into 2 wineglasses and top off with Champagne.
(Alternatively, serve drinks over ice in highball
glasses.) Serves 2.

Frozen Watermelon Margaritas ○+

a 3-pound piece watermelon
1 cup white Tequila
½ cup fresh lime juice (from about 4 limes)
¼ cup sugar, or to taste

Remove rind from watermelon and cut enough
fruit into 1-inch pieces to measure 5 cups. (Leave in
some seeds for a speckled appearance.) *Freeze
watermelon in a sealable plastic bag at least 3 hours
and up to 1 week.*
    In a 5- to 6-cup blender blend frozen watermelon
with remaining ingredients until thick and smooth.
Makes about 6 Margaritas.

PHOTO ON PAGE 47

NON-ALCOHOLIC

Blackberry Lemonade ○+

about 6 lemons
4 cups water
1 cup sugar
½ cup picked-over fresh blackberries

Garnish: lemon slices

With a vegetable peeler remove zest from 4
lemons and squeeze enough juice from these and
remaining 2 lemons to measure 1 cup.

In a saucepan boil 2 cups water with sugar, stirring until sugar is dissolved. Add zest, lemon juice, and remaining 2 cups water and cool.

In a food processor or blender purée blackberries and stir into lemonade. Pour blackberry lemonade through a sieve into a pitcher or other container and chill. *Chill lemonade, covered, at least until cold and up to 2 days.*

Serve lemonade over ice in tall glasses, garnished with lemon slices. Makes about 6 cups.

PHOTO ON PAGE 44

Elderflower Coolers ☉

2 lemons
2 limes
12 fresh mint sprigs
1½ quarts chilled sparkling mineral water
    or seltzer
¼ cup elderflower concentrate*,
    or to taste
2 cups ice cubes

*available at some specialty foods shops and
    by mail order from Dean & DeLuca,
    tel. (800) 221-7714

Thinly slice lemons and limes and crush mint sprigs. In a pitcher stir together lemons, limes, mint, sprigs, mineral water or seltzer, and elderflower concentrate. Serve elderflower cooler over ice in tall glasses. Makes 6 drinks.

PHOTO ON PAGE 50

Minted Honeydew Limeade ☉

a 3-pound honeydew melon
1½ cups superfine granulated sugar
1¾ cups fresh lime juice
3 tablespoons chopped fresh mint leaves
3 cups cold water
1 cup ice cubes

Remove rind from melon, discarding it, and cut enough fruit into 1-inch pieces to measure 6 cups. In a blender purée melon in batches with sugar, lime juice, and mint until completely smooth and pour into a thermos or other container with water and ice. Shake or stir limeade before serving. Makes about 9 cups.

PHOTO ON PAGE 60

Agua Fresca de Pepino ☉
(Cucumber Cooler)

1 medium cucumber
2 cups cold water
1 cup ice cubes
¼ cup sugar
2 tablespoons fresh lime juice

Peel cucumber and cut into chunks. In a blender blend cucumber with remaining ingredients until completely smooth and pour into a glass pitcher. *Cooler may be made 6 hours ahead and chilled, covered.* Stir cooler before serving. Makes about 5 cups, serving 4.

PHOTO ON PAGE 46

CUISINES OF
THE WORLD

THE FLAVORS OF

INDIA

The vast subcontinent of India, home to nearly a billion people, is a complex, fascinating nation divided by religion, languages, and states, each with its own customs and traditions. (English is just one of the seventeen major languages and thousands of dialects spoken.) Hindus, who make up three-quarters of the population, are further bound by caste, the rigid system of hereditary social class. Although change is ongoing, caste still affects how one lives. India's disparities of wealth, education, and opportunity result from this hierarchical order.

While India has become self-sufficient in food production, for many, just having enough to eat is the daily challenge. For others, the metropolitan centers, humming with vitality and big business, offer upward mobility, even great prosperity. (Today, office space in the modern glass skyscrapers of Bombay commands some of the highest prices in the world.) Far from the deafening noise of congested cities are places of quiet, timeless beauty—the forested southern Nilgiri Hills, where birds, elephants, and even tigers still comprise most of the traffic; and Kashmir's Dal Lake, where glacial blue waters silently reflect the majesty of the surrounding Himalayan foothills. All are facets of India's beguiling, contradictory character.

Street Market, Delhi

The riches of India have always lured explorers. Black pepper, cardamom, ginger—a wealth of spices enticed travelers eager to make their fortunes. In return, India assimilated foreign ingredients. It's hard to imagine Indian food today without the tomatoes, potatoes, and chilies from the New World that arrived in the fifteenth century with Portuguese traders. A hundred years later, Mogul invaders developed a complex, rich cuisine that is considered by some to be the most refined form of Indian cooking. Even the British, whose colonial rule lasted until 1947, influenced Indian eating habits. Most notably, they introduced tea, now enormously popular, and cultivated plantations in Darjeeling, Assam, and the Nilgiri Hills, which continue to produce some of the world's finest teas.

Today, in cities like Delhi, Calcutta, and Madras, many restaurants are likely to offer pizza and burgers (lamb or veggie) on the same menu as traditional regional fare. Many innovative chefs are turning out lighter versions of the classics, and even creating East/West fusion dishes, contemporary by any standard. Still, in most rural areas, eating habits haven't changed much in thousands of years. Religious beliefs strongly influence diet and, consequently, over 600 million Indians are vegetarian. Hindus consider the cow and bull sacred, and raise them only for milk and field work. Indeed, these animals wander freely wherever they want to go, and they are pampered by household cooks and street vendors who feed them vegetable trimmings. Muslims, who make up the second largest religious group, never consume pork or shellfish, and so on. Sikhs, Jains, Buddhists, Christians, Parsis ... all coexist, each with their own customs and specialties. For people of all faiths, however, family celebrations, such as weddings, births, and holidays, are a welcome opportunity for an elaborate banquet.

Because India remains a predominantly agricultural country, cooks depend on seasonal harvests—from their own trees, gardens, and nearby fields. In cities, however, an extensive variety of produce, spices, and delicacies are available at sprawling outdoor markets; and peddlers still bring a selection of vegetables or fish door-to-door. Wives are in charge of the household and usually do the cooking, often for an extended family. (Secret recipes of grandmothers, mothers, and mothers-in-law are cherished.) Even when there are servants, it is the wife who plans and oversees meals. The rituals of cleanliness are nearly sacred: In the morning, before entering the kitchen, the cook bathes, and no one dares to enter without removing shoes and carefully washing hands and feet.

In rural areas and cities alike, kitchens remain simple, even rudimentary. For many of her tasks, the cook squats, resting on her heels, while she stirs pots, rolls out breads, or grinds spices and pastes. Most cooking is done on a low stove, which can be charcoal-, wood-, or dung-burning. Few utensils are used, but they are functional and well-made. Two of the most essential are the *tava* (cast-iron pan) for cooking breads and the *karhai* (similar to a wok) for stewing or deep-frying. Everyone has a pressure cooker for cooking *dal* (legumes), and grinding stones or an electric blender for crushing spices. Staples—rice, flour, *dal*—are stored in large airtight containers made of brass or steel, and spices are kept in a spice box. More and more households now have refrigerators, a sign of middle-class success.

Traditionally, Indians eat with their hand—the right hand only. In the North, grace is all-important and it is deemed impolite to have more than the first knuckle touch the food; in the South, it is acceptable to use more of the hand. Some households dine Western-style, seated on chairs around a table. In a more traditional or rural home, diners sit on the floor and eat at small individual tables called *chonkis*. When entertaining guests in the latter fashion, mats or soft cushions are provided for comfort. Hospitality and generosity are intrinsic to the dining experience in India, and guests are always encouraged to eat several helpings.

The day might begin with a light breakfast of seasonal fruit, or with a full savory meal, complete with spicy condiments. A hearty breakfast is considered essential by many South Indians who consume *idlis* (steamed rice and lentil dumplings) or *dosa* (rice and lentil crisp crepes) with *sambar* (lentil stew) and coconut chutney. Northerners quaff cups of sweet, milky tea—spiced with cloves or ginger in the winter—but in the South, coffee is preferred. Even in the cities, it's traditional to return home for lunch, the main meal of the day for many. For afternoon tea, a British vestige still enjoyed, deep-fried *pakoras* (fritters) and a fruit juice or frothy *lassi* (a yogurt drink) are as likely to appear as tea and finger sandwiches. While formal restaurants are still unusual outside of cities, fast food is everywhere: It is common to stop for a little refreshment, whether at a quick-service restaurant, a snack place, or *dhaba* (roadside truck stop). Carts sell savory, puffy, spicy snacks for eating on the run, and enticing stores specialize in sweet confections that are too time-consuming to make at home. At the end of the day, a light, easily digested late meal is enjoyed at 8 or 9 p.m.

On the following pages, three primers explore the essentials of Indian cooking: spices (page 239), the foundation of fine Indian cooking; rice, breads, and *dals* (page 243), the staples of every Indian meal; and condiments (page 246), an array of flavorful chutneys, pickles, and salads that round out every repast. Three menus follow. Although our recipes remain true to the spirit of a particular region, keeping Western cooks in mind, we've adapted some dishes to make them more accessible. For example, in order to serve breads piping-hot, an Indian cook must prepare them while others eat. To avoid this, we've included make-ahead steps in our bread (and other) recipes whenever possible. We've also considered the differences in kitchen equipment: In the *tandoori* preparations, we simply call for a grill or very hot oven. Traditionally, at Indian meals all the dishes are served at once. Each of our menus can be served Western-style, either as a sit-down dinner with individual courses or as a buffet that includes hors d'oeuvres, drinks, and desserts.

Our elegant North India Dinner (page 249) begins with an exotic cool tamarind drink and spicy chicken *tikka* skewers with *raita* (yogurt sauce) for dipping. You'll have plenty of *raita* left over to serve with the main course too. A spectacular leg of lamb, tender and richly spiced, is the centerpiece of the meal. The vegetable accompaniments, stewed eggplant and tart-flavored okra, offer contrasting textures, and the chewy yeast bread, *naan*, is worth some effort to make. (Substitute any heated store-bought flatbread, such as pita or *chapati*, if desired.) We've even included an aromatic *basmati* rice pilaf. A variety of condiments—chutney, *raita*, and pickles—provides sweet, cooling, and sour notes. (Look for the pickles at

Indian markets and many supermarkets.) *Kulfi*, a creamy mango ice cream usually reserved for special occasions, ends the meal on a rich note.

It's unlikely that our eclectic Vegetarian Indian Dinner (page 259) would be served in a traditional Indian home (where only their regional specialties are prepared), but it gives us the opportunity to showcase meatless dishes from several areas. To start, crunchy *pakoras* (fritters), made with green beans, squash, and lotus root (a popular Kashmiri vegetable), are served with tamarind chutney for dipping and a refreshing iced chamomile tea. The remaining dishes are best served buffet style. Peas and cubes of *panir* (fresh cheese), a comforting combination in a creamy, piquant sauce, is frequently enjoyed in the North. In contrast, large chunks of eggplant and potato are cooked in a traditional Bengali (eastern) manner that leaves the vegetables tender, yet slightly charred on the bottom. The *dal*, a mung-bean stew typical of Gujarat (in the west), has a spicy kick; and a mild, tender rice pilaf with cauliflower, seasoned with southern spices, blends well with the other complex flavors. *Chapatis* (griddle-cooked flatbreads), a crunchy salad, fresh chutney, and a cooling *raita* make impressive accompaniments. For dessert, we pulled out all the stops with *gulab jamun* (deep-fried milk balls in syrup), an extravagant treat.

South Indian regional cuisines are full of sweet and sour flavors, rice, fresh coconut, and plenty of spices and herbs. To set a casual tone for our relaxed dinner (page 269), we begin with spicy peanuts. (Feel free to serve them with either the tamarind coolers (page 253) or iced chamomile tea (page 262) from our other menus.) Because fish is abundant in coastal areas, our meal features tiger prawns simmered in coconut sauce. Alongside are two typical southern dishes, *sambar* (a lentil and vegetable stew) with *dosas* (rice and lentil crisp crêpes) for dipping. Steamed rice accompanies the shrimp, but you may want to enjoy the *sambar* with rice too. To balance the "wet" dishes, we offer spice-coated green beans, cooked "dry," without a sauce. Fresh chutney and a spicy salad provide contrast and crunch. Rice *payasam* (pudding) is a delicate, heavenly ending.

Authentic Indian food, especially vegetarian and South Indian fare, slowly is becoming more available at restaurants in America. With our menus in hand, however, you'll be able to try these flavorful dishes at home. If you are unfamiliar with this cuisine, try a recipe or two at a time, incorporating them into your meals. Or, divide a menu among your friends, and have each guest bring one dish for an exotic and unforgettable evening. Once you've discerned the regional cuisines you enjoy most, you can peruse in depth the many excellent cookbooks that are available. The tastes of India—flavorful, complex, varied, and always intriguing—are well-worth exploring.

SPICES AND OTHER FLAVORINGS

The creative use of spices makes Indian cooking one of the world's most exciting cuisines. Although India is a vast land with myriad regional foods, every cook knows how to handle spices to produce varied flavors. Beyond their culinary punch, spices and herbal brews are used to cure common ailments; spices also appear daily in temples where dishes are presented to honor the deities. The "magic" of these gifts from nature is cherished in India, and handed down from generation to generation with great care and pride.

Indian recipes often call for an astonishing number of spices (up to fifteen in an elaborate dish), but there is nothing arbitrary in their selection. Throughout history, the nature of each flavoring, from indigenous black pepper and cardamom to those introduced by invaders and traders, such as chilies and fennel seeds, was carefully studied and

catalogued. According to India's ancient science of *Ayurveda*, a holistic approach to health, some spices are known to "heat" the body (cinnamon), some to "cool" (garlic), some to act as digestives (asafetida), some as antiseptics (turmeric), and so on. Knowledgeable cooks intuitively understand these properties and carefully regulate their diet with them.

Indian food is frequently spicy but not always hot. Chilies, which were brought to India from the New World by the Portuguese in the late fifteenth century, provide different degrees of heat and flavor. (Black peppercorns have been used through the ages to add punch as well.) If you prefer a milder dish, decrease the number of chilies used (and/or remove the ribs and seeds, which are the hottest parts) or eliminate them altogether; the dish will remain authentic in flavor.

In every Indian kitchen you will find a spice

container with many individual compartments holding spices for everyday cooking. For maximum flavor, spices are kept whole and ground as needed with a spice grinder—a stone bowl with an oval grinding stone—or an electric blender. In fact, some traditional households employ a professional spice grinder, who arrives each morning to freshly grind all the spices needed for the day.

Specific ground spice blends are popular in different regions of India. *Garam masala,* meaning "hot spices," is reputed to warm the body and is the most popular blend of Northern India. Although recipes vary (see ours on page 254), cardamom seeds, cinnamon, cumin seeds, cloves, coriander seeds, and black peppercorns are usually included. Relatively small amounts (usually a tablespoon or two) are used in a recipe, but this spice blend's intensity and versatility merit a mention. Our leg of lamb (page 253) is infused with the warm spicy flavor of a paste made with *garam masala* and additional spices; while our peas and *panir* (fresh cheese) dish (page 263) gets a final boost of flavor when a tablespoon of the blend is added to the sauce. *Sambar masala* (see our recipe on page 273) is used throughout South India to flavor the ubiquitous *sambar dal* (lentil stew). This blend contains plenty of chilies to make the body sweat and cool.

Although prepared ground spice blends are available in Indian markets, often they are bulked up with cheaper spices, like coriander and cumin, and contain very little of the expensive spices, like cardamom. For the best flavor, we suggest that you buy whole spices, grind them, and make your own blends as Indian cooks do. It is interesting to note that commercial curry powder (the universally known Indian spice blend created to meet British demand) is rarely used in North Indian kitchens, and never used in the South (where it is always homemade). To confuse matters further, when speaking English, Indians use "curry" to refer to any sauced dish.

Different methods of cooking with spices are mastered by all Indian cooks. In a technique known as *tarka* (or *baghaar* or *chownk*), meaning "seasoning in oil," spices are usually left whole and dropped in hot oil (or *ghee,* Indian-style clarified butter) until they quickly pop, brown, swell, or otherwise change character. Generally, whole seeds intensify in flavor and aroma and develop a nutlike taste. This flavored oil (including the spices) is poured over cooked vegetables or *dals* (legumes), such as our mung bean stew (page 266), or uncooked foods, such as our cabbage and coconut salad (page 266), as a final intense seasoning. At other times a *tarka* is made to season the main ingredient as it cooks. For example, in our prawn coconut dish (page 272), coconut milk is added to a *tarka,* then the prawns simmer in this rich sauce.

Sometimes ground spices are mixed with water or another liquid to make a flavorful paste or purée. In our okra recipe (page 257), *amchoor* (mango powder) and other spices are mixed to a paste with water to coat the sautéed vegetable. At other times, whole spices are dry-roasted in a hot, cast-iron skillet and then ground. One simply shakes the pan until the spices turn a shade or two darker and release their fragrance. Dry-roasted cumin seeds add distinctive flavor to our spiced tamarind drink (page 253).

As you will see, the recipes themselves act as a primer on Indian spices. You will begin to notice that a spice takes on diverse flavors when handled in different ways. Spice combinations produce yet more surprises. And, by combining different spices *and* cooking methods, the taste possibilities seem endless. Slowly one comes to understand the "layering of flavors" that is so often used to describe Indian cooking.

Below is a list of spices (and herbs) used in our menus. Because freshness is key, we suggest that you shop in Indian and Pakistani markets, at natural foods stores, or by mail order (see sources on page 247). (Supermarket spices can be used in a pinch, but they are less likely to be fresh.) Most dried spices keep their intense flavor for a year if kept in airtight containers in a cool, dry, dark place (see exceptions below). It is best to buy small quantities of whole spices and grind them, as needed, yourself.

Traditional spice box

Ajwain Seeds. Popular in Northwestern cuisines, these tiny, greyish-green, oval seeds are peppery when raw, a bit more mild-tasting when cooked. They also help with digestion.

Amchoor (mango powder). Made from unripe, green mango slices dried in the sun, this camel-colored powder adds sour flavor to North Indian dishes. Although dried mango slices are available, it is best to buy the powdered form.

Asafetida. Grown in Afghanistan and Western Kashmir, this smelly resin adds a distinct flavor to dishes and acts as a digestive in *dals*. Generally a pinch is added to very hot oil before other foods are added. Buy ground yellow asafetida powder (Vani brand) in the smallest box available.

Bay Leaves. Introduced by the Moguls to India, bay leaves are used primarily in rice and meat dishes for their delicate aroma. Western bay leaves are similar and can be substituted. Bay leaves are most flavorful if used within 6 months.

Cardamom. This prized, expensive spice is the dried fruit of a ginger family plant. The oval pods, either smooth green or white (bleached), contain lots of brown aromatic seeds. Whole pods are used to flavor rice and meat dishes and are sucked on as a mouth freshener (pods are not meant to be eaten); the seeds are ground for *garam masala*. If possible, use only green pods, preferably from Kerala in South India. Ideally, buy whole pods and seed them by hand as needed.

Fresh Chilies. India is the largest producer and exporter of chilies in the world, and many savory Indian dishes contain them. Chilies range in color from bright green to deep red, depending on ripeness, although they can be used at any stage. Mexican *serrano* or *jalapeño* as well as Thai chilies can be substituted for hot, fresh Indian chilies. Store fresh chilies, chilled, unwashed, and wrapped in paper towels, in a plastic container.

Chili Powder. The heat of ground dried chilies depends on the type of chili used. Chili powder, often made in India from ground dried Kashmiri chilies, offers bright red color and mild heat. In our recipes, New Mexican chili powder and paprika are combined for similar color and taste. (Do not confuse Indian chili powder with the brown, American southwestern spice blend sold in supermarkets.)

Cinnamon. The inner bark of a laurel tree, whole-stick cinnamon is often used in Indian meat and rice dishes for warm, sweet flavor and aroma. The most aromatic and flavorful cinnamon powder is made by breaking sticks into small pieces and grinding them in an electric grinder.

Cloves. The dried, unopened flower buds of clove trees, cloves are often used whole to add woody flavor and aroma to meat and rice dishes. They are also ground for *masalas*. Indians often suck on cloves as a mouth freshener after a meal.

Fresh Coriander. Also known as *cilantro*, the leaves and stems of the delicate coriander plant add lemony astringency to fresh chutneys, salads, and cooked dishes. Coriander also is commonly used as a garnish in India. To store fresh coriander with roots attached, remove any rubber bands, and submerge the roots in water, covering the leafy tops with a plastic bag. It keeps, refrigerated, up to 2 weeks.

Coriander Seeds. These round, beige seeds from the coriander plant offer sweet flavor and a pine-like aroma. Both seeds and plant are used in many savory Indian dishes.

Cumin Seeds. Used in every region of India, these seeds range from sage-green to tobacco-brown and have long ridges. They are used in both ground and whole form and have a warm, somewhat bitter taste. Black cumin seeds, a rare and expensive variety, are smaller and sweeter.

Curry Leaves. These slightly bitter, almond-shaped, dark-green leaves are available fresh or dried. They are used in savories throughout South India (where you will find a small potted curry plant in many kitchens), and in Gujarat to embellish vegetarian dishes.

Fennel Seeds. Known for their warm, sweet licorice flavor, these seeds are green when fresh, yellow when dry. A mix of sugar-coated and plain fennel seeds is often served at the end of a meal as a mouth freshener and digestive.

Fenugreek Seeds. These small, strange-looking, ochre-colored seeds give curry powders their musky aroma. They are used in pickles, chutneys, and vegetarian dishes in North India; elsewhere, they season meat and fish dishes as well. Fenugreek seeds are most flavorful if used within 6 months.

Ginger. Most Indian meat and vegetable dishes include some fresh ginger. Look for pieces with taut, unwrinkled skin and store in a cool, airy place.

Fresh Mint. Native to Europe, fresh mint now grows well in India. It is used mostly in chutneys, *raitas*, and drinks for its refreshing flavor, but it also appears in rich meat or chicken curries, primarily in the North.

Mustard Seeds. Three varieties of mustard seed—white, reddish-brown, and black—are grown in India, but the reddish-brown seeds are the most commonly used. (Black mustard seeds are larger and stronger tasting than the other two.) The raw seeds have no smell but are bitter. When crushed they are pungent; when cooked in hot oil, they acquire an earthy aroma and a nutty, somewhat sweet taste.

Nigella Seeds. Also known as *kalonji* or black onion seeds, these ebony seeds, in fact, have nothing to do with onions; they are the dried, ripe, unopened flower buds of a small herb. Faintly nutty, oniony, and bitter-tasting, they are used in North Indian *naan* bread, fish, and salads.

Sesame Seeds. These cream-colored, small and glossy seeds are sweet and nutty when cooked. (Black seeds are stronger in flavor). Traditionally, sesame seeds are used to make sweets and chutneys, or they are sprinkled over breads before baking.

Tamarind. The pod of the tamarind tree contains fleshy pulp with brown, shiny seeds held together in a fibrous husk. The pulp is added to South Indian and Gujarati lentil dishes, chutneys, and curries for its pleasantly tangy flavor. Tamarind is available as a pliable slab or as a softer block of fruit paste. (Thai brands generally have more pulp and are better-flavored than Indian ones.) Once soaked, it is mashed slightly and the pulp and juices are passed through a sieve, leaving the husk, fibers, and any seeds behind.

Turmeric. India is the world's largest producer and exporter of this spice. It adds a bright yellow coloring and faint musky flavor to dishes. Because it's considered an antiseptic and a preservative, it also appears in most pickles and is often rubbed on fish. Buy turmeric in powdered form and use it within 4 months.

RICE, BREADS, AND DALS

Everyday over 600 million Indians consume a vegetarian diet that includes rice and/or breads, and *dals* (dried beans, lentils, or split peas). Food is eaten with the fingers, and rice and breads absorb liquids, making everything easier to handle. Although the average Indian eats at least a half pound of rice per day, some rarely consume it at all. Likewise, not all Indians eat wheat. *Dals*, on the other hand, are universally consumed at most meals, by vegetarians and non-vegetarians alike.

RICE

All Indians enjoy plain rice, either boiled or steamed, although South Indians and Bengalis are considered the primary rice-eaters. When a meal is served on a *thali* (large plate), plain rice is mounded in the center and surrounded by small portions of the other dishes and condiments. Similarly, a South Indian meal served on a banana leaf always includes a generous serving of rice. Although many types of rice are grown and eaten in India (such as Patna, Ambemohar, and the nutritious Red Patni Rice), *basmati* is favored everywhere. Grown in the foothills of the Himalaya mountains and in other parts of the North, aromatic *basmati* has thin, long grains that taper to points. When the grains are boiled or steamed, they expand four times their length and give off a buttery fragrance. *Basmati* rice is used in *pulau* (pilaf), a rice dish flavored with whole spices and often cooked in stock. Our menus offer a Northern version with cinnamon, bay leaf, and *garam masala* flavorings (page 255); and a Southern one with mustard seeds, cumin seeds, cardamom, and gingered cauliflower (page 265). It is best to buy aged *basmati* rice at Indian grocers and natural foods stores. American varieties, such as Texmati and Kasmati, can be found in supermarkets; they are

243

pleasant but less aromatic. Store rice in an airtight container, and be sure to wash and pick over the rice before cooking.

Throughout South India, rice dishes appear at every meal. In addition to plain steamed rice, our menu offers two favorites—*dosas* (page 274), popular thin, lacy crêpes made from a fermented rice and *urad dal* (split-pea) batter; and rice *payasam* (page 275), a typical milk-based rice pudding often served for festive occasions. We used long-grain white rice (not converted) for these recipes.

BREADS

In the north central regions of India (including Delhi, Punjab, Uttar Pradesh, and Madhya Pradesh), making bread at home is part of daily life. Indian breads (called *roti*) are usually unleavened and made with whole-wheat flour, although chickpea, barley, millet, cornmeal, and plain white flour also are used. To this day, in order to have the freshest flour possible, Indians buy whole-wheat grain and have it ground at the nearest mill. *Chapatis,* India's most commonly prepared flatbreads, are traditionally made with a simple whole-wheat flour and water dough. Rounds of dough are cooked on a cast-iron *tava* (curved griddle), then puffed like balloons over the fire. (The puffing step makes them softer but is not essential.) Our recipe (page 264), adapted to a Western kitchen, calls for a griddle or cast-iron skillet and a gas flame (or hot electric burner). Perfection, say the experts, lies in the art of rolling out the dough, and this takes a bit of time to master. Look for *chapati* flour (Indian wheat flour, also called *atta* flour; see sources on page 247), or simply blend whole-wheat flour with all-purpose white flour. *Parathas* (pan-fried flaky breads of the Punjab) and *poori* (puffy deep-fried breads) are also made with wheat flour.

Naan, a white-flour, flat yeast bread of North India (it rises only about ¾ inch), is traditionally made by slapping a ball of dough onto the inner wall of a blazing *tandoor* oven (a clay oven with a charcoal or wood fire). The bread stretches as it cooks into a teardrop shape. For our *naan* (page 256), the dough is rolled, then baked in a Western oven set at its highest temperature; the results are quite similar. Although *naan* can be plain, ours is flavored with poppy seeds and onion and topped with a seed mixture.

Chapati on tava

DALS

Dal is the term used to describe both dried legumes—dried beans, lentils, or split peas—and the dishes that are made with them. (Literally, the Hindi word *dal,* comes from the Sanskrit word meaning to divide or split—although not all *dals* are split.) Whole, split, and ground into flour, *dal* appears in puréed soups and whole-bean stews, thin crêpes, airy dumplings, crisp fried vegetable cakes, savory steamed cakes, and smooth gravies.

Simple *dal* soups or purées are consumed daily with either rice or bread by virtually everyone in India, and they are regarded as a primary source of protein. A variety of dried legumes are cooked in different ways from one region to another: They are combined with browned onions, cooked with tamarind paste and jaggery (an unrefined sugar), added to vegetables, and so on; and the final *dal* can be either thick (generally preferred) or soupy. A *tarka* (spiced oil) is poured over the *dal* for a final seasoning. The heat level of the finished dish will range from mild to scorchingly hot, depending on the spices used in the *tarka*. *Dals* can be difficult to digest, so ginger or *asafetida* is added.

Besides serving as a main ingredient, *dals* can also be used as a flavoring, especially in the South, where they frequently appear in spice blends. Although each has a traditional use in Indian dishes, *dals* are generally interchangeable. Larger dried legumes, however, need to be pre-soaked, and some take longer to cook than others. Before using *dals,* remember to pick them over, removing any stones and dirt, and then wash them several times. Below is a list of *dals* used in our menus. All can be found in Indian and Pakistani markets, in natural foods stores, or by mail order (see sources on page 247). They should be stored in airtight containers and used within 4 months.

Toor dal (yellow lentils, also known as *toovar* or *arhar dal*) are featured in our *sambar* (lentil stew, page 273). They are sold split into two rounded halves and often oiled to extend shelf life. Preferably, buy matte, unoiled ones. If you cannot get them, soak oiled lentils in hot water and drain. Regular yellow split peas (sold in supermarkets) may be substituted.

Moong dal (split mung beans), popular in northern and western India, are yellow when skinned and split. Whole mung beans (*sabat moong*) are small, oval, and dull green and are featured in our *sabat moong dal* (page 266).

Kala chana dal (small, yellow chick-peas with brown skins), widely used in India, are skinned and left whole, split, or ground into flour. They are stronger tasting than the large white variety and have a nutty flavor. Skinned, split *chana dal* resembles *toor dal* in appearance but is larger and coarser. Both our green bean *thovaran* (page 274) and our *sambar masala* (page 273) use skinned, split *chana dal* as a spice. Roasted chick-pea flour (*besan*) is used in our *pakoras* (page 262).

Urad dal (black lentils; also known as *arhad dal*), found throughout India, are left whole (with skins) in northern cooking, and skinned and split in the South. Both our *sambar masala* (page 273) and *dosa* (page 274) call for split *urad dal,* which is creamy, white, and matte with subtle aroma and flavor. Whole black lentils are small and oblong, and may be flecked with dark green or grey; they have a strong smell and rich taste.

CONDIMENTS

Sour or sweet, pungent or mellow, crunchy or creamy, cooling or incendiary, condiments are the versatile little dishes in Indian cooking that provide texture and intense bursts of flavor at every meal. Each household has its favorites; fresh chutneys are made daily for maximum piquancy, while pickles are prepared in huge batches just once a year. In a country where, until recently, refrigeration was a luxury, cooked chutneys and pickles preserved the produce of one harvest until the next. While there are a few condiments, such as sweet mango chutney and sour lime pickle, that are quite acceptable when store-bought, it is almost always best to make your own for the freshest flavor.

CHUTNEYS

In India, a chutney can be any spicy combination of chopped or ground ingredients, such as fruits, vegetables, herbs, nuts, and/or chilies. Basically, there are two kinds: cooked and fresh. The cooked variety is made of cut-up fruits or vegetables, and perhaps some onion or garlic, sweetened with sugar, molasses, or raisins, and soured with lemon juice, vinegar, or tamarind. (Cooked Indian chutneys are familiar to most Westerners because similar, though far less spicy, mixtures were eagerly adopted by the British Raj during Colonial rule and brought back to England.) Most cooked chutneys, especially those with fiery seasonings, improve when allowed to mature and mellow for a few days in the refrigerator, where they will keep for a few weeks. Our Gingered Tomato Chutney (page 254), although not excessively chili-hot, falls into this category.

Indian chutneys, however, aren't limited to sweet and sour, jamlike mixtures. Fresh chutneys, like our Coriander and Mint Chutney (page 266), Tamarind Date Chutney (page 262), and Coconut Chutney (page 275), don't require any cooking at all, and are intensely flavorful. They are made from fresh herbs or seasonal fruit as well as from dried staples that are available year-round. Fresh chutneys will last several days in the refrigerator, although the bright color of the herbs will fade.

When multiple chutneys are served at a meal, they should be contrasting: If one is cooked, sweet, and spicy, the other should be uncooked, with perhaps a crunchy texture from nuts, or a fresh, tart, herbal flavor. Leftover chutney makes a great snack: Spread cooked chutney on sandwiches or crackers, or serve it with a hard cheese; some chutneys can be mixed with yogurt for a quick vegetable dip; or try fresh herb chutney as a marinade for grilled chicken or shrimp.

PICKLES

Intended to provide an intense salty, sour, spicy note, Indian pickles differ from our Western brined versions. The most common variety is the oil pickle —usually made by combining mustard oil with vegetables, such as carrots or eggplant; or fruits, such as limes, mangoes, or gooseberries. Making pickles, like baking bread or making wine, depends on proper fermentation and can be a bit tricky. Pickles need to mature (in India, the pots are often set out in the sun), and while aging, they must be stirred occasionally. Use a recipe from any Indian cookbook to make your own, or try Patak's brand of sour lime pickle or mango pickle, available in many supermarkets.

While bottled oil pickles aren't as distinctive as homemade, they're a fine introduction.

RAITAS

These yogurt-based condiments can be made with cooked or raw vegetables, fruits, seeds, or even fried dumplings. Cooling, mild *raitas*, such as our zucchini *raita* (page 252), are seasoned with fresh herbs; zestier ones, such as our tomato *raita* (page 265), are flavored with hot spiced oil. Indian yogurt, traditionally made from buffalo milk, is rich, thick, tangy, and creamy. Look for plain whole-milk yogurt, available at Middle Eastern, Mediterranean, and natural foods stores, which is closest in flavor and texture to the Indian kind.

SALADS

Indian salads are made from fresh vegetables, fruits, beans, or sprouted beans, and dressed with lemon juice, herbs, and hot spiced oil. The main ingredients are usually finely chopped or shredded. Salads are served like condiments: In India, only a few tablespoons are taken to provide a bit of crunchy contrast to the meal. To adapt to Western habits, our recipes for carrot salad (page 275) and cabbage salad (page 266) yield larger quantities.

MAIL ORDER SOURCES

All specialty ingredients used in our recipes are readily available in Indian, Pakistani, and often Middle Eastern foods shops. However, if you do not have these shops in your area, you can find many items elsewhere: Whole-milk yogurt, *basmati* rice, *ghee*, and some spices and *dals* are available in natural foods shops; fresh chilies, lotus root, and Asian eggplants are available at specialty produce shops and some supermarkets; and, in a pinch, the spices found in supermarkets can be used. All non-perishable items can be ordered from the sources listed below.

Kalustyan's
123 Lexington Avenue, New York, NY 10016
tel. (212) 685-3451; fax (212) 683-8458

Seema Enterprises
10635 Page Avenue, St. Louis, MO 63132
tel. (800) 557-3362; fax (314) 423-0391

Jay Store
6688 Southwest Freeway, Houston, TX 77074
tel. (713) 783-0032

Purity Farms *(for organic ghee only)*
14635 Westcreek Road, Sedalia, CO 80135
tel. (800) 568-4433; fax (303) 647-9875

A NORTH INDIA DINNER

Tandoori Murghi
(Grilled Chicken Skewers)

Louki Raita
(Zucchini in Creamy Yogurt)

Panakam
(Spiced Tamarind Cooler)

•

Gosht Korma
(Slow-Roasted Leg of Lamb)

Tamatar Chatni
(Gingered Tomato Chutney)

Punjabi Baigan Pyaz
(Spicy Eggplant with Tomatoes and Onions)

Basmati Pulau
(Basmati Rice with Raisins and Cashews)

Masala Bhindi
(Sautéed Okra)

Naan
(Leavened Flatbreads with Mixed Seeds)

•

Aam aur Pista Kulfi
(Mango and Pistachio Ice Cream)

•

Serves 8

Slow-Roasted Leg of Lamb; Spicy Eggplant with
Tomatoes and Onions; Basmati Rice with Raisins and
Cashews; Sautéed Okra; Gingered Tomato Chutney

Mango and Pistachio Ice Cream

spices with remaining marinade ingredients until smooth.

Cut chicken breasts crosswise into ¼-inch-thick strips and in a large sealable plastic bag combine with marinade. Seal bag, pressing out excess air, and turn bag several times to coat chicken well. *Marinate chicken at least 1 day and up to 2.*

While chicken is marinating, soak skewers in water at least 1 hour. Prepare grill (or preheat oven to its highest temperature, 500° to 550° F.).

Remove skewers from water and pat dry. Thread 1 piece chicken lengthwise onto each skewer and grill on an oiled rack set 5 to 6 inches over glowing coals, turning over once, until just cooked through, about 5 minutes. (Alternatively, in a lightly oiled shallow roasting pan arrange skewers in one layer and roast in middle of oven.)

Serve skewers with *raita* and lime wedges. Makes 36 skewers, serving 8 as an appetizer.

Tandoori Murghi
(Grilled Chicken Skewers)

For marinade
2 teaspoons cumin seeds
3 whole cloves
¼ cup plus 2 tablespoons plain whole-milk
   yogurt (preferably Middle Eastern*)
3 tablespoons chopped garlic
3 tablespoons chopped peeled fresh gingerroot
1¼ teaspoons chili powder (preferably
   New Mexican)
1¼ teaspoons paprika
1 teaspoon salt

1 pound boneless skinless chicken breasts
thirty-six 7-inch bamboo skewers

Accompaniments:
zucchini *raita* (recipe follows)
lime wedges

*sources on page 247

Make marinade:
In an electric coffee/spice grinder finely grind cumin seeds and cloves. In a blender blend ground

Louki Raita ◔
(Zucchini in Creamy Yogurt)

3 medium zucchini
1½ cups plain whole-milk yogurt
   (preferably Middle Eastern*)
½ cup packed fresh mint leaves
¼ cup packed fresh coriander sprigs
1 teaspoon fresh lime juice,
   or to taste
¾ teaspoon ground cumin
¼ teaspoon salt
2 tablespoons whole milk
   if necessary

*sources on page 247

Grate zucchini on largest holes of a four-sided grater. In a large saucepan of boiling salted water blanch zucchini 1 minute. Immediately drain zucchini in a sieve and rinse under cold running water to stop cooking. Squeeze zucchini dry by small handfuls and transfer to a bowl. Stir in remaining ingredients, adding enough milk to reach desired consistency. *Raita may be made 2 days ahead and chilled, covered.* Serve *raita* at cool room temperature. Makes about 2½ cups.

Panakam
(Spiced Tamarind Cooler)

8 ounces tamarind from a pliable block*
6 cups boiling water
1½ teaspoons cumin seeds
¼ cup superfine sugar
8 fresh mint sprigs
four ½-inch-thick slices fresh gingerroot
a 3-inch cinnamon stick

*sources on page 247

In a large heatproof bowl break up tamarind and soak in boiling water at least 6 hours and up to 12. Pour tamarind-soaking liquid through a fine sieve into a bowl, pressing on solids to extract as much liquid as possible, and discard solids. (If clarity is desired, pour strained liquid through a sieve lined with a triple layer of cheesecloth.)

In a dry heavy saucepan dry-roast cumin seeds over moderate heat until fragrant, about 1 minute. Add tamarind liquid and remaining ingredients and bring to a boil. *Let mixture steep at room temperature 3 hours.* Pour drink mixture through a sieve into a pitcher. *Cooler may be made 1 day ahead and chilled, covered.*

Serve cooler in ice-filled tall glasses. Serves 8.

Gosht Korma
(Slow-Roasted Leg of Lamb)

For marinade paste
1 small onion
a 3- to 4-inch cinnamon stick
2 tablespoons cumin seeds
⅓ cup chopped peeled fresh gingerroot
3 tablespoons chopped garlic
2 tablespoons *garam masala**
  (page 254)
2 tablespoons water
1 tablespoon paprika
2 teaspoons salt

a 6- to 7-pound leg of lamb (bone-in),
  trimmed and tied by butcher
2 tablespoons unsalted butter
2 tablespoons honey

2 tablespoons fresh lemon juice
2 tablespoons fresh lime juice

Accompaniments:
gingered tomato chutney (page 254)
sour lime pickle* (store-bought)

*sources on page 247

Make paste:
Chop onion and halve cinnamon stick. In an electric coffee/spice grinder finely grind cinnamon and cumin seeds. In a blender purée onion with ground spices and remaining paste ingredients until smooth.

Lightly oil a roasting pan just large enough to hold lamb. Rinse lamb and pat dry. With a small sharp knife make 6 deep (to the bone) 1-inch long slits at about 1½-inch intervals on each of 3 sides of leg, being careful not to cut strings. Arrange lamb, meaty side up, in pan and season with salt and pepper. Rub lamb all over with paste. *Marinate lamb, covered with plastic wrap and chilled, at least 4 hours and up to 24. Let lamb stand at room temperature 1 hour before roasting.*

Preheat oven to 325° F.

Cover pan with several layers of foil, sealing tightly, and roast lamb in middle of oven 2 hours.

In a small saucepan melt butter with honey and stir in citrus juices. Uncover lamb and pour half of honey sauce over it. Roast lamb, pan tightly covered with foil, 1 hour more. Uncover lamb and pour remaining honey sauce over it. Roast lamb, pan tightly covered with foil, basting lamb twice with pan juices, 1 hour more. Uncover lamb and roast until meat is almost falling off bone, about 30 minutes more. If lamb begins to blacken, cover loosely with foil. (Note: lamb roasts about 4½ to 5 hours total.)

Transfer lamb to a platter and discard strings. Let lamb stand until cool enough to handle and skim fat from pan juices. *Lamb may be made 1 day ahead and cooled completely before being chilled, covered. Chill pan juices separately. Bring lamb to room temperature before reheating, covered, in a 350° F. oven and reheat pan juices.*

Serve leg whole with pan juices or pull meat from bone and drizzle lamb with juices. Serve lamb with chutney and pickle. Serves 8 generously.

1 cup chopped onion
¾ cup finely chopped peeled fresh gingerroot
2 tablespoons mustard seeds*
1 teaspoon salt

*sources on page 247

Coarsely chop tomatoes. Wearing rubber gloves, seed *jalapeños* and finely chop.

In a large heavy saucepan bring vinegar with sugar to a boil, stirring until sugar is dissolved, and stir in remaining ingredients. Simmer mixture, uncovered, stirring occasionally (stir more frequently toward end of cooking), about 1½ hours, or until thickened and reduced to about 4 cups. Transfer chutney to a heatproof bowl and cool. *Chutney keeps, covered and chilled, 3 weeks*. Makes about 4 cups.

Garam Masala ☺
(North India Spice Blend)

two 3-inch cinnamon sticks
2 tablespoons coriander seeds
1½ tablespoons cardamom seeds
  (removed from green pods*)
1½ tablespoons cumin seeds
1½ tablespoons black peppercorns
½ tablespoon whole cloves

*sources on page 247

Break cinnamon stick and in a bowl combine all spices. In an electric coffee/spice grinder finely grind spices a few tablespoons at a time, transferring to an airtight container. *Garam masala keeps in a cool, dark place 1 month*. Makes about ½ cup.

Tamatar Chatni
(Gingered Tomato Chutney)

2½ pounds vine-ripened tomatoes
2 large fresh *jalapeño* chilies
1½ cups distilled vinegar
1¾ cups sugar
1½ cups golden raisins

Punjabi Baigan Pyaz
(Spicy Eggplant with Tomatoes and Onions)

2 pounds Asian eggplants* (long, thin, and pale
  purple) or small Italian eggplants
2 medium onions
4 to 5 fresh hot green chilies such as *serrano*,
  Thai*, or *jalapeño*
1 pound vine-ripened tomatoes
about ⅓ cup vegetable oil
1½ teaspoons cumin seeds
½ teaspoon fenugreek seeds*
1½ teaspoons fennel seeds
2 tablespoons minced garlic (about 5 large cloves)
1½ tablespoons finely grated peeled fresh
  gingerroot
2 tablespoons unsalted butter or *ghee*
  (procedure on page 267)

*sources on page 247

Cut eggplant diagonally into 1-inch-thick pieces. Cut onions into 1-inch pieces. Wearing rubber gloves, finely chop 3 chilies. Cut each tomato into 8 wedges and cut each wedge crosswise in half.

In a 12-inch non-stick skillet heat 1½ tablespoons oil over moderately high heat until hot but not smoking and sauté eggplant in batches, without crowding, until browned on both sides, adding more oil as necessary. Transfer eggplant as browned with a slotted spatula to a plate.

In skillet heat 1 tablespoon oil over moderate heat until hot but not smoking and cook onions and chopped and whole chilies, stirring, until onions are golden, about 3 minutes. Add spices and cook, stirring, until fragrant, about 1 minute. Add tomatoes, garlic, gingerroot, and butter or *ghee* and cook, stirring, about 2 minutes. Add eggplant and salt and pepper to taste and cook, gently tossing, until heated through. *Eggplant mixture may be made 1 day ahead and cooled completely before being chilled, covered. Bring eggplant mixture to room temperature before reheating.* Serves 8.

Basmati Pulau
(Basmati Rice with Raisins and Cashews)

2 cups white *basmati* rice*,
   picked over
2 tablespoons vegetable oil
a 3-inch cinnamon stick
1½ tablespoons mustard seeds*
3 whole cloves

1 teaspoon *garam masala** (page 254)
¼ teaspoon turmeric
2 bay leaves
2 teaspoons salt
3 cups water
½ cup raisins
⅓ cup roasted cashews
¾ cup chopped fresh coriander
   (about 1 bunch)

*sources on page 247

In a bowl wash rice in several changes of cold water until water runs clear and drain in a fine sieve. In a large heavy saucepan heat oil over moderate heat until hot but not smoking and cook spices and bay leaves with salt, stirring, until fragrant. Add rice and cook, stirring, 1 minute. Stir in water. Bring mixture to a boil and cook, covered, over low heat, 20 minutes. Lifting lid briefly, add raisins (do not stir). Cook rice, covered, 5 minutes more, or until tender and liquid is absorbed. Remove pan from heat and let rice stand, covered, 5 minutes. Add cashews and coriander and fluff rice with a fork until combined. Serves 8.

Sweeping unmilled rice

Cooking naan in a tandoori oven

Naan
(Leavened Flatbreads with Mixed Seeds)

½ stick (¼ cup) unsalted butter
1 teaspoon active dry yeast
½ teaspoon sugar
1 tablespoon warm water (105° to 115° F.)
2½ to 3¼ cups unbleached all-purpose flour
¼ teaspoon baking soda
1 teaspoon salt
2 teaspoons black poppy seeds*
½ cup warm milk (105° to 115° F.)
½ cup plain whole-milk yogurt at room
    temperature
⅓ cup finely chopped onion
1 large egg, beaten lightly
1½ tablespoons mixed seeds such
    as *nigella**, sesame seeds, and/or
    white poppy seeds*
coarse salt for sprinkling

*sources on page 247

Melt butter. In a small bowl stir together yeast, sugar, and water and let stand until foamy, about 5 minutes. Into a large bowl sift together 2½ cups flour, baking soda, 1 teaspoon salt, and ½ teaspoon black poppy seeds. In another bowl stir together milk, yogurt, onion, and 2 tablespoons butter. Make a well in center of flour mixture and add yeast mixture, milk mixture, and egg, stirring until a soft and sticky dough is formed.

Transfer dough to a floured surface and with floured hands knead for about 10 minutes, adding enough of remaining ¾ cup flour to form a soft but not sticky dough. Form dough into a ball and put in a lightly oiled large bowl, turning to coat. Cover bowl with a kitchen towel. *Let dough rise in a warm place until doubled in bulk, about 2 hours.*

Set oven rack to lowest position and preheat oven to 500° F. Lightly oil a heavy baking sheet (preferably black metal).

Transfer dough to a lightly floured surface and quarter it. Roll out each quarter into a ⅛-inch-thick oval (12 inches long and 5 inches wide). Let dough stand, covered with a kitchen towel, 10 minutes. While dough is standing, heat baking sheet 10 minutes. In a bowl stir together remaining 1½ teaspoons black poppy seeds with remaining seeds.

Remove sheet from oven and immediately put 1 oval on it. Brush top of oval with some melted butter and sprinkle with one-fourth of seed mixture and some salt. Bake loaf in oven until edges are golden brown and bread bubbles (top will be an uneven golden brown), about 4 minutes. Keep *naan* warm, loosely covered with foil. Make more loaves, 1 at a time, in same manner without preheating baking sheet (it will already be hot). *Naan may be made 1 day ahead and cooled completely before being kept, wrapped in plastic wrap, at room temperature. Reheat naan, uncovered, on a baking sheet in a 475° F. oven until bottoms are slightly crisp, about 2 minutes.* Makes 4 large *naan.*

Masala Bhindi
(Sautéed Okra)

1½ pounds bright-green fresh okra
 (preferably small)
3 fresh *jalapeño* chilies
2 teaspoons ground *amchoor**
 (green mango powder)
½ teaspoon turmeric
½ teaspoon chili powder (preferably
 New Mexican)
¾ teaspoon freshly ground black
 pepper
½ teaspoon salt
2 tablespoons water
¼ cup vegetable oil

*sources on page 247

Rinse and pat dry okra and trim stems (do not cut into pod). Wearing rubber gloves, seed *jalapeños* and chop. In a small bowl stir together spices, salt, and water to form a spice paste.

In a 12-inch non-stick skillet heat oil over moderately high heat until hot but not smoking and sauté okra and *jalapeños,* stirring, until okra is barely tender, about 2 minutes. Add spice paste and sauté, stirring, until okra is crisp-tender, about 3 minutes. Serves 8.

Aam aur Pista Kulfi
(Mango and Pistachio Ice Cream)

4 cardamom pods*
¾ cup shelled natural pistachios
three 1-pound 14-ounce cans mango slices in
 syrup* (preferably Alphonso mangoes) or 4
 pounds fresh mangoes (about 8 large)
2 cups sweetened condensed milk, chilled
1½ cups well-chilled heavy cream

*sources on page 247

Preheat oven to 350° F.

Remove seeds from cardamom pods, discarding pods, and in a grinder finely grind seeds. In a shallow baking pan toast nuts in oven until one shade darker, about 7 minutes, and cool in pan on a rack.

If using canned mango, drain in a sieve. If using fresh mangoes, peel and pit and coarsely chop. In a blender purée mango until smooth and transfer 5½ cups purée to a large bowl. Stir in cardamom, milk, and cream until combined well. Chill half of mango mixture, covered, and freeze remaining half in an ice-cream maker. Transfer ice cream to a 1½-quart airtight container and fold in half of pistachios. Freeze ice cream in freezer. Repeat procedure with remaining mango mixture and pistachios. *Kulfi keeps 1 week*. Makes about 2 quarts.

AN INDIAN VEGETARIAN DINNER

Tinda Chai
(Iced Chamomile Tea)

Pakoras
(Squash, Bean, and Lotus Root Fritters)

Imli Chatni
(Tamarind Date Chutney)

·

Matar Panir
(Peas and Fresh Cheese in Creamy Tomato Sauce)

Baigan aur Aloo Charchari
(Eggplant and Potato with Fresh Coriander)

Chapatis
(Whole-Wheat Flatbreads)

Gobhi Pulau
(Rice Pilaf with Cauliflower)

Tamatar Raita
(Tomatoes in Mustard Seed Yogurt)

Dhaniya aur Pudina Chatni
(Fresh Coriander and Mint Chutney)

Sabat Moong Dal
(Whole Mung Bean Stew)

Bandhgobhi Kachambar
(Cabbage and Coconut Salad)

·

Gulab Jamun
(Fried Milk Balls in Syrup)

·

Ladies in Festive Saris,
Udaipur, Rajasthan

Serves 8

Rice Pilaf with Cauliflower; Eggplant and Potato with Fresh Coriander; Whole Mung Bean Stew; Whole-Wheat Flatbreads; Cabbage and Coconut Salad; Peas and Fresh Cheese in Creamy Tomato Sauce

Fried Milk Balls in Syrup

Tinda Chai ◐+
(Iced Chamomile Tea)

8 cups water
4 chamomile tea bags
8 green cardamom pods*
zest of 1 orange, removed in strips with a
    vegetable peeler
zest of 1 lime, removed in strips with a
    vegetable peeler
¼ cup sliced peeled fresh gingerroot
¾ cup sugar

*sources on page 247

In a 4-quart saucepan bring all ingredients to a
boil and simmer, covered, 15 minutes. Remove pan
from heat and cool mixture. *Steep mixture, covered
and chilled, at least 8 hours and up to 24.* Pour
mixture through a fine sieve into a pitcher. *Tea
keeps, covered and chilled, 1 week.*

Serve tea in ice-filled tall glasses. Makes about
2 quarts.

Pakoras
(Acorn Squash, Green Bean, and Lotus Root Fritters)

a ½-pound lotus root*
1 cup water
1½ cups roasted chick-pea flour* (*besan*)
1½ teaspoons *garam masala**
    (page 254)
1½ teaspoons salt
1 teaspoon ground cumin
½ pound green beans
half a 1-pound acorn squash
about 1 quart oil for deep-frying

Accompaniment: tamarind date chutney
    (recipe follows)

*sources on page 247

Peel lotus root. In a saucepan simmer root in
water to cover 15 minutes, or until crisp-tender,
and drain.

In a blender blend together 1 cup water, chick-pea
flour, *garam masala*, salt, and cumin until smooth.

Transfer batter to a bowl and whisk in enough water,
1 tablespoon at a time, to thin batter until it just coats
a bean. Let batter stand while preparing vegetables.

Trim green beans. Seed squash and cut crosswise
into ⅛- to ¼-inch-thick slices. Cut slices in half. Cut
lotus root into ⅛- to ¼-inch-thick slices and pat dry.

Preheat oven to 250° F. In a 4-quart saucepan heat
3 inches oil over moderate heat until it registers
350° F. on a deep-fat thermometer. Line a large shallow baking pan with paper towels.

Whisk batter 30 seconds. Dip vegetables, 1 piece
at a time, into batter to coat and fry in batches of 6
until evenly golden, about 2 minutes on each side.
Transfer *pakoras* as fried with tongs to baking pan
and keep warm in oven.

Serve *pakoras* with tamarind date chutney. Serves
8 as an hors d'oeuvre.

Imli Chatni ◐
(Tamarind Date Chutney)

⅓ cup tamarind from a pliable block*
    (about 4 ounces)
1 cup boiling water
⅓ cup packed dried pitted dates
¼ cup finely grated fresh coconut (procedure
    on page 274) or desiccated coconut*
1 teaspoon grated peeled fresh gingerroot
¾ teaspoon *ajwain* seeds*
2 tablespoons chopped fresh coriander sprigs

*sources on page 247

Break up tamarind and in a heatproof bowl soak
in boiling water 15 minutes. With a fork mash tamarind until pulp is dissolved. Pour tamarind-soaking
liquid through a fine sieve into a blender, pressing
on solids to extract as much liquid as possible, and
discard solids. Add remaining ingredients except
coriander and blend until almost smooth. Stir in coriander. *Chutney keeps, covered and chilled, 1 week.*
Makes about 1½ cups.

Matar Panir
(Peas and Fresh Cheese in Creamy Tomato Sauce)

2 pounds vine-ripened tomatoes
4 small hot fresh green or red chilies such
    as *serrano**, *Thai**, or *jalapeño*
1 tablespoon finely grated peeled fresh
    gingerroot
1 tablespoon ground coriander
1½ teaspoons turmeric
1 teaspoon paprika
3 tablespoons *ghee** (procedure on
    page 267) or vegetable oil
1 teaspoon mustard seeds* (preferably
    brown or black)
1 teaspoon cumin seeds
½ teaspoon fennel seeds
1 teaspoon salt
12 ounces *panir** (fresh cheese,
    recipe follows)
1 tablespoon vegetable oil
1½ cups water
¼ cup heavy cream
1 tablespoon *garam masala**
    (page 254)
3 cups fresh or thawed frozen peas
¼ cup chopped fresh mint leaves

*sources on page 247

Peel, seed, and chop tomatoes. Wearing rubber gloves, seed 2 chilies and mince all 4 chilies. In a small bowl combine chilies, gingerroot, coriander, turmeric, and paprika.

In a 3-quart heavy saucepan heat *ghee* or oil over moderately high heat until hot but not smoking and cook mustard seeds, cumin seeds, and fennel seeds, stirring, until mustard seeds begin to pop, about 1 minute. Add chili mixture and cook, stirring, 30 seconds. Stir in tomatoes and salt and cook, stirring frequently, until mixture forms a paste, about 5 minutes. Simmer paste, stirring occasionally, until *ghee* or oil begins to separate from tomato mixture, about 10 minutes. *Sauce may be made up to this point 4 hours ahead and chilled, covered. Reheat sauce before proceeding.*

While sauce is simmering, cut *panir* into ¾-inch cubes. In a large heavy non-stick skillet heat

1 tablespoon oil over moderately high heat until hot but not smoking and sauté *panir*, stirring occasionally, until golden, about 4 minutes. Transfer *panir* to paper towels to drain.

Into sauce stir water, cream, *garam masala*, and peas and simmer 5 minutes (for frozen peas) to 10 minutes (for fresh), or until peas are just tender. Stir in mint. Add *panir* and simmer 2 minutes more. Serves 8.

Panir ☽+
(Fresh Cheese)

10 cups whole milk
⅓ cup fresh lemon juice

In a 6-quart heavy kettle bring milk to a full boil, stirring occasionally. Reduce heat to low and gently stir in lemon juice. Cook mixture until it begins to separate. Remove pan from heat and let mixture stand 10 minutes.

Pour mixture into a colander lined with a triple layer of cheesecloth. Rinse cheese curds under lukewarm running water. Gather up edges of cheesecloth, twisting to squeeze out water, and transfer cheese in cheesecloth to a bowl. Weight cheese with a bowl filled with water or a large can. *Let cheese stand 1 hour, or until firm.* Remove cheesecloth. *Panir keeps, wrapped well in plastic wrap and chilled, 3 days.* Makes about 12 ounces.

Baigan aur Aloo Charchari
(Eggplant and Potato with Fresh Coriander)

¼ cup tamarind from a pliable block*
  (about 2 ounces)
1¾ cups boiling water
2 tablespoons *jaggery** or brown sugar
1 teaspoon salt
1 tablespoon minced peeled fresh gingerroot
1 teaspoon fennel seeds
1 teaspoon turmeric
¼ teaspoon freshly grated nutmeg
¼ teaspoon *asafetida* powder*
⅛ teaspoon ground cloves
2 large boiling potatoes (about 1 pound total)
1 large eggplant (about 1½ pounds)
4 tablespoons *ghee** (page 267) or
  vegetable oil
3 small hot fresh green or red chilies such as
  *serrano**, Thai*, or *jalapeño*
two 3-inch cinnamon sticks
2 tablespoons chopped fresh coriander leaves

*sources on page 247

Break up tamarind block and in a heatproof bowl soak in boiling water 15 minutes. With a fork mash tamarind until pulp is dissolved. Pour tamarind liquid through a fine sieve into a bowl, pressing on solids to extract as much liquid as possible, and discard solids. Stir in *jaggery* or brown sugar and salt.

In a bowl combine gingerroot, fennel seeds, turmeric, nutmeg, *asafetida*, and cloves. Peel potatoes and cut potatoes and eggplant into 2-inch pieces.

In a large heavy non-stick skillet heat *ghee* or oil over moderately high heat until hot but not smoking and sauté gingerroot mixture and chilies, stirring, 1 minute. Add potatoes, eggplant, and cinnamon sticks, tossing to coat. Stir tamarind mixture and add to vegetable mixture. Simmer mixture, partially covered, without stirring, 15 minutes, or until vegetables are tender. Uncover skillet and cook mixture at a rapid simmer, without stirring, until liquid is evaporated and mixture is slightly charred (but not burned) on bottom, about 15 minutes.

Remove skillet from heat and let stand, covered, 5 minutes. Gently stir vegetables to mix in charred bottom and sprinkle with coriander. Serves 8.

Chapatis
(Whole-Wheat Flatbreads)

2 cups *chapati* flour* (or 1⅓ cups whole-wheat
  flour plus ⅔ cup all-purpose flour) plus
  additional if necessary
¾ teaspoon salt
1 teaspoon vegetable oil
⅔ to ¾ cup warm water
¼ cup *ghee** (page 267) or unsalted butter

*sources on page 247

In a bowl stir together 2 cups *chapati* flour (or flour mixture) and salt and add oil, rubbing flour with fingers until oil is incorporated. Add ⅔ cup water, stirring to form a dough, and stir in enough additional water, 1 tablespoon at a time, to make dough pliable but not sticky. On a work surface knead dough, adding more flour if it becomes sticky or more water if too stiff, until very smooth, about 10 minutes. Form dough into a ball and put in a lightly oiled bowl, turning to coat. *Let dough stand, covered with plastic wrap, 1 hour. Dough may be made 1 day ahead and chilled, covered. Bring dough to room temperature before proceeding.*

In a small saucepan melt *ghee* or butter over low heat and keep warm. Heat a griddle or cast-iron skillet over moderately low heat. Divide dough into 12 pieces and roll each into a ball. Put balls on a plate and cover with a dampened kitchen towel.

Arrange 3 heatproof ramekins around another burner and top with a metal rack (rack should be about 1 inch over heat). Turn on burner to high if electric and moderate if gas. Line a plate with a large sheet of foil.

On a lightly floured surface with a rolling pin flatten 1 ball and roll out into a 6- to 7-inch round. Transfer round to griddle or skillet (if *chapati* wrinkles, wait a few seconds until bottom is firm and shake griddle to flatten) and cook until small bubbles begin to form on top and bottom has pale golden spots. Turn *chapati* over and cook 30 seconds more. Transfer *chapati* to rack over burner and cook, turning once with tongs, until it balloons and each side has charred specks, about 15 seconds total. Transfer *chapati* to plate and lightly brush with *ghee* or butter. Wrap *chapati* with foil.

Make 11 more *chapatis* in same manner, stacking them in foil package as cooked. (If a *chapati* cracks when set on rack for puffing and is tough, move griddle off heat for a moment so next *chapati* cooks more slowly.) *Chapatis may be made 1 day ahead and chilled, wrapped well in foil. Reheat chapatis, wrapped in foil, in a preheated 300° F. oven.* Makes 12 *chapatis*.

Gobhi Pulau
(Rice Pilaf with Cauliflower)

1 small head cauliflower (about ¾ pound)
1 tablespoon vegetable oil
1 tablespoon finely grated peeled fresh gingerroot
½ teaspoon turmeric
1 tablespoon *ghee** (page 267) or vegetable oil
1 teaspoon mustard seeds* (preferably
   brown or black)
1 teaspoon cumin seeds
4 green cardamom pods*
1 cup white *basmati* rice*, picked over
1½ cups water
½ teaspoon salt
2 tablespoons chopped fresh coriander sprigs

*sources on page 247

Cut cauliflower into 1½-inch flowerets. In a large heavy non-stick skillet heat 1 tablespoon oil over moderately high heat until hot but not smoking and sauté gingerroot and turmeric 30 seconds. Add cauliflower, tossing to coat, and sauté, stirring occasionally, 3 minutes, or until edges are golden but cauliflower is still firm. Season cauliflower with salt and transfer with a slotted spoon to a bowl.

In a 3-quart heavy saucepan with a tight-fitting lid heat *ghee* or oil over moderately high heat until hot but not smoking and cook mustard seeds, cumin seeds, and cardamom pods, stirring occasionally, until mustard seeds begin to pop. Add rice and cook, stirring, 1 minute. Stir in water and ½ teaspoon salt. Add cauliflower (do not stir), and simmer, covered, over low heat 15 minutes, or until most liquid is absorbed. Remove pan from heat and let pilaf stand, covered, 5 minutes. Add coriander and fluff pilaf with a fork. Serves 8.

Tamatar Raita ☺
(Tomatoes in Mustard Seed Yogurt)

1½ cups plain whole-milk yogurt (preferably
   Middle Eastern*)
1 pound vine-ripened tomatoes
2 small hot fresh green or red chilies such as
   *serrano**, Thai*, or *jalapeño*
1 tablespoon vegetable oil
1½ teaspoons mustard seeds* (preferably
   brown or black)

*sources on page 247

In a bowl stir yogurt until smooth. Cut tomatoes crosswise in half and remove seeds. Cut tomatoes into 1½-inch chunks and add to yogurt. Wearing rubber gloves, seed 1 chili and mince both chilies. In a small skillet heat oil over moderately high heat until hot but not smoking and cook chilies and mustard seeds, stirring occasionally, until mustard seeds pop. Add chili mixture and salt to taste to yogurt mixture and gently stir until combined well. *Raita may be made 3 hours ahead and chilled, covered.* Serves 8.

Dhaniya aur Pudina Chatni ◔
(Fresh Coriander and Mint Chutney)

3 cups packed fresh coriander sprigs
1¼ cups packed fresh mint leaves
¾ cup chopped onion
1½ teaspoons minced garlic
¾ teaspoon minced peeled fresh gingerroot
2¼ teaspoons minced hot fresh green chili
  such as *serrano**, Thai*, or *jalapeño*
1¼ teaspoons sugar
¾ teaspoon salt
¾ cup plain yogurt

*sources on page 247

Wash herbs and spin dry. In a food processor purée all ingredients except ¼ cup yogurt. Transfer purée to a bowl and stir in remaining ¼ cup yogurt until combined well. *Chutney keeps, covered and chilled, 3 days.* Makes about 2 cups.

Sabat Moong Dal
(Whole Mung Bean Stew)

1 cup *moong dal** (whole mung beans),
  picked over
5 fresh or dried curry leaves*
1 tablespoon *jaggery** or brown sugar
2 teaspoons finely grated peeled fresh gingerroot

1 teaspoon salt
¾ teaspoon cayenne
3 cups water
2 teaspoons coriander seeds
1 teaspoon cumin seeds
1 teaspoon mustard seeds* (preferably
  brown or black)
¼ teaspoon fenugreek seeds*
3 tablespoons *ghee** (procedure on
  page 267) or vegetable oil
2 tablespoons chopped roasted peanuts
¼ teaspoon *asafetida* powder*
2 tablespoons fresh lemon juice

*sources on page 247

In a bowl soak *moong dal* in water to cover by 3 inches for 5 to 8 hours.

Rinse and drain *dal*. In a 4-quart saucepan simmer *dal*, curry leaves, *jaggery* or brown sugar, gingerroot, salt, cayenne, and 3 cups water, uncovered, stirring occasionally, 1 hour, or until beans are very tender but still hold their shape.

In an electric coffee/spice grinder, finely grind coriander seeds, cumin seeds, mustard seeds, and fenugreek seeds. In a small skillet heat *ghee* or oil over moderately high heat until hot but not smoking and cook ground spice mixture and peanuts, stirring, 1 minute, or until nuts are one shade darker. Add *asafetida* and sauté, stirring, 30 seconds. Add spice mixture and lemon juice to *dal* and simmer, stirring occasionally, 10 minutes. Stir *dal* vigorously, breaking up some beans to thicken mixture slightly, and season with salt. *Dal may be made 1 day ahead and cooled completely before being chilled, covered. Reheat dal.* Serves 8.

Bandhgobhi Kachambar
(Cabbage and Coconut Salad)

½ head green cabbage (about ½ pound)
2 small hot fresh green or red chilies such as
  *serrano**, Thai*, or *jalapeño*
½ cup finely grated fresh coconut (procedure
  on page 274)
2 teaspoons coriander seeds
2 tablespoons vegetable oil

1 teaspoon cumin seeds
1 teaspoon brown mustard seeds*
2 tablespoons fresh lemon juice

*sources on page 247

Finely shred cabbage. Wearing rubber gloves, seed 1 chili and mince both chilies. In a bowl combine cabbage, chilies, and coconut.

With a mortar and pestle lightly crush coriander seeds. In a small skillet heat oil over moderately high heat until hot but not smoking and cook coriander seeds, cumin seeds, and mustard seeds until mustard seeds pop. Pour hot oil mixture over cabbage mixture and add lemon juice and salt to taste, tossing to combine well. Serves 8.

Gulab Jamun
(Fried Milk Balls in Syrup)

2½ cups sugar
2½ cups water
2 teaspoons rosewater*
1 cup whole milk
3 cups instant nonfat dried milk powder
2½ tablespoons self-rising flour
6 cups *ghee** (procedure follows)

*sources on page 247

In a saucepan stir together sugar and water and simmer, stirring occasionally, until sugar is dissolved. Remove pan from heat and stir in rosewater. Transfer syrup to a large bowl.

In a small saucepan heat milk over moderate heat until warm and transfer ¾ cup to a bowl. In another bowl whisk together milk powder and flour. Add powder mixture to milk in bowl, stirring, and if dough is stiff, stir in enough remaining milk, 1 tablespoon at a time, to form a pliable dough.

In a wide kettle heat *ghee* or clarified butter over low heat. Quarter dough and divide each quarter into 8 pieces. With lightly oiled hands roll pieces into smooth balls, transferring as formed to a plate.

Increase heat to moderately low and heat *ghee* or butter until it registers 220° F. on a deep-fat thermometer. Add balls to *ghee* or butter, 1 at a time,

until all are in kettle and cook, gently shaking kettle occasionally (to prevent balls from browning too much on one side), until balls rise to surface, about 5 minutes. Cook balls, gently stirring, 20 minutes, or until balls are chestnut-colored. (Temperature of *ghee* or butter will rise slowly during cooking; lower heat if it exceeds 250° F.)

To check doneness, with a slotted spoon transfer 1 ball to syrup and let stand 2 minutes. If ball collapses, return to *ghee* and cook all balls 5 minutes more, or until a ball holds its shape in syrup. Transfer balls to syrup. *Let gulab jamun stand in syrup at room temperature 2 hours. Gulab jamun may be made 2 days ahead and chilled, covered.* Skim ghee or butter from syrup.

Serve *gulab jamun* warm or at room temperature with syrup. Makes 32 *gulab jamun*, serving 8.

To make 6 cups of ghee, enough to deep-fry our gulab jamun, you will need 4 pounds (16 sticks) of butter. Not to worry, fresh ghee keeps 2 months and adds incomparable flavor. Once used for deep-frying, it can be strained (through a sieve lined with a triple layer of cheesecloth) and used in other recipes. Ghee is very similar to clarified butter which can be substituted.

To Make Ghee

1 pound (4 sticks) unsalted butter

Cut butter into 1-inch pieces. In a heavy saucepan bring butter to a boil over moderate heat. Once foam completely covers butter reduce heat to very low. Continue to cook butter, stirring occasionally, until a thin crust begins to form on surface and milky white solids fall to bottom of pan. Continue to cook butter, watching constantly and stirring occasionally to prevent burning, until sediment turns a light brown and butter is golden, translucent, and fragrant. Remove *ghee* from heat and pour it through a sieve lined with a triple layer of cheesecloth into a clean jar. (Butter will lose about one fourth of its original volume.) *Ghee keeps, covered and chilled, 2 months.* Makes about 1½ cups *ghee*.

Rice Pudding

A SOUTH INDIA DINNER

Verenaga
(Spicy Roasted Peanuts)

•

Thengai Konju Curry
(Coconut Tiger Prawn Curry)

Sadam
(Steamed Rice)

Kaya-Kari Sambar
(Mixed Vegetable Sambar Stew)

Dosa
(Rice and Lentil Crisp Crêpes)

Avarakka Thovaran
(Dry-Curried Green Beans)

Kothimira-Pachadi
(Shredded Carrot Salad with Mustard Seeds)

Thengai Chatni
(Coconut Chutney)

•

Payasam
(Rice Pudding with Cardamom and Raisins)

•

Serves 6

Coconut Tiger Prawn Curry;
Steamed Rice; Dry-Curried
Green Beans

Mixed Vegetable Sambar Stew

Rice and Lentil Crisp Crêpes   271

Verenaga ◔
(Spicy Roasted Peanuts)

1 tablespoon vegetable oil
1¾ teaspoons ground cumin
1½ teaspoons ground coriander
1 teaspoon freshly ground black pepper
2 cups salted roasted peanuts
   (about 12 ounces)
¼ teaspoon cayenne
½ teaspoon turmeric
¾ teaspoon sugar

In a heavy skillet heat oil over low heat until hot but not smoking and cook cumin, coriander, and black pepper, stirring, until fragrant, about 30 seconds. Add remaining ingredients and salt to taste and cook, stirring, until peanuts are coated well, about 2 minutes. *Peanuts may be made 2 days ahead and cooled completely before being kept in an airtight container at room temperature.* Serve peanuts warm or at room temperature. Makes 2 cups.

Thengai Konju Curry
(Coconut Tiger Prawn Curry)

2 garlic cloves
a ½-inch piece peeled fresh gingerroot
3 fresh hot green chilies such as *serrano**
2½ cups thinly sliced onion
¼ cup vegetable oil
1½ tablespoons ground coriander
1 teaspoon ground cumin
1 teaspoon turmeric
1 teaspoon salt
½ teaspoon freshly ground black pepper
¼ teaspoon ground cinnamon
⅛ teaspoon ground cloves
a 14-ounce can unsweetened coconut milk*
2 pounds jumbo tiger prawns or jumbo shrimp
   (about 24)

*sources on page 247

Mince garlic and gingerroot. Wearing rubber gloves, finely chop chilies.

In a deep 12-inch heavy skillet cook onion in oil over moderate heat, stirring occasionally, until edges are browned. Add garlic, gingerroot, chilies, and remaining ingredients except coconut milk and prawns or shrimp and cook over moderately low heat, stirring occasionally, 8 minutes. Stir in coconut milk and remove skillet from heat. *Sauce may be made 2 days ahead and cooled completely before being chilled, covered.*

Shell prawns or shrimp, leaving tails and first shell segments intact, and devein if desired.

Bring sauce to a boil, stirring. Add prawns or shrimp and simmer, uncovered, stirring occasionally, until just cooked through, 3 to 5 minutes. Serves 6.

Sadam ◔
(Steamed Rice)

6 cups water
2 teaspoons salt
3 cups long-grain white rice (not converted)

In a 3- to 4-quart heavy saucepan bring water with salt to a boil. Add rice and cook, stirring, until water returns to a boil. Reduce heat to low and simmer, partially covered, until most of water is absorbed and surface of rice is covered with steam holes, 8 to 10 minutes.

Cover pan and cook rice over very low heat until rice is tender and all water is absorbed, about 15 minutes more. Remove pan from heat and let stand, undisturbed, 5 minutes. Fluff rice with a fork. *Rice may be made 3 days ahead and cooled completely before being chilled, covered. Reheat rice in a lightly oiled colander set over a saucepan of boiling water and covered.* Makes about 9 cups, serving 6.

Kaya-Kari Sambar
(Mixed Vegetable Sambar Stew)

½ cup uncoated *toor dal** (yellow lentils)
6 cups water
¼ cup tamarind from a pliable block*
2 medium vine-ripened tomatoes
10 small shallots (about 1½ inches in diameter)
1 tablespoon vegetable oil
½ teaspoon brown mustard seeds*
½ teaspoon fenugreek seeds*
¼ teaspoon *asafetida* powder*
6 fresh curry leaves*
1 fresh hot green chili such as *serrano**,
 Thai*, or *jalapeño*
1 tablespoon *sambar masala** (recipe follows)
1½ teaspoons salt
1 large boiling potato

Accompaniment: dosa (page 274)

*sources on page 247

In a 2-quart saucepan simmer *toor dal* in 3 cups water, uncovered, until *dal* is very soft and falling apart, 30 to 40 minutes.

While *dal* is simmering, bring 1 cup water to a boil. Break up tamarind and in a heatproof bowl soak in boiling water 15 minutes. Pour tamarind-soaking liquid through a sieve into a bowl, pressing on solids to extract as much liquid as possible, and discard solids.

Coarsely chop tomatoes and peel shallots. In a 3-quart heavy saucepan heat oil over moderate heat until hot but not smoking and cook mustard seeds,

fenugreek seeds, and *asafetida*, stirring, until mustard seeds begin to pop. Add remaining 2 cups water, tamarind liquid, tomatoes, shallots, and remaining ingredients except potato and *dal* and simmer, stirring occasionally, 15 minutes, or until shallots are tender. Peel potato and cut into ⅓-inch pieces. Stir in potato and simmer, stirring occasionally, until potato is tender, about 10 minutes.

Add *dal* and simmer, stirring occasionally, 10 minutes. (*Sambar* will be soupy.) *Sambar may be made 3 days ahead and chilled, covered. Reheat sambar.*

Serve *sambar* with *dosa* for dipping. Serves 6.

Sambar Masala ◔
(South India Spice Blend)

½ teaspoon vegetable oil
¼ cup coriander seeds
1 tablespoon cumin seeds
1⅛ teaspoons fenugreek seeds*
1⅛ teaspoons black peppercorns
1⅛ teaspoons brown mustard seeds*
½ teaspoon *chana dal** (small yellow
 split chick-peas)
½ teaspoon *urad dal** (white split lentils)
a 1½-inch piece cinnamon stick
4 to 6 fresh curry leaves*
½ ounce dried whole hot red chilies (½ cup)
1 teaspoon turmeric

*sources on page 247

In a heavy skillet heat oil over moderate heat until hot but not smoking and cook coriander seeds, cumin seeds, fenugreek seeds, peppercorns, mustard seeds, *chana dal, urad dal*, and cinnamon, stirring constantly, 3 minutes. Add curry leaves and cook, stirring constantly, 5 minutes. Add chilies and cook, stirring constantly, until chilies darken, 2 to 3 minutes. Transfer spice blend to a plate and cool completely.

In an electric coffee/spice grinder finely grind spice blend, a few tablespoons at a time, transferring to a small bowl. Stir in turmeric until combined well. *Sambar masala keeps in an airtight container in a cool, dark place 3 months.* Makes about ½ cup.

Dosa
(Rice and Lentil Crisp Crêpes)

1½ cups long-grain white rice
  (not converted)
¾ cup *urad dal** (white split
  lentils)
1½ cups plus 5 tablespoons water
¾ teaspoon salt
about ½ cup vegetable oil
  for frying *dosa*

*sources on page 247

In separate bowls soak rice and urad dal in water to cover by 2 inches for 4 hours.

Drain *dal* in a sieve and in a food processor purée *dal* with ¾ cup water until light and fluffy, 3 to 5 minutes. Transfer *dal* to a large bowl. Drain rice in a sieve and in food processor purée rice with 5 tablespoons water until a gritty paste forms, about 1 minute. (Rice will not be as smooth as *dal*.) Stir rice and salt into *dal. Let mixture ferment, covered with plastic wrap, in a warm place (about 80° F.) 24 hours, or until doubled in bulk. (Mixture will be light and foamy.) Stir in remaining ¾ cup water. Let batter stand, covered, in a warm place 1½ to 2½ hours.*

Preheat oven to 250° F.

In an 8-inch heavy non-stick skillet heat 1 teaspoon oil over moderate heat until hot but not smoking. Fill a ⅓-cup measure with batter, gently scooping it, and pour into center of skillet (use a rubber spatula to scrape out batter remaining in measure). With back of a spoon quickly spread batter to thinly cover bottom of skillet. (*Dosa* will be lacy around edges.) Drizzle edge and top of *dosa* with 1 teaspoon oil and cook until underside is light golden and crisp, 1½ to 2 minutes. Turn *dosa* over and cook, pressing occasionally with a metal spatula, until underside is light golden, about 1 minute more. Roll *dosa* up loosely and transfer to an ovenproof platter. Keep *dosa* warm, covered loosely with aluminum foil, in oven and make more *dosa* in same manner. (*Alternatively, dosa may be made 1 hour ahead and kept, covered with aluminum foil, at room temperature. Reheat dosa in a 350° F. oven.*) Makes about 12 *dosa*.

Avarakka Thovaran
(Dry-Curried Green Beans)

1½ pounds green beans
2 teaspoons vegetable oil
1½ teaspoons brown mustard seeds*
1½ teaspoons cumin seeds
1½ teaspoons *chana dal** (small yellow
  split chick-peas)
1½ teaspoons *urad dal** (white split lentils)
1 small fresh hot red chili such as *serrano**,
  Thai*, or *jalapeño*, halved
4 fresh curry leaves*
½ cup water
½ cup finely grated fresh coconut
  (preferably by hand, procedure
  follows)

*sources on page 247

Trim beans and cut into ¼-inch pieces. In a heavy saucepan heat oil over moderate heat until hot but not smoking and cook mustard seeds, cumin seeds, *chana dal, urad dal*, chili, and curry leaves until mustard seeds begin to pop. Stir in beans, water, and salt to taste and simmer, covered, until beans are just tender, 6 to 8 minutes. Stir in coconut until combined well. *Beans may be made 6 hours ahead and chilled, covered. Reheat beans.* Serves 6.

To Crack and Grate Fresh Coconut ◌

1 heavy coconut without any cracks and
  containing liquid

Preheat oven to 400° F.

Pierce softest eye of coconut with a metal skewer or small screwdriver and drain liquid. Bake coconut in oven 15 minutes.

With a hammer or back of a heavy cleaver break shell and with point of a strong knife remove flesh, levering it out carefully. Remove brown membrane with a sharp paring knife or vegetable peeler if desired. *Fresh coconut keeps, chilled in an airtight container, 1 week.*

To grate coconut:

Grate coconut as needed on small holes of a 4-sided grater or in a food processor.

Thengai Chatni
(Coconut Chutney)

1 cup finely grated fresh coconut
  (procedure on page 274)
¾ cup packed fresh mint leaves
2 small hot fresh green or red chilies
    such as *serrano**, Thai*,
    or *jalapeño*
1 teaspoon grated peeled fresh gingerroot
2 tablespoons roasted peanuts
1¼ teaspoons salt
3 tablespoons *jaggery** or
    brown sugar
⅓ cup water

*sources on page 247

In a food processor pulse together all ingredients until finely chopped. *Chutney keeps, covered and chilled, 1 day.* Makes about 1½ cups.

Kothimira-Pachadi ◌
(Shredded Carrot Salad with Mustard Seeds)

¾ pound carrots (about 4 large)
1½ fresh hot green chilies such as *serrano**,
  Thai*, or *jalapeño*
1 tablespoon vegetable oil
1½ teaspoons brown mustard seeds*
¼ teaspoon *asafetida* powder*
6 fresh curry leaves*
1½ tablespoons fresh lemon juice, or to taste

*sources on page 247

Using a manual slicer or a food processor fitted with shredding disk, finely shred carrots. Wearing rubber gloves, mince chilies. In a heavy skillet heat oil over moderate heat until hot but not smoking and cook mustard seeds, chilies, *asafetida,* and curry leaves, stirring constantly, until mustard seeds begin to pop. Stir in carrots until coated well and transfer to a bowl. Toss salad with lemon juice and salt to taste. *Salad may be made 1 day ahead and chilled, covered.* Before serving, add additional lemon juice to taste. Serve salad warm or at room temperature. Makes 3 cups, serving 6.

Payasam
(Rice Pudding with Cardamom and Raisins)

4 green cardamom pods*
2 quarts (½ gallon) whole milk
¾ cup long-grain white rice
  (not converted)
a pinch saffron threads*
1 cup sugar
½ cup finely grated fresh coconut (by
  hand, procedure on page 274) or
  chopped unsalted roasted cashews
⅓ cup golden raisins

*sources on page 247

With back of a large knife, lightly crush green cardamom pods. In an 8-quart heavy saucepan simmer milk, rice, cardamom pods, and saffron, stirring frequently to prevent sticking and scorching, until reduced by half, 25 to 35 minutes. Discard cardamom.

Stir in remaining ingredients and simmer, stirring frequently, until thickened, 6 to 8 minutes. *Payasam may be made 1 day ahead and chilled, covered.* Serve payasam warm or cold. Serves 6.

A GOURMET ADDENDUM

GIFTS FROM YOUR KITCHEN

It's true—few gifts make a more lasting impression than one that's homemade. And, because opportunities to cook at leisure are so rare these days, gifts from the kitchen are especially appreciated. Here we offer extraordinary snacks, hors d'oeuvres, condiments, and sweets for year-round giving, each guaranteed to be remembered long after the last morsel is savored. You'll even want to make these goodies for yourself, to have on hand when friends are expected. To satisfy busy cooks, many of these recipes can be made in 45 minutes or less (Jerk-Spiced Peanuts, page 278, and Maple Apricot Butter, page 284, to name a couple). And, because there's always a need for holiday items, we've included Coconut Macadamia Macaroons (page 286) for Passover and a Spiced Berry Cordial (page 287) that would be especially festive for Christmas. Other items, such as Smoked Salmon Cream Cheese Spread (page 280) and Mushroom Walnut Pâté (page 280) make lovely hostess gifts.

As always, cooking with the freshest ingredients makes all the difference in flavor. (Pantry items, such as olives, nuts, dried fruit, dried herbs, spices, oils, and vinegars, are no exception.) Shop in stores with quick turnover, check expiration dates on jars and cans, and replace your dried herbs and spices after a year.

To keep a homemade gift fresh, it must be stored in an airtight container. Glass jars display condiments and sauces at their best, and because glass is non-reactive, it's ideal for storing liquids and moist foods (avoid aluminum and plastic). There are plenty of options, including old-fashioned and decorative jelly jars (available in 4- and 12-ounce sizes); wide-mouthed, tapered canning jars (8-ounce size); and French *confiture* jars (12- to 13-ounce capacity) with plastic lids. Glass-topped, European-style jars (1- to 2-quart capacity) with rubber rings and wire closures are great for foods with a high vinegar or alcohol content that can corrode metal lids. If reusing glass bottles or jars, be sure to clean and sterilize them. For baked goods, use tins and plastic containers.

Food safety is always a concern, and it's especially important when handling storage containers—all must be washed in hot soapy water (or in your dishwasher). Glass containers, in most cases (see recipes), must also be sterilized just before use.

Decorating your container adds a personal touch to your gift. For a homey look, cover the top of a jelly jar with a small round of gingham cut with pinking shears and secure it with ribbon, or for natural flair, tie raffia onto a thin-necked bottle. A basket filled with your homemade gift, a store-bought accompaniment, or even a handy kitchen gadget always makes a special presentation. For example, add a jar or two of mustard to enliven our pretzels, or a shrimp sheller to encourage the use of our shrimp spice mix. Remember, too, that baked goods and confections can be stored in a plastic bag, then nestled in a pretty ceramic pie plate or loaf pan (look for them at craft markets), and spreads and pâtés can be put in handsome crocks and ramekins. Be sure to write out the recipe on a pretty note card as part of your gift, and include suggestions for use, storage instructions, and the length of time it can be kept. If your gift is going into a decorative bag, punch a hole in the recipe card and thread it with ribbon to the handles. For bottled goods, affix a label that includes storage instructions and how long the item keeps.

MAIL ORDER SOURCES

Williams-Sonoma (800) 541-2233
European canning jars, Italian bottles, earthenware bowls and pie dishes, porcelain ramekins

The Container Store (800) 733-3532
Spanish glass bottles, plastic tubs, stacking jars, French canning jars, and square glass containers

Joe McCaffery at Narrow Land Pottery (508) 349-6308
Custom orders for pottery bowls and covered canisters

Peanuts come in jars with resealable airtight lids that make ideal containers for our spiced nuts. You can add your own label for a personal touch.

Jerk-Spiced Peanuts ◌

1 large egg white
1 tablespoon malt vinegar or distilled vinegar
3 tablespoons molasses
3 cups roasted peanuts
1 tablespoon sugar
2 teaspoons all-purpose flour
2 teaspoons salt
¾ teaspoon ground allspice
¼ teaspoon freshly grated nutmeg
¼ teaspoon cinnamon
¼ teaspoon ground ginger
¼ teaspoon freshly ground black pepper
⅛ teaspoon cayenne, or to taste

Preheat oven to 375° F. Line a large shallow baking pan with foil and lightly oil.

In a bowl whisk together egg white, vinegar, and molasses and add peanuts, tossing to coat well. In a small bowl stir together remaining ingredients and add to peanuts, tossing to coat well. Spread nuts in one layer in pan and roast in middle of oven, stirring occasionally, 15 to 18 minutes, or until golden brown. If desired, toss additional black pepper and cayenne into hot nut mixture. Cool nuts completely in pan on a rack. *Nuts may be made 1 week ahead and kept in an airtight container at room temperature.* Makes 3 cups.

You may want to try Greek sheep's milk feta for this recipe, although cow's milk feta, found in most supermarkets, is fine. Serve our marinated feta with pita bread or crackers or crumble it over a salad.

Herb-Marinated Feta ◌+

½ pound feta
1 tablespoon whole black peppercorns
6 to 8 fresh oregano sprigs
3 fresh mint sprigs
3 garlic cloves, sliced thin
4 thin lemon slices
1 to 1½ cups olive oil

Cut feta into 1-inch cubes and bruise peppercorns with side of a large knife. In a sterilized 1-pint jar (procedure follows) with a tight-fitting lid layer all ingredients except oil and add enough oil to cover. *Marinate cheese, covered and chilled, at least 2 days and up to 1 week.* Serve feta at room temperature. Serves 4 as an hors d'oeuvre.

To Sterilize Jars

Wash jars in hot suds and rinse in scalding water. Arrange jars, right side up, on a metal rack in a deep kettle, making sure that they do not touch side of kettle or each other, and cover with hot water by 1 inch. Bring water to a boil and boil jars 15 minutes. Turn off heat and let jars stand in hot water. Just before filling jars, remove carefully with tongs and dry, upside down, on paper towels. (Jars should be filled while still hot.) Lids, rubber seals, and corks should also be sterilized 5 minutes, or according to manufacturer's instructions.

ALEXIS SEABROOK

Our olive pesto is delicious served as a spread with crackers or sliced bread and mild goat cheese, Monterey Jack, or Cheddar. You can also use it as a pasta sauce: For 1 pound of cooked linguine or other pasta, whisk about 1 cup pesto with ⅔ cup hot pasta-cooking water and toss with drained pasta and some Parmesan.

Provençal Pesto ◔

½ cup dried tomatoes
¾ cup brine-cured black olives
¾ cup brine-cured green olives
¾ cup packed fresh parsley leaves
¾ cup packed fresh basil leaves
2 garlic cloves, chopped
1 flat anchovy fillet, chopped, if desired
½ cup olive oil
3 tablespoons drained small capers
2 tablespoons balsamic vinegar
2 tablespoons unsalted butter, melted

If dried tomatoes are not packed in oil, in a small heatproof bowl cover tomatoes with boiling-hot water and soak 20 minutes, or until softened. Drain tomatoes and coarsely chop. Rinse, drain, and pit olives. In a food processor pulse together all ingredients and pepper to taste until chopped but not smooth. Transfer pesto to sterilized jars (procedure on page 278) with tight-fitting lids. *Pesto keeps, chilled, 2 weeks.* Makes about 3 cups.

The next time you're invited to a picnic, bring along these chewy pretzels. For a clever presentation you can arrange them side-by-side in a long bread basket or loaf pan.

Soft Pizza Pretzels

1 cup warm water (110° to 115° F.)
1 teaspoon sugar
a ¼-ounce package (2½ teaspoons)
   active dry yeast
3¼ to 3½ cups all-purpose flour
⅓ cup minced pepperoni
⅓ cup finely chopped drained dried tomatoes
   (packed in oil)
¼ teaspoon dried oregano, crumbled

¼ teaspoon freshly ground black pepper
an egg wash made by beating together
   1 large egg and 1 tablespoon water
coarse salt to taste

In a large bowl stir together water, sugar, and yeast and let stand until foamy, about 5 minutes. Add 3 cups flour and beat until smooth. Add pepperoni, tomatoes, oregano, and pepper and beat until combined well. Beat in enough remaining flour to form a soft but not sticky dough. On a lightly floured surface knead dough 10 minutes and cover with inverted bowl. *Let dough rise until doubled in bulk, about 1 hour.*

Sprinkle 2 baking sheets with cornmeal or flour.

Roll out dough into a 15- by 12-inch rectangle and with a pizza wheel or sharp knife cut it crosswise into 12- by ½-inch strips. On baking sheets form strips into 4-inch pretzel shapes (see illustration below), arranging pretzels about 2 inches apart.

Preheat oven to 475° F.

Brush pretzels with egg wash and sprinkle with coarse salt. Let pretzels rise, covered loosely with plastic wrap, in a warm draft-free place 20 minutes. Bake pretzels in upper and lower thirds of oven 8 to 10 minutes, or until golden, and transfer to racks to cool. *Pretzels keep in an airtight container at room temperature 1 day or frozen 1 month. Reheat frozen pretzels on a baking sheet in a 300° F. oven until heated through.* Makes about thirty 4-inch pretzels.

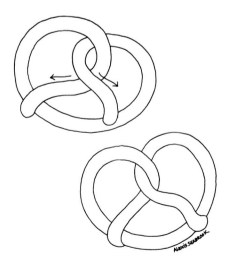

A bottle of Beaujolais Nouveau, a loaf of country bread, some cornichons, and coarse-grained mustard all make nice accompaniments to our pâté. To make several smaller gifts, pack the pâté mixture into small loaf pans or ovenproof crocks (totaling 6 cups capacity), wrap individually, and bake 1 hour.

Mushroom Walnut Pâté

3 leeks (white and pale green parts only)
1 cup chopped celery
½ cup chopped carrot
3 garlic cloves, chopped
1 stick (½ cup) unsalted butter
1 cup walnuts
2 pounds mushrooms, sliced
¼ cup dry Sherry or dry vermouth
2 teaspoons dried rosemary, crumbled
1½ teaspoons dried sage, crumbled
⅛ teaspoon ground allspice
⅛ teaspoon freshly grated nutmeg
1½ teaspoons salt
¾ teaspoon freshly ground black pepper
8 ounces cream cheese, cut into pieces
1 cup fresh bread crumbs
3 large eggs
¼ cup chopped fresh parsley leaves

Chop leeks and wash well and drain. In a large deep skillet or kettle cook leeks, celery, carrot, and garlic in butter over moderately low heat, stirring occasionally, until very soft but not browned, about 1 hour.

Lightly toast walnuts and cool. Chop nuts.

Preheat oven to 350° F. and butter a 9- by 5- by 3-inch loaf pan (6-cup capacity).

To vegetable mixture add mushrooms, Sherry or vermouth, rosemary, sage, allspice, nutmeg, salt, and pepper and cook over moderate heat, stirring, until liquid mushrooms give off is evaporated. Add cream cheese, stirring until melted, and transfer to a food processor. Add bread crumbs and pulse mixture until coarsely ground. Transfer mixture to a bowl and stir in nuts and remaining ingredients until combined well. Pack pâté mixture into loaf pan and rap on a hard surface to eliminate any air bubbles. Wrap entire pan in wax paper then in a double thickness of foil, leaving seam on top and crimping foil tightly around edges.

Bake pâté in middle of oven 1 hour and 15 minutes. Cool pâté, wrapped, to room temperature. *Chill pâté, wrapped, at least 8 hours and up to 2 days. Alternatively, pâté may be frozen, kept wrapped well and sealed in a freezer bag, 2 months.*

Run a knife around edge of loaf pan and invert pâté onto a plate. Serves 18 as an hors d'oeuvre.

Olive aficionados will enjoy the southern Mediterranean flavors of this snack. Glass-topped European-style jars ideally show off this mixture.

Mediterranean Marinated Olives ☺+

1 orange
2 cups mixed brine-cured olives
1 tablespoon fennel seeds
1 teaspoon dried hot red pepper flakes
4 fresh rosemary sprigs
1 to 1½ cups olive oil

Remove zest from half of orange with a vegetable peeler and cut into julienne strips. Rinse and drain olives. Lightly crush fennel seeds and pepper flakes with side of a large knife.

In a sterilized jar (procedure on page 278) with tight-fitting lid combine all ingredients, adding enough oil to cover. *Marinate olives, covered and chilled, at least 1 week and up to 1 month.* Serve olives at room temperature. Makes 2 cups.

For a complete breakfast gift to offer weekend hosts, bring along this spread, bagels or bialys, a sweet onion, and a bag of coffee.

Smoked Salmon Cream Cheese Spread ☺

8 ounces cream cheese, softened
2 tablespoons drained capers
1 tablespoon minced fresh dill leaves
2 teaspoons fresh lemon juice
¼ teaspoon freshly ground black pepper, or to taste
5 ounces smoked salmon, chopped (about ¾ cup)

In a bowl with an electric mixer beat cream cheese until smooth. Add capers, dill, lemon juice, and pepper and beat until combined well and capers are chopped. Fold in salmon and transfer spread to a large crock or a ramekin. *Spread keeps, covered and chilled, 3 days.* Makes about 1½ cups.

CONDIMENTS

This fruity vinegar, a welcome alternative in dressings and marinades, has a beautiful rose hue. The basil can be replaced with lemon verbena, sage, rosemary, or chervil. You may want to save your rice vinegar bottle for storing the flavored vinegar.

Plum Basil Vinegar ○+

1½ cups rice vinegar (not seasoned; a
   12-ounce bottle)
4 ripe black, purple, or red plums
2 small fresh basil sprigs
1 tablespoon sugar

Pour vinegar into a very clean 1-quart glass jar with a tight-fitting lid. Cut plums into eighths and add fruit with pits, basil, and sugar to vinegar. Shake mixture gently to dissolve sugar. *Let mixture steep, covered, in a cool, dark place 1 week.*
Pour vinegar through a fine sieve set in a funnel into a clean bottle and seal. Makes about 1½ cups.

You'll find all sorts of unexpected ways to use this relish: with cheese and crackers; on hot dogs, hamburgers, and other sandwiches; or as a condiment with poultry and fish.

Four Pepper Relish ○+

3 bell peppers in assorted colors
1 fresh green Anaheim or New Mexico
   chili*
1 cup chopped onion
2 garlic cloves, minced
2 teaspoons vegetable oil
⅔ cup sugar
½ cup distilled vinegar
½ cup water
2 teaspoons whole mustard seeds
1 teaspoon ground coriander seeds
½ teaspoon salt
freshly ground black pepper to taste

* available at specialty produce markets

Seed bell peppers and cut into ½-inch pieces. Wearing rubber gloves, seed chili and chop. In a large deep skillet cook onion, garlic, and chili in oil over moderately low heat until softened, about 10 minutes. Add bell peppers and remaining ingredients and boil, stirring occasionally, 20 minutes, or until liquid is syrupy. Spoon hot relish into sterilized jars (procedure on page 278) with tight-fitting lids and cool completely, covered. *Relish keeps, covered and chilled, 1 month.* Makes about 2½ cups.

ALEXIS SEABROOK

If you like the salad dressing typically served in Japanese restaurants, you'll love this one. It makes a great gift, especially when accompanied by a basket of fresh vegetables for dipping or greens.

Carrot, Ginger, and Miso Salad Dressing ☺

⅓ cup finely shredded carrot
1 tablespoon chopped peeled fresh gingerroot
1 tablespoon white or yellow *miso** (fermented soybean paste)
5 tablespoons rice vinegar* (not seasoned), or plum basil vinegar (page 281)
5 tablespoons vegetable oil
1 teaspoon soy sauce
½ teaspoon sugar
¼ teaspoon salt
freshly ground black pepper to taste

* available at Japanese markets and natural foods stores

In a blender blend together all ingredients until smooth. Pour dressing into a sterilized jar (procedure on page 278) with a tight-fitting lid. *Dressing keeps, covered and chilled, 1 week.* Makes about ¾ cup.

For a fun gift, put a bottle of this dressing into a salad bowl with a big wedge of Parmigiano-Reggiano.

Caesar Salad Dressing ☺

1 garlic clove
½ teaspoon salt
1 small flat anchovy fillet
¾ cup olive oil
⅓ cup freshly grated Parmesan
¼ cup fresh lemon juice
1 tablespoon mayonnaise
1 teaspoon Worcestershire sauce
1 teaspoon Dijon mustard
½ teaspoon freshly ground black pepper

Mash garlic and salt to a paste with a fork. Rinse anchovy and cut into pieces. In a blender blend garlic paste, anchovy, and remaining ingredients until emulsified. Transfer salad dressing to a sterilized jar

(procedure on page 278) and seal. *Dressing keeps, covered and chilled, 5 days.* Makes about 1 cup.

Louisianian flavor abounds in shrimp boiled in our spicy seasoning. For 1 pound of shrimp in shells: In a saucepan bring ½ cup water, ½ cup distilled vinegar, and 1 tablespoon shrimp spice mix to a boil and cook shrimp, covered, about 3 minutes. Serve shrimp with lime or lemon wedges and extra seasoning for dipping. The spice mix can also be rubbed on fish or chicken before grilling.

Shrimp Spice Mix ☺

2 tablespoons *ancho* chili powder*
1 tablespoon celery salt
1½ teaspoons ground cumin
1½ teaspoons ground coriander seeds
¾ teaspoons dried thyme, crumbled

* available at some specialty foods shops or by mail order from Chile Today–Hot Tamale, Inc., (800) 468-7377

In a small bowl stir together all ingredients and transfer to a very small jar with a tight-fitting lid. *Seasoning keeps, tightly covered, in a cool, dark place 6 months.* Makes about ¼ cup.

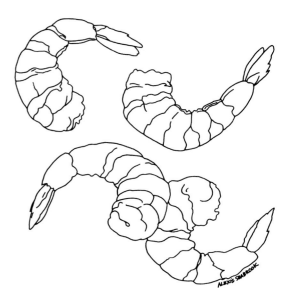

Although salsa is often served with tortilla chips for dipping, our black bean version also makes a great topping for rice or an accompaniment to grilled meats and fish.

Black Bean Salsa

1 cup dried black beans
2 teaspoons salt
1 large red or yellow bell pepper
3 scallions
1 fresh *jalapeño* or *serrano* chili, or to taste
3 tablespoons chopped fresh coriander,
    or to taste
3 tablespoons fresh lime juice
2 tablespoons fresh orange juice
2 tablespoons olive oil
½ teaspoon ground cumin

Pick over beans and rinse. In a large saucepan cover beans with cold water by 2 inches and bring to a boil. Simmer beans, partially covered, 30 minutes. Stir in salt and simmer until beans are tender but not falling apart, about 30 minutes more. In a colander drain beans and rinse briefly.

Chop bell pepper and thinly slice scallions. Wearing rubber gloves, seed chili and chop, reserving some seeds for hotter salsa if desired. In a bowl combine beans, bell pepper, scallions, chili, and remaining ingredients and toss well. *Chill salsa, covered, 1 hour.* Transfer salsa to sterilized glass jars (page 278) with tight-fitting lids. *Salsa keeps, covered and chilled, 2 days.* Makes about 3 cups.

This versatile condiment is the ketchup of Mexico's Yucatan. Try it with grilled meat or fish or on sandwiches. The onions' pink color is best shown off in a clear glass jar with fabric covering the lid.

Mexican Pickled Onions ◌+

1 pound red onions (2 medium)
1 fresh *jalapeño* chili
¾ cup distilled vinegar
½ cup fresh orange juice
¼ cup water
2 teaspoons sugar

1 teaspoon cumin seeds
1 teaspoon dried oregano, crumbled
1½ teaspoons salt

Cut onions into thin rings. Wearing rubber gloves, seed *jalapeño*, reserving some seeds for hotter pickled onions, if desired, and cut into very thin rings. In a large saucepan cover onions with cold water. Bring water to a boil and drain onions in a colander. In saucepan bring onions, *jalapeño*, and remaining ingredients to a boil. Transfer onion mixture to a sterilized jar (page 278) with a tight-fitting lid and cool completely, covered. *Marinate onions, covered and chilled, 1 day. Pickled onions keep, covered and chilled, 1 month.* Makes about 2 cups.

SWEET SAUCES

If you freeze sour cherries in June or July, you can make this sophisticated ice-cream sauce year-round: Pit cherries and freeze in single layers on paper-towel-lined trays. When they are hard, double bag the cherries in sealable plastic bags.

Sour Cherry Amaretto Sauce ◌

4 cups fresh or frozen sour cherries
    (about 1½ pounds)
1 cup sugar
⅓ cup DiSaronno Amaretto or other
    almond-flavored liqueur
1½ cups plus 3 tablespoons water
1 tablespoon fresh lemon juice
2 tablespoons cornstarch

Pit cherries if necessary. In a saucepan bring sugar, liqueur, 1½ cups water, and lemon juice to a boil, stirring. Add cherries and simmer 5 minutes. In a small bowl stir cornstarch into remaining 3 tablespoons water until dissolved and stir into cherry mixture. Simmer sauce, stirring, 2 minutes and pour into sterilized jars (procedure on page 278) with tight-fitting lids. Cool sauce completely, uncovered, and seal jars. *Sauce keeps, covered and chilled, 2 weeks.* Makes about 5 cups.

Since our sauce is so luscious over ice cream, you may want to dress up this gift with an ice cream scoop or parfait glasses.

Butter Pecan Bourbon Sauce ☼

1½ cups pecans
2 cups packed brown sugar
1¼ cups heavy cream
1 stick (½ cup) unsalted butter, softened
¾ teaspoon salt
a generous pinch freshly ground black pepper
2 tablespoons bourbon or rum
1 teaspoon vanilla

Lightly toast pecans and coarsely chop. In a saucepan bring pecans, brown sugar, cream, butter, salt, and pepper to a boil, stirring. Simmer mixture, stirring, 10 minutes and remove pan from heat. When bubbling stops, stir in remaining ingredients and pour sauce into sterilized jars (procedure on page 278) with tight-fitting lids. Cool sauce completely, uncovered, and seal jars. *Sauce keeps, covered and chilled, 1 month.* Makes about 4¼ cups.

A little of this butter goes a long way on croissants, scones, or biscuits.

Maple Apricot Butter ☼+

1 cup dried apricots
⅔ cup water
3 tablespoons pure maple syrup
   (preferably dark)
2 tablespoons brandy or fresh orange juice
1 tablespoon fresh lemon juice
¼ teaspoon cinnamon
⅛ teaspoon freshly grated nutmeg

In a small saucepan simmer all ingredients, covered, 10 minutes and remove pan from heat. *Let mixture stand, covered, 1 hour.* In a food processor or blender purée mixture, scraping down side frequently, until smooth. Spoon apricot butter into sterilized small glass jars (procedure on page 278) with tight-fitting lids and chill, covered, until firm. *Apricot butter keeps, covered and chilled, 3 weeks.* Makes about 1¾ cups.

A tin of our slightly sweet biscotti along with a bottle of Vin Santo make a fabulous present. (Alternatively, biscotti may be arranged, standing up, in wide-mouthed glass canisters.)

Orange Cranberry Walnut Biscotti

½ navel orange
3 large eggs
1 cup sugar
1 teaspoon vanilla
3 tablespoons unsalted butter,
   melted
3¾ cups all-purpose flour
¾ teaspoon baking powder
½ teaspoon baking soda
½ teaspoon salt
1½ cups dried sweetened cranberries
   (about 7 ounces)
1¼ cups walnuts, chopped coarse

Preheat oven to 350° F. and butter a large baking sheet.

Cut orange half into chunks (including peel and discarding any seeds) and in a food processor purée until smooth. In a large bowl with an electric mixer beat together eggs and sugar until light and creamy. Add ½ cup orange purée and vanilla and beat until fluffy, about 5 minutes. Add butter, flour, baking powder, baking soda, and salt and stir until just combined. Stir in dried cranberries and walnuts until just combined.

On baking sheet roughly shape dough into 3 long mounds. With wet hands pat and form mounds into three slightly flattened 12-inch logs (each about 2½ inches wide). Bake logs in middle of oven 30 minutes, or until golden. Cool logs on sheet on a rack 10 minutes and transfer to a cutting board. With a serrated knife cut logs diagonally into ½-inch-thick slices. Arrange slices, cut sides down, on 2 baking sheets and bake in upper and lower thirds of oven 12 to 15 minutes, or until golden. Transfer *biscotti* to racks and cool. *Biscotti keep in an airtight container at room temperature 1 week or frozen in sealable plastic bags 4 months.* Makes about 72 *biscotti*.

Kugelhopf is a classic Alsatian cake made in a special fluted pan. Our miniature versions, made in muffin tins, are jazzed up with dried fruit, hazelnuts, and chocolate chips.

Kugelhopf Muffins

¾ cup chopped dried cherries, cranberries,
    or apricots
½ cup dried currants
3 tablespoons triple sec or fresh
    orange juice
2 teaspoons vanilla
¾ cup hazelnuts
¾ cup warm milk (110° to 115° F.)
two ¼-ounce packages (5 teaspoons total)
    active dry yeast
½ cup granulated sugar
3 large eggs
1 stick (½ cup) unsalted butter, melted
    and cooled
4 cups all-purpose flour
½ cup semisweet chocolate chips
¾ teaspoon salt
confectioners' sugar for dusting
    muffins

In a small bowl stir together dried fruits, triple sec or orange juice, and vanilla and macerate 30 minutes.

Preheat oven to 350° F.

In a baking pan toast nuts in one layer in middle of oven 10 to 15 minutes, or until lightly colored and skins blister. Wrap nuts in a kitchen towel and let steam 1 minute. Rub nuts in towel to remove loose skins (do not worry about skins that do not come off) and cool. Chop nuts.

Butter twelve ⅓-cup muffin tins.

In bowl of an electric mixer stir together milk, yeast, and 1 teaspoon granulated sugar and let stand 10 minutes, or until foamy. Add eggs and butter, stirring until smooth. Add 3 cups flour and remaining granulated sugar and beat until mixture forms a smooth and sticky dough. Beat in macerated fruits with liquid, hazelnuts, chocolate chips, and salt until combined well. Beat in remaining cup flour, a little at a time, until dough is smooth. (Dough will still be sticky).

Divide dough among muffin tins and with floured hands press dough into tins. Let dough rise, covered loosely with oiled plastic wrap, in a warm, draft-free place 30 minutes.

Preheat oven to 375° F.

Bake muffins in middle of oven 15 to 20 minutes, or until golden brown. Turn out muffins onto a rack and cool completely. *Muffins keep in an airtight container at room temperature 2 days or frozen in doubled freezer bags 1 month. Thaw frozen muffins completely and heat in a preheated 350° F. oven until heated through.*

Just before serving, dust cooled muffins generously with confectioners' sugar. Makes 12 muffins.

Meringue cookies such as these macaroons ideally should be baked on a dry day so they will stay crisp.

Coconut Macadamia Macaroons ☺

3 large egg whites
⅛ teaspoon cream of tartar
⅔ cup sugar
3 cups sweetened flaked coconut
1 cup macadamia nuts,
   chopped

Preheat oven to 350° F. and line 2 large baking sheets with parchment paper.

In a bowl with an electric mixer beat whites until foamy. Add cream of tartar and beat until whites hold soft peaks. Gradually beat in sugar and beat until sugar is dissolved, about 4 minutes. Working quickly, fold in coconut and nuts thoroughly.

Drop cookie batter by rounded tablespoons ½ inch apart onto parchment and bake in upper and lower thirds of oven, switching position of sheets halfway through baking, 20 minutes, or until cookies are dry to the touch. Cool macaroons on sheets on racks and carefully peel off parchment. *Macaroons keep, layered between sheets of wax paper, in an airtight container 1 week.* Makes about 34 macaroons.

For the richest flavor use fine-quality bittersweet chocolate, such as Lindt or Valrhona for our toffee.

Chocolate-Covered Butter Toffee

1 stick (½ cup) unsalted butter
1 cup sugar
¾ teaspoon salt
2 tablespoons water
2 teaspoons vanilla
⅔ cup semisweet chocolate chips or
   chopped bittersweet chocolate
   (not unsweetened)

Line a baking sheet with foil and lightly oil foil.

In a saucepan bring butter, sugar, salt, and water to a boil, stirring, and continue to boil, stirring, until mixture registers 310° F. on a candy thermometer and is a pale honey color. Remove pan from heat and stir mixture until it stops bubbling. Stir in vanilla until toffee mixture is smooth and pour onto foil. Cool toffee completely.

Melt chocolate and spread half onto top of toffee. Let chocolate harden slightly and cover top with a sheet of foil. Invert a second baking sheet over toffee and invert toffee onto second sheet. Peel off top sheet of foil and spread remaining chocolate on top of toffee. Chill toffee until chocolate is hardened. Peel off remaining foil and break toffee into pieces. *Toffee keeps, layered between sheets of plastic wrap in an airtight container and chilled, 2 weeks.* Makes about ½ pound.

ALEXIS SEABROOK

When rolling truffles, cool your hands every few minutes by holding them in a pan of ice water for a moment. Dry your hands well before continuing to roll. Small coffee bags or coffee mugs make clever containers.

Chocolate Espresso Truffles

12 ounces fine-quality bittersweet chocolate
   (not unsweetened)
½ cup heavy cream
1 tablespoon instant espresso powder
⅛ teaspoon salt
½ stick (¼ cup) unsalted butter, cut into bits
   and softened
3 tablespoons Kahlúa
about 60 chocolate-covered espresso beans or
   chocolate coffee beans
For coating truffles
¼ cup unsweetened cocoa powder
2 tablespoons confectioners' sugar
½ teaspoon instant espresso powder

Finely chop chocolate. In a heavy saucepan stir together cream and 1 tablespoon espresso powder and bring just to a boil. Remove pan from heat and add chocolate, stirring until melted. Add salt and butter, a little at a time, stirring until mixture is smooth. Stir in Kahlúa and transfer to a small bowl. *Chill mixture, covered, 4 hours, or until firm.*

Chill a shallow baking pan.

Using a teaspoon, scoop truffle mixture and push a chocolate espresso bean into center. With cool hands, quickly roll scoop into a ball and transfer to chilled pan. Make more truffles in same manner and chill 10 minutes.

Coat truffles:

Into a bowl sift together coating ingredients. Working with about 5 truffles at a time, drop truffles into coating mixture and swirl bowl until truffles are thoroughly coated. *Truffles keep, layered between sheets of plastic wrap or wax paper in an airtight container and chilled, 2 weeks.* Makes about 60 truffles.

Delicious at tea time, these tart cakes also make a fine alternative to fruitcake during the holidays.

Zesty Lime and Almond Cakes

1 cup blanched almonds
1 stick (½ cup) unsalted butter,
   softened
1⅓ cups sugar
1 teaspoon finely grated fresh lime zest
½ teaspoon almond extract
1 teaspoon salt
2 large eggs
2 cups all-purpose flour
2 teaspoons baking powder
1 cup milk
⅓ cup fresh lime juice

Preheat oven to 350° F. Butter and flour four 6- by 4- by 2-inch loaf pans or two 8-inch round cake pans.

In a food processor finely grind almonds.

In a bowl with an electric mixer beat together butter and 1 cup sugar until light and fluffy. Add zest, extract, and salt and add eggs, 1 at a time, beating well after each addition and until mixture resembles whipped cream. Beat in 1 cup flour, almonds, and

baking powder. Add milk and remaining cup flour alternately in batches, beating well after each addition, and until batter is smooth.

Divide batter among pans, smoothing tops, and bake in middle of oven until a tester inserted in centers of cakes comes out clean, about 40 minutes for cake rounds and 50 minutes for loaves. Transfer cakes in pans to racks.

In a small bowl stir together lime juice and remaining ⅓ cup sugar until sugar is dissolved. With a wooden skewer prick tops of cakes all over and spoon lime syrup evenly over tops of warm cakes. Cool cakes completely and turn out of pans. *Cakes keep, wrapped in wax paper and chilled in an air-tight container, 1 week or frozen in doubled plastic bags, 3 months.* Makes 4 small loaves or two 8-inch rounds.

This spicy cordial, with its bright-red hue, makes a festive holiday gift. You may also want to keep a bottle on hand to share when company stops by.

Spiced Berry Cordial ☺+

1 orange
1½ cups fresh or unthawed frozen cranberries
3 cups vodka
1 cup fresh or unthawed frozen raspberries
   (not in syrup)
1¾ cups sugar
1 teaspoon whole coriander seeds
½ cinnamon stick
½ cup water
four ¼-inch-thick slices peeled fresh
   gingerroot

With a vegetable peeler remove two 4-inch strips of zest from orange. In a food processor pulse cranberries until coarsely chopped.

In a very clean 2-quart jar with a tight-fitting lid combine zest, cranberries, and remaining ingredients. Seal jar and shake gently until almost all sugar is dissolved. *Let mixture stand in a cool, dark place, shaking occasionally, 6 weeks.* Pour cordial through a fine sieve into a pitcher or large measuring cup. Transfer cordial to very clean bottles and seal. *Cordial keeps in a cool, dry place indefinitely.* Makes 4 cups.

Page numbers in *italics* indicate color photographs
◌ indicates recipes that can be prepared in 45 minutes or less
◌+ indicates recipes that can be prepared in 45 minutes but require additional unattended time
🥬 indicates recipes that are leaner/lighter

INDEX OF RECIPE TITLES

Page numbers in *italics* indicate color photographs

TABLE SETTING ACKNOWLEDGMENTS

To avoid duplication below of table setting information within the same menu, the editors have listed all such credits for silverware, plates, linen, and the like in its most complete form under "Table Setting."

Any items in the photograph not credited are privately owned.
All addresses are in New York City unless otherwise indicated.

Back Jacket

Fallen Chocolate Cake Squares à la Mode with Butterscotch Sauce: See Table Setting credits for Celebrating Father's Day.
Picnic Setting: See Table Setting credits for Lazy Sundaes.

Frontispiece

Peppermint Chocolate-Chunk, Strawberry, and Blueberry Ice-Cream Cones (page 2): Italian frosted double Old Fashioned glass—Neiman Marcus, (800) 937-9146. Linen napkin with raffia fringe—for stores call Archipelago, (212) 334-9460.

Table of Contents

Strawberry Pistachio Mille-Feuillantine (page 6): Ceramic dessert plate—Wolfman • Gold & Good Company, 117 Mercer Street.
Corn Chowder with Basil (page 6): White dinner plate and blue-and-white "Gingham" salad plate—Crate & Barrel, 650 Madison Avenue. "Denimware" soup bowl and cotton tablecloth—for stores call The Ralph Lauren Home Collection (212) 642-8700. Soup spoon—Calvin Klein, 654 Madison Avenue.
Place setting (page 7): *Photographed at Hôtel Le Toiny, Saint Barthélemy, French West Indies.*

The Menu Collection

Table Setting (page 10): See Table Setting credits for A Pacific Northwest Thanksgiving.

Dinner for Two

Baked Oysters in Jackets with Bacon Cognac Butter; Crisp Potato Canapés with Caviar (pages 12 and 13): Limoges spotted plates by Sandrine Ganem—Bergdorf Goodman, (800) 218-4918. "Murano" flatware—The L•S Collection, 469 W. Broadway. "Neapolitan" Champagne flutes—Snyder's Glass, Inc. (707) 745-2614. Napkins—Barneys New York, Madison Avenue at 61st Street. Silver-leaf glass bottles (flowers)—Troy, 138 Greene Street. Italian parchment-topped table, circa 1940—Fred Silberman, 83 Wooster Street. Velvet sofa and ottoman from the Big Mama Collection by Massimo Josa Ghini—Modern Age, 102 Wooster Street. Screen—Einzigart & Co., 88 Wooster Street. Antique needlepoint rug—Coury Rugs, Inc., 515 Madison Avenue. Peking Stripe wallpaper—Clarence House, 211 E. 58th Street.
Mocha Mousse with Kumquat Cranberry Sauce and Phyllo Pecan Crisps (page 15): Limoges charger by Sandrine Ganem—Bergdorf Goodman, (800) 218-4918.

New Year's Eve Buffet Party

Apricot Almond Shortbreads (page 16): English sterling and glass tiered tray, circa 1910—Bergdorf Goodman, (800) 218-4918.
Four Hors d'Oeuvres (page 17): Bamboo tray (crêpes)—William-Wayne & Co., 850 Lexington Avenue. Vintage crystal stand (mousse); vintage spreaders, circa 1930 (pâté)—Bergdorf Goodman, (800) 218-4918. "Nobel" wineglasses by Orrefors (nori rolls)—Galleri Orrefors Kosta Boda, 58 E. 57th Street.

Chinese New Year

Chinese Chicken Noodle Soup with Spinach and Garlic Chives (page 18): Chinese plates and soup bowls—available at many Chinese and other Asian housewares shops. Crystal wineglass—Hoya Crystal Gallery, 689 Madison Avenue. Napkins—Barneys New York, Madison Avenue at 61st Street. Cotton sateen fabric (place mats)—Silk Surplus, 235 East 58th Street. Nineteenth-century padded silk figures; eighteenth-century Chinese bamboo table and chairs—William Lipton Ltd., 27 East 61st Street.

Breakfast in Bed

Herbed Yellow Pepper Scrambled

Eggs with Chive Sour Cream on Brioche; Broiled Brown-Sugar Apple with Bacon; Passion Fruit Mimosa; Cappuccino (pages 20 and 21): "Etched Rose" ceramic plates, cup, and saucer; "Cone" double Old Fashioned glass; sycamore tray—Calvin Klein, 654 Madison Avenue. Norstaal "Chaco" stainless-steel flatware—for stores call Norstaal, (800) 404-5199. Napkin—William-Wayne & Co., 850 Lexington Avenue. Cotton duvet cover—Frette, 799 Madison Avenue.

Easter Dinner

Table Setting (pages 22 and 23): "Agate" earthenware plates—Bennington Potters, Inc., (802) 447-7531. "Garance" porcelain dinner plates—Bernardaud, 499 Park Avenue. Pewter-handled flatware; pewter beakers—Pierre Deux French Country, 870 Madison Avenue. Wineglasses—Simon Pearce, 500 Park Avenue at 59th Street. Napkins—Ad Hoc Softwares, 410 W. Broadway. Flowers—Zezé, 398 E. 52nd Street. "Tulip" cotton quilt, circa 1925—Woodard & Greenstein, 506 E. 74th Street. Decorative pine column, circa 1780—Guild Antiques, 384 Greenwich Avenue, Greenwich, CT, (203) 869-0828.
Pork Loin with Morel Stuffing; Roasted Celery Root; Minted Spring Vegetables (page 24): Platter—Crate & Barrel, 650 Madison Avenue.
Rhubarb Raspberry Meringue Cake (page 25): Glass platter—Hoagland's, 175 Greenwich Avenue, Greenwich, CT, (203) 869-2127.

Desktop Dining

Chicken Cashew Chili; Cheddar Corn Bread (page 26): Hand-painted plates and bowl by Barbara Eigen; "Scof" flatware; cotton napkin; cotton place mat—Wolfman•Gold & Good Company, 117 Mercer Street. Glass tumbler—Simon Pearce, 500 Park Avenue at 59th Street.
Poached Pear with Ginger and Port (page 27): Footed glass bowl—Crate & Barrel, 650 Madison Avenue.

Spring Dinner

Warm Camembert Croûte with Dandelion Greens and Red Currants (page 28): "Café Paris" porcelain salad plate—Bernardaud, 499 Park Avenue.
Asparagus Crudités with Mayonnaise Verte (page 29): "Provence" crystal wineglasses (water)—Baccarat, 625 Madison Avenue. "Nugget" hand-sewn place mats—The Dining Trade, 306 East 61st Street. Glazed flowerpot and saucer—Takashimaya, 693 Fifth Avenue.
Lavender and Thyme Roasted Poussins; Vegetables Printanier (page 30): Blue "Basique" earthenware plates by Jars—Marel, (516) 466-3118. Brass chargers—Crate & Barrel, 650 Madison Avenue. "Claridge" flatware by Scof—Brodean, 338 Columbus Avenue.
Frozen Lemon Mousses with Strawberry Mint Sauce (page 31): "Robin's Nest" earthenware dessert plates—for stores call Essex Collection, (800) 337-1416. Flowers—Paul Bott Beautiful Flowers, 1305 Madison Avenue.
Photographed at Paul Bott Beautiful Flowers.

Dessert Party

Table Setting (page 32): Cotton fabric (tent), available through decorator—Sonia's Place, 979 Third Avenue. Antique blue-glass cake stand—More & More Antiques, 378 Amsterdam Avenue. "Dom Perignon" Champagne flutes—Baccarat, 625 Madison Avenue. "Laura" resin-handled teaspoons—Villeroy & Boch Creations, 974 Madison Avenue. Polka-dot napkins—for stores call Archipelago, (212) 334-9460. Green napkins, cotton fabric (tablecloth)—for stores call Necessities, (718) 797-0530. Crystallized edible flower petals—Meadowsweets, (800) 484-7347, code 4884. Worcester saucer, circa 1820—Bardith, 901 Madison

Avenue. All other items credited below.
Dessert Assortment (page 35): (Tart) Worcester saucer and dessert plates, circa 1820—Bardith, 901 Madison Avenue. Antique sterling server—F. Gorevic & Son, Inc., 635 Madison Avenue. (Brandy snaps) "Lipari" Limoges cup and saucer—Bernardaud, 499 Park Avenue. Antique wineglass—More and More Antiques, 378 Amsterdam Avenue. Antique sterling coffee and tea service—Bulgari, 730 Fifth Avenue. (Bombe) Coalport dessert plates, circa 1830; decanter, circa 1860—Bardith, 901 Madison Avenue. Mother-of-pearl-handled dessert forks, circa 1875—S. Wyler, 941 Lexington Avenue. Cordial glasses—Baccarat, 625 Madison Avenue.

A Swedish Midsummer Party

Aquavit (page 36): Nineteenth-century Swedish and Norwegian bottles—Evergreen Antiques, 1249 Third Avenue. "Vega" crystal vodka glasses—Baccarat, 625 Madison Avenue.
Buffet Setting (page 37): Vintage wooden table and slatted chairs—Intérieurs, 114 Wooster Street. Painted iron chairs—Zona, 97 Greene Street. Luncheon plate by Les Toiles du Soleil—Bergdorf Goodman, 754 Fifth Avenue. Other items credited below.
Matjes Herring with Red Onion and Dill, Boiled Potatoes; Savory Sandwich Torte, Shrimp Tart; Grilled Swedish Meatball Kebabs; Pickled Cucumbers, Boston Lettuce with Radishes (page 38): Glass jam jar (herring); glass cake stand—Intérieurs, 114 Wooster Street. SoHo "Mt. Auban" vintage English basket-weave platter (kebabs)—Bergdorf Goodman, 754 Fifth Avenue. Nineteenth-century Scandinavian footed glass salad bowl—Evergreen Antiques, 1249 Third Avenue.
Strawberry Cream Cake (page 39): Blue-etched glass dessert plates—Aero Ltd., 132 Spring Street.

Celebrating Father's Day

Chunky Clam and Bacon Dip with Pita Toasts (page 40): Pewter bowls by Keith Tyssen—Simon Pearce, 500 Park Avenue at 59th Street.
Table Setting (pages 40 and 41): "Denimware" earthenware dinner plates; "Winslow Stripe" cotton-linen fabric (napkins, draped over chairs, and runner)—for stores call The Ralph Lauren Home Collection (212) 642-8700. Italian platinum-glazed ceramic chargers—The Dining Trade, 306 East 61st Street. "Silver Braid" stainless-steel flatware by Trupco—for stores call Reading China & More! (800) 747-7224. Wineglasses; Madeira glasses—Simon Pearce, 500 Park Avenue at 59th Street. Glasses (water)—Wolfman•Gold & Good Company, 117 Mercer Street. Potted grass—Christian Tortu at Takashimaya, 693 Fifth Avenue.
Grilled Porterhouse Steaks; Mixed Olive Relish (page 42, lower left): Platter—Wolfman•Gold & Good Company, 117 Mercer Street.
Fallen Chocolate Cake Squares à la Mode with Butterscotch Sauce (page 43): "Coupe" plates—Takashimaya, 693 Fifth Avenue. Glass pitcher—Simon Pearce, 500 Park Avenue at 59th Street.

Picnic on the Beach

Picnic Assortment (page 44): Glasses—Fishs Eddy, 889 Broadway. Steel bowl by iittala—for stores call Hackman, (800) 448-8252. Lidded glass container (dip)—ABC Carpet & Home, 888 Broadway. Enamel-on-steel rimmed dish (chips) and plates—MacKenzie-Childs, Ltd., 824 Madison Avenue. Striped napkins—Pottery Barn, 117 East 59th Street. "Frame" cotton towels—Calvin Klein, 654 Madison Avenue. Wood and nylon-net beach chair—Island Pursuit, 2 Straight Wharf, Nantucket, MA, (508) 228-5117.

¡Taquiza!

Piquant Crab on Jícama Wedges;

Cucumber Coolers (page 46): Ceramic blackware—Geomancy, 337 East 9th Street. Glasses—Pottery Barn, 117 East 59th Street.
Taquiza Assortment (page 47): Etched stemmed glasses, mortar, and glass pitcher—Bazaar Sabado, 54 Greene Street.
Place Setting (page 48): "Rope" ceramic service plates—Bloomingdale's, 1000 Third Avenue. Dinner plates, napkins, table runner, terra-cotta serving bowls (poblano strips and avocado), wood serving spoons—Pan American Phoenix, 857 Lexington Avenue. "Stonehenge" flatware—Pottery Barn, 117 East 59th Street. Ceramic blackware—Geomancy, 337 East 9th Street.
Mango, Cactus-Pear, and Lime Sorbets (page 49): Wood serving bowl—Jamson Whyte, 832 Collins Avenue, Miami Beach, FL, (305) 535-2224.

An Herb Garden Lunch

Table Setting (page 50): "Verdures" porcelain plates—Christian Tortu at Takashimaya, 693 Fifth Avenue. Stainless-steel chargers by Mepra—Frank McIntosh Home Collection at Henri Bendel, 712 Fifth Avenue. "Flemish" sterling flatware—Tiffany & Co., 727 Fifth Avenue. "Phalsbourg" crystal wineglasses—Lalique, 680 Madison Avenue. Highball glasses—Barneys New York, Madison Avenue at 61st Street. Pitcher—Crate & Barrel, 650 Madison Avenue. Potted herbs—L. Becker Flowers, 217 East 83rd Street. Organdy tablecloth and napkins with embroidered leaf appliqués—for stores call Dransfield and Ross, (212) 741-7278. Steel chairs with beechwood seats—Gardeners Eden, (800) 822-9600.
Grilled Shellfish and Potato Salad with Avocado Salsa, Scallion Oil, and Plum Coulis (page 52): Glass pitcher (with scallion oil) from sugar-and-milk set designed by Arnour Visser—The MoMA Design Store, 44 West 53rd Street.

Summer Berry Basil Kissel; Sweet Lemon-Thyme Crisps (page 53): "Laguna" footed crystal bowls—Rogaska, 685 Madison Avenue.

Lazy Sundaes

Picnic Setting (page 54): "Scott Plaid" ceramic platter—for stores call Square One, (800) 316-8080. "Cancan" footed glass bowl (macaroni salad) designed by Kjell Engman for Kosta Boda—Galleri Orrefors Kosta Boda, 58 East 57th Street. Acrylic-handled flatware—Pottery Barn, 1965 Broadway. Frosted stemmed glasses—Frank McIntosh Home Collection at Henri Bendel, 712 Fifth Avenue.
Ice-Cream Fixings and Ice Creams (page 56): Beakers by Bodum—Bloomingdale's, 1000 Third Avenue. "Dewdrop" bowls by iittala; "Quadro" footed bowl—Crate & Barrel, 650 Madison Avenue. "Cambridge" spoons by Scof—for stores call Mariposa, (800) 788-1304. Wood tray by Axis—Alphabets, 2284 Broadway.
Strawberry Ice-Cream Sundae with Blackberry-Raspberry Sauce and Crystallized Mint Leaf; Lemon Meringue Ice Cream with Candied Orange and Lemon Zest (page 57): Compotes designed by Cristina Salusti for Fossilglass—Barneys New York, Madison Avenue at 61st Street.

Picnic on the Pond

Picnic Sandwiches and Accompaniments (page 58): Tin mold (corn salad)—Broadway Panhandler, 477 Broome Street. Wooden spoon (in chutney)—Dean & DeLuca, 560 Broadway.
Explorateur Cheese and Assorted Crackers; Minted Honeydew Limeade (page 60): Sheathed knife (cheese)—Williams-Sonoma, 20 East 60th Street. Tumblers—Wolfman • Gold & Good Company, 117 Mercer Street. Blue Mason jar—Broadway Panhandler, 477 Broome Street.
Nectarines, Plums, and Blueberries in Lemony Ginger Anise Syrup; Choco-

late-Chunk Cookies with Pecans, Dried Apricots, and Tart Cherries (page 61): Rush bottleholder; "Catalina" Champagne flutes—Wolfman • Gold & Good Company, 117 Mercer Street. Bandanas (on pillows)—Outdoor Traders, 2 Greenwich Avenue, Greenwich, CT, (203) 862-9696. Wooden bowl—Dean & DeLuca, 560 Broadway. Vintage glasses (fruit)—Ad Hoc Softwares, 410 West Broadway.

Come for Cocktails

Buffet Setting (page 62): Mother-of-pearl plate—Gordon Foster, 1322 Third Avenue. "Lumière" crystal bowl (crudités); "Medusa d'Or" wineglasses designed by Gianni Versace for Rosenthal—Gianni Versace, 647 Fifth Avenue.

Four Hors d'Oeuvres (page 65): Italian silver-plate trays—S. Wyler, Inc., 941 Lexington Avenue. "Gloria" Martini glasses (mussels)—Frank McIntosh Home Collection at Henri Bendel, 712 Fifth Avenue. "Le Voyage de Marco Polo" porcelain serving platters designed by Gianni Versace for Rosenthal (negimaki and tart)—Gianni Versace, 647 Fifth Avenue.

A Traditional Thanksgiving

Caramelized Chestnuts (page 66): Hand-painted bowl—Barneys New York, Madison Avenue at 61st Street.

Roast turkey and Accompaniments (page 67): English sterling platter (turkey); sterling sauceboat; and vintage wood-and-sterling salt and pepper cellars—S. Wyler, Inc., 941 Lexington Avenue. "Tortoise" glass chargers by Sol Designs—for stores call (800) 605-8366. Earthenware plates by Lindt-Stymeist—At Your Service, Bloomingdale's, 1000 Third Avenue. "Spiral Cone" wineglasses; silver-plate and bronze candlesticks—Calvin Klein Home Collection at Calvin Klein, 654 Madison Avenue. "Tortoise" glasses—Bloomingdale's, 1000 Third Avenue. Coasters—Barneys New York, Madison Avenue at 61st Street.

Emile Henry ovenproof baking dishes—Zabar's, 2245 Broadway. Footed bowl (cranberry kumquat compote)—for stores call Mesa International, (603) 456-2002.

Dried-Fruit Tart with Brandied Crème Anglaise (page 68); Pumpkin Pie "Pumpkin" (page 69): "Tortoise" porcelain plates by Nicole Miller—for stores call Sakura, Inc., (212) 683-4000. Enameled stainless-steel servers by Mike & Ally—Barneys New York, Madison Avenue at 61st Street. Pitcher—for stores call Crusader Glass, (518) 672-4393.

Photographed at The J. Harper Poor Cottage in East Hampton, New York.

A Pacific Northwest Thanksgiving

Table Setting (page 70): Earthenware chargers; candlesticks; and tray (flowers) designed by Michael Vanderbyl and Peter Fishel for Pentimento—Frank McIntosh Home Collection at Henri Bendel, 712 Fifth Avenue. "Bernadotte" sterling flatware—Georg Jensen, 683 Madison Avenue. "Bourgueil" crystal wineglasses by Lalique—for stores call (800) 993-2580. Japanese etched water glasses and ceramic fruit—Takashimaya, 693 Fifth Avenue. "Tuckered Out" linen-and-organdy place mats and napkins designed by Angel Zimick—ABC Carpet & Home, 888 Broadway.

Spinach and Lentil Salad (page 71): Glass salad plate by Fossilglass—Barneys New York, Madison Avenue at 61st Street.

Cedar Planked Salmon with Accompaniments; Roasted Pears with Hazelnut Syrup (pages 72 and 73): Black ceramic plate (biscuits) and ceramic tray (pears) by Michael Vanderbyl and Peter Fishel for Pentimento—Frank McIntosh Home Collection at Henri Bendel, 712 Fifth Avenue.

Come A Caroling

Sugared Anise Rosettes; Chocolate Coconut Squares; Kumquats (page

75): "Snowflake" porcelain dessert plates by Philippe Deshoulieres; sugar bowl from "Platinum Deco Collection" ceramic coffee service—Bloomingdale's, 1000 Third Avenue. Pewter tray—Wolfman • Gold & Good Company, 117 Mercer Street.

Beef en Croûte with Coriander Walnut Filling; Haricots Verts and Red Peppers with Almonds; Scalloped Fennel and Potatoes (page 76): "Carat" porcelain dinner plate by Philippe Deshoulieres—for store information call Lalique N.A., (800) 993-2580. "Chinon" silver-plate flatware—Pavillon Christofle, 862 Madison Avenue. Venetian pewter bowl—Portantina, 895 Madison Avenue.

Buffet Setting (page 77): "Montaigne" crystal wineglasses (special order only)—Baccarat, 625 Madison Avenue.

An Austrian Christmas Dinner

Roast goose and Accompaniments (page 78): Salt-glaze platter, circa 1760 (goose)—Bardith, 901 Madison Avenue. Earthenware service plate by Gien; "Perfection Rhine" wineglass (shown in blue)—Baccarat, 625 Madison Avenue. "Mayfair" porcelain dinner plate by Nina Campbell—for stores call Rosenthal, (800) 274-3374. Wood-handled flatware—Takashimaya, 693 Fifth Avenue. Red Venetian tumblers, circa 1910—James II Galleries, 11 East 57th Street. Linen napkins—ABC Carpet & Home, 888 Broadway.

Place Setting (page 80): Lusterware pitcher, circa 1860—Ages Past, 450 East 78th Street.

Chocolate Orange Dobostorte (page 81): Creamware dessert plates, circa 1800; Crystal port glasses, circa 1860—Bardith, 901 Madison Avenue. Raised cake stand by Carol Dirahoui for Classic Cakestands—Wolfman • Gold & Good Company, 117 Mercer Street.

Photographed in Beaver Creek, Colorado courtesy of Slifer, Smith & Frampton/VARE Real Estate.

317

A Vegetarian Menu

Chilled Minted Cucumber Honeydew Soup; Roasted Peppers Stuffed with Chick-Pea and Eggplant Purée and Mushrooms (pages 82 and 83): French acrylic/stainless-steel flatware—Barneys New York, Madison Avenue and 61st Street.

Ease into Autumn

Peach and Passion-Fruit Phyllo Tart; Veal Scallops with Squash, Tomatoes, and Roasted-Garlic Basil Sauce; Lemon Wild Rice (pages 84 and 85): "Luna" porcelain dinner and dessert plates; heavy-stem all-purpose wineglass—Calvin Klein, 654 Madison Avenue. "Cheverny" flatware—William-Wayne & Co., 850 Lexington Avenue. Cotton napkin—Ad Hoc Softwares, 410 West Broadway.

Have Your Steak...

Poached Filets Mignons with Horseradish Sauce; Butternut Squash, Turnip, and Green-Bean Quinoa (page 87): Alabaster dinner plates—Michael Dawkins, 33 East 65th Street.

A Recipe Compendium

Raspberry Chocolate-Chip Pancakes (page 88): Glass syrup pitcher—Bridge Kitchenware, 214 East 52nd Street. Striped pillow—Ad Hoc Softwares, 410 West Broadway.

A North India Dinner

Entrée, Accompaniments, and Dessert (pages 249-251): Peter Crisp glass plates—for information call Peter Crisp (Australia), 61 6 2276073 (tel.); 61 6 2276107 (fax). Some plates available at Barneys New York, Madison Avenue at 61st Street, (212) 826-8900.

An Indian Vegetarian Dinner

All items in photograph are privately owned.

A South India Dinner

All items in photograph are privately owned.

CREDITS

Grateful acknowledgment is made to the following *Gourmet* readers for permission to reprint their recipes which were previously published in *Gourmet* Magazine:

Ric Andersen: Crostini with Garlic Pea Purée and Roasted Asparagus (page 104).

Matt Cabot: Beef Goulash Soup (page 118).

Lynne Ciuba: Lamb Stew (page 141).

John M. Frase: Pimiento Cheese (page 109).

Sari Schlussel Leeds: Radish Canapés (page 103).

Aliza Levenson: Cinnamon and Currant Sweet Rolls (page 114).

Priscilla Nesbitt: Cornmeal Buttermilk Waffles (page 156).

Jane Rinden: Corn Fritters (page 153).

Rozz Rusinow: Chive Pepper Popovers (page 115).

Judy P. Seibels: Pulled Turkey Barbecue (page 152).

The following photographers have generously given permission to reprint their photographs. Some of these photographs have previously appeared in *Gourmet* Magazine.

Jean Marc Giboux: "The Maharana of Mewar" (page 7) Copyright © 1995; "North Fort Gate, Chittorgarh, Rajasthan" (page 248) Copyright © 1997; "Ladies in Festive Saris, Udaipur, Rajasthan" (page 258) Copyright © 1995.

Roberta Gleit: "Street Market, Delhi" (pages 234 and 235) Copyright © 1997.

Ernie Hulsey: "Fishing Nets, Cochin, Kerala" (page 268) Copyright © 1997.

Ted Voigt: "Camel Fair, Pushkar, Rajasthan" (pages 232 and 233) Copyright © 1997.

If you are not already a subscriber to *Gourmet* Magazine and would be interested in subscribing, please call *Gourmet*'s toll-free number, 1-800-365-2454.

If you are interested in purchasing additional copies of this book or other *Gourmet* cookbooks, please call 1-800-438-9944.